The Autonomy of Morality

In *The Autonomy of Morality*, Charles Larmore challenges two ideas that have shaped the modern mind. The world, he argues, is not a realm of value-neutral fact, nor is reason our capacity to impose principles of our own devising on an alien reality. Rather, reason consists in being responsive to reasons for thought and action that arise from the world itself. In particular, Larmore shows that the moral good has an authority that speaks for itself. Only in this light does the true basis of a liberal political order come into view, as well as the role of unexpected goods in the makeup of a life lived well.

Charles Larmore is W. Duncan MacMillan Family Professor in the Humanities and Professor of Philosophy at Brown University. He is the author of *The Morals of Modernity* and *The Romantic Legacy* and a member of the American Academy of Arts and Sciences. In 2004, he received the Grand Prix de Philosophie from the Académie Française for his book *Les pratiques du moi*.

In memory of Marlowe

The Autonomy of Morality

CHARLES LARMORE

Brown University

CAMBRIDGE
UNIVERSITY PRESS

CAMBRIDGE UNIVERSITY PRESS
Cambridge, New York, Melbourne, Madrid, Cape Town, Singapore, São Paulo, Delhi

Cambridge University Press
32 Avenue of the Americas, New York, NY 10013-2473, USA

www.cambridge.org
Information on this title: www.cambridge.org/9780521717823

First published 2008
Reprinted 2009

Printed in the United States of America

A catalog record for this publication is available from the British Library.

Library of Congress Cataloging in Publication Data

Larmore, Charles E.
The autonomy of morality / Charles Larmore.
    p.   cm.
Includes bibliographical references and index.
ISBN 978-0-521-88913-1 (hardback) – ISBN 978-0-521-71782-3 (pbk.)
1. Ethics.   2. Reasoning.   I. Title.
BJ37L37   2008
170'.42–dc22   2007045635

ISBN   978-0-521-88913-1 hardback
ISBN   978-0-521-71782-3 paperback

Contents

Acknowledgments

I would like to thank Beatrice Rehl, my editor at Cambridge University Press, for her help in the preparation of this volume. My thanks to Ronald Cohen, who edited the manuscript with great care and made many helpful comments and suggestions. I am also indebted to many colleagues and audiences, too numerous to mention, for their comments and criticisms over the years as I wrote and presented various versions of the essays collected here.

Finally, I owe everything to my dear wife Amey, who keeps me going.

All of the previously published essays in this volume have been significantly and extensively revised, and I would like to thank the original publications and publishers that kindly granted me permission to use them here:

Chapter 1, "History and Truth." Originally published in *Daedalus* (summer 2004), pp. 46–55. Copyright © 2004 American Academy of Arts and Sciences. Reprinted with permission.

Chapter 2, "Back to Kant? No Way." Originally published in *Inquiry* 46(2) (June 2003), pp. 260–271. Copyright © 2003 Taylor & Francis. Reprinted with permission.

Chapter 3, "Attending to Reasons." Originally published in Nicholas Smith (ed.), *Reading McDowell* (London and New York: Routledge, 2002), pp. 193–208. Copyright © 2003 Routledge Ltd. Reprinted with permission.

Chapter 4, "John Rawls and Moral Philosophy." Originally published under the title, "Lifting the Veil" in *The New Republic*, 5 February 2001. Copyright © 2003 Charles Larmore. Reprinted with permission.

Chapter 5, "The Autonomy of Morality," is new.

Chapter 6, "The Moral Basis of Political Liberalism." Originally published in *The Journal of Philosophy* 96(12), December 1999, 599–625. Copyright © 1999 *The Journal of Philosophy*. Reprinted with permission.

Chapter 7, "The Meanings of Political Freedom." Originally published under the title "A Critique of Philip Pettit's Republicanism" in *Noûs: Philosophical Issues* (Oxford: Blackwell, 2001), vol. 11, pp. 229–243. Copyright © 2001 Blackwell. Reprinted with permission.

Chapter 8, "Public Reason." Originally published in Samuel Freeman (ed.), *The Cambridge Companion to Rawls* (Cambridge: Cambridge University Press, 2003), pp. 368–393. Copyright © 2003 Cambridge University Press. Reprinted with permission.

Chapter 9, "Nietzsche and the Will to Truth." Originally written in German and published under the title "Der Wille zur Wahrheit" in O. Höffe (ed.), *Nietzsche: Zur Genealogie der Moral (Klassiker Auslegen)* (Berlin: Akademie-Verlag, 2004), pp. 163–176. Copyright © 2004 Akademie-Verlag.

Chapter 10, "The Idea of a Life Plan." Originally published in *Social Philosophy & Policy* 16(1), 1999, 96–112. Copyright © 1999 Cambridge University Press. Also published in E. F. Paul et al. (eds.), *Human Flourishing* (Cambridge: Cambridge University Press, 1999). Copyright © 1999 Cambridge University Press. Reprinted with permission.

Introduction

Response and Commitment

In an earlier collection of essays, *The Morals of Modernity*,[1] I argued that our moral self-understanding, even at its most fundamental, needs to draw upon the distinctive forms of modern experience. All our thinking is shaped by our historical context. Philosophy is no exception and, committed as it is to being fully explicit about its assumptions and goals, it ought to acknowledge the ties of time and place that give it substance and direction. I have not abandoned this conviction, as many of the essays in the present volume attest. Yet I have also gone on to pursue a lot further another theme in the earlier volume that is very much at odds with a dominant strand of modern thought.

The principles by which we determine what to believe or do must in the end, so it is often held, be principles of our own making. Once the Enlightenment has undone the notion that they are imposed on us by a higher being, and the Scientific Revolution shown that they cannot be read off the fabric of the world, which is now seen to be normatively mute and devoid of directives, the conclusion appears inescapable that we alone must be their source. The authority of any principle of thought and action is an authority we bestow upon it ourselves. This idea of the *autonomy* of reason, far more common than the Kantian tradition from which the term itself derives, seems to me profoundly mistaken. Reason, indeed thought in general, involves an essential responsiveness to reasons. We cannot believe or do even the most insignificant of things except insofar as we see some basis or reason for doing so. Far from being the authors of the principles by which we live, we must conceive of them as binding on us from without, not only in moral matters but in every area. The point is not our need for divine tutelage. Quite the contrary, it is the need to revise the reigning image of what the world itself is like. To make sense of how we think and what we care about, we have to see reality as embodying

---

[1] *The Morals of Modernity* (Cambridge: Cambridge University Press, 1996).

a normative dimension. Commitment is unintelligible except as a response to the existence of reasons.

Now my very dissatisfaction with so pervasive a tendency of the modern mind might be taken as evidence of a general truth to which the idea of historical rootedness fails to do justice. However much we may be a part of our time and place, we retain the capacity to question accepted opinion and set out on a path of our own. This is undeniable. Yet nothing in the idea of rootedness, properly understood, really goes to deny it. After all, holding to some belief or practice, be it ever so firmly, entails being able to stand back and see ourselves from the outside. For we are not moved by reasons as we are by mere causes, but only in virtue of acknowledging their force, which means that on reflection (though then only by reference to other reasons) we must be able to weigh the value of committing ourselves as they demand. Though Hegel rightly spoke of reason's need to reconcile itself to its place in history, we can never come to feel so fully at home that we lose that inner distance to our commitments, that ability to have determined otherwise, which the Romantics whom he loathed called the element of irony in even our most serious of endeavors.[2]

All the same, I would also point out that my opposition to the modern notion of reason as autonomous has to do with what I take to be a self-misunderstanding. The target of my discontent is not, at least primarily, the moral and political principles characteristic of modern thought at its best, but rather its conception of what must be the basis of our allegiance to them – though this conception does embody a certain ideal of freedom with substantial implications for how we are to live our lives. My primary ambition is to have us see more clearly where we stand. And so, here too, philosophical argument remains moored in the present.

The first chapter of this book, "History and Truth," takes up again this refrain of the earlier book, showing why a sense of history ought not to produce a diminished devotion to truth. But it will be helpful if in this Introduction as well I describe in some detail the historically minded view of moral philosophy to which I have long been wedded. Then I can return to explain the principal theme of the present book, the responsiveness of our deepest commitments to an independent order of principles, and show how the two concerns fit together.

THE IMPORTANCE OF HISTORY

The Morals of Modernity grew out of my conviction that moral philosophy should be pursued with a historical sensibility. Such is not the spirit in which moral philosophers ordinarily go about their work. Their usual procedure is to treat the nature of morality as though it were essentially

---

[2] See my book, *The Romantic Legacy* (New York: Columbia University Press, 1996), pp. 76–83.

timeless in character, unaffected by any deep historical shifts in the way people conceive of their world and themselves. Reference may be made to great thinkers of the past, but they are invoked for their insights or mistakes about a subject matter presumed to be fundamentally unchanging. Even when the focus becomes some specifically modern development, the approach often remains the same. Liberal democracy, for instance, is regularly seen as a form of political life whose distinctive principles could have been known all along to define the proper goals of government and the dignity of the individual.

There have been, to be sure, notable exceptions to this tendency. But it is the norm, and it represents a mistake. Philosophy in general is wrong to aim at standing free from the vicissitudes of history. For then it must either fail to achieve anything of substance or misunderstand the conditions of its own success. Moral philosophy is no exception. Systematic reflection about the nature of the good and the right cannot hope to find much guidance in formal concepts of practical rationality, which tell us in essence only that we should pursue efficiently the things we hold to be valuable (that we should maximize expected utility, according to the technical jargon), but not what it is that we ought in fact to value. (I develop this point at some length in Chapter 5 of this book.) Nor will we make much headway if we simply bring in a knowledge of the essentials of the human condition along with a stock of moral truisms such as "promises are to be kept" and "the innocent are not to be harmed." To get a handle on the philosophical questions that matter – for instance, the relation between the demands of morality and the pursuit of our own good, the basic unity or instead heterogeneity of what we owe to others as well as of what constitutes the human good, the proper goals of political association – we must turn to the resources that our own historical situation provides us. We need most of all to make use of one of the cardinal lessons of modernity, which is that the ultimate ends of life are bound to be an object of reasonable disagreement and that a core morality, binding on all despite their differing ideals of the human good, is therefore an institution of immeasurable value. We must also rely upon the traditions of moral thought, various and contingent though they are, that have shaped our sense of what is obligatory, noble, or unconscionable and given us what are indeed substantive principles of judgment and action. So we do anyway, if only implicitly or unknowingly, whenever we manage to say something of real moment (which does not, it is true, happen all that often in moral philosophy). To recognize the need to base ourselves on historical givens, instead of aspiring to some transcendent point of view, is thus to remove a crippling source of error and confusion.

Reflection, even in philosophy, cannot but base itself on commitments we already have, since its essence is to be the response to a problem. We do not reflect for the pure pleasure of reflecting, but because some idea or experience has disrupted our ordinary expectations, obliging us to find a way of revising them, and we could not even identify the problem, much less work out a solution, except in the light of our existing beliefs and interests. Reflection is always situated. To take this truth to heart is to see the merits of what I call a "contextualist" epistemology.[3] What is it for a belief, moral or otherwise, to count as justified? Answers to this question have generally fallen into two opposing molds, "foundationalist" or "coherentist": either the reasons to accept some view are thought to rest in the end upon a special class of beliefs that we can see to be true in some immediate fashion, without appeal to yet further beliefs, or the reasons to accept it are held to turn upon its forming an integral part of some broad web of belief whose various elements lend one another mutual support. This conflict is a recurrent feature of the philosophical landscape, and yet the two warring camps share a crucial and dubious assumption. They both suppose that no view is really justified unless the considerations serving to warrant its acceptance have themselves the status of being justified. As a result, they both maintain that all our existing beliefs stand in need of justification simply by virtue of our having them at all. Otherwise, it is thought, we would not be entitled to rely upon them in figuring out what else we should accept.

The common idea that every justifying belief, and thus every belief as such, should be justified mistakes the point of justification, however. Asking whether some view ought to be accepted is one of the things we do when we reflect. It is a response to a problem, and only what is problematic calls for justification. Whether we should adopt a belief we do not yet have certainly counts as a problem, and that is why we are right to seek its justification, determining whether there are positive reasons to think it true. The fact that we already hold a belief does not, by contrast, constitute a problem – unless, of course, we have come upon reasons to think it might be false (one such reason cannot be merely the fact that we possess it), and so only under such circumstances must we set about ascertaining its credentials. The proper object of justification is not belief but rather changes in belief. We need to worry about the grounds for some view when it is one we are deciding whether to adopt or one we already hold but have reason to contemplate modifying or rejecting. Questions of justification arise within a context of existing beliefs that do not themselves have to be justified. They need not even be regarded as having been justified once upon a time, nor of course do they count as justified by virtue of the mere fact that they are held. Their status consists in being understood as true,

---

[3] The term "contextualism" is used in epistemology today to mean many different things, not all of which I am inclined to endorse. I have in mind a certain view about the justification of belief. My ultimate source of inspiration is C. S. Peirce, and I am also indebted to the writings of Isaac Levi, such as *The Enterprise of Knowledge* (Cambridge, MA: MIT Press, 1980).

since such is the sense in which they function as beliefs: to believe that *p* consists in being disposed to think and act in accord with the presumed truth of *p*.[4] Existing beliefs define the setting in which problems take shape and provide the premises from which solutions can be devised. They are not in themselves a problem.

In this light, it ought to be clear why moral philosophy should proceed in a historical spirit, taking its bearings from the traditions of thought and forms of experience that have made us who we are. It is a matter of doing more consciously, and so more knowledgeably and carefully, what we must do in any case if we are to achieve something of consequence. Outside philosophy, inquiry can afford to ignore its historically conditioned character. There, the leading aim is to solve the problems at hand, in order to be better able to handle others in the future. Not so in philosophy, whatever the particular domain. Progress here means not just solving problems, but also making as explicit as possible the assumptions guiding the way we go about it. To say this is not to dictate in some substantive way what it is that philosophy should be. Attempts to delimit its peculiar methods or subject matter, which is the form substantive definitions regularly take, never succeed since they simply reflect the predilections of some particular philosophical movement. But something more general does appear distinctive of all philosophy, as shown by both those attempts and the exposures of their failure, and that is its commitment to being fully self-aware. To take this ideal seriously, I maintain, is to keep in view the historicity of the problems we face and of the resources we bring to bear on them.

In *The Morals of Modernity*, I sometimes held up Hegel as a pioneer of this approach. But I am no Hegelian. Much of his "system" strikes me as wrong, outlandish, or unintelligible. There is, in particular, his conviction that as our ideas of what counts as rational belief or action change over time, they develop in accord with an inner logic, following a necessary path that is the course of human history itself. Few today could endorse such a view. Once it has been discarded, however, a certain skepticism may seem inescapable. Must not a rejection of the notion that history has a meaning, when combined with an awareness of how reason depends on history, lead us to doubt whether we can really claim to have access to truth itself, as opposed to the picture of the world licensed by our current but changing standards? If the grounds we have for our present views turn on the contingencies of tradition and experience, what more can we really mean by saying that our predecessors were wrong than that they did not happen to think like us?

Skepticism of this sort is now widespread. It drives the different currents of so-called post-modernism that have proven so influential in

---

[4] This account of belief is defended in Chapter 5, §8.

contemporary culture. Although the work of others may be more famous, the clearest statement of the post-modernist outlook remains an early and programmatic essay by Jean-François Lyotard. Once we have seen through the grand modern stories about finding outside history or in the movement of history itself an objective – that is, non-parochial basis for the evaluation of all human endeavor – we are left, he argued, only with our various language games themselves, each with its own rules, but without any impartial standpoint to settle the conflicts between them.[5] This looks like the recipe for a rather facile relativism, and that is what post-modernism has indeed become. Thus there has occurred the expectable reaction of insisting that we can after all pry ourselves loose from the grip of history and latch onto timeless standards of belief and action.

Both attitudes miss what was Hegel's genuine insight, and which we can recast in a form more compatible with our own greater sense of contingency. Like him, we need to comprehend our rootedness in a particular time and place as the very means by which we gain access to truth, though now without any guarantee that where we happen to stand is an inevitable moment in the human mind's (or *Geist*'s) quest for knowledge of itself and of the world. Our changing views about the proper principles of thought and action represent a learning process in which we come to see better how to determine what to think and do, a learning process that proceeds in much the same way as deciding upon beliefs and actions themselves – namely, by judging how to make the best sense of our experience in the light of what we already know. The key is to understand our finitude as opening us outward rather than hemming us in. As noted before, Chapter 1 in this book gives a general defense of such a position. There I look chiefly at the case of scientific inquiry. Most of the other chapters focus on questions in moral and political philosophy, and in them the same conception is at work.

THE NATURE OF REASON

The essays in this book are also united by a second concern, which has to do, as I have said, with our need to break with the modern idea of the autonomy of reason and to recognize the dependence of our thinking, particularly in the moral and political realm, on principles that bind us from without. "Autonomy" is itself a term with many meanings, and I should make clear at the outset which sense I have in mind. Sometimes it means our capacity to grasp and do what is right regardless of threats or rewards coming from some superior, human or divine, our right to think for ourselves instead of having to defer to custom or coercion. In this

---

[5] Jean-François Lyotard, *La condition post-moderne* (Paris: Minuit, 1979). See also his book, *Le différend* (Paris: Minuit, 1983).

sense, the term denotes a certain kind of independence that we can or should enjoy in our relations to others. It is not the object of my critique. But autonomy can also refer to the nature of our relation to the principles themselves by which we think and act. Their authority, it is supposed, comes from us alone, since there can be no reasons to do one thing rather than another except insofar as we take them to be reasons: it is up to us to decide what import, if any, the facts as they are will have for our conduct. That the world itself is normatively mute except for the principles we impose upon it – this is the idea of autonomy, running through so much of the moral, political, and even scientific thought of modernity, which I contest in various ways during the course of this book.

Let me therefore explain a bit more why such an idea has seemed so persuasive and why it ought nonetheless to be replaced by a different view of the mind as essentially responsive to reasons. What this different view involves and how it fits together with my other theme, the essential historicity of reason, also deserve some general remarks, even though the essays that follow explore these matters in considerable detail.

Ever since the Scientific Revolution, a naturalistic picture of the world as a realm of value-neutral facts has grown in prestige and has encouraged in turn the view that how we ought to think and act is ultimately a matter of principles whose authority derives from us alone. Though not always explicit, the alliance between these two outlooks has proven extraordinarily influential. For instance, modern conceptions of freedom, whether their focus is individual conduct or political association, typically gravitate toward the idea of self-determination, claiming that we ourselves are responsible, if not for the conditions we find ourselves in, then for the terms on which we deal with them. Thinking moves so easily along these lines because of the background assumption that, were it not for the norms we introduce, there would exist only the things that natural science has come to take as its domain – matter in motion, along perhaps with minds (unless they too are but matter in motion), but nothing outside us to point us one way rather than another. The necessity we face of having to impose a rational order of our own construction on an alien world is held to constitute our very dignity as human beings. It is in this regard that Kant has been the paradigmatic philosopher of modernity. Quite apart from his more particular doctrines, he was the first to recognize clearly that, once we accept the naturalism of the scientific worldview, reason must be seen as essentially self-legislating or "autonomous" if we are to believe that it exists at all.

I am convinced that this conception of mind and world, however influential, is fundamentally mistaken. A number of essays in this book, particularly Chapters 2 through 5, are devoted to showing, by reference to certain issues in moral philosophy and also by way of generalization, that a different approach is necessary. Thus I argue in Chapter 5, against some of the central strands of modern thought, that there is no way to reason ourselves into the moral point of view from some supposedly more basic position outside it: morality speaks for itself, and we must simply see and acknowledge that another's good is in itself a reason for action on our part. This lesson, which I term "the autonomy of morality" (to underscore the contrast with the Kantian ethic of autonomy), has general implications. Thought is unintelligible unless understood as guided by reasons that are not of our own making. We cannot, for instance, believe at will (say, that the number of stars is even), but can only believe what we see there to be some reason to regard as true. Though freedom is the power to choose independently of external constraint, choosing entails heeding the reasons we regard as favoring one thing rather than another. The idea of self-determination misses the way that the freedom that makes us the beings we are involves both active and passive moments, commitment as well as response. It cannot be right to say that we impose our reason on a normatively mute world. For reason itself consists in a responsiveness to reasons, reasons that prescribe how we ought to think and act.[6]

"Naturalism" is invoked today in a number of different senses. Some of them – that knowledge rests on experience, that explanations appealing to the supernatural should be avoided – are not at issue. The naturalism I oppose is the view, increasingly hegemonic in modern times, that all that there is, properly speaking, is what the natural sciences say to exist – physical and psychological facts, in other words, and thus nothing intrinsically normative, no facts about what we ought to do. This naturalism, despite its deference to modern science, is not a theorem of any scientific theory. It is a metaphysical position, according to which the scientific image of nature answers our philosophical questions about the ultimate makeup of reality. As a piece of metaphysics, it is to be judged, as all metaphysical theories have to be, by considering how well it ties together our experience as a whole. In this regard, it does quite poorly, I maintain. If we cannot make sense of reason, or indeed of thinking in general, except as involving a responsiveness to reasons, then reasons must be seen as themselves a part of what there is.

The idea that we are in the end bound only by principles we institute ourselves has had a wider currency than these rather abstract remarks might suggest. It has played a pervasive role in modern culture, from the individualist celebration of experiments in living to the aesthetic ideologies of the avant-garde. It comes to powerful expression in the writings of Friedrich Nietzsche, whose constant refrain – every value we honor, even the obligation to truth, is a means we have willed, and could have willed

---

[6] I develop this claim, not only in a number of essays in this book, but also in a book I have published on the nature of the self, *Les pratiques du moi* (Paris: Presses Universitaires de France, 2004).

otherwise, to give shape and meaning to our lives – continues for all its fundamental incoherence (see Chapter 9) to exercise a continuing fascination on the contemporary mind. The idea of autonomy knows indeed no party allegiances, since it also inspires a common way of commending the political ideals of modern liberal democracy, of which Nietzsche himself was no friend.

In many people's eyes, it has seemed axiomatic that the ideal of democratic self-government consists in a people or its representatives laying down themselves, in a legislative assembly or more firmly by way of a constitution, what the rules establishing their common life together shall be. The principles by which they are to be bound, defining the powers of the state and the rights of citizens, must be principles whose authority stems from them alone. This is a deep misunderstanding. As I explain in Chapters 6 through 8, it misses the moral framework within which alone liberal democracy acquires its distinctive character. No supposed expression of the people's will can count as authoritative, no appeal to what would be the object of reasonable agreement can serve as the standard for the basic terms of political association, as in the "political liberalism" of Rawls and similar thinkers (myself included), unless "democratic will" and "reasonable agreement" are defined by reference to a moral principle of respect for persons. This principle, requiring that the necessarily coercive rules of political life be nonetheless acceptable to all whom they are to bind (acceptable on the assumption that they themselves endorse such a principle), has therefore an authority independent of the democratic order itself. For democracy to be possible, citizens must be understood as standing under the obligation to respect one another as persons, in advance of the laws they give themselves.

No doubt my insistence that reasons form part of the fabric of reality, that the world contains a normative dimension to which our reason is responsive, will strike many as simply extravagant. This impression will not be lessened by my having sometimes chosen to call the position "platonistic," in allusion to this one element of common ground with Plato's theory of Forms. Just as Plato held that in addition to trees and our ideas of trees there must exist the Form, or what it is to be a tree, so I claim that not all that exists is physical or psychological in character. Reasons, which are irreducibly normative, must also figure among what is real. "On the Platonistic picture," writes Allan Gibbard, "among the facts of the world are facts of what is rational and what is not ... If this is what anyone seriously believes, then I simply want to debunk it." Gibbard's scorn turns out, however, to be little more than an expression of his own *parti pris*, for he justifies it by adding, "Nothing in a plausible, naturalistic picture of our place in the universe requires these non-natural facts."[7] To be sure,

---

[7] Gibbard, *Wise Choices, Apt Feelings* (Cambridge, MA: Harvard University Press, 1990), p. 154.

nothing in a naturalistic worldview allows that there exist such things as reasons and thus facts about what is rational. But the question is precisely whether that worldview is in the end a tenable one.

It is often said, in company with Max Weber, that in modern times the world has become "disenchanted" (*entzaubert*). I am not contesting the phenomenon. But it is essential to understand aright what it consists in. Perhaps it is true (though many will disagree) that we can no longer in good conscience suppose that the world harbors any element of the divine or the sacred, which is what Weber meant by disenchantment.[8] Yet this does not entail that the world is barren of all normative distinctions. Sometimes naturalism has leaned upon such an argument, as though reasons for belief and action must draw their authority from someone – either God or us. That assumption is incoherent, however. Reasons have their own authority, and persons acquire authority because of the reasons we see to trust or honor them. If we ought indeed to endorse the disenchanted view of the world, then presumably there are good grounds for doing so distinct from anyone's say-so or from what happens to be the spirit of the times, grounds that really do obtain.

Some have promised that we can have "objectivity without objects," that we can regard our statements about reasons as true or false without falling into the platonistic illusion of supposing that there actually are reasons that make them true or false.[9] Unsurprisingly, this *via media* proves elusive. Statements are true in virtue of things being as they claim, and to back away from their objects having to exist means equivocating about their really being true. Ultimately, the charge of metaphysical extravagance is but the reflection of an unbudging allegiance, doctrinaire or implicit, to a pre-given notion of the world. Though there is no point postulating entities beyond necessity, there is also no point deciding *a priori* what can and cannot exist – which includes (as I stress in Chapter 3) refusing to own up to the implications when we do accept that thinking is essentially responsive to reasons.

Still, I can dispel some misconceptions if I note right away – I examine the matter at length in Chapter 5 (§7) – that I am not imagining reasons to occupy some ethereal, platonic heaven, cut off from the natural world here below. Reasons for belief and action depend on the physical and psychological facts being as they are. There is a reason to take an umbrella only if it is indeed raining, or a reason to get a drink of water only if I happen to be thirsty. Similarly, reasons exist only insofar as beings exist capable of doing things for reasons (such beings including, I would add,

---

[8] See, for instance, his famous essay, *Wissenschaft als Beruf* (Berlin: Duncker & Humblot, 1996).

[9] A recent example is Hilary Putnam, *Ethics without Ontology* (Cambridge, MA: Harvard University Press, 2004), Chapter 3.

not just human beings, but all higher animals to which we can attribute beliefs and desires). A reason is a reason for someone, and for someone able to take up the possibility the reason endorses. In short, reasons are relational in character: they consist in certain features of the natural world *counting in favor of* possibilities of thought and action belonging to intelligent beings. Yet a relation of this sort is not only irreducibly normative, given that "counting in favor of" resists explication by reference to natural facts alone. It also obtains independently of our beliefs or wishes about whether it does so. That our situation gives us reason to believe this or to do that is a fact we discover, sometimes immediately and sometimes only as a result of reflection.

Now it may appear puzzling how this conception of reasons can be squared with the background theme of this book, which is the historicity of reason itself. We always deliberate from within a body of inherited belief, even when we set about evaluating and changing where we stand. Yet if all our thought and action holds itself accountable to an independent order of reasons, do we not thereby aspire, whatever our eventual success in reasoning as we ought, to transcend the circumstances in which we happen to find ourselves? In one respect, I have already disposed of this worry. What we have reason to do depends, as I have said, on the way the world is as well as on our possibilities. As these factors change, so too can the reasons to which they give rise. Far from its being true that we must transcend our own time and place in order to make contact with the reasons there are, the only way to determine what it is that we ought to do is by attending to the actual situation before us. To make sure that I have a reason to take an umbrella, I need to look out the window once more.

In another respect, however, a more serious conflict may seem to drive apart the two leading themes of this book. *Principles* purport to settle in advance how we ought to proceed when determining what to believe or do, as opposed, say, to policies that it may be expedient to adopt at one time rather than another. But if they then amount to reasons that there always are – independent of changing circumstances – to think and act in certain ways (as my "platonistic" approach would imply), then supposing that such things as principles exist may appear difficult to reconcile with the idea that what we see reason to do turns, as a rule, on our historical context. How can we guide ourselves by the timeless reasons that principles embody if our reason itself is a creature of time?

Here too I am convinced that the tension is only apparent. It vanishes once one thinks in the right way about the rather obvious distinction between truth on the one hand and our access to it on the other. All truth as such is timeless. If it is true that Socrates entered the agora on a certain day, then it is always true; the proposition can never change its truth-value. Even so, our ability to ascertain some truth may depend on beliefs and standards that would not have been ours, had our traditions and experience been different. Our access to that truth may in this sense be historically contingent. And yet – here is the crucial point – this fact alone does not undermine our confidence in the truth of what we have discovered; or at least it ought not to do so if we have no positive grounds to think that those beliefs and standards might be incorrect. A central tenet of the contextualist epistemology outlined earlier is that we need to worry about the worth of our existing commitments only insofar as we have some reason to think they may be faulty, and such a reason cannot be the mere fact that we hold them or hold them as the result of a history that might have turned out otherwise. A reason for doubt must be one that indicates how we may have actually gone wrong. The historical contingency that lies at the heart of our finitude is not, I have been urging, an obstacle to be overcome or a cause for regret, but the very means by which we lay hold of truth.

Now amongst the truths we take ourselves to possess are not only truths about the natural world, but also truths about how in general we ought to think and act – truths, that is, about what principles should shape our conduct, intellectual and practical. They too, if they have some substance instead of being truisms such as "contradictions are to be avoided," are likely to have recommended themselves for reasons we could appreciate only because previous thought and experience happened to have gone a certain way. But though time-bound in their availability, they are still timeless in scope. Nor do they warrant anything less than our unqualified allegiance unless, once again, we have uncovered some reason to believe that they may not, after all, be correct principles to endorse. Being part of history means having a place to stand from which we can discern the way things really are.

FREEDOM AND PHILOSOPHY

It may seem that in these essays I have been eager to come up with ways in which we are not really so free as we imagine. But a better description of my purpose would be that I have been concerned to bring out the preconditions for there being such a thing as human freedom. Without a responsiveness to reasons and a rootedness in history, choosing what to do and thinking for ourselves would be unintelligible, and it has been a failing of modern philosophy to have denied or neglected these forms of dependence that make being our own person possible.

More specifically, it is a central claim of this book that freedom cannot be elevated, as it so often is in modern thought, to the status of being the supreme political value. We cannot in general make sense of what we prize as freedom except by reference to other human goods. How else, as I explain in Chapter 7, can we distinguish, among the various influences and rules that govern our behavior, those that act as harmful constraints and those that serve instead as enabling conditions? It is just this fact that explains why freedom is not a univocal concept, but takes on many different senses (none of them the supposedly "true meaning" of freedom), depending on the other goods with which it is connected.

Thus, in particular, both individual liberty and self-government have in modern liberal democracy the general shape they do because, so I argue in Chapter 6, they draw upon the even deeper value of respect for persons. Respect is itself, of course, a term with many meanings. The relevant sense in this case has to do with the distinctive nature of political principles that sets them off from the other moral principles to which we may hold people's conduct accountable. The principles that structure political life, insofar as they become a part of law, have an essentially coercive character. Compliance is effected by force, if need be. But the essential liberal conviction is that the use of coercion is legitimate only if the fundamental principles of political association are rationally acceptable to all who share indeed a commitment to living together on mutually acceptable terms. That conviction expresses a basic kind of respect for persons. For to seek compliance by the threat of force alone is to treat citizens merely as means. It is to engage their essential capacity to think and act for reasons solely so as to ensure public order. To respect them as ends, as persons whose reason is of equal moment with our own, is by contrast to impose on them only those principles whose grounds they too can appreciate. This idea of respect may seem so evident that we barely notice the way it frames our thinking. Yet it defines the moral "we" that we are. And however much it may for us go without saying, to hold that the rules of political society must accord with the reason of its members is not a deliverance of reason itself. It represents a contingent development, one quite alien to other cultures of the past and of the present too, for which the crucial demand on any political form of life is, for instance, that it be pleasing to God.

That is not the only way in which I have sought to put the idea of freedom into proper perspective. The last chapter of this book (Chapter 10) charts the limits of a widespread notion of how we ought to live our lives that expresses in effect a particular ideal of individual freedom, an ideal going back far before modern times to the beginnings of Western philosophy. It is the view that we ought to take charge of our own existence, weigh our abilities, circumstances, and interests so as to devise a rational plan of life, instead of letting ourselves become the hostage of chance and whim. Only then, it is supposed, can we grasp the nature of our good and set about achieving it; only then, in Plato's words, can we become the "masters and architects of ourselves" (*arxanta auton hautou kai kosmesanta*).[10] So comprehensive an attitude of foresight and control misses, I believe, a key dimension of what makes for a life lived well. We would be the poorer if our lives unfolded

---

[10] Plato, *Republic* 443d.

according to a plan, however well thought out that plan might be, for then we would be without those strokes of good fortune that befall us when we least expect them and often transform our very sense of what is valuable. Indeed, our good itself is never something whose character is already settled. In many ways it takes shape only in and through the process of living itself. For as our abilities and circumstances change, often in ways we could not have foreseen, so too do the forms of human flourishing we thereby have reason to pursue. Self-mastery is a flawed ideal.

I want to conclude with two remarks about the spirit in which I have written these essays. First, I remain committed to the "political liberalism" that I have championed in earlier works and develop further here as well. This means that I continue to distinguish between the considerations relevant for defining the basis, the publicly shareable basis, of a liberal political order and the more complete story we may tell ourselves of what those considerations really entail about man and his place in the world and about the things of ultimate value in life, a story that is likely to be the object of reasonable disagreement among our fellow citizens. Many of the points I am most concerned to establish in this book – the historicity of reason, the "platonistic" account of reasons, the flaws in the ideal of living in accord with a rational plan of life – belong in the second category. I do not regard them as essential to our self-understanding as liberal citizens (far from it!), though I do not think of them as any the less correct. Liberalism, as Michael Walzer once aptly observed, is "the art of separation."[11] It involves learning to live with others on terms that embody only part, and perhaps not the deepest part, of the truth as we fully conceive it. Still, I also believe that we as citizens do well to see that our political life is founded upon a principle, the principle of equal respect, whose authority does not derive from our collective will since it serves to define the democratic ideal itself. In this regard, my critique of the modern idea of being subject only to principles we institute ourselves points to a sense of being bound from without that we ought to share as citizens, and no doubt do, if only implicitly.

The second remark is a note of modesty. Philosophy is in my view a wrestling with problems that always threaten to elude our best efforts at solution. No sooner do we manage to dispose of one aspect than another looks all the more difficult to accommodate. It is what I call at the beginning of Chapter 3, in a sort of philosophical profession of faith, "*the law of the conservation of trouble*," and I point out there how it applies to my realism about reasons no less than to other matters. I have had this law continually in mind as I wrote and rewrote all the essays in this book. Philosophical problems are not, I believe, illusory just because they defy

[11] Walzer, "Liberalism and the Art of Separation," *Political Theory* 12:3 (August 1984), pp. 315–330.

anything like definitive answers. Nor is there any profit in being diffident or cagey about the conclusions that appear, perhaps only provisionally, to be on balance the best. The views I defend in this book embody what I hold to be true, and presenting them forthrightly makes them all the more accessible to criticism. And thus, if I reject the naturalism underlying so much of contemporary philosophy, I do not do so in the way that opposition to it today too often adopts. I have no sympathy with the philosophical quietism that draws its inspiration from Wittgenstein and holds that in philosophy theories are to be avoided since the problems at issue are to be dissolved rather than solved. Quietists merely keep quiet about the theoretical positions on which they actually rely. I prefer to do my thinking out in the open.

Part I of this book contains a number of essays that expound in a general way and from different angles the two principal themes of the book, the historicity of reason and the responsiveness to reasons inherent in all our thinking. Parts II and III then develop these themes in the areas of moral and political philosophy. In Part IV, I propose in the same spirit some reflections about why we cannot fail to care about truth and why living well requires remaining open to the unforeseeable ways our good itself changes over time.

PART I

REASON AND REASONS

1

History and Truth

History, according to Schopenhauer, teaches but a single lesson: *eadem, sed aliter* – the same things happen again and again, only differently. "Once one has read Herodotus, one has studied enough history, philosophically speaking."[1] If, like Schopenhauer, we survey human affairs from afar, assuming the stance of a neutral spectator, suspending all our own interests and commitments, we will certainly have to agree. At so great a remove, what else will we see but, as he said, countless variations on the same old theme of people pursuing dreams that they never achieve, or that they find disappointing when they do?

Consider the cardinal cases where history is held to do more than repeat itself, where it is said to show direction and progress. Theories that scientists in one age endorse nonetheless meet with refutation in the next. Technological innovations aimed at easing man's estate go on to create new needs and burdens. Modern democracies, despite their promise, do not end the domination of the many by the few. Progress is bound to seem an illusion, if we look at life from the outside, abstracting from our own convictions about nature and the human good. For then we cannot make out the extent to which our predecessors, despite their defeats, were still on the right track. All that we will perceive is their inevitable failure to accomplish the ends they set themselves. History will serve only to remind us that man's reach always exceeds his grasp.

Yet, ordinarily, we think quite differently from Schopenhauer about the past, and about modern times in particular. In reflecting on the course of the last 500 years, we usually conclude that great strides have been made in understanding nature and in creating a more just society. Patterns of scientific and moral progress come into view, once we lean on established conceptions of nature and scientific method, of individual rights and human flourishing. Classical mechanics constituted an advance over

---

[1] Arthur Schopenhauer, *Die Welt als Wille und Vorstellung*, Ergänzungen, §38.

Aristotelian physics, we then say, because it came nearer to the truth about matter, force, and motion, and perceived more clearly the importance of results expressible in the form of mathematical laws. So too in the moral realm: for all its imperfections, the rise of liberal democracy represented a turn for the better, when measured against the conviction that political life, particularly where coercive force is involved, ought to respect the equal dignity of each of its members.

1. HISTORICIST SKEPTICISM

When we abandon the view from nowhere and turn to appraising the past by our present standards, new doubts arise, however. Relying as they must on our current ideas of what is true, important, and right, our judgments about progress can begin to appear irredeemably parochial. We may wonder whether they amount to anything more than applauding others in proportion to their having happened to think like us. Is not the notion of progress basically an instrument of self-congratulation? What can we say to someone who objects that our present standpoint is merely ours, with no greater right than any other to issue verdicts upon earlier times?

One way of handling this worry has long proved immensely influential; indeed, it taps into a dominant strand of Western philosophy. Philosophers since Plato have generally believed that there exists a body of timeless, universally valid principles governing how we ought to think and act, and also that we discover these principles by becoming, as it were, timeless ourselves. Standing back from all that the contingencies of history have made of us, viewing the world *sub specie aeternitatis*, we then can take our bearings from reason itself.[2]

Theories of scientific and moral progress are very much a modern phenomenon, of course. But the Enlightenment, which pioneered them, still found congenial the age-old ideal of reason as transcendence when articulating its vision of the progressive dynamic of modern thought. A prime example of this tendency is Condorcet's famous essay on progress (*Esquisse d'un tableau historique des progrès de l'esprit humain*, 1793). Once people in the West, he argued, threw off the yoke of tradition and recognized at last that knowledge arises only through careful generalizations from the givens of sense experience, scientific growth and moral improvement were bound to accelerate as they had done since the seventeenth century.

---

[2] I am alluding here to an important but often neglected distinction between two senses of "universal" as applied to principles – "universally binding" and "universally accessible or justifiable" – a distinction I have discussed at length in *The Morals of Modernity* (Cambridge: Cambridge University Press, 1996), Chapter 2, §5. The distinction will prove pertinent in what follows.

In a similar spirit, we may believe that our present point of view amounts to more than just the current state of opinion, because we have carefully worked over existing views in the light of reason. We may regard ourselves as having achieved a critical distance toward our own age, even as we avoid the detachment of Schopenhauer's neutral spectator. For reason is not a view from nowhere. It lines up the world from a specific perspective, defined by the principles of thought and action it embodies. It allows us to determine which of our present convictions may rightly serve as standards for the evaluation of the past. Consequently, the judgments we then make about scientific and moral progress will not simply express our own habits of mind.

Or so it seems. The rub is that our conception of the demands of reason always bears the mark of our own time and place. To be sure, some rules of reasoning, such as those instructing us to avoid contradictions and to pursue the good, are timelessly available. But they can do little by themselves to orient our thinking and conduct; they have to work in tandem with more substantive principles, if we are to receive much guidance. The reason to which we appeal when critically examining our existing opinions must therefore combine both these factors. And yet, the more concrete aspects of what we understand by reason involve principles we have come to embrace because of their apparent success in the past, or because of our general picture of the mind's place in nature. As these background beliefs change, so does our conception of reason, and earlier conceptions sometimes turn out to look quite mistaken.

Once again, Condorcet's essay offers a perfect illustration. His confidence in the existence of elementary sensations, uncolored by prior assumptions and conceptual schemes, belongs to a brand of empiricism, triumphant in his day through the influence of Locke, which we can no longer accept.[3] Our own notions of reason, however self-evident they seem to us, may well encounter a similar fate. But even if they do not meet with rejection, they will certainly appear dated, shaped as they are in their formulation by the particular historical path that our experience and reflection have taken up to the present.

Doubts of this sort about progress have intensified over the past few centuries, as reason has shown itself to be less a tribunal standing outside history than a code expressing our changing convictions about how we ought to think and act. It was already in this spirit that Hegel undertook to

---

[3] Consider the very first sentences of Condorcet's *Esquisse*: "L'homme naît avec la faculté de recevoir des sensations; d'apercevoir et de distinguer dans celles qu'il reçoit les sensations simples dont elles sont composées, de les retenir, de les reconnaître, de les combiner; de comparer entre elles ces combinaisons; de saisir ce qu'elles ont de commun et ce qui les distingue; d'attacher enfin des signes à tous les objets, pour les reconnaître mieux, et en faciliter des combinaisons nouvelles."

"historicize" reason, though in a way designed to hold on to the idea of progress. The "Bacchanalian revel" in which one conception of reason has succeeded another exhibits in hindsight, so he claimed, a pattern with an inner necessity: each understanding of reason proved unsatisfactory in its own terms – its methods and goals failing to cohere, for instance – and could only be remedied by its successor, until there emerged the conception that we (or rather Hegel) possess at present, which alone lives up to its expectations.

Today, our sense of contingency is far too acute for any such story to appear credible. We may certainly believe that our present conception of reason has improved upon preceding ones, which themselves rightly corrected the errors of those before them. Still, we have to admit that different improvements might also have been possible, and that our present view too may someday have to be revised. Even though the standards we invoke for judging ourselves and the past may be functioning perfectly, they can seem too much a hostage of chance and circumstance to justify any conclusions about progress.

2. GROWTH AND PROGRESS

In order to grasp the exact import of these doubts, we need to attend to the crucial difference between *growth* and *progress*. Take the case of modern natural science. No one can plausibly see it as a mere succession of different theories, each one a fresh speculation about the world. In antiquity and the Middle Ages, the study of nature did often look like that – and parts of the social sciences still do today. Beginning in the seventeenth century, however, physics and then chemistry and biology turned themselves into cumulative enterprises. They set their sights on securing conclusions solid enough to be passed on as guiding premises for future inquiry. In large part, it was the combination of mathematics and experiment that made this possible; experimental laws in mathematical form lend themselves to precise testing and, once confirmed, are unlikely to be discredited later, even if they have to be fine-tuned in the face of new data. At the same time, their precision helps to orient further research, setting limits on the hypotheses that henceforth are to be taken seriously. Not by accident, the history of modern science displays a clear line of development leading to our present conception of nature. Each stage along the way has extended and corrected the achievements of its predecessors. Growth in this sense is unmistakable.

To be sure, growth has not always proceeded by simple accretion. Sometimes, new theories have appropriated previous results by recasting them within very different conceptual vocabularies. Sometimes, well-corroborated theories have had to be rejected because they failed to square with newly available evidence. And sometimes these two kinds of theory-change have gone together – as in the "scientific revolutions" so dear to Thomas Kuhn, in which one "paradigm" supposedly replaces another by means of a "gestalt-switch." It is nonetheless true that the revolutions occurring within the modern sciences of nature, as opposed to those that preceded or inaugurated them, have typically carried over an accumulated stock of experimental laws. Maxwell's equations of the electromagnetic field, for instance, survived the advent of relativity theory, even though they had to be reconceived so as to make no reference to a luminiferous ether.

Kuhn complained that science textbooks write the history of their discipline backward from the present, disguising its dramatic twists and turns as step-by-step contributions to the present-day edifice of knowledge.[4] No doubt they do distort the past. Yet only in modern times have such textbooks played much of a role at all, and that is in itself a significant fact. Only recently has it become possible (and indeed essential to scientific training) that past results be expounded as a body of systematic doctrine, complemented by problem sets and answer keys. The very prominence of these texts testifies to the cumulative character of modern science.

Growth is not the same as progress, however. Progress means movement toward a goal, whereas growth is essentially a retrospective concept, referring to a process in which new formations emerge by building upon earlier ones. Progress generally entails growth, but it posits, in addition, a terminus toward which that growth is thought to be advancing. Now, common opinion holds that science aims at the truth and that therefore its astounding growth in the modern era represents progress in the direction of that goal. No doubt so simplistic a view calls for some immediate qualifications. The modern sciences of nature do not seek truth in general, as though scientific knowledge were the only sort worth having (a scientistic prejudice). They focus on the natural world, and they devote their energy not to merely piling up truths (the more the better) but to assembling truths that can help explain the workings of nature. Moreover, the so-called search for truth really encompasses two distinct goals – acquiring truths and avoiding error (to see the difference, note that if we were interested solely in acquiring truths, we would believe everything, and if we wanted only to avoid error, we would believe nothing), and scientists must pursue the two in tandem and according to their willingness to risk making mistakes for the sake of obtaining new information about the world.[5] Finally, the truth at which science aims need not be a single, rock-bottom order of things, as defined, for example, by microphysics. Nature may embrace (as I believe in fact it does) an irreducible plurality of levels of reality.

---

[4] Thomas S. Kuhn, *The Structure of Scientific Revolutions*, 2nd ed. (Chicago: University of Chicago Press, 1970; orig. ed., 1960), pp. 136ff.
[5] For some details, see my essay, "Descartes and Scepticism," in S. Gaukroger (ed.), *The Blackwell Guide to Descartes' Meditations* (Oxford: Blackwell, 2005).

Yet these amendments do not address the fundamental objection that the common view of modern science has come to provoke – namely, that the idea of scientific progress appears suspect, once we recognize the historical contingency of the standards we use to judge the present and the past. If our current view of nature counts as well-founded only by reference to a conception of reason that itself arises from the vicissitudes of experience, how can we maintain that its improvement on previous views represents progress toward the truth? The question does not challenge the existence of scientific growth: plainly, there has been since the sixteenth and seventeenth centuries a steady accumulation of experimental laws, and where earlier theories met with difficulty they were corrected in ways that produced the body of knowledge now expounded in the textbooks of the various disciplines. But with what right can we regard this process as leading to anything other than simply the prevailing opinions of the day? Why should we suppose that it has at the same time brought us closer to the goal of discovering the truth about nature?

Kuhn was himself an eloquent exponent of this widespread sort of skepticism. Though he continued to refer to "progress," the term as he used it meant solely growth in puzzle-solving ability. Progress toward the truth seemed to him an idle notion, irrelevant to the analysis of modern science: "Does it really help to imagine that there is some one full, objective, true account of nature and that the proper measure of scientific achievement is the extent to which it brings us closer to that ultimate goal?" His answer was no, since "no Archimedean platform is available for the pursuit of science other than the historically situated one already in place."[6] Scientists do not decide among rival theories by invoking truth as a standard. Or, if they do, it is but shorthand for the principles on which they actually rely – namely, the methods and scientific values sanctioned by the present state of inquiry. Truth – that is, nature as it is in itself – makes sense as a goal only so long as reason is thought to offer the means for pulling ever closer to it. Once the ideal of reason as transcendence loses its plausibility, giving way to the recognition that science always takes its bearings from a historically determined body of beliefs, our understanding of the aim of science must become similarly more modest. Its goal, Kuhn claimed, consists in solving the puzzles that current doctrine happens to pose.

This mode of argument has become a familiar refrain in many areas of contemporary thought. It fuels, for example, the vast company of post-modern theorists who regard the idea of science progressing toward the truth as the paradigm of those illusory stories, or "meta-narratives," by which modernity has sought to give its achievements a universal

---

[6] Kuhn, *The Structure of Scientific Revolutions*, p. 171, and *The Road since Structure* (Chicago: University of Chicago Press, 2000), p. 95.

legitimacy.[7] In my view, historicist attacks on scientific realism (to give them a name) stem from an important insight. Contrary to one of the deepest aspirations of the Enlightenment, if not of philosophy in general, reason does not pry us free from the contingencies of time and place. Substantive principles of rationality are always framed in the light of beliefs and practices bequeathed by a past that could have turned out otherwise.

All the same, the contemporary skepticism about progress also trades upon a false assumption, which it shares with the very ideal of transcendent reason it rejects. The givens of history are not obstacles, but rather means. Reasoning from where we find ourselves is the very way by which we match our claims against the world. Creatures of chance though we are, the world itself remains the object of our thinking, and the reasons we find to prefer one belief to another must be understood as the reasons we have to think we are drawing closer to the truth.

3. AGREEING AND COPING

There is no better way to develop these points than to look in some detail at the most famous skeptic of recent years. I mean Richard Rorty, a self-styled "left-wing Kuhnian," who provides the most illuminating example of all that is right but also wrong-headed in the antirealist philosophies so common in our culture. Unlike many other friends of truth and progress, I shall not engage in a round of Rorty-bashing in order to declare victorious, as though by default, all the orthodox views he sought to overthrow. Enough has already been said, I trust, to evidence my sympathy with the historicized concept of reason that serves as the springboard of his thinking. I intend instead to bring out the single line of argument that, amidst his changing formulations and copious references to other figures, ties together his work as a whole. My object is to locate the precise spot in this argument where insight turns into error.

Common sense says that there is a world "out there," existing independently of the mind, and Rorty wisely denied that it was his wish to deny so plain a fact. Even where we do shape the world to suit our purposes, we proceed by exploiting the laws of nature at work in the things around us. But truth, Rorty insisted, is not similarly out there. Truth is a property of the sentences we utter, a property we judge that they have by standards we ourselves establish. Although sometimes the relevant standard may demand that we simply look and let the physical world determine the truth or falsity of a given statement (for example, "the cat is on the mat"; "the proton has crossed the cloud chamber"), our very idea of when perception can decide an issue, as well as the interpretation we then place on what we see, depend on a whole web of other beliefs and ways of dealing with the world. To call

---

[7] See Jean-François Lyotard, *La condition post-moderne* (Paris: Editions du Minuit, 1979).

a statement true, he claimed, amounts to saying that those who share with us a certain framework of belief have equally reason to endorse it. The only substantive thing we can mean by talk of truth is that a given statement coheres, in a way sanctioned by present standards, with our existing body of settled belief. To maintain that a true proposition "corresponds" to the way the world really is can signify no more than this, since all that we can mean by "the world" is "whatever the vast majority of our beliefs not currently in question are currently thought to be about."[8]

Being true is not, of course, the same as being justified. Yet, for Rorty, the fact that a statement justified by our lights might still turn out false signified only that a better view of things may come along in which the statement would no longer pass muster. The distinction between "true" and "justified" serves, he argued, simply a cautionary function, warning us that we may always find reason to change our minds. "True" does not refer to some final point of view that we are laboring to attain and that, once achieved, will show us the world as it really is. Or, more exactly, Rorty's position was that we do not need to think in these terms. The idea of such a viewpoint plays no part in our actual decisions about what to believe. Truth, not being "out there," does not therefore constitute a goal of inquiry, and scientific progress cannot consist in getting closer to the truth. What progress meant for him, as for Kuhn, is not strictly progress at all, but rather growth: an increased ability to make successful predictions and to solve the problems posed by existing doctrine.[9]

"The world does not speak," Rorty liked to quip, "only we do." We have no other vocabularies than the language games we have invented ourselves. Since truth is always judged by their means, he occasionally went on to announce, in an evident desire to disconcert, that truth is something *made* rather than *found* in a reality lying outside our forms of speech.[10] It is tempting to snap back that, while our sentences are manifestly our own creation, what renders them true or false – namely, the world – is not. True statements are made, but their truth is not made; it is discovered.[11] This easy rejoinder misses the point, however. It fails to do justice to the historicist insight inspiring Rorty's and many others' rejection of traditional ideas of truth and progress. What sense can there be in holding that truth is found, if the very standards by which we determine truth and falsity – in other words, the roles we have the world play in shaping our thinking – are as much a product of human history as the beliefs they serve to evaluate? Reason, it

---

[8] Richard Rorty, "The World Well Lost" (1972), as reprinted in his *Consequences of Pragmatism* (Minneapolis: University of Minnesota Press, 1982), p. 14.

[9] Rorty, *Truth and Progress* (Cambridge: Cambridge University Press, 1998), pp. 5, 39.

[10] Rorty, *Contingency, Irony, and Solidarity* (Cambridge: Cambridge University Press, 1989), pp. 6–7.

[11] See John Searle, "Rationality and Realism," *Dædalus* 122 (4) (Fall 1993), pp. 55–83.

then seems, does not teach us how to let the world itself make our statements true or false; it shows us how the world as presently conceived bears on the statements we happen to utter. If truth is not found, why not then conclude that it must be made?

Nonetheless, precisely because he considered truth to be of little consequence in our actual decisions about what to believe, Rorty eschewed in his more careful moments the contrast between making and finding. If truth is indeed an uninteresting notion, it scarcely deserves to be the object of so striking a theory. His point was instead to discard as an empty slogan the idea that science and morality aim at "the truth" about nature and the human good, however truth may be understood. Rorty's more considered proposal was that we learn to regard them as activities whose goal is to expand the horizons of intersubjective agreement, accommodating new experience and hitherto neglected or flouted interests. His favored contrast then became one between objectivity and solidarity. If objectivity means taking our bearings from reality itself, it needs to give way, so he claimed, to the more coherent ideal of striving for solidarity, the unforced agreement with others. We do better to make hope rather than knowledge – reasoning together rather than answerability to the world – our highest aspiration.[12] For science itself does not undertake to discover more and more of the truth about how nature works. Its purpose is instead, Rorty averred, to devise by reasoned argument ever more satisfactory syntheses of theory and experiment. So, too, our moral thinking is most profitably understood, not as trying to determine what we truly owe to one another, but as constructing increasingly inclusive communities in which free and open discussion replaces the use of force. Agreement, not truth, was Rorty's preferred idiom for formulating what he called his "pragmatism."

Now the classical pragmatists (Peirce, James, and Dewey) always looked with suspicion at philosophy's habit of setting up dualisms, particularly those that oppose the absolute and permanent to the relative and changeable. Theory and practice, reason and experience, duty and desire do not exclude one another, they insisted, but work together from different angles to help us make sense of the world. Rorty too prided himself on being an antidualist. Yet he seemed unable to state his position without resorting to one or another philosophical dualism of just this sort – if not finding versus making truth, then objectivity versus solidarity. This dualist rhetoric was not accidental. *Le style, c'est l'homme même.* Rorty liked to play off a historicized concept of reason against the idea that inquiry aims at the truth. The traditional antithesis between timeless truth and human

---

[12] Rorty, *Philosophy and Social Hope* (London: Penguin, 1999), and "Solidarity or Objectivity?" in Rorty, *Objectivity, Relativism, and Truth* (Cambridge: Cambridge University Press, 1991), pp. 21–34.

mutability structured his thought from the outset, and he scarcely escaped its hold by arguing, as he did, that only the latter, not the former, matters.

Herein lay Rorty's fatal mistake. For consider how far from obvious it is that solidarity stands opposed to objectivity. Agreement with others can take a variety of forms, depending on the motives that move us to pursue it. Sometimes, for instance, going along with whatever our fellows happen to say affords a cozy kind of companionship. But what makes *reasoned* agreement a good worth achieving if not that it is a sign of our having grasped the way things really are? If we justify a view not only to our own satisfaction but also in a way that others find convincing, have we not thereby all the more reason to think that it is true? The opposition between solidarity and objectivity proves illusory. The best way to see this is to look again, but now more closely, at the nature of reason and justification.

4. OVERCOMING DUALISMS

Deliberating about whether to accept a problematic statement consists, as Rorty rightly said, in determining how well it fits with our existing beliefs. Reason may guide the appraisal, but the requirements that we see reason imposing reflect the changing self-understanding of the community of inquiry to which we belong. All this is correct.

Yet it offers no basis for denying that truth forms the object of our endeavors – and truth conceived as correspondence with reality in the non-technical and everyday meaning of "correspondence," which signifies simply fitting the way the world really is. Indeed, the practice of justification makes no sense without that idea. For what serves to justify or disqualify a statement under scrutiny is not the psychological fact that we happen to hold the beliefs to which we appeal. Our own state of mind, in and of itself, has no bearing on the issue. The probative consideration is rather that the beliefs, so we presume, are true – in other words, that the world is as they describe it to be. (Otherwise, we might just as well "justify" the statement by reference to views of ours we simply entertain, without affirming.) Successfully justifying a claim means, in turn, showing that it deserves to stand alongside our established beliefs, to join them in their role as premises for the resolution of future doubts. It follows that when we examine the credentials of a problematic proposition, our intention is to settle whether it matches the way the world really is. Naturally, background beliefs may themselves be mistaken. We can always err in what we say about reality. Fallibility, however, does not make truth any less our goal. Rorty was right that justification proceeds by appeal to what we already believe, seeking conclusions that others equipped with similar beliefs can equally see reason to embrace. Yet this very activity is indissociable from making our thought responsive to the world. Solidarity and objectivity go hand in hand. Coherence as the test of truth only makes sense if truth itself is understood as correspondence to the way things really are.

A similar verdict applies to the allied dualism he often deployed between coping and copying. He correctly noted that different descriptions of the same thing can prove to be appropriate, depending on which of our various purposes we are pursuing and which audience we are therefore addressing. Sometimes we speak of water as a collection of H_2O molecules, sometimes as an essential nutrient for all of life. Does this mean, as Rorty argued, that our talk aims merely at being useful, not at representing or "copying" the way the world is in itself? Once again, we are given a false alternative – utility and truth are inseparable. We cannot cope with the things around us unless we consider how the world looks from the particular angle we have chosen. Agreed, no single description is the one and only true description. But the existence of many equally true ones mirrors the fact, alluded to before, that the world itself comprises multiple and irreducible levels of reality.[13] Water is both those things and a lot more besides.

These remarks imply that scientific growth must also count as progress toward the truth, when the series of later theories building upon earlier ones yields some element of our present understanding of the natural world. I do not mean to suggest that the two concepts – growth and progress – are synonymous after all. But the only way in which growth may fall short of being progress is by failing to produce beliefs of the sort we ourselves have reason to endorse. (Thus, in Ptolemy's hands, the geocentric theory grew in sophistication, without moving any closer to the truth about the planetary motions.) For to believe that something is the case means holding it to be true, and to the extent that our current beliefs about nature are the result of a self-correcting process, which the history of modern science has undeniably been, we may justifiably regard them as the outcome of progress toward the truth. Where past views do not fit our present convictions, they must be deemed false, and where, having been corrected, they have led to the views we presently hold, we must conclude that we have drawn closer to grasping the world as it really is.

To be sure, truth is then being judged by existing standards. Yet, one might ask, what other standards should we use instead? Like Rorty, many others today continue to endorse a defining assumption of the traditional notion of progress they seek to overturn. They assume that we would only be entitled to consider ourselves nearer the truth than our predecessors if we could rise above our historical situation and vindicate our present views from a vantage point outside the shifting teachings of experience. That is why, arguing rightly that our idea of reason is part and parcel of our changing web of belief, they go on to reject truth as the goal of inquiry.

[13] Cf. John Dupré, *The Disorder of Things* (Cambridge, MA: Harvard University Press, 1993).

Precisely this assumption, however, is the dogma we need to dispel. The real revolution in philosophy would be to regard the contingencies of history as the very means by which we lay hold of reality. We cannot look back (as Hegel supposed) and see in the developments leading to our current body of belief a path that mankind was destined to travel. What we can do is show how our present views represent an improvement over earlier ones, solve the problems they left unanswered, and, to the extent that we can do so, we ought to conclude that the reasons for preferring the new to the old are reasons for thinking we have now a better comprehension of the way the world is.

The principles by which we make these judgments may themselves change as our conception of nature changes. But reason, even though understood in a historicized manner, does not lose its authority to regulate our thought and to determine the progress we have achieved. To have good grounds to alter our beliefs is to have learned from our mistakes, and such are the terms in which we should view the changes our very notion of reason has undergone. As the history of science demonstrates, we have learned how to learn in the very process of learning about the natural world.[14] The principles of rationality we have come to accept are themselves truths, discoveries we have made about how we ought to think and conduct our inquiries into nature. For, in general, principles of thought and action are standards indicating the sorts of reasons there are for what to believe and do; what are called principles of rationality are the most fundamental among such standards. Reasons as well as the principles that identify them are objects of knowledge, and our beliefs about them have the same basic features as our beliefs about other sorts of things.[15] The principles of rationality we endorse are ones we presume to be timelessly, universally valid, just as any belief that is true is one that cannot change its truth-value. But insofar as our grasp of principles is the result of a learning process, they can fail to be timelessly accessible, just as the basis for accepting other sorts of beliefs may depend on the way our experience has happened to go.

5. MORAL PROGRESS

So far I have focused chiefly on progress in the sciences, rather neglecting the idea of moral progress. But this idea too lends itself to a similar reconstruction, and does so even when the term "moral" is taken quite broadly so as to cover all the different elements of a life lived well and not just the duties we owe to others. (Sometimes, a contrast is introduced here between the "moral" and the "ethical," but I will not follow this usage.)

[14] Cf. Dudley Shapere, *Reason and the Search for Knowledge* (Dordrecht: Reidel, 1984), p. 233.
[15] That reasons are an object of knowledge is a theme I pursue in later chapters of this book, particularly in Chapters 3 and 5.

To a significant extent, we can indeed talk of there having been such a thing as moral progress. But as I am suggesting, we must tread carefully here and add some important qualifications. The reason is the need to distinguish between our moral thinking on the one hand and the actual morality exhibited by our deeds and institutions on the other. The two cannot be completely separated, of course. Whether there has been actual moral progress depends in part on whether there has been progress in our moral understanding. Still, one might easily conclude (a quick glance at the twentieth century should suffice) that advances in understanding have not gone hand in hand with a great deal of improvement in the ways we actually treat one another.

Now some will dispute whether progress is a term that can properly be applied even to our moral thinking, taken by itself. For moral progress in this sense presupposes that there can be such a thing as moral knowledge, and it has long been controversial whether our moral judgments really aim at knowledge and whether there is anything in the world about which they can rightly be said to be true or false. I have explained elsewhere, including in some essays in the present book,[16] why moral knowledge is both a possibility and a reality. It is, I have argued, the knowledge we possess of certain kinds of *reasons for action.* I shall not rehearse this argument here, or justify the further claim that also seems to me correct – namely, that the history of moral thought is indeed a history of progress in the apprehension of the truth about what we owe to others and about what makes up human flourishing. I want instead to focus on the point where the parallel between moral progress and scientific progress comes nonetheless to an end. It is the area of life itself, where thinking gives way to action. In part, as I have indicated, this difference is due to our notorious failure to live up to the ideals we profess. But it also reflects an intrinsic feature of what it is that our moral thinking is about.

Agents and not just knowers that we are, we want not only to deepen our understanding of the right and the good, but also to act better in our dealings with others and help to create a better world. Yet there is more than one reason why history offers few signs of progress on the latter score. To be sure, people remain by and large as weak, as thoughtless, and as cruel as they ever were, for all their greater knowledge about what they owe to others. But it is also the case that one of the moral truths we have come to grasp, and which illustrates the progress we have made at the level of moral reflection, is that in general no way of life can secure some things of value except at the expense of others. The human good is not all of a piece. It embraces a motley of fundamental ends that pull in contrary directions and that easily conflict in practice. Martial valor rules out Christian humility; modern democracy may prove incompatible with high

---

[16] See my book, *The Morals of Modernity,* Chapter 5 ("Moral Knowledge"), as well as Chapters 3 and 5 in the present book.

cultural achievement. This "pluralist" outlook, which Isaiah Berlin so memorably championed in our time,[17] has taught us rightly to expect that gains come invariably with losses. As a result, we often find it difficult, if not impossible, to say that one form of life, not just in certain respects, but taken as a whole, represents a moral improvement over another.

Science does not pursue so diverse a range of ends. Because such goals as explanatory power or precision matter only insofar as they serve to move inquiry closer to its ultimate objective, which is knowledge of the natural world, our judgments about scientific progress do not require a similarly problematic balancing of pluses and minuses. There is only the need, as I mentioned earlier (§2), to weigh against one another the two component goals in the pursuit of knowledge – the acquisition of truths and the avoidance of error. Our moral thinking, too, aiming as it does at understanding what is right and good, does not face essentially greater obstacles to progress than does scientific theorizing. But life is different. We may unhesitatingly agree that modern democracy represents an improvement over earlier forms of political rule. Yet if we look also at its cultural consequences, at the vulgarization and commercialism that seem inevitably to accompany it, we may be far less certain about its superiority overall as a form of life to others in the past.

One thing is clear, however. In reflecting on the nature of science and morality, we must break the grip that the old dualisms still maintain upon the philosophical mind, even among those who claim to fight against them. Overcoming dualisms does not, of course, mean abolishing distinctions. We may continue, for example, to distinguish between making our beliefs answerable to the world and seeking reasonable agreement with others, between objectivity and solidarity. The crucial point is to see that we are not obliged to choose between two conceptions of inquiry, each based on one of these aims to the exclusion of the other, since the distinction captures interdependent aspects of a single process.

Truth itself is timeless; if Newtonian mechanics now appears importantly mistaken, then it was always false, even in its heyday. Our thinking, by contrast, takes place necessarily in time, and has no other resources than those that the past and our own imagination happen to provide us. Yet the finitude that marks every step we take tracks the world that lies beyond. Reasoning from where we find ourselves means reasoning about the way things really are. As T. S. Eliot wrote in Burnt Norton, "only through time time is conquered."

---

[17] See I. Berlin, "The Pursuit of the Ideal," in *The Crooked Timber of Humanity* (New York: Knopf, 1991), pp. 1–19.

2

Back to Kant? No Way

In 1798, Kant was challenged to reveal his thoughts about the recent claims by Karl Leonhard Reinhold and Johann Gottlieb Fichte that they had recast the true spirit of Kant's philosophy in a more perspicuous and better-argued form. "There is an Italian proverb," Kant replied, "May God protect us especially from our friends, for we shall manage to watch out for our enemies ourselves." Karl Ameriks quotes this remark near the beginning of his provocative book, *Kant and the Fate of Autonomy*.[1] There is no mistaking his fundamental agreement about the relationship between the Critical Philosophy and the various movements of the succeeding decades, usually labeled "German Idealism," which claimed inspiration from Kant at the same time as they sought to go beyond him.

Kant, of course, did not live long enough to become acquainted as well with the writings of Schelling and Hegel. Nor can it be said that these four post-Kantians marked out similar paths in their attempts to move beyond the inadequacies they perceived in Kant's thinking. Nonetheless, Ameriks maintains, they were at one in failing to appreciate the complexities of Kant's own transcendental idealism, and their failure had a common source. It was Reinhold's image of Critical Philosophy, his diagnosis of Kant's aspirations and failings, that set the agenda for the developments that came afterward. Ameriks' book is meant as a "prolegomenon to a rehabilitation of orthodox Kantianism" (p. 269). He wants to rescue Kant from the massive distortions that, in his view, Reinhold bequeathed to his successors, Fichte, Schelling, and Hegel. The point is not that German Idealism was simply a mistake. But the achievements of post-Kantian German philosophy are better measured, he believes, by the new themes and ideas it introduced than by its criticisms of Kant (p. 339). Where Reinhold, Fichte, and Hegel found fault with the

---

[1] Ameriks, *Kant and the Fate of Autonomy* (Cambridge: Cambridge University Press, 2000), p. 2. All further references to this book will be given in the text. For Kant's statement, see his *Gesammelte Schriften* (Berlin: Preussische Akademie der Wissenschaften, 1900–), vol. 12, p. 371.

master, they were largely in the wrong. Kant himself, by contrast, was onto the truth, or so it would appear from Ameriks' deeply sympathetic account. His book adds a new and important strain to the now more than a century old cry, "Back to Kant!"

1. KANT'S MODESTY

For Ameriks, Kant's thought is defined by his "modest" conception of the goals that philosophy can reasonably set itself and of the sort of systematicity it can achieve (p. 25). Kant began with the idea that our experience consists essentially not in a string of sensations or impressions but instead in our judging that things are thus and so. He proceeded to determine by way of transcendental arguments the necessary conditions for experience to have the structure that our judgments about things presuppose. A metaphysical account of mind and world, called "transcendental idealism," was then proposed to make sense of these conditions for the possibility of experience: our knowledge is limited to the realm of experience as constituted by our forms of sensibility and the categories of our understanding, and cannot extend to the nature of things as they are in themselves. And finally, mind so understood was declared to be free, though its freedom could not be directly ascertained, but only inferred (again by way of a transcendental argument) from a consideration of that particular area of experience that is the moral life.

"Modesty" is probably not the first word one would use to describe a four-point theoretical program such as this, and certainly not a word that typically occurs to most of Kant's readers. But what Ameriks means by the term comes into focus by way of contrast with Reinhold's influential reformulation of the Critical Philosophy. If the *Briefe über die kantische Philosophie* of 1786–87 were a popularizing work intended to win for Kant's thought the public recognition it deserved, Reinhold's book of two years later, the *Versuch einer neuen Theorie des menschlichen Vorstellungsvermögens*, had a different purpose. Transcendental idealism, Reinhold believed, had to be given a more systematic exposition than Kant himself had presented. The result, as Ameriks explains, was an ambitious conception of philosophy that outstripped Kant's own with regard to each of the four elements in the Kantian program.

For Reinhold, the proper starting point was not the structure of experience, but rather the more fundamental and supposedly incontestable notion of representation (*Vorstellung*). "In consciousness," he declared, "a representation is distinguished from what is represented and from what does the representing and is set in relation to them both." Philosophy could take on the shape of a rigorous science once it set about deducing the various consequences of this single first principle, or *Grundsatz*. Among them there supposedly figured, moreover, an argument far simpler than any Kant advanced to show that things-in-themselves are unknowable, an argument that Ameriks calls the "short argument to idealism" (see §2 in this chapter). A further advantage, Reinhold averred, was that the mind's ability to initiate its own representing activity provides in and of itself an immediate proof of human freedom.

Reinhold's reworking of the Critical Philosophy thus makes Kant's efforts appear modest in several important respects. He proposed to ground a philosophical theory of mind and world upon one ultimate principle, instead of taking our common experience and scientific knowledge as givens and then determining their conditions of possibility. In addition, he claimed that the unknowability of things-in-themselves as well as the certainty of our freedom flow immediately from this new basis, there being no need for the more complicated arguments that Kant presented to secure these results. Through these changes, Reinhold set the terms for the way Kant's philosophy was appropriated by the more illustrious figures who came afterward. Fichte, for example, Reinhold's successor at the University of Jena, followed his lead in holding that philosophy needs to take its bearings from a single supreme principle. His disagreement with Reinhold had to do only with the nature of that principle: not representation, but subjectivity or the I (*das Ich*) forms the necessary starting point since Reinhold himself, he pointed out, was obliged to define representation by reference to two activities (distinguishing and relating) whose source can only be the subject itself.[2] Thus there occurred, on Ameriks' telling, that fateful transformation by which Kant's philosophy was turned into a "strong foundationalism" (pp. 25, 85). As Schelling famously wrote to Hegel in a letter of 6 January 1795:

Philosophy is not yet at an end. Kant has given us conclusions, but the premises are still lacking. And who can understand the conclusions without the premises?

Why did Reinhold feel impelled to recast the Critical Philosophy in this form? According to Ameriks, the demand for an ultimate foundational principle grew out of a quest for certainty that Kant's own exposition was not thought to satisfy (p. 63). Kant had made his starting point the central features of experience – our ordinary perceptual dealings with things, our scientific knowledge of the world, the nature of the moral life; he had uncovered their conditions of possibility and then had sought to show how these underlying principles do not conflict but instead cohere with one another. Such was the respect in which philosophy for Kant was an essentially "apologetic" enterprise (pp. 66–68). It aimed at vindicating the coherence of

---

[2] Sometimes, in fact, Reinhold's writings of the early 1790s presented the fundamental principle as saying that "In consciousness, a representation is distinguished by the subject from the subject and the object and is set in relation to them both." But it was Fichte who forced him to recognize that the key notion was therefore subjectivity, not representation. For details, see Manfred Frank, *Unendliche Annäherung* (Frankfurt: Suhrkamp, 1997), pp. 221, 287.

common experience against the various doubts that may arise. In Ameriks' view, demonstrating the unity of reason in this sense is the sort of systematicity to which Kant believed that philosophy could legitimately aspire.

Kant's style of argument takes for granted, however, that we agree about what are the basic features of our experience. In particular, it assumes that we all recognize in our conscience that we are subject to categorically binding moral obligations. Given this conviction, we can then see, so Kant argued, that we must be free, able to rise above what experience has made of us in order to comply with obligations that are ours whatever our interests and desires happen to be. True, the *Grundlegung zur Metaphysik der Sitten* (1785) had suggested in passing an argument for practical freedom – or more exactly for the fact that any rational being having a will must suppose that it is free, must act "under the idea (*Idee*) of freedom" – which appealed merely to the activity of making judgments: in taking our judgments to be based upon reasons, we thereby assume that they do not arise from impulses stemming from our place in the natural order of cause and effect.[3] Such an argument is one therefore that even a moral skeptic wishing to deny the existence of categorical obligations would be obliged to accept. Yet by the time of writing the *Kritik der praktischen Vernunft* (1788), Kant had given up all hope in this strategy.[4] Not only does having to suppose that we are free amount to a lot less than knowing that we are free, but the argument in question fails to ensure that our basing our judgments and actions on reasons is not itself the result of deeper causes operating upon us from the outside. Some might welcome the idea that freedom is in this way quite compatible with necessity. But for Kant, the freedom we must possess as moral beings is an absolute freedom, undetermined by "alien causes." And thus, he now insisted, it can only be inferred from the antecedent "fact of reason" that we are subject to the demands of morality.[5] Though constituting an expression of our rational nature insofar as we understand ourselves as moral beings, freedom cannot be derived from any more fundamental principle of rationality that even the moral skeptic would have to endorse.

---

[3] Kant, *Grundlegung zur Metaphysik der Sitten*, pp. 447–448 in his *Gesammelte Schriften*, vol. 4. The idea of using such an argument to establish human freedom and thereby to prove the bindingness of the moral law, as an essential expression of that freedom, had long held an attraction for Kant. See, for example, his review of J. H. Schulz's *Anleitung zur Sittenlehre für alle Menschen* (1783), in ibid., vol. 8, pp. 9–14.

[4] In some other essays, reprinted in his book *Interpreting Kant's Critiques* (Oxford: Clarendon Press, 2003), Chapters 6 and 9, Ameriks has charted very insightfully the development of Kant's thinking on this issue.

[5] Notoriously, it is sometimes the moral law, sometimes our consciousness of the moral law, and sometimes the autonomy of practical reason, that the Second Critique calls a "fact of reason." What is certain is that Kant had come to hold that our freedom can be recognized only through our awareness of the moral law. His vacillation had to do with which of these terms to count as the "fact of reason."

In Ameriks' view, it was reliance of this sort upon common experience, crystallized in Kant's claim that our sense of freedom rests on acknowledging that we are bound by the moral law, which prompted Reinhold and then Fichte to insist on the need to begin instead from first principles (pp. 63, 75, 105). Such arguments appeared too hypothetical in scope, assuming views that some would dispute. They could not provide a genuinely universal basis for that recognition of human freedom that Reinhold and Fichte regarded as the most important achievement of the new Critical Philosophy. Kant's method needed to be revamped in order to assure the triumph of his message. A single supreme principle had to be found that would be at once incontrovertible yet also sufficient to ground the key theses of transcendental idealism.

So ambitious a project, however, was doomed to failure, and in its impossibility Ameriks sees a decisive corroboration of Kant's own theoretical modesty. No principle can satisfy the two requirements in question (p. 122). If it is substantial enough to explain the cardinal features of the mind's relation to the world, it is too rich in content to count as self-evident, since only trivialities are absolutely certain. Such a principle will therefore appear disputable to some, and the only way to justify its validity lies in showing that it coheres with various things that are commonly, even if not unanimously, believed. Thus we must rely in the end on a philosophical method not unlike the one practiced by Kant himself.

2. DUALISMS AND ULTIMATE PRINCIPLES

As Ameriks observes (pp. 64f), this criticism of Reinhold and Fichte was not unknown in Jena in the early 1790s. A number of other thinkers living there and inspired by Kant – particularly Immanuel Carl Diez and Friedrich Niethammer – had already argued the point against Reinhold before Fichte arrived in 1794. To them, Fichte's inaugural lectures on the *Wissenschaftslehre* appeared to rest on the same mistake.

Yet Ameriks passes over the lesson that Niethammer, for example, drew from his critique. It is not to be concluded, Niethammer believed, that the philosophical search for a fundamental principle to explain the relation between mind and world should be abandoned. Much can be learned from the systematic account of experience that a principle of this sort can provide. The important thing is to recognize that no such principle can claim apodictic certainty: its justification must instead be piecemeal and provisional, measured by how well it organizes the other things we believe, and philosophy is therefore an essentially unending enterprise.[6]

---

[6] For Niethammer's very interesting views on the nature of philosophy, see Dieter Henrich, *Der Grund im Bewußtsein* (Stuttgart: Klett-Cotta, 1992), pp. 113–126, and Frank, *Unendliche Annäherung*, pp. 424–431, 512ff.

Reinhold himself became persuaded by this conception, and in 1794 presented an appropriately modified version of his *Grundsatzphilosophie.* Toward the later Reinhold, however, and thus by implication toward Niethammer too, Ameriks strikes a rather dismissive attitude. The change in methodology, he asserts, was "not so crucial for the specific purpose of Kant interpretation" (p. 114n). Ameriks takes this view, I believe, because he does not do justice to the fact that more was involved than just a quest for certainty in the post-Kantian project of finding a single supreme principle of philosophy. A second and powerful reason for this systematizing effort was the unsatisfactory state in which Kant had left the various dualisms essential to his thought.

Chief among these dualisms was the one between sensibility and understanding – that is, between the passive faculty of the mind through which the objects of experience are given to us and the active faculty by which we apply concepts to our experience. The distinction between sensibility and understanding shaped all Kant's other characteristic dualisms, such as those opposing appearances to things-in-themselves, the sensible to the supersensible, and inclination to duty. Dualisms are not in themselves objectionable. But when they serve to distinguish contrasting capacities of a single being, and when particularly – as in the case of sensibility and understanding – these capacities must work together to engender a significant outcome – namely human knowledge – something also needs to be said about their underlying unity.

At the end of the Introduction to his First Critique, Kant had himself acknowledged that sensibility and understanding may "spring from a common, but to us unknown, root."[7] Subsequent developments had made an investigation of this common root appear a necessity. Friedrich Heinrich Jacobi's *David Hume über den Glauben oder Idealismus und Realismus* of 1787 had demonstrated *in nuce* that Kant did not have one of his own key dualisms under firm control: things-in-themselves were said to lie beyond the applicability of the categories of our understanding (such as causality), yet also to act causally upon the mind through our sensibility. Throughout the 1790s, other Kantian dualisms too came under attack for their apparent inconsistency, or because they seemed too crude and severe. (In his essay, *Über Anmut und Würde*, of 1793, Schiller brought the latter sort of charge against the opposition between duty and inclination).

Reinhold was but the first among many who reasonably concluded that all these dualisms would receive their proper definition if expounded within a unitary framework, and that such a framework would have to uncover the common root of that fundamental opposition on which all

---

[7] Kant, *Kritik der reinen Vernunft*, A15/B29. All subsequent references to the First Critique will be given in the text, identified by "A" and "B" preceding the pages of the first (1781) and second (1787) editions.

the others turned – namely, the dualism between sensibility and understanding. Moreover, the idea that Reinhold fixed on in order to lay bare this common root – the idea of representation – seemed an obvious candidate. For both sensibility and understanding are faculties through which the mind, according to Kant himself, forms representations of things. Fichte only deepened this natural line of argument when he insisted that "representation" itself had to be explained through the more basic notion of subjectivity or the I's own (self-positing) activity.

None of this implies that the "short arguments" for idealism that Reinhold and Fichte devised on the basis of their favored principles have any cogency. On this point, I completely agree with Ameriks (pp. 127–133, 179–183). To argue that things-in-themselves, or things as they exist independently of our forms of representation, are unknowable or even inconceivable because to think of them at all is to form a representation of them is to trade in sophisms. (One might just as well argue for immortality by saying that one cannot think of the world existing except by virtue of being there to think about it). But the reasons for attempting to reformulate the Critical Philosophy in terms of a single ultimate principle were not limited to the lure of short arguments or to the hope of achieving philosophical certainty. There were difficulties and inconsistencies in Kant's own writings that appeared to call for such a reformulation. That is why Niethammer, no devotee himself of short arguments or apodictic certainties, could still see a point in the enterprise. "Although I believe," he wrote in 1794,

> that a single proposition, whatever it may be, is unlikely ever to provide a foundation (*Fundament*) for the whole edifice [of knowledge], it is still not to be denied that philosophy has already been significantly advanced through these efforts to find a foundation-stone [*Grundstein*] for the whole edifice.[8]

To my mind, Ameriks wrongly depicts Kant's thought as enjoying a kind of equilibrium that only extraneous concerns could have induced his contemporaries to find problematic. In reality, the Critical Philosophy was plainly in trouble (as philosophy always is). It could not remain in its current condition. Finding an ultimate principle to define the mind's relation to the world had much to recommend it as a way to set things right while preserving what many took to be Kant's genuine insights.

3. KANT ON REASON

This first point of disagreement between Ameriks and me is connected with a second. Ameriks can attribute to Kant a "modest" conception of philosophy's goals only because he underplays the important role that

---

[8] Niethammer in a letter to F. P. von Herbert of 2 June 1794, cited in Frank, op. cit., p. 431.

Kant assigned to reason (*Vernunft*) as distinct from the understanding (*Verstand*). His Kant is a Kant who, beginning with experience as it is articulated in our judgments, brings to light its conditions of possibility and shows on this basis that, though our knowledge cannot therefore reach to things-in-themselves, we must be free if we are to understand ourselves as moral beings. Absent from this picture is Kant's conviction that human reason has a "natural tendency" to move beyond the limits of possible experience (A642/B670). This tendency sometimes leads of course to the mistake of supposing that we possess knowledge of such things as God and the soul that can form no part of our experience. But reason for Kant is not merely a source of illusion. In what he calls its "regulative" use, it performs a positive and fundamental task. Indeed, Kant's view is that experience would not have the shape it has, were it not structured by a faculty of reason that pushes us in the direction of what lies beyond its bounds.

The understanding is the faculty by which we subsume the material of our experience under concepts – that is, under rules. Reason, by contrast, is the faculty by which we organize our conceptually articulated experience under principles. For Kant, it is a higher-order capacity, operating on the deliverances of the understanding, as when we draw a conclusion from given premises according to principles of inference (A644/B672, A664/B692).[9] Yet reason is not limited to the strictly "logical" function of drawing inferences. It also, wrote Kant, has a "transcendental" capacity in that it introduces concepts of its own, having to do with the Unconditioned. The conclusion of an inference is grounded (*begründet*) in premises that provide the condition (*Bedingung*) of its validity. But reason, according to Kant, requires that the premises too must be grounded, the condition of the condition must be sought in turn, and so on in a process that aims inevitably at the totality of conditions. Reason therefore contains a principle peculiar to itself, which is to "find for the conditioned knowledge obtained through the understanding the unconditioned whereby its unity is brought to completion" (A307/B364).

Though the Unconditioned can never become an object of knowledge, it has an indispensable function as a regulative ideal. Reason directs us to approach ever nearer to the Unconditioned. We are to build up and organize our knowledge in a systematic fashion so that, Kant himself declared, it hangs together as far as possible in terms of *a single ultimate principle*:

If we consider in its full extent our knowledge obtained through the understanding, we find that what reason characteristically prescribes with regard to it and what it seeks to achieve is the *systematization* of knowledge, that is, its interconnection on the basis of one principle (A645/B673).

---

[9] This account of Kant's theory of reason draws on both his discussion at the beginning of the Transcendental Dialectic (A298/B355-A309/B366) and the appendix devoted to the regulative employment of the ideas of pure reason (A642/B670-A668/B696).

Once this conception of reason is brought into the picture, Ameriks' contrast between Kantian modesty and post-Kantian hubris begins to look a bit overdrawn. Philosophy for Kant must involve more than just the apologetic task of showing that the principles underlying the different areas of experience do not really conflict but cohere. It must also heed reason's demand for system and indeed for a single ultimate principle by which the totality of experience can be explained. In fact, Kant himself went so far in this context as to talk of reason's aspiration toward the Absolute (A324/B380-A326/B383). Reinhold and Fichte were not therefore engaged in substituting their own extravagant conception of system for the more restrained one favored by Kant. On the contrary, they were following Kant's lead. Their object was to bring the Critical Philosophy closer to a realization of reason's ultimate goals as Kant himself understood them, and precisely because in their eyes the very coherence of his philosophy required nothing less. For Kant, of course, the complete systematization of experience could only be approximated, never fully achieved. But in that regard, his position did not differ materially from the one espoused by Niethammer or by the later Reinhold.

There is a further point on which Reinhold and Fichte were not in these matters so very far from their master. Reason's interest in the Unconditioned, they all believed, springs from reason itself, since nothing in experience, nothing that partakes of the conditioned, could be sufficient to give rise to it. The "demand of reason" that there be a single ultimate principle from which all else follows, this *Forderung der Vernunft* (A332/B389), is therefore one that reason imposes upon itself. Reason for Kant is self-legislating not only in its practical, but also in its theoretical employment. This theme comes to expression, for example, in the famous passage of the Second Preface to the *Kritik der reinen Vernunft*:

Reason has insight only into that which it produces after a plan of its own, and ... it must not allow itself to be kept, as it were, in nature's leading-strings, but must itself show the way with principles of judgment based upon fixed laws, constraining nature to give answer to questions of reason's own devising (Bxiii).

Now, if theoretical reason is self-legislating in its drive to systematize experience, it would appear to be as well-suited as practical reason to provide a basis for the recognition of our freedom. In this light, there seems no reason for a Kantian to fault Reinhold and Fichte for thinking that freedom must be an immediate consequence of a first principle having to do with the very activity of thinking, instead of being derivable only from the nature of the moral life. As I observed earlier, Kant himself ventured an argument along these lines in the *Grundlegung zur Metaphysik der Sitten*. "We cannot," he claimed, possibly conceive of reason as being consciously directed from outside in regard to its judgments: for in that case the subject would attribute the determination of his power of judgment, not to his reason, but to an impulsion. Reason must look upon itself as the author of its own principles independently of alien influences.[10]

The *Kritik der praktischen Vernunft*, it is true, abandoned this line of argument in favor of the doctrine that freedom can be deduced only from our awareness of the moral law, not from any deeper principle of rationality. This doctrine Ameriks regards as essential to Kant's mature conception of philosophy, and certainly it was a step in which Reinhold and Fichte were loath to follow him. But the question remains whether Kant was right – by which I mean here, right given his views about morality and reason – to retrench in this fashion.

What more powerful grounds are there for thinking that practical reason in its moral capacity must truly be self-legislating and thus free than for thinking that theoretical reason must be so? To invoke the key worry (mentioned in §1 earlier) that convinced Kant to jettison the *Grundlegung* argument: what feature of morality must move us to suppose that moral self-legislation cannot ultimately be an illusion – that "that which, in relation to sensuous impulses, is entitled freedom, may not, in relation to higher and more remote operating causes, be nature again" (A803/B831) – that does not have its counterpart in theoretical reason? It would be a mistake to reply that in morality alone we understand ourselves as subject to categorical obligations, binding whatever may be our desires and interests and therefore addressed to us as free beings. For theoretical reasoning as well finds itself bound by norms that are categorical in just this sense – by the rules of logic, for instance, and, if we are to believe Kant, by the requirement that experience be systematized.[11] Nor would it be right to reply (and there is evidence to suggest that this point too may have led to Kant's change of view) that freedom, if it exists, is a feature of the will and therefore forms an integral assumption of practical reason alone. For theoretical reasoning is equally an exercise of the will. Though we cannot believe just anything at will, reasoning about what to believe, when it arrives at some conclusion, typically moves us to believe what we have inferred. Coming to believe is something we do. Accordingly, it is no less subject to the will's pathologies than our reasoning about what to do. Sometimes, for instance, through

---

[10] Kant, *Grundlegung zur Metaphysik der Sitten*, p. 448.

[11] Note that there are two routes by which Kant considers that we may arrive at a grasp of our freedom – by way of the idea of categorical obligations, and by way of reason understood as self-legislating. That is because his notion of free action has both a *negative* dimension – not being determined by external causes (a freedom that we must believe to be available to us if we take ourselves as able to comply with categorical obligations, binding whatever our experience has made of us), and a *positive* one – heeding a law one gives to oneself. For the distinction, see, for example, *Grundlegung zur Metaphysik der Sitten*, pp. 446–447.

a cognitive sort of "weakness of will," we fail to accept what we see we have every reason to believe.

I hasten to add that I do not make these remarks with the intention of siding with Reinhold and Fichte against the Kant of the Second Critique. Nothing could be farther from my mind! For if I do believe that theoretical and practical reason are in the same situation with regard to the idea of freedom, I do not think that self-legislation – or, in a word, autonomy – offers the key to an understanding of reason. There is no essential link between categorical norms and autonomy. Thus I come to a final, and more general, point of disagreement with Ameriks.

4. THE FATE OF AUTONOMY

Near the beginning of his book, Ameriks very graciously includes me in a group of well-known philosophers who "are all united in making a loud and clear call for an exploration and defense of autonomy" (p. 5). Yet my name does not really belong on this list. To be sure, I agree that the notion of autonomy needs exploring. But in part this is because any philosophical notion about which no one has apparently a bad word to say seems to me to call for some skepticism. Either the term has ceased to have any clear-cut meaning, or people are not thinking about it hard enough. Chiefly, however, my interest in autonomy has to do with the fact that, far from wishing to defend the notion, I have set out to attack it, or more exactly to attack the foundational role that Kant and the Kantian tradition have awarded it in their accounts of reason and morality.

I shall not expound here in detail my opposition to the idea of autonomy, since later chapters lay out my views at some length.[12] For present purposes, a summary account will suffice. It can indeed serve as an introduction to the more thorough treatment that will come later.

It was Kant himself who introduced the idea of autonomy, originally a political term, into discussions of the nature of reason and of its relation to morality. In his hands, it did have a distinct meaning – namely, self-legislation: principles of thought and action acquire their authority by virtue of rational beings imposing them upon themselves, instead of sup-posing them endowed with an independent validity to which they must simply assent. Now, some principles having to do with our intellectual or practical conduct are indisputably of this character. Think, for example, of rules stipulating the acceptable margins of experimental error or of rules determining the frequency of elections. But, I claim, the idea of autonomy cannot provide a complete account of the "normativity" that structures all

---

[12] An earlier expression of my misgivings about the idea of autonomy occurs in *The Morals of Modernity* (Cambridge: Cambridge University Press, 1996), chapter V. But the critique is developed more thoroughly in Chapters 4 and 5 of the present book.

our thought and action. For, first of all, when we do impose principles on ourselves, we presumably do so for reasons: we suppose that it is fitting for us to adopt them, or that adopting them will advance certain of our interests. Self-legislation, when it does occur, is an activity that takes place in the light of reasons that we must antecedently recognize, and whose own authority we therefore do not institute but rather find ourselves called upon to acknowledge. Moreover, such cases differ palpably from the more basic way we go about determining whether to accept some principle, where the reasons we invoke are reasons for thinking the principle correct, not for making it valid in the first place. Indeed, some principles of conduct are so fundamental (think of the rules of logical inference, for example) that we can frame no coherent notion of what it would be like not to recognize their validity, and thus no coherent notion of how we would go about determining that we ought to impose them on ourselves. Being responsive to their authority is a precondition for thinking and acting at all. And even though the moral point of view does not figure at this deepest stratum of our self-understanding, the principles defining it are still not ones we can find grounds to embrace without already thinking in moral terms. We cannot reason ourselves into the moral point of view, beginning from outside it (see Chapter 5), and this fact alone shows that morality cannot belong to the in reality quite limited domain of reason's self-legislation. Fundamental moral principles present themselves as categorically binding, whatever our interests and desires – about this Kant was right, but it does not follow (here Kant went wrong) that their authority stems from our imposing them on ourselves.

Why has the conception of reason as autonomous or self-legislating proven nonetheless so enduringly attractive? Because of the dominance in modern times of a *naturalistic* worldview, according to which reasons for thought and action can form no part of the world itself, which viewed through the lens of the natural sciences is normatively blank. If we are not to despair of reason, then the only way to make room for reasons in such a picture is to regard them as authored by the very faculty of reason with which we confront a silent world. To be sure, those inspired by Kant have been keen to reject the reduction of reason to a mere expression of the needs and desires we have as part of nature. All the same, the naturalistic conception of the world provides the impetus to conceive of reason as the autonomous source of the principles it endorses.

How then should we proceed, if we agree that theories of reason as self-legislating are doomed to failure? One task is to challenge the pervasive hold that naturalism has over the modern mind. But equally, I believe, we must conclude, in a very un-Kantian spirit, that reason at bottom is a *receptive* faculty. It is the capacity to recognize and heed the independent validity of reasons. In the eyes of Kant and the Kantian tradition, I must count then as having a "heteronomous" conception of reason. I accept the characterization, though not the implied criticism. Reason does have an inherent connection to freedom, but in my view it must be freedom conceived, not as autonomy, but rather as the ability to be moved by reasons instead of by mere causes.

It is no surprise that Ameriks, by contrast, remains committed to the idea of autonomy. True, he voices doubts about recent theories of "moral constructivism" (such as those of John Rawls and Christine Korsgaard), which in his view make morality too much of a "human creation."[13] Rawls interpreted Kantian autonomy as the thesis that moral principles draw their validity from being derived in accord with a certain procedure (the universalization of maxims) from an ideal of moral personhood.[14] That seems indeed a natural way to explain the metaphor of self-legislation, and it does not clearly warrant the charge of forgetting that morality for Kant applies not just to human beings but to all rational beings. Be that as it may, Ameriks proposes in *Kant and the Fate of Autonomy* his own account of the meaning of autonomy, and it confirms all the doubts I have expressed. In the case of both practical and theoretical reason, he claims, the basic principles by which we operate

are ... not external to our *essential nature*, which for Kant is our sheer rationality. In this way they in one sense have a significant 'internal' source – they come from something 'in' us. (p. 14)

Though the statement is meant to be somewhat vague, I could not ask for a more concise expression of the error that I see lying at the heart of the Kantian notion of autonomy. If my preceding remarks have been on the mark, then reason – that is, our "sheer rationality" – is at bottom a receptive, not a self-legislating faculty. It cannot therefore be the source of the authority that the fundamental principles of thought and action have for our conduct. Rather, reason is the capacity that enables us to recognize the authority they possess in and of themselves. Reason works by responding to the reasons there are.

To be sure, we should hold fast to the idea that rational beings are *self-governing*: they are moved to heed the reasons they discern by virtue simply of recognizing their cogency, without having to be pushed by further desires or incentives. In particular, we should see our moral life as capable of being an expression of reason in this sense. Each us is able to grasp and to do what is right regardless of the threats or rewards that others (human or divine) may hold out. But self-governance falls well short of

---

[13] See *Kant and the Fate of Autonomy*, p. 13, and also Ameriks' essay, "On Schneewind and Kant's Method in Ethics," *Ideas y Valores* 102 (1996), pp. 28–53, reprinted in his book, *Interpreting Kant's Critiques*, pp. 263–274, particularly pp. 268–269.

[14] For more on Rawls' and Korsgaard's moral constructivism, see Chapters 4 and 5.

self-legislation.[15] And I, for one, see no reason why in morality or elsewhere we should hope for more.

In a reply to these criticisms, Ameriks has suggested that I wrongly think of self-legislation as imposing principles on ourselves by way of some "causally efficient" act. If reason is understood more as the "formal" cause, as "determining" or "defining" the proper standards of thought and action, then the Kantian idea of autonomy, he argues, proves immune to the objections I raise.[16] This rejoinder misses the point, however. I quite agree that the question concerns, not so much the *causes* by which we come to see principles as binding on us, as the *reasons* that make those principles authoritative for our conduct. My complaint is that we cannot coherently hold that our fundamental principles draw their authority from reason itself, since reason is in the last analysis a receptive faculty, responsive to reasons that exist independently of it. Any standards that reason is in a position to "determine" – that is, to make authoritative – are ones that there must appear to be good reasons to institute.

In general, I see no way "back to Kant" that can promise satisfaction. To those who believe that Kant was on the right track, his own dualisms as well as his celebration of autonomy offer ample grounds for going even further and heading in the direction of German Idealism. To those, like myself, for whom autonomy represents a flawed idea of reason, getting beyond the whole Kantian tradition is the task at hand.

---

[15] On this important distinction, see J. B. Schneewind, *The Invention of Autonomy* (Cambridge: Cambridge University Press, 1998).

[16] Ameriks, "On Larmore and Self-Legislation in Kant," pp. 274–282 in his book, *Interpreting Kant's Critiques*. Sebastian Rödl, in his book *Self-Consciousness* (Cambridge, MA: Harvard University Press, 2007), pushes this line of argument even further. He holds that "autonomy" for Kant has nothing to do with instituting the authority of the laws of thought and action – in other words, with "the origin of the law" (p. 117) – but instead with "the logical form" of the law: reason is autonomous in that it operates by laws referring only to its own nature. Yet, clearly, Kant meant by the term a lot more than this, and precisely the idea that reason institutes or authorizes the principles by which it proceeds. For in the *Grundlegung* (p. 448), he wrote that reason is the "author" or "originator" (*Urheberin*) of its principles, a point confirmed by his frequent talk of reason giving (*geben*) itself its laws (pp. 432, 434, 435, 441). One may regret that Kant said this sort of thing (I certainly do), but there is no hiding that it is what he said.

3

Attending to Reasons

1. INTRODUCTION

First published in 1994, John McDowell's book, *Mind and World*,[1] has already won recognition as a philosophical classic. Few works of the past 100 years have managed to challenge so profoundly the host of preconceptions that prevent modern empiricism from truly being the philosophy of experience it aims to be. Ever since Locke, empiricist appeals to "experience" have remained trapped behind a "veil of ideas," unable to make contact with the world itself. The mind has been understood as having immediate experience, not of things themselves, but only of its own impressions, and as therefore having to build up from these givens a picture of the reality beyond. Yet every attempt to bridge this gap between inner and outer has fallen short. In fact, the very notion of something simply "given" in experience has proven impossible to articulate clearly. Others before have tried to forge a way out of this cul-de-sac, though often at the price of abandoning the idea that experience forms a tribunal for our beliefs about the world. McDowell presents a new understanding of mind and world that looks better poised to redeem the empiricist ideal.

Despite my admiration for his accomplishment, the two of us differ greatly in our conceptions of philosophy itself, however. This difference in outlook colors my large measure of agreement with the details of his remodeled empiricism, leading me to see new problems arising where McDowell believes he need not push further. My dissatisfaction centers on his treatment of a theme we share – namely, the mind's responsiveness to reasons. But before I jump into this topic, I want to say a word about the broader views that divide us.

---

[1] John McDowell, *Mind and World*, 2nd edition, with a new Introduction (Cambridge, MA: Harvard University Press, 1996). Page references to this book are given in the text.

Philosophical reflection, I believe, has no natural end. The answer we propose to a philosophical problem usually brings in its wake new difficulties we did not face before. We may find it necessary to rethink our other commitments. Or we may run up against further questions whose existence we did not previously suspect. Philosophy is subject to a law we might call "*the conservation of trouble.*" To a certain extent, the situation is no different in the various sciences and other organized forms of knowledge, or indeed in life itself. It is a general truth that the more we learn, the more we see that we have yet to figure out. In philosophy, however, the conservation of trouble takes on a more complex and daunting form, because of the nature of the problems at issue. Philosophical problems are typically fundamental in character, their implications ramifying through different areas of our experience, and as a result many disparate considerations turn out to be relevant to their solution. At the same time, they also show a remarkable cohesiveness. Their various elements tend to be so interconnected that our judgment about how well any particular aspect has been handled hinges on our conception of the problem as a whole. These two features conspire to give the problems of philosophy their special intractability. Only a comprehensive solution will do, yet generally none seems able to tie together in a convincing way the many diverse factors involved. The theory that recommends itself when certain elements are regarded as crucial looks doubtful or even wrongheaded when the problem is approached from another angle, where different considerations weigh more heavily.

As a result, piecemeal resolutions of the sort employed in the sciences seldom work in this domain. Philosophical problems resist being broken down into manageable puzzles solvable to everyone's satisfaction and deeper questions that we can leave for a later time. Notoriously, philosophy achieves few settled results. Everything stands open to question from some, not implausible, point of view. Reflection seems fated never to be at rest. No argument or vision succeeds in one regard without falling short in another.

Most philosophers would doubtless agree that such a picture fits the course of philosophy up to them. Yet few have felt at home in this state of affairs, and many have imagined that they, single-handedly or as part of a movement, had managed to get beyond it. Some, of course, have persuaded themselves that they have arrived at definitive answers. Others have supposed that they possessed a method by which philosophical problems would eventually yield to a step-by-step resolution after all. Neither sort of stance wins many converts or keeps them for very long. A third reaction, increasingly common over the past century, has been to seek a more radical means of escape. The problems of philosophy have proven so intractable, it is said, because they rest upon assumptions that, though naturally seductive, are bound up in confusion. Progress is to be achieved, not by the solution but by the dissolution of problems, not by the construction of theories but by the diagnosis of the misconceptions that give rise to the apparent need for theory. Philosophy at its best consists in curing us of the philosophical impulse.

No one championed this conception more ardently than Ludwig Wittgenstein. "The real discovery," he exclaimed in the *Philosophical Investigations*, "is the one that makes me capable of stopping doing philosophy when I want to. – The one that gives philosophy peace, so that it is no longer tormented by questions which bring *itself* in question."[2] Wittgenstein's quietism has been enormously influential, despite the inescapable paradox that lies at its heart. For how, we must ask, can showing up the mistaken assumptions underlying some philosophical problem amount to anything other than putting better views in their place? And must not these views be of a similar scope and thus provide the makings of a positive theory of the phenomena in question?

Many readers of Wittgenstein, dismissing his quietism, have undertaken to expound the actual positions implicit in his writings. Not surprisingly, these ideas exhibit the traits of all good philosophical theory: they accord well with certain things, but have to strain to accommodate others. In philosophy, there is no genuine escape from difficulty. The only way that philosophy can be at peace with itself is to accept that tranquility of mind must forever elude it. The unendingness of philosophical reflection is the true expression of the human condition, and Montaigne provides a better model than Wittgenstein. "There is no end to our inquiries," Montaigne wrote, "our end is in the other world. It is a sign of narrowness of mind when the mind is content, or of weariness."[3] Or as Thomas Nagel has formulated this outlook, "It may be that some philosophical problems have no solutions. I suspect this is true of the deepest and oldest of them. They show us the limits of our understanding. In that case such insight as we can achieve depends on maintaining a strong grasp of the problem instead of abandoning it ... Unsolvable problems are not for that reason unreal."[4]

These meta-philosophical remarks define the spirit in which I shall discuss the central theme of McDowell's *Mind and World*. For he is in these matters very much the disciple of Wittgenstein.

---

[2] Wittgenstein, *Philosophische Untersuchungen* §133: "Die eigentliche Entdeckung ist die, die mich fähig macht, das Philosophieren abzubrechen, wann ich will. – Die die Philosophie zur Ruhe bringt, sodaß sie nicht mehr von Fragen gepeitscht wird, die *sie selber* in Frage stellen."

[3] Montaigne, *Essais* III.13 ("De l'expérience"): "Il n'y a point de fin de nos inquisitions, notre fin est en l'autre monde. C'est signe de raccourcissement d'esprit quand il se contente, ou de lasseté." I give a more detailed account of Montaigne's style of skepticism, if that is indeed the proper term, in my essay, "Un scepticisme sans tranquillité: Montaigne et ses modèles antiques," in V. Carraud and J. -L. Marion (eds.), *Montaigne: Scepticisme, Métaphysique, Théologie* (Paris: Presses Universitaires de France, 2004), pp. 15–31.

[4] Thomas Nagel, *Mortal Questions* (Cambridge: Cambridge University Press, 1979), p. xii.

Modern philosophy, McDowell observes, has found insuperable the problem of understanding how thought can be both shaped by experience and responsive to reasons. Experience is regarded as the way the world impresses itself upon us in accord with causal laws, yet experience can serve as a tribunal for our thinking only if it provides us with reasons for belief, and reasons involve a normative relation to the world. McDowell's claim is that this problem proves so difficult because of the dominance of what he calls, following Max Weber, the "disenchanted" image of the world that in modern times has divested it of everything normative (70, 85, 181). I think that the crippling *Weltbild* ought rather to be termed the *naturalistic* conception of the world. For Weber's famous account of modern disenchantment (*Entzauberung*) had to do with the disappearance of God from the world, whereas the idea that the world is barren of all normative distinctions really comes from thinking that the world consists only of what the natural sciences see it to be.[5] McDowell chooses a different terminology and on grounds that, as I shall explain, are far from innocuous. According to him, we need to adopt a broader naturalism than has become current, one that does not reduce nature to the domain of law-governed processes described by modern science. If we recognize that the way we are caught up in the natural world through our sense experience already involves the exercise of conceptual capacities, which training and tradition have made our "second nature," we will be able to see ourselves as at once part of nature (broadly conceived) and guided by reasons. We will have bridged the deep-seated dualism of mind and world and discerned how norms, reason, and thus freedom too – understood not as the absence of constraint, but as the heeding of reasons – fit into the natural order.

No book undertaking to establish so much could fail to represent a bold project, and the philosophical ambition of *Mind and World* is matched by the power of its results. Nonetheless, McDowell's book is also importantly flawed by his professed quietism, his Wittgensteinian refusal to own up to the true character of his enterprise. He resolutely denies being engaged in expounding a substantive philosophical theory. "Naturalized platonism" is the name he gives his views, meaning that though reasons are to be understood as being "there anyway," whether we recognize them or not, this platonistic thought is tamed by the insistence that our responsiveness to reasons betokens nothing supernatural, only that second nature that stems from appropriate upbringing. Despite its technical sound, this naturalized platonism is not meant to be "a label for a bit of constructive philosophy" (95). It is supposedly no more than shorthand for a set of "reminders" that dispel the assumptions responsible for the chief problem

---

[5] See Weber's essay *Wissenschaft als Beruf*. I have explained in the Introduction (§3) how I think the idea of disenchantment should be understood.

of modern empiricism. It represents the sort of discovery, McDowell declares in echo of Wittgenstein, that "gives philosophy peace" (86). His aim too is to cure the philosophical impulse, even if the affliction is bound to recur (177).

Yet McDowell is in no position to promise peace. In reality, he has embarked upon the construction of a comprehensive theory of mind and world, and his failure to see that undertaking for what it is keeps him from realizing how his answer to one problem leaves him, in turn, faced with another, no less difficult. The notion of "second nature" identifies the means by which the mind is responsive to reasons. But it does not tell us what reasons themselves are, if reasons are supposed to be, as he himself avers, "there anyway," forming a possible object of knowledge. What precisely is a reason, and how can there exist, independently of our beliefs about them, normative entities of this sort? What must the world be like, if it is to be understood as containing reasons? McDowell believes that such questions will evaporate if only we take to heart the import of the idea of second nature. "The response we should aim at being entitled to, if someone raises a question like 'What constitutes the structure of the space of reasons?,' is something like a shrug of the shoulders" (178). Shrug his shoulders he certainly does. Yet the problem remains, all the same. The very things he says to explain how experience can function as the tribunal of belief make it necessary to wrestle with understanding how reasons can form part of reality.

Once we follow through the implications of holding that reasons are there anyway and that they are (as McDowell also realizes) essentially normative in character, there can be little point in calling the resulting position "naturalism," even if we add, as he does, that it is a "broader" or "relaxed" naturalism. For then we will have acknowledged that the world, as the totality of what exists, contains more than just the physical and psychological facts of which the natural sciences speak. It will be plain that what we have done is to replace one metaphysics with another we find better.

2. EXPERIENCE AND REALITY

To see why the nature of reasons cannot be dismissed as an idle question, let us look more closely at McDowell's analysis of the travails of modern empiricism. The enduring difficulty, he remarks, has been that the idea of "experience" is expected to contain two distinct features that seem to resist combination. Experience is a causal notion, denoting the way the world impinges upon us. But it is also a normative notion, signifying a source of reasons for belief: the world having being found to be thus and so is supposed to give us reason to believe this or that. In the now standard terminology of Wilfrid Sellars favored by McDowell, experience belongs to

the "logical space of reasons," defined by relations of warrant and implication, at the same time as it apparently falls within that space of causal
processes that forms the object of modern scientific inquiry and has no
place for normative relations. Whence the perplexity.

One common solution has been to hold that relations of justification
find their terminus in experiences of the world where certain contents of
thought, often called "sense data," directly impose themselves upon the
mind. Experience can appear to be a notion at once causal and normative
if it grounds our beliefs about the world in the way that the world, at the
outermost bounds of our conceptualization of it, acts causally upon us.
The ultimate basis of belief will then be the (sensible) Given. But the well-
known trouble with this "foundationalist" approach is that the Given
cannot serve as a justification for belief if it lacks conceptual articulation;
yet to the extent that it is shaped by an understanding of the world we
already possess, it cannot count as simply "given."[6] The alternative to the
Myth of the Given, notes McDowell, has usually been some species of
coherentism, which rejects the idea that the world itself provides any
rational constraint upon our beliefs. Part of the causal order though they
obviously are, beliefs find their warrant only in how they cohere with our
other beliefs. "Nothing can count as a reason for holding a belief," writes
Donald Davidson, McDowell's paradigm of the coherentist, "except
another belief."[7] Experience itself, understood as the tribunal at which
belief is held accountable to the world, no longer has then a role to play.
The trouble with this position is also familiar. Coherence theories of
knowledge turn the very possibility of knowledge of the world into
a mystery. They threaten to make our web of beliefs appear "a frictionless
spinning in a void" (50), whereas knowledge involves thought's answerability to the way things are – that is, to the world itself. The dilemma,
however, is that in pursuing this latter intuition, we seem destined to end
up again at the idea of the Given.

To cut the Gordian knot, McDowell argues, we must jettison the
assumption that underlies both these positions and that creates the
problem in the first place. The mistake is to assume that the points at
which the world acts causally upon us do not involve already the exercise of
our conceptual capacities. Foundationalists suppose that such points serve
to initiate conceptual thinking, and coherentists counter that they are, by
their nature, unsuited to instruct our thought. But, in fact, the conceptual

---

[6] The difficulty finds perfect expression in C. I. Lewis, *Mind and the World Order* (New York:
Scribner's, 1929). Without the Given, he writes, "there would be nothing which
[knowledge] must be true to" (p. 39), yet "in a sense," he goes on to acknowledge, "the
given is ineffable, always" (p. 53).

[7] Donald Davidson, "A Coherence Theory of Truth and Knowledge" (1983), quoted by
McDowell on p. 14 of *Mind and World*.

is unbounded, extending all the way into our causal dependence on the world. We need to hold on to the idea that the world is given to us in experience, yet also recognize that it is given as already possessed of conceptual structure, and therefore already bound up in relations of warrant and implication. In McDowell's view, the obstacle to acknowledging this truth, the preconception responsible for perpetuating the seesaw debate between foundationalists and coherentists, is, as I have said, a modern, impoverished idea of nature, one that strips nature of everything normative and immures it within the space of law-governed processes. The receptivity of experience, properly construed, shows up the deficiency of that idea. For at such moments, the mind is at once part of nature, in being shaped by it, and also participant in the "space of reasons."[8]

"In experience," so McDowell puts his position, "one takes in, for instance sees, that things are thus and so" (9). Clearly, the content of such experience – "that things are thus and so" – is not a preconceptual Given, to which we could only point, speechlessly as it were. Yet for such experience itself to embody a receptivity to the world, that content also cannot be a judgment we make *about* what is given to us, for then the given element in experience would have been located, once again, beyond the bounds of the conceptual. Instead, that very content must be what is given in experience, and it thus must be, in the absence of error, part of the world itself. Anything short of this conclusion reintroduces the Myth of the Given, and the only other alternative is to reject altogether the receptivity of experience, denying the existence of an independent reality, as an idealist might, or refusing it any epistemological significance, as the coherentist does. Our thought ought not therefore to be understood as forever operating at one remove from the world, as though what it immediately conceives were always some picture or "representation" of things and not the things themselves. Much of modern philosophy has adopted this representationalist outlook, but that is the deep-set prejudice that now needs to be overcome. Through experience, the mind latches directly onto reality and follows the conceptual articulations of the world itself.

McDowell is in no doubt about this implication of his views. "*That things are thus and so,*" he argues,

is the conceptual content of an experience, but if the subject of the experience is not misled, that very same thing, *that things are thus and so*, is also a perceptible fact,

---

[8] It is therefore wrong, McDowell argues (71, fn 2), to suppose that the proper contrast with "the space of reasons" is "the space of causal relations." Nature as the disenchanted object of modern science really forms the space of "law-governed processes," since reasons themselves can be causes. There is an important problem here for McDowell's approach – namely the question of how indeed reasons can be causes, and I take it up in §5.

an aspect of the perceptible world.... Thinking does not stop short of facts. The world is embraceable in thought" (26, 33).[9]

Yet it is also significant, I believe, that he sometimes slips in laying out his conception. Later on in *Mind and World*, he remarks that he does not want to "disallow the question what the conceptual contents that are passively received in experience bear on, or are about," and his answer is that "they are about the world, as it appears or makes itself manifest to the experiencing subject" (39). Disallowing such a question, however, is precisely what McDowell should have done. The content of experience ought not to be regarded as being *about* the world, since then thought could not be understood as reaching up to reality itself; it would have to stop short at some representation of it. Experience may count as being *of* the world, but the content of experience – that is, *what* we experience – had better belong to the world itself insofar as it makes itself manifest to us. For the only reason not to identify the content of experience with the very fact that things are thus and so is the notion that what is strictly speaking given in experience must be something – a preconceptual something – out of which the thought that things are thus and so is constructed. Then, conceptual content will have been restricted to the judgments we make about experience, to our "spontaneity" (following the Kantian terminology of which McDowell is so fond), instead of figuring in our "receptivity" as well. And such, of course, is the misstep to be avoided.[10]

I point out this lapse, not simply to make clear McDowell's actual position, but also to underscore how unconvincing and indeed obfuscating is his denial that he is proposing a piece of "constructive philosophy." True, McDowell has rejected an assumption – the idea that experience cannot be at once given, that is, causally dependent on the world, and conceptually structured – that has been a large part of the problem in seeing how experience can act as a tribunal of belief. And I am convinced that he is right to do so. But what he puts in its place goes well beyond a mere reminder or "a truism dressed up in high-flown language" (27). His arguments contain the makings of a full-scale theory of the mind's relation to the world that is no less ambitious than the modern representationalism that, as I have indicated, forms the ultimate object of his attack. The fact that his conception hews more closely to what our self-understanding would be, if freed from that assumption, does not make it any less

---

[9] See also his essay, "Knowledge and the Internal," pp. 395–413 in McDowell, *Meaning, Knowledge, and Reality* (Cambridge, MA: Harvard University Press, 1998).

[10] For a very interesting argument to the effect that the passage in question is not so much a slip as a symptom of a pervasive mistake that McDowell makes about the nature of concepts in laying out his empiricism, see Richard Gaskin, *Experience and the World's Own Language. A Critique of John McDowell's Empiricism* (Oxford: Oxford University Press, 2006), p. 14 (fn 30) and *passim*.

a theoretical construct – that is, any less a set of theses requiring systematic elaboration and giving rise to further questions.

For consider: McDowell is committed to regarding the world itself, not just our understanding of it, as conceptually structured. "We have to suppose," as he declares elsewhere, "that the world has an intelligible structure, matching the structure in the space of *logos* possessed by accurate representations of it."[11] This proposition is scarcely an innocent truism. It is a claim of considerable moment and brings into play an age-old spur to metaphysical speculation. How can we avoid wondering why there should be this sort of natural sympathy or pre-established harmony between mind and world? If the mind does not impose its own order on an alien world, but finds its standards of right thinking woven into the very fabric of reality, then why not see the mind as the way in which the world comes to an awareness of itself, or why not seek some common source of both mind and world? It is no surprise, therefore, that philosophers resolved to be "post-metaphysical" want nothing to do with McDowell's idea of the mind's intimacy with the world.[12] I share his conviction that in experience the world impresses itself upon us as the knowable world it is.[13] But nothing is gained by pretending that such a view does not stake out a substantive philosophical position.

3. EXPERIENCE AS A TRIBUNAL

McDowell's approach removes one obstacle to conceiving how experience can serve as a tribunal of our thinking, yet other obstacles remain, and they embody questions that cannot be exorcised, but have to be tackled. Let us grant that it is the world itself in articulate form, the fact that things are thus and so, that is given to us in experience. Certainly the thesis is not without its points of obscurity. If, for example, receptivity involves the exercise of conceptual capacities, then the way we experience things to be must be capable of error, and not just of errors that reflect the limits of the capacities deployed (as when our perception leads us astray in cases of

---

[11] McDowell, "Two Sorts of Naturalism" (1995), p. 178 as reprinted in McDowell, *Mind, Value, and Reality* (Cambridge, MA: Harvard University Press, 1998).

[12] Such has been the reaction, in their different ways, of Richard Rorty ("The Very Idea of Human Answerability to the World: John McDowell's Version of Empiricism," pp. 138–152 in his *Truth and Progress. Philosophical Papers*, vol. 3, Cambridge: Cambridge University Press, 1998) and Jürgen Habermas (*Wahrheit und Rechtfertigung*, Frankfurt: Suhrkamp, 1999, p. 43).

[13] Some may object to McDowell's taking the world to be "everything that is the case" (27), the totality of facts, in other words, and not the totality of objects about which facts can be asserted. The supposed distinction amounts, however, to little more than alternative ways of speaking. The objects that make up the world are not bare "things-in-themselves," but objects having such and such features, their having them being what is meant by the facts being thus and so.

optical illusion), but also of errors that consist in failing to exercise these capacities correctly – as when in normal cases we simply mistake the color of the table before us. How, one might wonder, can such mistakes be understood, if not (as McDowell would have to deny) as judgments wrongly made about what was given to us in sense?[14] I mention this difficulty as a minor illustration of the "law of the conservation of trouble." But, again, I want to grant the thesis (indeed, I believe it to be true) since my aim is to focus on a larger problem still remaining – namely, the fact that the thesis falls crucially short of explaining how experience can have the function of a tribunal.

In order for the experienced world to be something to which we are accountable, it has to be such as to provide us with reasons for believing this or doubting that. We may be given in experience the world itself, or the fact that things are thus and so, but unless that fact gives us in turn reasons for belief, experience cannot instruct us what to think. To be a tribunal, experience must present us, not merely with facts, but with facts seen to have a bearing on the course of our thinking; otherwise, experience cannot be said to stand in judgment over our attempts to understand the world. McDowell may thus be right that in experience the mind can grasp directly the way things are. But that truth does not suffice to establish the sort of empiricism he intends to redeem. For the fact that things are thus and so cannot be equated with the reason we thereby think we possess to believe this or that, nor does McDowell show any inclination to make such an identification.[15] After all, we might agree about the fact, yet dispute the existence of the reason, as can easily happen when the belief we supposedly have reason to adopt is not about the fact but about what can be inferred from it. (Though seeing that it is raining, one might deny that one ought therefore to take an umbrella.) There is, to be sure, a relation between the two: without the fact, the reason would not obtain. But the fact that things are thus and so is not the same as the reason to believe this or that; it "gives" us that reason or "constitutes" that reason, or, as we may more impressively put it, the reason is "supervenient" on that fact.

We will not therefore have vindicated experience as a tribunal, until we have made sense of how it can yield reasons for belief. One account would be that the ways things are made manifest to us in experience serve as

---

[14] To this concern, McDowell has replied as follows, in his response to the original version of this essay (*Reading McDowell*, ed. Nicholas Smith, Routledge: London, 2002, p. 295): "But why can [such mistakes] not be mistakes in judgment, badly based on what is given to us in sense, about what is perceptually present to us?" The trouble I have in mind, however, is that the given element thus taken to be the basis of mistaken judgment threatens to become, as of old, a preconceptual given. I do not mean that this result is inevitable, but certainly a problem arises here which needs further attention.

[15] He writes, for example, that appearances – the way we experience the world as being – "constitute" (not "are") reasons for judging the world to be that way (62).

reasons solely to the extent that we take them as such or give them that role. Reasons are not something we discover, so it might be said. They consist only in a status we confer upon the things in the world that we do discover, a status expressing our decision about the evidential force that those things will be held to possess. Deep philosophical pressures push in the direction of this perspective, and I will come back to them in §5. For the moment, however, I want to point out that our self-understanding usually runs along different lines. Reasons, we suppose, are in general something we discover. They are not created by us; they are there waiting to be discerned, and we may miss them, if we have not learned enough or focused our minds enough to make them out. From this point of view, experience can serve as a tribunal for our thinking precisely because the reasons for belief we draw from it are reasons we suppose it discloses by way of the facts it makes known to us. Were we ourselves to fix what weight, if any, those facts have for our thinking about the world, experience would be a tribunal only in some etiolated sense.[16]

McDowell's own statements show that he shares a robust conception of experience and of the reasons it provides. He observes, to be sure, that even if "how one's experience represents things to be is not under one's control, ... it is up to one whether one accepts the appearance or rejects it" (11). Yet the judgment one then makes, though an exercise of spontaneity or freedom, is regarded by McDowell as being *responsive* to reasons (79, 84): indeed, freedom he seems inclined, and rightly so, to identify with responsiveness to reasons (xxiii), which are "there anyway" (82, 91), "whether we know it or not" (79). A reason, so conceived, cannot consist in our own taking one thing to count in favor of another; it has to be a relation of warranting that really obtains and that it is our business to acknowledge. The mind's responsiveness to reasons is a theme pervading McDowell's book as a whole and fueling his attempt to rehabilitate the basic truth of empiricism. All the more dismaying, therefore, that he shrugs off the need to explain the nature of reasons themselves. Without such an account, he has not made clear how experience can be, not just an "openness to the world" (111), but also (by way of that) a tribunal for belief. He has only asserted that it is so.

Why this reluctance to face the question squarely? I have already noted McDowell's professed hostility to "constructive philosophy," belied though it is by his actual practice. Not by accident, I suspect, this aversion to positive theory becomes particularly inflexible, when the character of reasons as such would seem to call for analysis.

To see why this may be so, let us pause for a moment to consider what we have to be willing to say about the space of reasons, if we regard it as

---

[16] This is precisely the perspective that Rorty, in his critique of McDowell (see fn 12), urges that we should adopt.

constituting an order that is "there anyway," awaiting our response. Suppose that some fact of physical nature gives us a reason for accepting a belief about the world. The reason, as I have observed before, cannot be identified with that fact itself, if only because people can agree upon the fact, yet deny or be unsure that it provides any warrant for the belief. The reason is the *bearing* that fact has upon what we are to believe: it consists in that fact being such as to *count in favor of* the belief in question.[17] True, if people do not recognize that a particular fact of nature gives them reason to adopt a certain belief, it is generally because they have not taken into account other facts in the situation. Yet a person apprised of all the relevant facts might still be unable to see the reason he has to believe a certain thing if, as we indeed say, he fails to reason properly: he fails to grasp the import of the facts before him. Reasons therefore are not part of physical nature, though they may well depend on its being as it is.

But neither can reasons be equated with anything psychological – at least if our point of departure is that reasons are an object of knowledge and not merely an expression of our own commitments, a status we bestow upon the facts we meet with. The belief that we have a reason cannot be the same as the reason itself, since that belief turns on our assuming that we would have the reason, even had we not discovered it.

Some philosophers hold that the only reasons a person has are ones that he can grasp by deliberating on the basis of his existing beliefs and desires. Such a view has found its canonical formulation in a famous essay by Bernard Williams,[18] and though he focused solely on reasons for action, his distinction between "internal" and "external" reasons is easily extended to belief as well. The reasons a person supposedly has to believe something count then as "internal" or "external" depending on whether he can come to discern them by deliberating from his present point of view (his given "motivational set," as Williams put it). So let us consider the thesis that internal reasons for belief and action are all the reasons there really are. Whatever its truth (and I cast doubt on it in Chapter 5, §7), internal reasons themselves cannot be reduced to elements of our psychology. Someone who infers from his present convictions that he has a reason for belief or action does not suppose he has this reason because he believes he has it; he believes he has it because he supposes it is his in point of fact,

---

[17] On this point, as on the matters discussed in the next few paragraphs, cf. T. M. Scanlon, *What We Owe to Each Other* (Cambridge, MA: Harvard University Press, 1998), Chapter 1, and my book, *Les Pratiques du moi* (Paris: Presses Universitaires de France, 2004), Chapter 3, §2.

[18] Williams, "Internal and External Reasons," in *Moral Luck* (Cambridge: Cambridge University Press, 1981), pp. 101–113. McDowell himself has argued against this view in "Might There Be External Reasons" (1995), pp. 95–111 in his *Mind, Value, and Reality*. Important though it is, this debate leaves untouched the question of the metaphysical nature of reasons.

deliberation making no sense if not aimed at figuring out what reasons one really has. Indeed, the definition of internal reasons, properly stated, is that they are reasons a person can grasp by deliberating *correctly* on the basis of his existing beliefs and desires. Though the internal reasons a person has depend on his perspective being as it is, they are not therefore any item in his mind. Such reasons obtain in virtue of where he stands, yet he may fail to recognize their existence, and if he succeeds, his grasp is a grasp, not of his thought at the time or in its future tendency, but of demands (conditional, to be sure, yet no less prescriptive) about the way he ought to think.

Moreover, a reason cannot, even if internal in character, consist in a belief we already have combined with a given desire, our reason to take an umbrella amounting then to our belief that it is raining conjoined with our wish to remain dry.[19] Even if it is true (which is not obvious) that I ought to carry an umbrella only if I want to stay dry (shouldn't I take one anyway and care more about my health?), the reason to do so does not depend on my happening to believe that it is raining; it is the fact that it is raining that gives rise to the reason. After all, you inform me that I needn't take the umbrella by pointing out that it is no longer raining, even though you do not doubt for a second that I still believe that it is. A reason is the possible object of a belief, and not itself a mental state.

In general, reasons are essentially normative and resist identification with anything physical or psychological. McDowell too perceives their *sui generis* character. Reasons, he insists, cannot be reduced to physical phenomena belonging to the domain of the natural sciences, as the proponents of what he calls "bald naturalism" suppose to be possible. Nor for him can they come down to simply an expression of our own commitments, for then one could hardly say of reasons, as he does, that they represent "requirements of reason that are there whether we know it or not" (79). These convictions would appear to entail a fundamental rethinking of the reigning conception of what there is. The world, the totality of what exists, would have to encompass not only the two dimensions of physical nature and of minds, both the object of the natural sciences, but also a third, normative order of reasons. The proper conclusion would seem to be that naturalism in any form is an inadequate conception of reality. Only some version of platonism, denying that solely the physical and mental are real, would seem able to do justice to the essence of reasons. No wonder that, given his quietism, McDowell is determined to skirt the challenge, declaring that "there is no need for constructive philosophy, directed at the very idea of norms of reason"

[19] An influential statement of this view of reasons is the essay by Donald Davidson, "Actions, Reasons, and Causes" (1963), reprinted in his collection, *Essays on Actions and Events* (Oxford: Clarendon Press, 1980), pp. 3–19.

(95). He may call his position a "relaxed" naturalism (89), but the sense of relaxation comes from not venturing to take up the consequences of his own assertions.

In the end, this indifference only cripples McDowell's own enterprise. Without some account of what reasons are and of how they fit into the architecture of the world, we can have no real comprehension of what is meant by our responding to them. To that extent, we will have failed to show how experience can work as a tribunal.

4. PLATONISMS

This conclusion will impress itself on us all the more if we look at the way that McDowell, using moral thought as a paradigm, proposes to talk about responsiveness to reasons without worrying about what reasons themselves may be. It is in virtue of our "second nature," he declares, drawing on Aristotle's discussion of ethical character, that we are keyed in to the space of reasons. "The ethical is a domain of rational requirements, which are there in any case, whether or not we are responsive to them" (82), but we are able to grasp them only because of the upbringing and cultivation of sensibility that endow us with the conceptual capacities necessary to discern them. They are not visible in the absence of character. The demands of ethics will not come into view, if one looks at ethical life "sideways-on" (83), taking up a standpoint outside it and checking its forms of thinking against the way the world appears from that detached perspective. The study of ethics, as Aristotle remarked,[20] is of little profit to young people lacking moral experience.

In just this way, McDowell argues, reasons in general – not only moral reasons, but the full gamut of reasons for belief and action – will disappear from sight if we seek them in the world as it must look if dissevered from our conception of it as placing demands on our thinking. Then the world will appear as merely the realm of law-governed processes, the object of modern natural science. Our eyes are open to the reasons there are, only so long as we deploy those forms of understanding that training has made our second nature and that show us a world to which our thought is answerable (84).

There is much to be applauded in McDowell's theory of second nature. One of its strengths is the insight that, in regard to the question of objectivity, moral judgment stands on a par with other species of normative judgment, including those at work in the sciences. Far too often the debate about whether morality is a form of knowledge proceeds as though

---

[20] Aristotle, *Nicomachean Ethics* 1095a2–4, 1095b4–6, 1142a11–16. See McDowell, *Mind and World*, p. 80 (fn 13), and also his essay "Two Sorts of Naturalism" in *Mind, Value, and Reality*, pp. 167–197.

morality were a special case, to be taken up once the rest of one's world-view is already in place. If moral judgments can properly be said to be true or false, what sort of things, it is asked, can they be considered to be true of? That the world should contain, along with mind and matter, such things as moral values then strikes many (as it did J. L. Mackie) as too "queer" to be believed, and thus it becomes easy to regard moral judgments, not as descriptive, but as only expressing our own preferences. Expressivism, however, looks far less hospitable, once we recognize that moral judgments are essentially judgments about the moral reasons we have and that they thus form one kind of judgment, amongst others, about the reasons there are. For then expressivism's rejection of the idea of moral knowledge entails that there can also be no knowledge of how in general we ought to think, even about the realm of physical nature. The perennial debate about whether there can be moral knowledge really concerns the possibility of normative knowledge as such.[21]

McDowell was not always so clear about this point. In the early 1980s, he sought to rescue the notion of moral knowledge by exploiting a parallel between values and secondary qualities such as colors, each possessing a reality that is at once dependent on forms of human sensibility and robust enough to be the object of true and false judgments. Even then, however, he put his finger on the key disanalogy: the object of a moral judgment is taken to "merit" our response, whereas a dispositional property such as a color can merely cause it.[22] McDowell's move to a more satisfactory view was signaled in his Lindley Lecture of 1987, where he observed that a proper epistemology of moral judgment should center on "the notion of susceptibility to reasons."[23]

A second strength of McDowell's theory of second nature is its overcoming of the common opposition between reason and tradition. We learn from experience only to the extent that our thinking is shaped by forms of sensibility and understanding that are ours primarily because we have been brought up in them. Such traditions of thought are not of course immune to scrutiny and correction, but critical reflection, as McDowell likes to say, is best compared to Otto Neurath's famous image of the sailor who repairs his ship at sea. Only within our existing web of belief can we find the resources essential to determining which elements have become problematic and what solutions would count as appropriate, so that revision is always piecemeal, though sometimes radical all the same (81).

Thus the exercise of reason does not consist, as a certain modern individualism supposes (98), in peeling away the force of tradition so that we may stand face to face with the real. The *Bildung* we receive through our

---

[21] I pursue this theme in *The Morals of Modernity*, Chapters 4 and 5.

[22] See McDowell, "Values and Secondary Qualities" (1985), p. 143 in *Mind, Value, and Reality*.

[23] McDowell, "Projection and Truth in Ethics," p. 162 in *Mind, Value, and Reality*.

place in history is our very avenue to reality.[24] Stripped of all the standards
and habits of mind it has inherited, and forced to begin again from
scratch, our moral thinking must lose its bearings, and the same is true for
our ability to grasp every sort of reason for belief or action. Even scientific
thinking, setting about as it does to describe the world as a system of law-
governed processes, normatively mute, proceeds by adapting its inheri-
tance from the past. Reliance on tradition is not a second-best mode of
inquiry, whose results need to be relativized in the light of a more direct
confrontation with the world as it is. It is the very nature of reasoning.
Nothing, McDowell points out,[25] could be more wrong-headed than to
argue (as the position he calls "bald naturalism" is wont to do) that the
world of modern natural science alone is real because reasons for belief
and action only come into view against the backdrop of some given way of
conceiving the world. On such grounds, any form of articulate thought
would have to count as but a "projection."

Yet, for all its virtues, this conception of second nature is not a point at
which philosophy can come to rest, much as McDowell would like to believe
so. Once "the bare idea of *Bildung* is in place," so he maintains, "no genuine
questions about norms" remain (95). But that is simply not true. We have
been told the conditions under which we are able to apprehend reasons, but
not what reasons are themselves. How can any account of our responsiveness
to reasons be complete if it skimps on a systematic explanation of the
object of our response and of its place in the overall scheme of things?
McDowell's refusal to take on this topic amounts to a failure to show that
experience – and experience as he wants to understand it, as an openness to
the world itself – is truly a tribunal for belief.[26]

---

[24] Cf. also "Some Issues in Aristotle's Moral Psychology," p. 37 in *Mind, Value, and Reality*. On
this point too, I feel particularly close to McDowell. See my *Morals of Modernity*, Chapter 2,
as well as "History and Truth," Chapter 1 in the present book.

[25] See, in particular, McDowell, "Two Sorts of Naturalism," p. 187 in *Mind, Value, and Reality*.

[26] In "Self-Determining Subjectivity and External Constraint" (in *Internationales Jahrbuch des
Deutschen Idealismus*, vol. 3, de Gruyter: Berlin, 2005, pp. 21–37), McDowell rightly notes
that the authority of reasons cannot coherently be understood as conferred on them by
rational subjects, individually or collectively. Their authority is one they possess "anyway"
and that rational subjects must "acknowledge." (I develop at length a similar critique of
the Kantian approach in Chapter 5 of the present book.) McDowell also rightly observes
that "the capacity to recognize the requirements of reason, still seen as authoritative
anyway, not owing their authoritativeness to their being recognized, is acquired by
initiation into suitable communal practices," by what elsewhere he calls *Bildung* (p. 36).
Yet these points do not tell us how, positively, we should understand the inherent
authority of reasons. The most he is willing to say here is that the fundamental norms of
thinking are "constitutive of the practice of thinking" (p. 35). True enough – but the term
"constitutive" only hides the need for further (and inevitably metaphysical) analysis,
particularly as thinking is being understood as "acknowledging" reasons that obtain
"anyway."

Of course, laying bare the nature of reasons, when one credits them with being irreducible to anything else and with being there independently of our knowledge of them, can hardly prove an innocent business. As I have indicated, it runs in the face of the prevailing view of the world as consisting in but mind and matter. Pursuing this question can only lead to the kind of constructive or substantive theorizing that McDowell aims to shun. He himself mentions but one sort of speculation about the ontology of reasons, the position he calls "rampant platonism," and this undoubted piece of philosophical extravagance serves as his excuse for refusing to get into the subject. Rampant platonism views reasons as "constituted independently of" (77) or "in splendid isolation from anything merely human" (92), and as a result it turns our ability to respond to them into something "occult or magical": it fails to see "the demands of reason [as] essentially such that a human upbringing can open a human being's eyes to them" (92). Such a theory does not indeed seem very attractive. But is this really the shape our thinking must take if we do not believe that the idea of second nature tells us everything we would like to know about reasons as such? Is this the only form a platonism of reasons can assume?

Describing the order of reasons as a third ontological dimension of the world (a way of talking McDowell would surely deplore), I observed at the same time how reasons, though irreducible, depend on the physical and psychological facts being as they are. If it turns out not to be raining, or if I do not care about getting wet, then I no longer have a reason to carry an umbrella. Nothing in the willingness to take seriously the reality of reasons and the questions it raises obliges us to suppose that they inhabit some remote Platonic heaven. To deny an essential connection between the reasons there are and the circumstances of our existence would seem in fact to betray an ignorance of the very notion of what a reason is. Reasons, as I have suggested, are relational in character: they consist in the bearing that physical or psychological facts have on our possibilities, in their counting in favor of certain beliefs or actions.

Nor are we driven to reject training and tradition as the means by which we tune in to the demands of reason, just because we think that the irreducibility of reasons calls for a deeper account and one that will prove to be nothing less than metaphysical – but also no more metaphysical than the naturalism we are then rejecting. After all, second nature can only count as a mode of access if it enables us to lay hold of something that is distinct from itself. McDowell's "naturalized" platonism combines an insistence on reasons "being there anyway" with a refusal to describe what is exactly their mode of being. Such a position is hardly satisfactory, and it seems motivated by the fear that if we venture beyond a focus on second nature itself, we will find ourselves launched into the outlandish sort of platonism he rightly rejects. But forsaking quietism does not entail losing touch with the human condition. We can make out the lineaments of

a platonistic account of reasons that does justice to their distinct ontological status while keeping them very much a part of our world. We have
no need to take refuge in the oxymoron of "naturalized platonism."

5. THE CONSERVATION OF TROUBLE

I do not want, however, to paint an irenic picture of where speculation
about these matters will lead. On the contrary, trouble waits just around
the corner.

Reasons, I have argued, cannot be physical or psychological in character, if they are to enjoy the sort of objectivity that both McDowell and I
attribute to them. How then can they operate as causes, as reasons certainly must do if their "being there anyway" is to explain our coming to
grasp them? Our usual understanding of causes involves locating them in
space and time. Yet how can a reason occupy a spatial or temporal
position? Perhaps reasons can be placed in time, as when we say that
a certain reason obtains at one time and not at another. But assigning
reasons a spatial location, as though one could talk about the distance
between them, is manifestly ridiculous. As a rule, we suppose that cause
and effect are spatially contiguous, or that the one leads to the other along
some path in space, or (as in so-called mental causation) that they are
successive states of some spatially situated entity. Have we any real idea of
how the denizens of the "space of reasons" can act in the world, if they
have no locus in physical space? The physical and psychological features of
the world that give us reasons for belief and action are certainly in space,
and no mystery surrounds how they can act on us. But reasons themselves,
it will be recalled, cannot be identified with these features, however much
they may depend on them. The snag, therefore, is conceiving how reasons
as such are able to move us.

Loath to delve into the question of what reasons actually are, McDowell
never addresses this difficulty, of course. But he does make a point of
observing that, for his vindication of experience as a tribunal to succeed,
reasons must be able to act as causes (71, footnote 2).[27] After all, the idea
of a responsiveness to reasons makes no sense if reasons are denied

---

[27] See also McDowell, "Naturalism in the Philosophy of Mind," in M. De Caro and D. Macarthur
(eds.), *Naturalism in Question* (Cambridge, MA: Harvard University Press, 2004), pp. 91–105
(esp. pp. 92, 96). The point is an essential part of his critique of Davidson's coherentism. See,
in particular, McDowell's essay, "Scheme-Content Dualism and Empiricism," pp. 87–104 in
Lewis Hahn (ed.), *The Philosophy of Donald Davidson* (Chicago and La Salle: Open Court,
1999). Oddly, he writes in "Two Sorts of Naturalism" (pp. 186–187 in *Mind, Value, and Reality*)
that while science is led to its conclusions "because of the causal influence of the fact
that things are thus and so, ... there is no analogue to that in ethics." So great a difference
there cannot be, if ethical thinking, like scientific thinking, hinges on a responsiveness to
reasons.

a causal influence. Where there is no action, there cannot be a response. That is why McDowell quite rightly insists that the proper contrast to the space of reasons – the organizing principle, in other words, of the modern scientific image of nature – is not the space of causal relations, but the space of law-governed processes. And thus the predicament I have just sketched is his, whether he chooses to acknowledge it or not.[28]

The problem of how reasons can be causes, when irreducible to physical or psychological phenomena, provides one of the strongest motivations for maintaining that the truth must lie instead with that view of the world that McDowell rejects under the name of "bald naturalism." There is only confusion, it can seem, if we imagine that the space of reasons consists ultimately in anything other than the law-governed processes of the natural world, explicable in the terms of modern science. To many, reasons will look "spooky," despite all McDowell's assurances to the contrary (94, 95), if they are assumed to be, as he himself must grant, both *sui generis* and causally active in the world. The sensible approach, one easily concludes, is to regard reasons for belief and action as simply the expression of our own commitments, and not as something "there anyway," awaiting our discovery: the reasons there are are simply the reasons we take there to be. For our commitments themselves are psychological phenomena, and their place in the causal order of the world poses no similar problem of intelligibility.

Far be it from me to want to argue that this sort of naturalism is in the end the position to embrace. Even more formidable obstacles lie in that direction. Chief among them is indeed the expressivist analysis of reasons it typically begets, since that analysis implies that strictly speaking there can be no such thing as normative knowledge, no truths to be discovered about how it is that we ought to think and act.[29] My own belief, like McDowell's, is that the mind's answerability to the reasons there are forms an indispensable part of our self-understanding. But the price we must pay to hold on to this conviction is recognizing that we must ultimately face the difficult problem of understanding how reasons can be causes.

Better on balance, I believe, to accept the perplexity than a crippled notion of human reason. But it means that we cannot deny the significance

---

[28] In his response to the original version of this essay (*Reading McDowell*, p. 296), McDowell replies that the worry can be dissolved if we focus instead on how "*someone's having a reason can be causally relevant* ... to their acting or to their forming a belief." But nothing is gained by this strategy. Having a reason causally shapes our action or belief only insofar as we grasp the reason (no one is moved by a reason he fails to see), and thus the question immediately returns: how is it that reasons act on us, when we grasp or respond to them?

[29] A good example of this alliance of (bald) naturalism with an expressivist theory of norms is Allan Gibbard, *Wise Choices, Apt Feelings* (Cambridge, MA: Harvard University Press, 1990). For some detailed criticisms of expressivism, see my book, *The Morals of Modernity*, Chapter 5 (revised version published as "La connaissance morale," in R. Ogien (ed.), *Le réalisme moral*, Paris: PUF, 1999, pp. 382–419).

of these questions, nor also the need to weigh pluses and minuses. By refusing to enter into the discussion about what reasons actually are and how it is that we respond to them, McDowell fails to show what he sets out to establish – namely, that experience can indeed be a tribunal. Standing in his way is a conception of philosophy that serves him ill. Denying the constructive vision that animates his work blinds him to the problems he has yet to face. They are not problems that melt away once we break loose enough from a scientistic view of the world to see in our second nature an attunement to the demands of reason. They are problems his own platonism, tame though it be, is obliged to reckon with, and their difficulty accounts in large part for the enduring attraction of the kind of modern naturalism he opposes.

On these fundamental matters, there can then be no peace in philosophy. Here, as elsewhere, philosophy is always in trouble, and to seek a cure that will give it rest is to mistake for an affliction the very vitality of thinking. Skepticism, if that means suspending judgment, is not the answer either. In philosophy, too, we need to heed the reasons there are, and we do so when we let our reflection follow where it is pulled, instead of hankering to bring it to a close. In Chapter 5, I develop more systematically the "platonistic" conception of reasons that I believe is, on balance, the best route to take (see particularly §§6 and 7). But nothing I say there should be understood as denying that this theory, like every philosophical position, remains beset by difficulties. There is most particularly the problem of just how it is that reasons can be causes, a problem that I do not yet feel myself able to address properly.

PART II

THE MORAL POINT OF VIEW

4

John Rawls and Moral Philosophy

1. THE ONE AND THE MANY

The mind's relation to the world is often considered the fundamental problem of philosophy, as the discussion in the previous chapter would seem to confirm. The nature of thought, the basic categories of experience, the sources of knowledge – for most philosophers the changing opinions about these topics define the essential history of their enterprise. That the world is peopled not by one, but by many minds, each with its own point of view, seems a secondary matter. Questions arising from the manyness of minds and having to do with the relation in which persons stand to one another – in other words, the questions of moral and political theory – are admitted to be important, but they play a minor role in the dominant image of what philosophy is all about. They are supposedly derivative questions, anchored in the deeper issue of mind and world. The so-called "linguistic turn" in twentieth century thought, emphasizing the way that thought is shaped by the social institution of language, did little to alter this predilection for mind in the singular. Its concern was with the shared forms of understanding in which each of us must participate to be capable of coherent thought and action. Perhaps philosophers tend to regard the relation between mind and world as their primary subject because of a professional conceit. They like to imagine that through them Man himself is coming to understand his place in the world.

This view underlies the canonization of Wittgenstein and Heidegger as the two giants of twentieth century philosophy. In their different styles, they both demolished the representationalist theory of the mind that had

This chapter serves to introduce many of the key themes and concerns of the next two parts of the book. An earlier version appeared as a review of Rawls' *Lectures on the History of Moral Philosophy* (ed. Barbara Herman, Cambridge, MA: Harvard University Press, 2000) in *The New Republic* of 5 February 2001. I have largely kept the informal style.

held sway ever since the seventeenth century. Their common project was to show how thought does not operate at a remove from the world, framing to itself "ideas" of the way things are, but instead inhabits the world itself through the public rules and practical entailments that alone give it content. But neither found much to say about ethics. Wittgenstein declared in a lecture on the subject that "if a man could write a book on Ethics which really was a book on Ethics, this book would, with an explosion, destroy all the other books in the world" – which probably explains why he never wrote one.[1] Heidegger held that in our present spiritual disarray, we are not ready to think about ethics, and clearly he was ill-prepared himself, rallying to the Nazi movement and continuing long after 1945 to extol its "inner truth and greatness."[2] The striking one-sidedness of Wittgenstein's and Heidegger's genius may be as good a proof as any that the mind's relation to the world does not offer the master perspective for making sense of everything else. The "many-minds" problems of moral and political philosophy are no less fundamental, and they come into focus only when considered in their own terms.

   To take stock of the achievements of twentieth century philosophy, we need therefore to broaden our view and see in ethics a domain of equal and independent significance. What names would we want to place next to those of Wittgenstein and Heidegger in this more inclusive picture?

   No thinker, I believe, has a greater right to stand alongside them than John Rawls. His book of 1971, *A Theory of Justice*, has become a classic and changed forever the landscape of moral and political philosophy. Like Wittgenstein and Heidegger, Rawls also showed a remarkable capacity for self-criticism. Like them, he went on to revise in significant ways the doctrines that first established his fame. *Political Liberalism*, published in 1993, recast his liberal theory of justice in a more flexible and accommodating form. It showed a greater appreciation for modernity's deep disagreements about the nature of the human good as well as about the proper roles of tradition, community, and individualism in our pursuit of it. There is a "Rawls$_1$," and a "Rawls$_2$," just as there is an earlier and later Wittgenstein or Heidegger.

   One reason Rawls has been so central a figure is the clarity with which he saw the real relation between ethics and the rest of philosophy. In 1974, he gave a Presidential Address before the American Philosophical Association entitled "The Independence of Moral Theory."[3] Its title was not meant to suggest that moral philosophy should become yet one more

---

[1] "Wittgenstein's Lecture on Ethics" (1929–30), in *Philosophical Review* 74 (1) 1965, pp. 3–26 (7).
[2] See Heidegger, *Einführung in die Metaphysik* (Tübingen: Mohr, 1953), p. 152.
[3] The address is reprinted in Rawls, *Collected Papers* (Cambridge, MA: Harvard University Press, 1999), pp. 286–302.

sub-field specializing in problems only experts can understand. To reflect upon the basic notions of the right, the good, and moral worth and upon their connections to human psychology and society is to wrestle with the most important question we all confront: how should we live our lives? But in pursuing this subject, we ought, Rawls maintained, to expect little help from the latest advances in metaphysics, the theory of meaning, or epistemology. Moral philosophy has its own distinctive concerns, and the only way to do them justice is to tackle them directly on their own terms.[4]

This conviction inspired Rawls' work as a whole, both his writings and his many years of teaching, mostly at Harvard. No less than his own positive theories, it is part of his enduring legacy. Rawls taught his students and readers to appreciate the integrity of moral thinking. At a time when ethics seemed the poor cousin of the rest of philosophy, riveted on the formal analysis of moral language and inclined to regard value judgments as little more than expressions of preference or tools of persuasion, Rawls shifted attention back to the great questions of substance such as what we owe to others and what relation there can be between a commitment to justice and the pursuit of our own good. He made them once again the object of detailed argument and theory. Indeed, one of the principal themes of his ethical thought was the manyness, or as he put it, the "separateness" of persons.[5]

Rawls' lead is not always to be followed, however, particularly in fundamental matters. About the nature of practical reason, for instance, he seems to me importantly mistaken. His so-called "constructivism" presents an untenable account of what makes for the authority of moral and political principles. In the following pages, I focus chiefly on these foundational questions. The discussion is therefore often critical, and though disagreement too is testimony to a philosopher's greatness, my criticisms are not meant to take away from what are Rawls' undoubted achievements. He saw far more clearly than most the distinctive object of moral thinking, which is the good of others as persons in their own right, each of them an independent source of demands on our attention. This insight animates much of the substance of his theorizing about morality and justice, as I shall also be at pains to point out. The trouble is that Rawls failed to find the right overall framework for his thought.

---

[4] Though this is so, I also believe, as the next chapter shows, that moral philosophy can suggest important lessons for other areas of philosophy.

[5] The manyness of persons or human "plurality" was also a leitmotif of Hannah Arendt's thought, as when she observed that "men, not Man, live on the earth and inhabit the world" (*The Human Condition*, Chicago: University of Chicago Press, 1958, p. 7). But Arendt failed to appreciate the need for systematic reflection in ethics. See my article, "Arendt for Beginners," *Internationale Zeitschrift für Philosophie* 7 (1) 1997, pp. 5–19.

2. THE CRITIQUE OF UTILITARIANISM

A Theory of Justice has, quite naturally, a more specific focus than the whole of morality. It is a treatise in political philosophy, presenting an account of justice as "the first virtue of social institutions." To meet Rawls' conception of modern ethics as a whole, the understanding of its characteristic themes and problems on which he drew in working out his theory of justice, we need to look at some other of his writings, particularly his *Lectures on the History of Moral Philosophy* (published only in 2000), and also to pay close attention to certain key passages in his three principal works in political theory – not just *A Theory of Justice*, but *Political Liberalism* and *Justice as Fairness* as well.[6] The *Lectures* are especially helpful. They begin by discussing some of the apparent differences between classical Greek and modern moral philosophy and then focus on Hume, Leibniz, and Kant, closing with two chapters on Hegel. Naturally there are insightful analyses of all these figures, particularly of Kant, who was Rawls' philosophical hero. But the real importance of this work is the light it sheds on the deepest strata of Rawls' own moral and political thought.

Part of the excitement that greeted *A Theory of Justice* in the 1970s stemmed from its frequent use of the techniques of modern rational choice theory and welfare economics. Some readers applauded, and others lamented, what they saw as the attempt to turn social justice into the object of something like a science. Their impression was that Rawls wanted to derive, as an economist might, a set of principles for the distribution of rights and resources by showing that rational agents, each seeking to maximize his own advantage under circumstances that make cooperation beneficial, would converge upon these principles as the best bargain they could make with one another.

This reading could not have been more wrong-headed, however. For Rawls, political philosophy had its basis, not in economics, but in moral theory, as these *Lectures* make plain. *A Theory of Justice* asks us, it is true, to imagine an "Original Position" in which principles of justice are chosen by mutually disinterested and rational agents, efficiently pursuing their own interests. But this social contract is only a thought experiment, not an agreement that has been or ever should be made, and the reason we ought to heed its terms has to do with the constraints under which it is envisioned as taking place. We are to assume, according to Rawls, that the

---

[6] Two essay-length texts by Rawls on the foundations of ethics are "Kantian Constructivism in Moral Theory" (1980) (*Collected Papers*, pp. 303–358) and "Themes in Kant's Moral Philosophy" (1989) (*ibid.*, pp. 497–528); they both draw on the *Lectures* in many places. To all these works may now be added his *Lectures on the History of Political Philosophy* (Cambridge, MA: Harvard University Press, 2007). See my review in *The New Republic* of 27 February 2008, pp. 43–47 ("Behind the Veil").

parties are ignorant of their particular abilities, social position, and conception of the good, since it would not be *right*, but rather partisan and self-serving, to base one's idea of justice on such information. What they are taken not to know is what we ought to consider morally irrelevant when deliberating about the terms on which we should live with one another.

The "veil of ignorance" imposed upon those hypothetical choosers reflects therefore a set of moral convictions that ought to govern our own thinking about justice. At their heart stands a commitment to what Rawls called being "reasonable," a readiness to engage with others in forms of cooperation that all, as free and equal persons, have a similar reason to adopt.[7] Reasonableness he distinguished from rationality in the sense of that term now widely used in the social sciences and that signifies the efficient pursuit of one's own interests. To be sure, we must as rational persons take into account what other people are likely to do, and we may even give their well-being an important place in our deliberations. But in the end it is our own interests, be they self-or other-directed, that we aim to pursue as best we can. If we seek to advance the good of others, then only because it happens to figure among our desires. Reasonableness, by contrast, requires that we reason from the perspective of others no less than from our own, since the goal is to find a way of living together that each person has reason to accept. When being reasonable, we seek conclusions that square with the good of all those involved, independently of the extent to which we may already care about how well they fare. In this case, the manyness of persons does not represent merely a fact to be acknowledged and handled from the point of view of our own concerns. It serves as the very basis on which we deliberate.

Rawls did not claim, of course, that we should be reasonable instead of rational. Both kinds of thinking are necessary, and the essential thing is to grasp their respective roles. Each underlies one of what he termed our two basic "moral powers."[8] To frame an idea of the good or of human flourishing, we must exercise rationality, fashioning and ordering our ends into a coherent vision of a life lived well. But to develop a sense of justice, we need to be reasonable and look for the basis of a common life that people holding different ideals of the human good can have similar grounds to accept.

For my past, I do not believe that the capacity to devise a conception of our own good really counts as a *moral* power, even if such conceptions typically give some role to moral endeavors. Morality consists in seeing in another's good a demand on our attention that is as direct, as unmediated by ulterior considerations, as the concern we naturally feel for our own.

---

[7] Rawls, *Political Liberalism* (New York: Columbia University Press, 1996), p. 305.

[8] See Rawls, *A Theory of Justice* (Cambridge, MA: Harvard University Press, 1971) §77, and *Political Liberalism*, p. 19.

The ability to look beyond our own interests, whatever they may be, and to take an interest in another's good simply because it is his or hers – that is the essence of moral thinking. One way, if not the only one, in which we can exercise this ability lies in seeking common ground that all can occupy starting from their different perspectives. So reasonableness as Rawls defined it is certainly a moral power – though not, I think, our capacity for morality in its most fundamental form. Moreover, Rawls seems to me absolutely right in holding that rationality and reasonableness are two distinct powers and that in particular the latter cannot be derived from the former.[9] For this is to recognize the crucial truth that morality, as I explain in the next chapter, constitutes an autonomous realm of value. There is no way we can reason ourselves into the moral point of view from a standpoint lying outside it and consisting in the rational pursuit of our own good.[10]

The distinction between the rational and the reasonable has often been missed, most notably in modern utilitarianism. A primary aim of *A Theory of Justice* was indeed to challenge the hegemony that utilitarian thought had enjoyed in England and America since the time of Jeremy Bentham and John Stuart Mill. Utilitarianism holds that social institutions are properly arranged when the general happiness, the net sum of everyone's gains and losses, is as great as possible (or, according to some versions, when the average happiness is maximized). Justice, so conceived, would thus allow that a given individual's prospects might rightly be enhanced or diminished to any degree whatsoever, depending on which social policy would bring about the most welfare overall. In this way of thinking, society itself takes on the aspect of a single person, a giant "We" whose good is to be pursued in the same cost-benefit terms that a prudent individual would use to calculate his own. For utilitarians, the cardinal virtue is therefore sympathy: to be just, we must become impartial spectators who identify imaginatively with the interests of others and balance them in our own minds as though they were ours.

The main difficulty with utilitarianism is therefore that it does not take seriously the manyness or, as Rawls said, the "separateness" of persons.[11] It too readily sacrifices the individual to the whole. This kind of complaint had often been voiced since the middle of the nineteenth century, but no one had managed to move beyond the criticism and come up with a rival, equally comprehensive conception of justice. No one, that is, until Rawls. He was the first to work out systematically the idea that the just society consists in how we stand to one another and only secondarily in how much

9 Rawls, *Political Liberalism*, pp. 51ff.
10 In Chapter 10 ("The Idea of a Life Plan"), I examine critically Rawls' account of what it is to develop a conception of our own good.
11 Rawls, *A Theory of Justice*, pp. 27, 29.

overall good is brought about. It is the essence of his theory of "justice as fairness," evident in each of its two basic principles – a set of equal basic civil and political liberties and the arrangement of social and economic inequalities so that they be tied to positions open to all, through equality of opportunity, and render the least advantaged better off than they would be under any alternative distribution. Not sympathetic identification but, we might say, respect for one another as distinct individuals is its moral foundation.[12] Justice has to do with the principles that persons can freely acknowledge before one another as the mutually acceptable basis of their life together. Utilitarianism, he claimed, looks at social life with the eye of an administrator, charged with allocating benefits and burdens among a given population in the most efficient or welfare-maximizing fashion possible. The ideal of fairness, by contrast, concerns the relation that the citizens themselves should assume in regard to one another. Utilitarians – or "consequentialists" as they more demurely call themselves today – have not, of course, vanished from the scene, for the notion that our basic duty is to bring about as much good as possible has its undeniable attraction. But Rawls made clear the basic issue at stake and showed that there exists a systematic alternative to the utilitarian paradigm.

To expound his conception of justice, Rawls chose to return to the tradition of social contract theory. Principles of justice are to be understood as valid if reasonable people (our representatives, as it were) would agree on them in the Original Position. The contractarian idiom may have been a mistake, for the very idea of a contract appears redundant and obfuscating. Instead of holding that a conception of justice is justified by virtue of its being the object of reasonable agreement under hypothetical conditions embodying certain basic moral values (as Rawls acknowledges the Veil of Ignorance to do), one could just as well say, and a lot more simply, that its validity consists in its following from those deeper values that already count as settled. To suppose that people under the stipulated conditions would find it reasonable to agree to some principle comes to no more than claiming that there is good reason to accept that principle, given the premises. Actual contracts are not of course superfluous: they institute obligations that would not otherwise exist, since the parties have really made an agreement. But hypothetical contracts do not, being hypothetical, bring anything about. Whatever authority they may seem to have is a borrowed luster. All that can be meant by the notion that certain principles would be the object of fair and reasonable agreement is that considerations of fairness provide good reasons to accept those principles.

---

[12] Rawls himself shied away from invoking the idea of respect, largely I believe because of his reluctance to spell out the moral foundations of his thought, and this for reasons I explore in §4. See, too, Chapter 6.

This sort of criticism seems to me in large measure correct.[13] Both the substance and the arguments of Rawls' theory of justice do not depend essentially on the contractarian language he favored. Not even the special weight he gave to the separateness or manyness of persons requires it, though the metaphor of a contract does have the virtue of bringing out an important feature of his ideal of fairness. As I explain in Chapter 8 (§1), this feature is that proper principles of justice are such that the reason each person has to accept them turns on others too having reason to accept them, just as one is bound by an agreement only if the other parties are similarly bound by it.

3. HUME VS. KANT

In *A Theory of Justice*, Rawls explained at some length how justice as fairness lends itself to a "Kantian interpretation."[14] In fact, Kant exercised a pervasive influence on his moral and political thought. One reason to be grateful for the publication of his *Lectures on the History of Moral Philosophy* is that they reveal just how deeply Rawls drew upon Kant's writings.

Rawls begins the *Lectures* with some insightful observations on the characteristic differences between ancient and modern ethics. These differences, he remarks, have less to do with the content than with the basis of morality. How do we distinguish right from wrong, and what is it in the nature of moral beliefs that they appear able by themselves to move us to action? Following Henry Sidgwick, Rawls observes that the Greeks typically regarded morality as an "attractive" ideal, as an essential dimension of our own flourishing that we come naturally to value in discovering our true good; modern ethics, by contrast, has generally conceived of morality in "imperative" terms, as fundamentally a body of obligations by which we are bound and which we owe to others. However, he goes beyond Sidgwick in the historical explanation he offers of this difference. No doubt Christian theology, with its concept of the law of God, played a role. But just as important was the fact that in early modern times the nature of the human good came to appear so intractable an object of disagreement (often violent, as in the age of religious wars) that the need became plain to understand morality as a body of demands binding on each of us, whatever our views on this controversial subject. Here again we note how Rawls put at the center of his moral thinking the manyness of persons, in this case our

---

[13] It was made early on by Ronald Dworkin in his famous review of *A Theory of Justice*, reprinted in his *Taking Rights Seriously* (Cambridge, MA: Harvard University Press, 1978), chapter 6. Rawls never adequately responded to it.

[14] Rawls, *A Theory of Justice*, §40.

natural tendency to disagree with one another about the ultimate purposes of existence.[15]

What can be the basis of morality if understood as a body of demands binding upon us? One answer would be to posit some external authority. If an appreciation of moral right and wrong is not seen as making up an essential part of our own flourishing, then it might seem to have to derive from some outside source such as God's will, social convention, or the state. This approach has had its adherents. But as Rawls makes plain, the two canonical figures of modern ethics – Hume and Kant – pursued a different path. For them, as for their many followers, the moral order arises

> from human nature itself and from the requirements of our living together in society... The knowledge or awareness of how we are to act is directly accessible to every person who is normally reasonable and conscientious. ... We are so constituted that we have in our nature sufficient motives to lead us to act as we ought without the need of external sanctions.[16]

Yet, at the same time, Humeans and Kantians have disagreed profoundly about what this self-standing basis of morality is like. Their disagreement marks in fact a fundamental divide in modern ethical theory. Rawls sides with Kant, and the account he developed of the Kantian position provided the inspiration for own theory of justice as fairness.

According to Hume, our moral judgments express the particular sort of desire we feel for other people's good when considering their situation sympathetically from the impartial standpoint of the "judicious spectator." In one regard, he therefore counts as one of the founders of the utilitarian tradition and shares in the collectivistic bias that Rawls attributes to it as a whole. But just as significant is another drawback in this stance – namely, Hume's contention that morality is rooted in our affective, not in our rational nature. Our moral judgments, he insisted, are not to be imagined as embodying a form of knowledge, as though there existed some independent realm of moral facts that we were attempting to describe. The position he had in mind had been influentially expounded by Samuel Clarke in his *Discourse Concerning the Unchangeable Obligations of Natural Religion* of 1705, but others too have explicitly held it, not only then (Leibniz, for example) but in the twentieth century as well (H. A. Prichard and W. D. Ross) and in our own day – I count myself an adherent. Rawls calls the view "rational intuitionism," somewhat misleadingly given the obscurity of the term "intuition." He himself is eager to reject it, though not on the grounds that Hume adduced. For Hume believed he had

---

[15] Rawls, *Lectures on the History of Moral Philosophy*, pp. 1–8. I believe that Rawls is quite right in his conjecture, and I have extended Sidgwick's ideas in a similar manner. See *The Morals of Modernity* (Cambridge: Cambridge University Press, 1996), Chapter 1 ("The Right and the Good").

[16] Rawls, *Lectures*, p. 11.

something of a "knockout" argument for disposing of the notion that moral judgments can properly aim at knowledge, and Rawls objects, quite rightly in my view, that this argument carries far too high a price.

Hume's argument – still quite popular in various versions among contemporary "expressivists" who follow him in this regard – went basically as follows: In general, reason alone cannot move us to act. The knowledge we acquire by its means, if not combined with some desire, has no effect on the will since it merely serves to portray the way things are. Our moral judgments, by contrast, generally incline us to act as they demand, even if sometimes too feebly to overcome our other interests; they involve a commitment to make things go as we judge that they should. Morality cannot therefore be fundamentally a matter of knowledge. It is instead, Hume concluded, our affective nature, our desires and "passions," to which our moral judgments give voice.[17]

In Rawls' view, the trouble with this argument is that it leaves no room for there being such a thing as practical reason at all – that is, the capacity of reasoning out how we should act in given circumstances. When Hume, in keeping with his analysis of moral judgments, famously declared that "Reason is and ought only to be the slave of the passions," he might seem to be granting reason at least the function of calculating the most efficient means to the ends we happen to desire. Yet even this modest role was further reduced by the way he understood that "general appetite to good" that impels us to look to the future no less than to the present and thus to match means and ends in a spirit of efficiency. This appetite, according to Hume, is itself but another passion. It shapes our thinking, depending on how strong it is, but there can be no sense in supposing that it expresses a demand of reason – that it has, in other words, an *authority* distinct from its *strength*. "'Tis as little contrary to reason," he thus wrote in an equally famous phrase, "to prefer even my own acknowledged lesser good to my greater." In the end, as Rawls concludes, Hume really had no conception of practical reasoning.[18]

Where exactly is the error in Hume's master argument? For my part, I would place it in the first premise – namely, in the assumption that knowledge, if unaccompanied by desire, has no effect on the will. Whether or not they qualify as knowledge, beliefs do aim at describing the world: to believe something is to hold it to be true, to maintain that things are as they are thus portrayed as being. But a belief is more than just a holding-to-be-true.

---

[17] Hume, *Treatise of Human Nature*, ed. L. A. Selby-Bigge (Oxford: Oxford University Press, 1968), pp. 456f. The leading "expressivists" today are no doubt Allan Gibbard and Simon Blackburn. For a lengthier critique of the Humean argument, see Chapter 5, § 8, as well as *The Morals of Modernity*, Chapter 5.

[18] Rawls, *Lectures*, pp. 37, 50, 69, 84. For the two quoted passages from Hume, see *A Treatise of Human Nature*, pp. 415f.

It involves the commitment to think and act in accord with the presumed truth of what is believed. Someone announcing that he believed a certain thing but had no intention of ever conducting himself accordingly would scarcely count as really believing it. Beliefs are not therefore motivationally inert. In and of themselves, without the accompaniment of some desire, they move the will. A belief, as C. S. Peirce aptly said, is a "rule for action," and how it directs us to think and act depends on its specific content. The beliefs that moral judgments express are beliefs about the reasons we have to act in certain ways. Consequently, there ought to be no difficulty in understanding how, contrary to Hume, moral judgments can both move us to action and embody knowledge.

Rawls did not take this route. It would have led him toward the "rational intuitionism" that he joined Hume in rejecting. His own rejection of it consisted in complaining that such a view "sees moral thought as a form of theoretical as opposed to practical reason."[19] I think a better characterization would be, as my own defense of the position implies, that it does not regard the supposed distinction between theoretical and practical reason as in any way fundamental: there is a single faculty of reason whose exercise may be styled as "theoretical" or "practical" depending on whether its subject matter is belief or action. Rawls, by contrast, believed the distinction to be of profound significance. In this, he showed the extent of his debt to Kant, who made it central to his philosophy.

Unlike Hume, Kant maintained that practical reason is a reality. Its existence is manifest, for instance, in the difference we cannot fail to grasp between the strength and the authority of motives. When we consider what we are to do, we may well observe that there are some things we desire quite a lot. But our object is to determine what we ought to do, so that even if we decide to act on our strongest desire, and do so because of its intensity, we are assuming that the strength of this desire counts as a good reason to satisfy it. Deliberation, Kant argued, takes place within a "practical point of view," in which we regard ourselves as free beings who are moved by reasons. To conduct ourselves self-consciously as agents, or simply to look back at what we have done and see in it actions we have performed, entails supposing that we guide ourselves by what we hold to be reasons. Rawls summarizes Kant's thesis in these terms: "As we deliberate, we must not believe that our powers of reason are determined by anything external to our reason, or allow anything to influence us except the reasons and evidence that are relevant for our consideration."[20]

We may also, of course, look at ourselves from the same "theoretical point of view" that we adopt toward the natural world, seeing ourselves as but one more phenomenon governed by the physical laws of cause and

[19] Rawls, *Lectures*, p. 69.
[20] *Ibid.*, p. 286.

effect. Many of Kant's successors, and sometimes Kant himself, got tied up in knots trying to explain how these divergent perspectives can both be valid. Do we simultaneously live in two different worlds, one where our actions are free and another where they are caused? Or do we as free agents intervene in the world of cause and effect, initiating from the outside a chain of events that then unfolds according to physical law? Or, yet again, are our actions at one and the same time both free and caused? According to Rawls, Kant in his best moments pursued a less metaphysical and more promising tack. His solution was that theoretical and practical reason are animated by different interests, the one directed at a systematic explanation of the world as given in experience, the other at a systematic ordering of our ends, both individual and collective. Both interests are legitimate, and their results are in harmony so long as neither trespasses on the other's terrain and one does not pretend, for example, that science has shown freedom to be an illusion.[21] At bottom, writes Rawls echoing Kant, philosophy is "defense." Its goal is not to devise a single, ultimate picture of the world in which everything, causality plus freedom, has its place. It is instead to defend reason in all its forms against various threats of skepticism.

I doubt that there can be so neat a division of labor between practical and theoretical reason. Even though, as I would like to say, they differ (and differ simply) in virtue of their subject matter – the one directed toward action, the other toward belief, action itself is possible only if it can figure, as the very action it is, among the objects of belief. Certainly, acting requires focusing on what remains up to us, on what is not already settled or set to happen anyway. That is why we do not deliberate about what we believe is or will be the case independently of our decision. But it is also why, in envisioning some possible action, we see it as taking place in the world we know. Indeed, to act for reasons is to intend that our action occur in the world in precisely this way – not, that is, as some bare physical movement, but as an action motivated by reasons. We cannot understand ourselves as agents without regarding our agency as part of the way things are. In the end, acting for reasons must be either an illusion or a theoretically intelligible feature of the world. Resolving this issue has, of course, long been one of the chief problems of metaphysics, and little progress has been made over the centuries. That may be a reason why moral philosophy need not overly trouble itself with it, which was Rawls' counsel. But the problem will not disappear by means of the legerdemain that Kant performed.

Connected with this Kantian contrast between practical and theoretical reason was another that had a far deeper influence on Rawls' moral philosophy. Whereas theoretical reason endeavors to discover truths about

---

[21] *Ibid.*, pp. 275ff., 322ff.

the way things are (in our experience, Kant cautioned), practical reason does not seek conformity with some independent order of moral principles. No more than supposedly its operations do its objects occupy some place in the world as conceived by the theoretical understanding. Instead, practical reason legislates for itself the principles of right and wrong.[22] This is the doctrine that Rawls recast in the form of what he called "constructivism."

4. MORAL CONSTRUCTIVISM

Though Kant differed from Hume in recognizing the need for a conception of practical reason, he did not believe that our judgments about what we ought morally to do aim at some kind of knowledge. There is no such thing as moral knowledge, if that notion means the grasping of moral distinctions that are there anyway, awaiting our discovery. For Kant, we determine the rightness or wrongness of an action by reference to moral principles we impose on ourselves, for practical reason consists in devising laws of conduct that are worthy of our nature as beings who must "legislate" (*Gesetze geben*) for themselves. Rawls preferred to talk of "constructing" moral principles, and this idiom makes the point even plainer. Legislation (in parliaments) may sometimes be meant to give the force of law to principles regarded as having an antecedent validity. But the Kantian thesis is that the very authority of moral principles derives from our reason enacting them for itself. It stands therefore in sharp opposition to the view that Rawls called "rational intuitionism" and that regards our moral judgments as aiming to correspond to an order of moral principles existing independently of our reason. We are ourselves, in exercising our practical reason, the authors of the moral law. As constructed, moral principles may of course figure in our knowledge; we can say, if we like, that we know what is right and wrong. The claim is that they are not in the first instance objects of knowledge. It is not by our knowing them, but by our endorsing them, that they show themselves to be binding on us.

To the extent that we act in accord with the true nature of practical reason, we exhibit what Kant called "autonomy." As the etymology of the term suggests, *auto-nomous* agents are ones who give themselves the rule or law by which they act. It is not simply that they subordinate their desires and interests to a sense of duty, apart from all concern for reward and punishment, showing themselves to be – as St. Paul said of the Gentiles – "a law unto themselves."[23] So-called rational intuitionism is more than able to accommodate that sort of stance. For there to be autonomy as Kant and

---

[22] Actually, Kant held that theoretical reason too must be in certain basic respects self-legislating or "autonomous." See Chapter 2, §3.

[23] "*heautois eisin nomos*" in St. Paul, *Letter to the Romans* 2.14.

Rawls understood it, this sense of duty cannot be beholden to some prior and independent moral order. It has to arise out of our practical reason alone. "Pure practical reason," as Rawls put it, "must construct out of itself its own object."[24]

Kant's analysis of the prohibition against false promises illustrates the view nicely. We do wrong to make false promises because, so the story goes, the policy of doing so whenever convenient, were everyone to adopt it, would destroy the practice of making and accepting promises of which our action seeks to take advantage. No such policy could be coherently "universalized" – that is, propounded as a universal rule of conduct: we could not be willing for everyone to act upon it at the same time as we chose to pursue it ourselves, since deceit of this sort only works if others share in a general culture of honesty and trust and are thus disposed to take us at our word. It follows that the principle of making only promises we intend to keep, even when it runs contrary to our interest, is a principle we have reason to impose on ourselves as a categorically binding duty. Such is, in outline, the procedure (Rawls called it the "CI-procedure") by which we supposedly legislate or construct the "categorical imperatives," the absolute do's and don'ts of morality, that we use to judge particular actions and institutions. The claim is not anything as silly as that liars contradict themselves. As mere liars, they do not. But they do run into contradiction if they also think of themselves as acting according to a policy to which they would want others to adhere as well. Liars have to suppose, if they give any thought to the matter at all, that they are somehow special, entitled to make an exception for themselves when it comes to the rules of social intercourse. When we act morally, by contrast, our standpoint is one of universalizing. We impose on our own conduct the very same rules that we could wish others to impose on theirs.

Moral constructivism depends, therefore, on our being able to think of ourselves as laying down or legislating principles of conduct for all that each, thinking in the same vein, would have reason to adopt. If it does not appeal to some independent order of moral values, it does build upon a substantive notion of the sort of beings we must be if we are to take an interest in morality. For Rawls, this notion makes up the very heart of the constructivist position. "It is characteristic of Kant's doctrine," he wrote, "that a relatively complex conception of the person plays a central role in specifying the content of his moral view." He then went on to spell out this conception in the terms that he himself favored. To be moral agents, he held, we have to regard ourselves as being not just rational, able to pursue our own good efficiently, but most of all *reasonable*, committed to

---

[24] Rawls, *Lectures*, p. 226. See, too, "Kantian Constructivism in Moral Theory," in *Collected Papers*, pp. 308 and 315.

regulating our dealings with one another by rules we all have equally reason to accept. Rational intuitionism, by contrast,

> requires but a sparse conception of the person, based on the idea of the person as knower. That is because the content of first principles is already given, and thus persons need only be able to know what these principles are and to be moved by this knowledge.[25]

For Rawls, the idea that practical reason, being self-legislating, is fundamentally different from theoretical reason was one of the great virtues of the Kantian position. It expresses our nature as doers, not knowers, and in the specific case of moral reasoning, as doers devoted to setting up the basis for a common life together. The advantages of this view can seem obvious. There is, first, its metaphysical economy. Those who hold that moral principles exist independently of our reason so as to be in the first instance an object of knowledge have the difficulty of explaining how they can form part of the world. Where exactly are such moral facts to be located in the fabric of reality? The question can seem unanswerable once the world is understood as the world of modern natural science, which has no room for values. Second, constructivism can appear to offer a more plausible view of moral agency than theories that conceive of our judgments about right and wrong as descriptive in intent. Why we care about moral distinctions would be a mystery if they were merely further facts we might come to know. If instead they grow out of the effort to create a shared code of conduct, it becomes readily intelligible why they matter to us, why to hold that something is morally right or wrong is thereby to be moved to act accordingly. The Humean approach may also recommend itself in these regards. But its signal disadvantage is the lack of any real conception of practical reason. The desideratum, it would seem, is an account of how we can reason about the moral thing to do without having to attribute to our conclusions a validity independent of this very process of reasoning. Constructivism is thus the ideal solution. So Rawls believed, and so too a number of other contemporary moral philosophers who, often inspired by his interpretation of Kant, have followed his lead.[26]

Nonetheless, constructivism cannot work, and the easiest way to see this is to note that it fails to explain on its own terms the whole of morality. The image that it proposes of us as the architects of morality relies on moral principles that must be presumed to have an antecedent validity. We are depicted as constructing principles of morality by virtue of a commitment to being reasonable. Yet reasonableness, as Rawls understood the notion,

---

[25] Rawls, *Lectures*, p. 237.
[26] See, particularly, Christine Korsgaard, *The Sources of Normativity* (Cambridge: Cambridge University Press, 1996). My critique of this book in the next chapter develops at greater length the points that I go on to make here.

embodies an allegiance to what is nothing less than a moral principle in its own right. To seek a basis for living together that all can have reason to accept is to regard one another as free and equal persons whose relations are to be grounded upon mutual respect. The construction of morality that Rawls envisioned builds on a moral foundation that must already be in place, which is not itself constructed.

Oddly enough, Rawls was prepared to concede the point:

> Not everything can be constructed. Every construction has a basis, certain materials, as it were, from which it begins. While the CI-procedure is not constructed but laid out, it does have a basis: the conception of free and equal persons as reasonable and rational, a conception that is mirrored in the procedure.

He also acknowledged that reasonableness has the character of a moral commitment; it is "a particular form of moral sensibility."[27] But this laudable candor does not change the fact that constructivism fails to offer a complete account of morality. It is obliged to attribute to our deepest moral commitments a status that its defining ambition means to deny to moral beliefs in general. Either these commitments lie outside the scope of reason, or their basis in reason must consist in our grasping the antecedent validity of the moral principles they reflect. If morality is a rational enterprise (as I join Kant and Rawls in holding), there is no way around having to recognize that we take our moral bearings from an independent order of right and wrong.

The essential incompleteness of constructivism is, I believe, the symptom of a more basic failing that I examine at length in the next chapter (see especially §5). It is the failure to properly appreciate the truth that reason is a faculty we exercise by reasoning and that reasoning involves being responsive to reasons. In general, when we deliberate about what to do, we are seeking to discover the reasons there are to do one thing rather than another. The principles underlying these reasons must therefore be understood as having an authority independent of our own devising, an authority we come to grasp because they are, in the first instance, an object of knowledge. There is no mystery about why knowledge can of itself lead to action, for as I observed earlier (§3), belief is not motivationally inert. If our moral judgments do not leave our will unmoved, it is not because we construct the moral distinctions they refer to, or because (as Hume thought) these distinctions are the objectification of our feelings, but because we respond to the difference between right and wrong as reasoning beings respond to reasons generally, be they reasons for belief or action – namely, by adjusting their thought and conduct accordingly. Contrary to the Kantian tradition, theoretical and practical reason differ only in their respective subject matters, and autonomy represents an incoherent ideal.

[27] Rawls, *Lectures*, p. 240, and *Political Liberalism*, p. 51.

The same criticism applies to Rawls' more specifically political philosophy. Consider, again, the Original Position, the device he used to expound his theory of justice: we are to imagine ourselves as represented by parties who choose, subject to certain constraints (embodied in a Veil of Ignorance), to impose on themselves principles of justice that will henceforth be binding. Here he was deploying, of course, the idea of a social contract. But he combined it with the Kantian paradigm, so as to produce what he called his "political constructivism." Unlike other contract theorists such as Locke, who held that agreement upon principles of justice must defer to "an independent order of moral and political values," Rawls intended to dispense with any such appeals to "natural law."[28] Instead, the hypothetical contract was to model our political autonomy as citizens, for whom "the political values of justice and public reason are not simply presented as moral requirements externally imposed," but who instead shape their common life by their own authority, according to "the liberal principle of legitimacy":

Our exercise of political power is proper and hence justifiable only when it is exercised in accordance with a constitution the essentials of which citizens may reasonably be expected to endorse in the light of principles and ideals acceptable to them as reasonable and rational.[29]

Yet, as the final phrase implies, this principle has a moral foundation, not itself legitimated by the constructivist procedure supposedly at work. It is the commitment to reasonableness. Nor should we be surprised to find it there, given that for Rawls it shapes not only the way we must think of ourselves as agents of moral construction, but also (see §2) the constraints under which, in the Veil of Ignorance, agreement upon principles of justice is conceived as taking place. Political autonomy, too, cannot be complete. In a liberal democracy, citizens should indeed be able to see their political principles as having an authority they themselves have collectively given them. But they can do so only if they are committed to being reasonable and thus accept the antecedent validity of the even deeper principle of mutual respect which that commitment affirms. As I argue in Chapter 6, liberal democracy cannot make do without appeal to "an independent order of moral and political values." Contrary to Rawls, the idea of natural law has an abiding element of truth.

In the political realm, constructivism can play a circumscribed, if not comprehensive role. It mirrors the democratic ideal according to which citizens be able to see the terms of their political life as deriving from their own collective will – though only up to the principles serving to define their collective will, for those must have another, and independent, basis.

[28] Rawls, *Lectures on the History of Political Philosophy*, p. 112.
[29] Rawls, *Political Liberalism*, pp. 93, 98, and 217.

The situation is different in our moral thinking more generally. There, I have suggested, constructivism is inappropriate. It offers a distorted view of what it is to reason; it misses the responsiveness to reasons which reasoning involves. Why this difference?

It comes from the fact that political principles, though a province of morality, stand out from other moral principles by virtue of being coercive. We may fault people morally for failing to adhere to certain rules, but these rules do not become political until we also hold that people may be forced to comply with them when need be. The democratic ideal consists in placing a certain constraint on this use of coercion. It requires that political principles be such that those whom they bind must also be able to find reason to accept them. Only on this condition do they become politically legitimate, whatever may be their moral validity in themselves. This constraint is none other than what Rawls called the "liberal principle of legitimacy," and it may be understood as demanding that political principles, if they are to enjoy political authority, be "constructed" or authorized by the citizens themselves. But this demand is itself, clearly enough, a moral principle in its own right, and one, moreover, whose own political authority is an exception to that rule. It represents the point at which in a liberal democracy the collective will of the citizens finds itself subject, even politically speaking, to an independent order of moral values.

Constructivism has then a role in the political realm it cannot have in morality as a whole because there is a specific moral principle that gives it that role. This conclusion suggests in turn that the idea of respect that that principle embodies has a quite specific content. It does not involve all that we may mean by respect for persons. It has, instead, to do with the sort of respect we owe one another in the political realm – that is, in relationships where the possibility of coercion is involved. The principle holds that coercive rules (not moral rules in general) are valid only if justifiable to those whom they are to bind.[30]

As I noted, Rawls readily acknowledged that the idea of reasonableness, a moral principle underlying his constructivism, is not itself constructed. So one might reply that this part at least of my criticisms – the charge that constructivism must be at best an incomplete account of morality and political legitimacy, if not the more basic complaint that it misses the essentially responsive nature of practical reason – contains nothing that Rawls himself did not admit. In a way, this is true. But it is also a sign that he never found the right overall conception in which to house his thinking about the moral and political significance of the irreducible manyness of persons. Constructivism proves inadequate, as does social contract theory (§2). Perhaps Rawls' greatest mistake was to look for support in certain philosophical traditions of the past when he had himself moved beyond their confines.

[30] For more on this difference between political and moral principles see Chapter 6, § 3.

5

The Autonomy of Morality

1. THE PROBLEM WITH MORALITY

Why should we be moral? This question is not simply one more puzzle that philosophers have contrived for their own amusement. Fortunate are they who live in such harmony between obligation and interest that they have never wondered whether they should really do as morality requires. Or rather, not so much fortunate as unthinking and out of touch with the human condition. For every reflective person is bound to ask himself this question at one time or another. No surprise, therefore, that it goes back to the beginnings of Western philosophy. It received its first systematic expression in the request that Glaucon addressed to Socrates at the beginning of Book II of Plato's *Republic* (357b). "Show us," he demanded, "that it is better without exception to be just than unjust."

I want to take up again this ancient question, though not in order to propose an answer, or anyway not one of the sort that Plato and so many others have sought. My focus will be the question itself or, more exactly, the form it has generally assumed in the philosophical tradition. With few exceptions, philosophers have understood it to mean that the moral life stands in need of justification, that we cannot truly have reason to heed its demands unless we can reason our way into acknowledging their authority, beginning from premises that are ours independent of any allegiance to morality. The challenge, they have supposed, is to show how the deepest elements of our humanity direct us to embrace the moral point of view, for only then will we have a firm basis on which to resist the contrary desires that prompt the question, "Why be moral?" Thus Plato had Socrates argue that justice alone ensures the harmony of the soul to which we ultimately

This chapter, not previously published, has a remote ancestor in "L'Autonomie de la morale," a lecture I first gave before the Société philosophique du Québec in May 1997 and published in *Philosophiques* 24 (2), 1997, pp. 313–328.

aspire. And equally a part of this tradition have been the moral skeptics or nihilists who, denying that any such argument can succeed, conclude that morality has no essential claim upon us as rational beings.

Thinking along these lines, however, changes the setting and thus the character of that question as it arises in everyday life. Ordinarily, we are not asking for an argument that, starting at some point outside morality, would suffice to convince even the knave or the amoralist to change his ways. We are seeking reassurance about the moral commitments we already have, and we find it (if we do) only by bringing more vividly before our mind the substance of those commitments themselves, or of the conflicting interests that look possibly more important. In other words, the question "Why be moral?" in its everyday context is one in which we are wondering whether we must really do some particular morally required action, whereas the philosophical tradition has tended to turn it into a question about whether to heed moral requirements at all – as though only in this way could a truly adequate answer to the initial worry be found.

Yet more is at stake than just the proper formulation of the question. Fueling the traditional approach, I believe, is a failure to recognize that morality forms a realm of irreducible value. We cannot explain why it should matter to us by appealing to interests and motivations that are presumably more basic. In that, I agree with the moral nihilist, but I am no nihilist myself, since my position is that moral reasons possess an intrinsic authority. Morality speaks for itself. This truth has too often been missed or obscured by philosophical theory, and not least by the ethics of autonomy, which draws its inspiration from Kant and aims to ground the moral point of view in a conception of human freedom as self-legislation. All the more appropriate, it seems to me, to reverse the terms and to speak instead of *the autonomy of morality*. There is no way to reason ourselves into an appreciation of moral value from some standpoint outside it. Morality only makes sense in its own terms.

What the "moral point of view" itself amounts to has proven, of course, to be a controversial matter. The debate between deontological and consequentialist theories promises to go on forever. My own conviction is that our ordinary moral beliefs are best interpreted as giving expression not simply to one, but to a number of ways of moral reasoning different enough from one another to warrant talking about "the heterogeneity of morality."[1] If morality speaks for itself, it does not always speak with a single voice. Still, these different perspectives do have something important in common, which we can regard as the distinctive feature of moral thinking as a whole. Morality in general involves seeing another's good as a reason for action on my part. The widespread notion that

---

[1] Larmore, *Patterns of Moral Complexity* (Cambridge: Cambridge University Press, 1987), chapter 6.

morality stands in need of an external validation is therefore the idea that the grounds for taking this sort of interest in another person's interests must derive from even more basic interests of my own.

My purpose is to challenge this notion by examining critically the two main strategies – the one inspired by Hobbes, the other by Kant – that modern philosophers have adopted to give morality an extra-moral rationale. Determining where these theories go awry is instructive in the way that negative results in philosophy often are when the illusions they dispel have a natural and recurrent appeal. My aims are also positive, however. First and foremost, we will find ourselves in a better position to understand the true constitution of the moral world. For the moral point of view really consists in taking an interest in another's good that is as direct, as unmediated by ulterior considerations, as the interest we naturally take in our own. "Love thy neighbor as thyself" is the way the Bible formulates this truth.[2]

To see in another's good a claim on our attention no less direct than the claims of our own entails regarding these claims as equal. But I should add right away that the morally best action need not always be the action that, all things considered, we have most reason to do. Nor does it follow that if we do hold ourselves to treating everyone's good as of equal moment, we should devote ourselves to bringing about the most good overall. The claims of morality need not always be paramount, nor are they essentially consequentialist in character, and nothing I say in this chapter should be construed as favoring such views. My point will be only that morality, rightly conceived, turns on taking an interest in another's good simply because it is his good.

My positive aims go beyond just a proper understanding of morality, however. They have to extend further, given how formidable are the obstacles that stand in its way. Some further preliminary remarks about the nature of the question "Why should I do what I ought morally to do?" may help to explain why this larger agenda is necessary.

It is a general truth that philosophical questions seldom admit of uncontroversial answers. That is not surprising, given that rival responses usually go hand in hand with different notions of what the question means and demands. Working out a solution and defining the problem prove inseparable. In the end, we have to judge which overall view, which combination of question and answer, is intellectually more satisfying, and judgments of this kind, given the distinctive depth of philosophical

---

[2] *Leviticus* 19:18; *Matthew* 19:19, 22:39; *Mark* 12:31. Note that this precept is quite different from the Golden Rule of doing unto others as we would have them do unto us (*Matthew* 7:12), at least when the latter is understood as a norm of reciprocity, for then it ties our treatment of others to what would be conducive to our own interests. On the idea of morality as reciprocity and its failings, see §2.

questions, inevitably draw upon our deepest, and often opposing, convictions concerning man's place in the world. The present case is no exception. The answer we give to the question "What reason have I to be moral?" cannot fail to reflect our underlying conceptions of reason and of morality themselves.

True, the question itself first seizes our attention in rather everyday circumstances, and as a result of the moral commitments we already have. For one reason or another, we are forced to realize how sharply these convictions may clash with other interests that we are loath to abandon or set aside. We find ourselves asking whether we really ought to do what morality demands, not because we are unmoved by moral considerations, but rather because we are moved by other things as well. And that is why it ought to seem odd – odder, I have suggested, than it generally does – that typically this original context disappears from the systematic treatment that philosophers bestow upon the question. The standard philosophical approach is to ask whether a rational agent, aware of the general features of the human condition, characterized by certain basic needs and interests, endowed with the general powers of reason – *but without any antecedent allegiance to morality* – would discover grounds to take up the moral point of view. Once we recall the sort of situation giving rise to the question, this reformulation can therefore simply look like a distortion of what is really at issue.

Such was the reaction of H. A. Prichard in a famous essay published in 1912, "Does Moral Philosophy Rest on a Mistake?"[3] "Yes," he replied, insofar as it regards its principal task as one of determining whether each of us can be brought, by a line of non-moral reasoning, to an acknowledgement of morality's claims. It should come as no surprise that I share much of Prichard's dissatisfaction. His essay contains many invaluable insights that deserve to be rescued from his otherwise often peculiar views. One of the few to keep squarely in mind that our doubts about whether to be moral spring from a state of inner conflict, a struggle between "the force of the various obligations in life" and "the irksomeness of carrying them out," he also saw that the only remedy, if we are to find our way back to the moral life, is a renewed effort at moral reflection. To be sure, the "ought" in the question "Ought I to act morally?" is not the moral "ought" (for then the question would be trivial). It is an overall "ought" or, as is often said today, the general "ought of deliberation": we are asking ourselves, "ought I, all things considered, to do what I suppose I ought morally to do?" But we are not compelled by this fact alone to conduct our deliberation from a standpoint that prescinds from all our existing moral beliefs. If we find ourselves torn between our moral

---

[3] Reprinted in Prichard, *Moral Obligation* , ed. J. O. Urmson (Oxford: Oxford University Press, 1968), pp. 1–17.

obligations and our other interests, the proper way to proceed – and this was Prichard's point – is to attend more closely to what they severally involve.[4]

Yet despite my admiration for Prichard's acuity – and here I return to the magnitude of the problems before us – I cannot agree that the way of thinking I join him in opposing is merely a "mistake." Its roots lie too deep for that. Pushing philosophers toward the idea that the moral point of view needs an external validation are, as I intimated, some broader and more basic assumptions. The question "What reason have I to be moral?" can appear to require just such an approach, if reason and morality are themselves understood along certain lines. As a result, the critique of the Hobbesian and Kantian traditions I present will have to focus on these guiding presuppositions. This is why my positive aims include more than a defense of the autonomy of morality. The nature of reason, indeed the very nature of mind and world, will need to be reconceived in ways quite different from the dominant strands of modern philosophy.

2. MORALITY AND ADVANTAGE

Morality involves seeing other people's good as a reason for action on my part. But how can I have reason to take this sort of interest in another, except by having concluded that it is in my interest to do so? Moral demands, so this thinking goes, present themselves as a body of restraints on individuals determined to pursue their own good, and thus they will only prove to be rationally acceptable, if they are shown actually to profit, on balance, those whom they purport to bind. Rules of mutual restraint have to be rules of mutual advantage if they are to exercise authority over human conduct. Here we meet, in outline, one influential notion of why morality requires an extra-moral rationale. Though receiving in modern times increasingly sophisticated expositions, it has no doubt been attractive from time immemorial. Its enduring appeal, as we can perceive already, stems from its underlying conceptions of morality and practical reason.

The great modern pioneer of this approach was Thomas Hobbes. Without a commonly acknowledged code of restraint, he observed in the famous passage of the *Leviathan* (I.13.ix), life would be "solitary, poor,

---

4 Contrary to Christine Korsgaard (*The Sources of Normativity*, Cambridge: Cambridge University Press, 1996, pp. 38f., 42f.), Prichard did not therefore fail to distinguish the question of whether we ought to comply with moral demands from the question of whether a certain action is required by morality. His point was that we cannot answer the first question in favor of those demands unless we engage in moral thinking. No doubt Korsgaard believes that Prichard did not do justice to that question because she herself is certain it must be handled in precisely the fashion that he rejects – namely, by way of arguing us into morality from the outside (see §6).

nasty, brutish, and short." In general, Hobbes claimed, what we view as good is the expression of our own desires, and reason serves only to modify these desires as the facts require and then to determine the most efficient means to their satisfaction. Since material goods are generally scarce, and the goods of the mind reduce to one or another form of glory, which "is nothing if everybody has it, since it consists in comparison and preeminence,"[5] we cannot help but find ourselves in a "war of all against all." Or so it must be, if we do not reason well about our situation and conduct ourselves accordingly. For the very feature of human nature that leads to conflict – the pursuit of our own desires – can also move us beyond it. Reckoning death to be the worst of evils since it spells the end of all desire, reason tells us that in circumstances where the threat of death is ever-present we ought to seek peace above all else and that peace entails giving up the freedom to do as we please if others are willing to do so as well. Thus we enter the realm of morality, understood as a system of mutual restraint and advantage, and come to accept its principles of "natural law," Hobbes argued, in virtue of heeding a minimal conception of rationality that we already endorse – namely, the efficient pursuit of our own interests.[6] The moral "ought" emerges as a theorem from the "ought" of prudence.

There is no sense, however, in limiting our freedom without the assurance that others stand ready to limit theirs. Nothing would be more contrary to reason (understood as the efficient pursuit of the objects of our desires) than to adhere to principles of restraint when others continue to pursue unfettered their own desires. It has become customary to describe the apparent snag in game-theoretic terms, as a so-called Prisoners' Dilemma: rational agents, acting so as to maximize their expected utility (always choosing, in other words, the option most likely to yield them the greatest benefit),[7] will certainly prefer peace to the absence of restraint, but they will prefer even more to violate the articles of peace whenever convenient, and knowing that others will reason similarly and that complying when others do not is the height of folly, they will refuse to

---

[5] Hobbes, *De cive* I.2: "gloriatio, sicut et honor, si omnibus adsit, nulli adest; quippe quae comparatione et praecellentia constant."

[6] See *De cive* II.1: "By right reason in man's natural state I mean ... man's own true reasoning about actions of his which may conduce to his advantage, or other men's loss" ("Per rectam rationem in statu hominum naturali, intelligo ... ratiocinationem uniuscujusque propriam, et veram circa actiones suas, quae in utilitatem, vel damnum caeterorum hominum redundare possint"). See also *Leviathan* I.13.xiv, 14.iii–iv, 15.iv–v. Since all law requires a legislator, Hobbes maintained, the natural laws yielded by "right reason" are not law (*lex*) in the strict sense, but only counsel (*consilium*), their authority deriving from their content and not from a person commanding them. They do not acquire the status of natural law until understood as being the word of God. Nonetheless, they still obligate (telling us what we "ought" to do) in the way that all demands of reason do. See *De cive* III.33 and *Leviathan* I.15.xli.

[7] More formally, maximizing expected utility is defined as choosing that option for which the probability of its success times its value to the individual is greatest.

adopt the constraints necessary for peace and thus remain trapped in the lawless condition they like far less. Morality, along with the advantages it procures, will prove inaccessible to reason.

Notoriously, Hobbes held that the only remedy lies in instituting a "Sovereign" whose coercive power makes it in everyone's interest never to defect. Yet this solution suffers from two core weaknesses that, as we shall see, continually beset the attempt to base morality on the rational pursuit of one's own desires, even once the idea of a Sovereign is abandoned: the reasoning adduced proves inadequate, while the image of the moral world that appears to invite this sort of vindication is itself a grave distortion. In Hobbes' case, there is first of all the difficulty that rational agents lacking sufficient reason to cooperate will scarcely be able to join together and establish a common Sovereign. And an initial sign of the second sort of flaw is that morality appears quite able to engage our allegiance without the presence of an enforcer.

Today, Hobbesian views about the rational basis of morality are most often developed without appealing to a centralized source of coercion. Yet their proponents (who are legion) remain wedded to the same conception of reason that Hobbes invoked, which is prudence or, as I shall generally call it, the "instrumental" notion of reason and which enjoins us to choose the most efficient means to the satisfaction of our own desires, duly adjusted to the facts.[8] The project is still one of explaining how this starting point provides our entry into the moral world. Accordingly, morality itself continues to be understood as a device for mutual advantage. I take the combination of these underlying conceptions of reason and morality as a warrant to term the approach as a whole, and in all its forms, *instrumentalism*.

One popular version of contemporary instrumentalism, dispensing with all reference to a Sovereign, claims that we have sufficient reason to comply with principles of restraint that others too are disposed to observe, so long as we can expect to be in continual contact with them, the person we decide to deceive today being around tomorrow to retaliate. Assume, in other words, that we foresee ourselves interacting with others into the

---

[8] The term "instrumental reason" is used in a variety of senses, some quite expansive. Sometimes it means determining efficient means to given ends, the ends themselves not having to involve the satisfaction of the agent's own interests, and in this very broad sense it thus has a place even in the conception of morality that Hobbesians reject – seeing in another's good as such a reason for action on our part. Sometimes the term is used to mean the concept in rational choice theory of maximizing expected utility. As will become apparent, I think it is wrong to equate, as many do, this sense of the term with the one given in the text – the notion of practical reason that Hobbesians regularly assume. Finally, even instrumental models of rationality in this last (Hobbesian) sense differ depending on whether they focus on (a) our given interests at present, (b) the interests we take to be ours both at present and over the longer term, or (c) our present and long-term interests duly informed by the available facts. In general, Hobbesians have favored (c), their guiding conviction being that morality derives from our own interest well conceived.

indefinite future, so that our situation has the form, not of a single, but of an "iterated game," an ongoing series of encounters. (It is important for this view that our dealings be open-ended in time, otherwise we may have a preemptive reason to defect.) Then, so the argument goes, we no longer face any dilemma at all.[9] Even in the absence of a coercive authority, individuals aiming to achieve their own good have reason to regard mutual restraint as superior, not only to its general absence, but also to the option of selective cheating, for the best policy is one of *reciprocity*, of doing unto others as we would have them do unto us. Reciprocity can assume somewhat different forms, depending on the specific rule chosen. There is for example "tit for tat": one begins by complying and then responds in kind to the reactions of others, so that if they comply too, one continues to do likewise, and if they do not, one retaliates by inflicting on them a similar harm – no more and no less, leaving them the choice of either mending their ways or incurring a continued denial of the benefits of cooperation. But whatever the version of reciprocity favored, the argument remains that anyone tempted to take unfair advantage of other people's compliance is failing to look beyond the immediate present. To ensure our long-term good, we ought to respect others to the extent that they are ready to show us a similar respect.

The flaws in this line of thought should be obvious, however. It provides no disincentive for those who believe that they can violate the principles of mutual restraint without detection, deceiving others into supposing that they are trustworthy members of the community. It also offers no reason why we should not treat as we please any people we know will never pass our way again; we would not have to worry that our acquaintances would then consider us unreliable, since they would presumably understand why strangers are bound to weigh less heavily in our deliberations than they themselves must do. So, too, the argument gives us no reason to respect those who happen to be too weak, mentally or physically, ever to benefit us in return. In sum, individuals reasoning instrumentally about how to advance their own interests need not adopt a rule of reciprocity, and even if they see reason to do so, the principles of conduct they then would honor fall woefully short of what we expect of a conception of morality.

These defects are not accidental. They afflict every version of the idea that morality is a system of mutual advantage, adopted for reasons of individual prudence (that is, for instrumental reasons), whatever the particular strategies of argument deployed. They epitomize the resistance that morality cannot fail to show to this way of approaching it, not in its own terms, but from the outside.

---

[9] See, for example, Robert Axelrod, *The Evolution of Cooperation* (New York: Basic Books, 1984); Michael Taylor, *The Possibility of Cooperation* (Cambridge: Cambridge University Press, 1987); Ken Binmore, *Natural Justice* (Oxford: Oxford University Press, 2005).

One reason often given today for regarding morality as a system of mutual advantage, founded upon reciprocity, is that then its existence can be explained by reference to how it has enhanced over the millennia the chances for survival of human groups. I have my doubts about the present-day fad of armchair evolutionary theorizing. But I will play along with the game for a bit. Let us imagine that a disposition to practice reciprocity became widespread as the result of some mix of biological and cultural evolution; those who practiced it had a better chance of survival. The appearance of such a disposition may well have been an important first step in mankind's coming to understand what it is to think morally. For in order to calculate how one can best advance one's own interests through cooperation, one needs to be able to look at the world from the standpoint of others (plotting how they are likely to act as a result of what one does oneself), and this ability to take up another person's point of view is essential to learning to see another's good as in itself a reason for action. But manifestly it is not enough. The practice of reciprocity falls short of the kind of impartiality in which one sees another's good as of equal importance with one's own. A gap remains, and it is the gap that divides instrumental reasoning, in which one determines how best to satisfy one's own interests, from taking an intrinsic interest in another's interest. To continue the evolutionary story (or fable), what must have happened, once human beings became able to reason instrumentally about the advantages of cooperation, is that someone of great imagination came along and observed that adopting another's point of view, essential for strategic thinking, is also worth doing for its own sake since other people's good should be valued just because it is theirs. Only then did morality emerge.

The defects I have noted in the Hobbesian conception all stem from its incapacity to cross this divide. To appreciate just how inescapable they are, let us examine what can look like the obvious solution to the first of them.

3. INSTRUMENTALISM AND ITS FAILURE

Planning to take advantage of other people's cooperativeness, it will be said, is in reality an irrational attitude, contrary to the judicious pursuit of one's own interests. Hobbes himself may have had something of the sort in mind. "The fool" was his name for anyone who "questioneth whether injustice, taking away the fear of God . . . , may not sometimes stand with that reason, which dictateth to every man his own good."[10] In part, he found it an easy matter to dismiss such thinking, since in his view there would be no justice at all, no general practice of mutual restraint for the person to exploit, without a coercive Sovereign or "mortal god," whose power of enforcement everyone had reason to fear. Yet in the absence of this *deus ex*

---

[10] Hobbes, *Leviathan* I.15.iv. Hobbes' reply to "the fool" comes in the following paragraph.

machina, where is the folly? Another part of Hobbes' response to the fool seems more promising. People suspected of making it a habit to cheat whenever convenient cannot expect others to welcome them into the folds of society: "he which declares he thinks it reason to deceive those that help him, can in reason expect no other means of safety, than what can be had from his own single power." Only those known to honor their commitments can hope to reap the benefits of cooperation. The fool aims to be selective, deciding on an *act-by-act basis* whether to comply with principles of justice. Hobbes' words suggest that this plan is foolish because others, if rational, will offer cooperation only to those whom they believe stand ready to cooperate in return, and the surest way to secure this reputation is to follow a *standing practice* of playing fair.

Such is David Gauthier's reading of this passage in *Leviathan*, and whatever its merits as an interpretation of the text, it has inspired him to develop the philosophically richest version of the Hobbesian scheme available today.[11] People can reason themselves into the moral point of view, Gauthier claims, once they shift from being straightforward to being constrained maximizers, a change of *disposition* that it is in their rational interest to effect. "Morality," he announces, "can be generated as a rational constraint from the non-moral premises of rational choice."[12]

I do not believe that this innovation fares any better. It too succumbs to the twin difficulties we have noticed before. Not only does the reasoning proposed fail to yield the desired outcome, but the goal itself expresses an unacceptably crude notion of the moral life. Here, as elsewhere, the instrumentalist is fated to distort the very nature of morality in the attempt to explain the authority of its demands. Yet Gauthier does give considerable attention to the underlying conceptions of reason and morality that propel this way of thinking, and a close look at his theory will therefore make all the plainer the defining errors of the instrumental approach.

As one would expect, the starting point of his argument is a state of nature ("a morally free zone") in which individuals are imagined as thinking and acting without any limitation by moral constraints. Insofar as they are rational, they seek to maximize their expected utility, by which Gauthier means that it is their own interests, reflectively examined, that they aim to satisfy, and in such a way as to achieve over the long term the greatest possible satisfaction. In other words, they do not operate by a "universalistic" conception of rationality, which would require them to think impartially from the outset and thus consider the interests of each person equally before determining what they have reason to do. Impartiality is itself a moral norm, and the fundamental question, so Gauthier

---

[11] David Gauthier, *Morals by Agreement* (Oxford: Clarendon Press, 1986). The discussion of Hobbes and the fool occurs on pp. 158–165.

[12] *Ibid*, p. 4.

claims, is why a person should ever be moved to accept this sort of constraint on deliberation.[13] Maximizing expected utility supposedly provides the appropriate baseline from which that question is to be answered. For who, he argues, could dispute that reason means at its core determining the most efficient means to the satisfaction of one's own considered interests? It is, for instance, the notion of rationality that the social sciences use to explain human action.

To be sure, the interests in question need not be solely interests *in the self*. People can be assumed, even without morality, to be more than just self-interested, to have feelings of sympathy for their fellows and to take an interest in their welfare. Hobbes himself often invokes psychological egoism as the truth about human nature, but such a model is neither plausible nor necessary. The crucial premise, Gauthier insists, is that all one's interests are at bottom interests *of the self* – that is, interests that one pursues because they are one's own, be they self- or other-regarding, and not because they are other people's interests that one pursues for that very reason. (The phrase "pursuing one's own interests" is ambiguous between these two senses.) Since moral thinking begins when we take an impartial interest in the good of others, it therefore needs to be justified in terms of the efficient handling of the interests that are one's own. The maximization of expected utility thus understood – and I shall return to this point – corresponds to what I called earlier "instrumental" rationality.

Gauthier's argument, as I have said, is that entering the moral point of view does become reasonable, once people realize that it is in their interest to cease looking at every situation as an opportunity to secure their own greatest good, and to show others respect as a matter of course, to share in a way of life that is to the good of all.[14] Honesty must become a habit of mind, and not merely the best policy, which as such will appear to admit of exceptions. For only the truly honest person, disposed to treating others

---

[13] Gauthier represents the Kantian tradition as supposing that practical reason is universalistic from the start (p. 6). But as we shall see (§5), the true starting point of Kantian conceptions is not a commitment to reasoning impartially, but rather the conviction that reason must itself lay down what shall count as reasons for action.

[14] *Ibid*, pp. 2–8: Oddly, Gauthier likes at times to declare that "morality arises from market failure" (p. 84). Only when people's efforts to better their condition by exchanging goods and services would cease to be perfectly competitive, by virtue of enhancing or reducing the welfare of others who are not involved, will they have reason to counter these "externalities" by introducing moral demands to the effect that everyone should contribute to public goods that all will enjoy or desist from actions that harm others. This claim is odd, because as Gauthier readily acknowledges on the very next page, no market is possible, however perfect, unless people respect one another's physical integrity and property. It is morality that makes markets possible. Any argument purporting to show that individuals concerned to maximize their utility have reason to impose moral constraints on their actions cannot assume them to be already able, in the absence of such constraints, to achieve a limited sort of social order through free exchange.

impartially instead of being forever on the lookout for his own advantage, will be trusted enough by others to be welcomed into their company and allowed to share in their cooperative endeavors.[15] It is important to remember, however, that this change of outlook (from "straightforward" to "constrained" maximization) supposedly recommends itself, not because of its intrinsic value, but because it conduces to one's own interest, well understood. The impartial interest one then takes in other people's good is rooted in the efficient pursuit of one's own interests. For Gauthier, instrumental rationality continues to be the means by which we reason ourselves into the moral point of view. Morality reveals itself to be to everyone's advantage, once each acquires a standing disposition to adhere unfailingly to its requirements on the condition that others do so as well. That is why no one can afford to heed these rules when encountering people like "the Fool" who remain determined to seek their own good at others' expense; they have put themselves outside the moral pale and must accordingly be treated in kind.

We cannot, of course, change our character at will, but the argument in question does not imagine that we can. What we can do when we please is reflect upon the human condition, see the utility of adhering to rules of mutual restraint, and resolve to act in accord with them. Over time, this deliberate activity will turn into a settled disposition, and we will have become people who do the right thing naturally, without calculating each time whether it pays.

I shall not go into the specific principles that, according to Gauthier's "contractarian" theory, people so disposed would agree to impose on their dealings with one another, nor into the conditions of fairness (his so-called proviso) that they would allegedly require all such agreements to satisfy. My concern is with the general shape of this argument and with its essential failings. And surely the first, most striking deficiency is one that I have noted before – namely, the conception of morality that the Hobbesian conception deploys, here as elsewhere. Morality is understood as a system of cooperation, founded upon mutual advantage: the limits it places on the pursuit of our good are held to be in our own best interest when others too comply with these restraints. No less than the cruder versions of this idea, Gauthier's construction therefore excludes from the domain of moral concern two groups of people whom it would seem to be the business of morality to move us to treat better than we would otherwise be inclined to do. It give us no reason to care about those with whom we do not expect to be in frequent contact and who are therefore unlikely ever to contribute to our own good. Similarly, it ratifies the lack of attention we all too easily exhibit toward those who have neither the power nor the ability to enhance or jeopardize our interests in any way, however

---

[15] *Ibid.* pp. 170, 182ff.

often we may cross their path. Morality conceived as a cooperative scheme for mutual benefit fails to embody so fundamental an element of the moral point of view as the respect we owe to *strangers* and to *the weak*.

This is not a small imperfection, a failure to account for some marginal aspect of morality, which might be remedied by adding to the theory further refinements or auxiliary notions. A hallmark of the moral point of view is precisely the respect it requires us to show toward people who, through circumstance or misfortune, may never be in a position to benefit us in return. As a matter of fact, we act toward the powerful and the useful in a moral and not simply prudent fashion when we behave as we would even if they lacked those assets that make them of interest to our own endeavors. We treat them with the respect they are due as human beings, not merely with the sort of circumspection we exercise in dealing with the various forces in our environment. As John Locke once memorably observed, "An Hobbist with his principle of self-preservation whereof himself is to be judge, will not easily admit a great many plain duties of morality."[16]

Gauthier quotes this remark himself, yet only in order to dismiss its pertinence, explicitly putting "beyond the pale of morality" anyone ill-equipped to participate in a scheme of mutual advantage. He is prepared to admit that morality, such as his constrained maximizers would develop it, may fit only roughly our ordinary ideas of moral right and wrong. But, he insists, we ought to trust theory rather than intuition and deny any weight to "plain duties" or everyday moral judgments that fail to be confirmed by his approach.[17] Why this self-assurance? Because, allegedly, there is no other choice. Today, Gauthier claims, morality faces "a foundational crisis." The traditional picture of the world as purposively ordered, and as thereby providing a rationale for moral constraints that extend beyond those endorsed by individual prudence, has been lost beyond retrieval. If we are to find any justification for moral limits on human conduct, we now have no other resource than the instrumental conception of rationality, which still makes sense in a purposeless world, and it will ratify only those moral rules that enable us to maximize our expected utility.[18]

This analysis of our intellectual situation is not very convincing, however. Though the religious and metaphysical conceptions of the past certainly pictured the world as shaped and governed by a moral order, their intention

---

[16] Quoted from a manuscript by John Dunn, *The Political Thought of John Locke* (Cambridge: Cambridge University Press, 1969), pp. 218–219.

[17] Gauthier, *Morals by Agreement*, pp. 268–269; see also pp. 17–18.

[18] See Gauthier, "Why Contractarianism?" pp. 15–30, in Peter Vallentyne (ed.), *Contractarianism and Rational Choice* (Cambridge: Cambridge University Press, 1991), and especially pp. 15–20, which spell out some of Gauthier's deepest philosophical motivations.

was to reinforce an authority the demands of morality were already thought to enjoy. After all, God or the Cosmos could not play a legitimating role except in virtue of the moral perfections they were presumed to possess. Morality – and morality understood more generously than the dictates of mutual advantage will allow – must therefore be intelligible in its own terms. It must be able to speak for itself, if people once sought support for moral beliefs of this sort in what they took to be the moral fabric of the universe. I myself, it is true, turned to the Bible when declaring at the outset (§1) that "Love thy neighbor as thyself" is the very soul of the moral point of view, which demands that we regard another's good as having the same direct claim on our attention as our own good expectably does. And those wedded to an instrumentalist approach will naturally refuse to attach any rational sense to this idea, holding that our allegiance to morality has to be grounded in the pursuit of our own interests, and finding themselves therefore unable to explain why our moral attention should extend to strangers and to the weak, as it obviously must if another's good weighs with us independently of our own. Yet though I have quoted Scripture to bring home the import of a non-instrumentalist conception of morality, can one really maintain that it makes sense only within a religious worldview? Do we not judge the worth of a religion by moral principles we know in our heart of hearts to be right, including the very one in question?

Before exploring this non-instrumentalist conception further, however, let us look at the second principal defect in Gauthier's theory. It is that his derivation of a morality of expediency does not in fact succeed. Rational agents, aiming to bring about their own good, will no doubt realize how counterproductive it is to take advantage of others whenever the opportunity arises. They will understand that it is in their interest to develop the habits and dispositions that will recommend them to others as trustworthy members of the community. Nonetheless, they need not therefore have reason to become the sort of persons who adhere in good faith to the rules of morality. Others before me have pinpointed the fatal gap in the argument, and I will only push their criticism a bit further.[19] Gauthier's assumption is that we are neither fully transparent to one another nor inscrutably opaque; we are "translucent" beings such that others have a better than equal chance of figuring out how we are likely to act the more evidence they get. Knowing this, we ought supposedly to commit ourselves to respecting those inclined to show us respect in return, so that we may thereby share in the benefits of mutual restraint and cooperation. The trouble is that we have just as much reason to make ourselves into a rather different sort of person – namely, people devoted to providing

---

[19] See, in particular, Geoffrey Sayre-McCord, "Deception and reasons to be moral" and David Copp, "Contractarianism and moral skepticism," both in P. Vallentyne (ed.), *Contractarianism and Rational Choice*, pp. 181–195 and 196–228 respectively.

others with plenty of misleading evidence of our reliability, in order eventually to seize the best moment to take advantage of their trust. We may stand to gain the most if we become like Hume's "sensible knave" who, generally observant of the moral proprieties, gratefully praising the benefits they bestow, is yet continually alert to the possibility of breaking the rules when it "will make a considerable addition to his fortune without causing any considerable breach in the social union and confederacy."[20]

For consider that, in general, none of us waits for others to form an opinion of our character. On the contrary, we all expend considerable energy trying to influence their judgment through our words and deeds, whether it be to deceive, to ingratiate, or to seek a confirmation in their eyes of our own sense of who we are. The character our acquaintances attribute to us is to a great extent the character we endeavor to project, and though this image is bound to reflect attitudes and dispositions we really possess, and so offers a basis for predicting our behavior, it may also spring from motives that remain hidden from their view. Recognize though we may how self-defeating it is to view every situation as a chance to get ahead at others' expense and how invaluable is a reputation for fair dealing, we need not conclude that reality ought to match appearances. Even under these conditions, morality is not necessarily the optimal strategy for securing our own good. In determining what sort of person to be, we will invariably be deciding what sort of impression we want to make on others, and if our principal aim is to prosper ourselves, long-term deception, involving only the most cautious, though lucrative, episodes of wrongdoing, may well deliver equal, if not greater, payoffs. In light of this fact, who could feel sure that others truly intend to keep faith as a matter of course, their only reason for doing so being the pursuit of their own interests? And why should one then keep faith oneself, the precondition for doing so supposedly being the confidence that others stand ready to comply as well?

It is hard to see how any version of the instrumentalist approach can get round the two fundamental flaws I have analyzed. If morality is understood as a system of constraints we reason ourselves into for the sake of advancing our own good, it harbors no intrinsic basis for including within its scope people unlikely or unable to benefit us through participation in such a scheme. Nor need it command more than a qualified and dissembling allegiance.

It might be thought that, despite the defects in Gauthier's theory, its guiding assumption is sound: only if the basic requirements of morality can be shown to be acceptable to agents bent on maximizing the satisfaction of their interests, can these requirements possess any rational authority for their conduct. For is he not right to hold that the idea of maximizing expected utility forms the core of what is meant by rationality?

---

[20] Hume, *An Inquiry concerning the Principles of Morals*, Conclusion, Part II.

In a sense, this last claim is true, but only if it is suitably – that is, very broadly – construed.

Let us note, to begin with, that nothing can count as part of the very essence of rationality if there are clear cases where we would have reason to think or act contrary to what it would require. Thus, maximizing expected utility had better not be understood as entailing that rational action consists in choosing the most efficient means to ulterior ends. For sometimes we engage in activities that we have good reason to regard as worthwhile for their own sake, and not because they advance some further goal, or even because of the pleasure or satisfaction that doing them well may provide. Furthermore, the idea of maximizing expected utility, applying as it does to whatever may be the options before us, offers by itself no support for the view that we can see no grounds for adhering to moral requirements unless they advance the desires we have independently of the moral point of view. It requires only that we pursue efficiently whatever interests we happen to have, and these may well include already a commitment to do what is morally right for its own sake. Precisely because maximizing expected utility takes as given a person's interests, without regard to their origin, it does not give special weight to those that are fundamentally *interests of the self,* pursued on account of their being one's own, as opposed to the *interests of others that for that reason one has made one's own.* In fact, within the moral domain itself it does not, strictly speaking, privilege "consequentialist" over "deontological" ways of reasoning, despite the common perception of an elective affinity between maximization and consequentialism (which holds that one is to act so as to bring about the most good overall). For the deontologist maximizes too when he conforms as best he can to the moral principle he holds supreme, which is that one is to respect certain rights, whatever the consequences, even for the extent to which others may in turn respect these rights.

In sum, the notion of maximizing expected utility implies nothing of substance about the nature of value in general, or about the status of moral reasons in particular. It directs us simply to do the best we can, given what we already, and substantively, believe to be good.[21] From these beliefs alone spring the disagreements about whether deontological norms are reasonable or not, and about whether morality can speak for itself or needs to be justified in other terms. Gauthier cloaks his argument in the mantle of the unexceptionable idea of reason as maximization. But in fact he relies on a narrower and quite disputable notion of rationality, predicated on a certain preconception of what our fundamental purposes must be

---

[21] I doubt that so-called "satisficing" constitutes a notion of rationality distinct from maximization. In doing what is "good enough," rational agents are choosing the option that is best with respect to certain constraints – with respect, in other words, to the other things they value for which they want to leave time and energy.

like. It is the notion I defined earlier as *instrumental* rationality, according to which the basic desires we must seek to satisfy efficiently all amount to desires *of the self*: any interest we take in another's good is presumed to be based in an antecedent desire of our own (as when we want to do right by another because of the pleasure it gives us or because that person happens to be dear to us), and not to derive directly from our understanding of that person's own interests. If one begins with this idea of rationality, the moral point of view cannot but appear a way of thinking into which we must reason ourselves from the outside – but only because one has effectively assumed from the outset that moral considerations cannot speak for themselves.

Whence the hold this notion of rationality exercises on so many minds, making it appear incontrovertible that morality stands in need of an external validation? No doubt it has more than one source: perhaps a certain cynicism about human motives, and probably also a taste for thinking of morality in a way that goes hand in hand with this conception of reason – namely, as a device for mutual advantage. In any case, to have laid bare the presuppositions of the instrumentalist approach is to have dispelled its seeming irresistibility. Why can we not take an interest in another's welfare as immediate as the interest we indisputably take in our own? Instrumentalists in the Hobbesian tradition assume that we cannot, and build that denial into their very notion of practical reason. Thereby they place morality itself out of reach.

4. LETTING MORALITY SPEAK FOR ITSELF

All that the preceding critique of instrumentalism has shown, however, is that this way of reasoning us into morality cannot succeed. It does not establish that moral considerations truly carry an authority of their own. In particular, it does not rule out drawing a very different conclusion. For one might insist that all our interests really are rooted in desires of our own, or that any independent interest we might take in another's good arises from confusion or from some delusion on our part. Moral claims could therefore weigh with us only if propped up by some line of instrumental reasoning, and since no such justification looks workable, one would conclude that morality lacks a basis in reason. In other words, the failure of the Hobbesian project might well be understood as vindicating the truth of moral nihilism. The instrumental model of rationality is certainly a substantial and disputable conception, as the purely formal idea of reason as maximization is not. But, for all that, it might nonetheless in the last analysis fit the actual shape of human motivation.

It is hard to imagine what a positive argument would look like to prove that morality speaks for itself. Where would such an argument begin? What premises could it invoke if the thesis is true, other than premises already expressive of the moral point of view? The best one can do by way of argument, it would seem, is to point out the mistakes and prejudices that stand in the way of recognizing this truth. Consider, as an analogy, how we would go about changing the mind of someone who perceives no reason, in deciding what to do, to take into account the desires that he will surely have later even if they are not his at present. We can expose the erroneous assumptions that move him to deny the value of prudence (such as the notion that reasons for action are but the expression of given desires). But if negative arguments of this sort do not suffice, we can only say to him, "Think about what you will no doubt want one year from now. Don't you see that you therefore ought to act accordingly?" If he does not, there is no more to be done. You can lead a horse to water, but you can't make him drink. In the end, people must simply acknowledge that there exist reasons of prudence. There is no way to argue them into this conclusion from a standpoint lying outside prudence itself. And that is because reasons of prudence are *sui generis*, intelligible only in their own terms.

In this regard, morality is just like prudence. It forms an irreducible domain of value. Indeed, the case of prudence ought to make it plain that there is nothing bizarre about the good in general being marked by discontinuities of this sort – though again, the point serves only as a negative argument in support of the autonomy of morality itself. The necessity simply to recognize certain basic kinds of good for what they are reflects, moreover, a fundamental truth about the nature of reason as a whole. This truth is that reason consists in a *receptivity or responsiveness to reasons*, and I shall often return to this theme later, as part of what I call the positive task of moral philosophy. But for now we can note that, if the authority of moral claims truly stems from their own nature alone, the only way we can hope to answer the question "Why be moral?" when it arises in the course of our lives is the way I described at the beginning of this chapter. We must attend more closely to the very demands of morality whose troublesomeness moves us to ask that question, examining, for instance, their connection to other moral commitments that appear less problematic. Or we may need to think more deeply about the other interests of ours that conflict with those demands. ("Do they really mean that much to me?" we may ask.)

Gauthier himself mentions the idea, though only to dismiss it, that deliberation of this sort is all that is required, morality admitting of no extra-moral foundation.[22] Yet his grounds for rejecting it are ones we now know to be specious. Only if the world, he claims, were still regarded as purposively ordered could morality amount to more than what individual prudence can ratify – whereas, in fact, the religious worldviews of the past rely on the presumed intelligibility of thinking about morality in its own terms. Maximizing expected utility, Gauthier also claims, provides "an alternative mode for justifying our choices and actions," one that is "clearly

---

[22] Gauthier, "Why Contractarianism?" pp. 18–19.

more basic" – whereas, in fact, this principle of rationality is far too formal to represent an alternative to moral reasoning, the latter being also an instance of aiming to do the best we can, given what we hold to be good. There can be, as I say, no proof that the moral point of view speaks for itself. But it is possible to remove misconceptions such as these that stand in the way of appreciating that truth.

When we acknowledge the authority of moral claims, despite the allure of contrary desires and independently of appeals to our own interests, we are commonly said to be listening to our conscience. The call of conscience is in this sense none other than morality speaking for itself, and that is why it stands in need of no higher validation. Seeing more clearly than most the irreducible nature of moral value, Rousseau had the Savoyard Vicar sum up the moral teaching of his *Emile* in the eloquent phrase, "*la conscience dépose pour elle-même.*"²³ Conscience testifies for itself; it does not need to be backed up by extra-moral argument. Rousseau's conviction had in turn a profound impact on Immanuel Kant. After reading *Emile* and long before writing his *Critiques*, Kant remarked around 1763–64, "Rousseau set me straight" ("*Rousseau hat mich zurecht gebracht*").²⁴ The message he met there was that it is not by a piece of clever reasoning that we come to appreciate morality's claims; the learned too can only grasp their force through that distinctive part of our humanity that is the ability to recognize directly another's good as mattering to us irrespective of our own.

Kant failed, however, to take the message truly to heart. The ethical theory he went on to develop became the paradigm of the other great strand of modern philosophy that has sought to ground the authority of morality in concerns that are presumably more basic – in this case, not in the efficient pursuit of our interests (as in the Hobbesian tradition), but instead in the affirmation of our freedom or "autonomy." It is to a critique of this Kantian tradition that I now turn. I shall begin with Kant's own views, including the opportunities he missed to see that morality speaks for itself. But then I shall look in some detail at an important contemporary refor-mulation of his ethics of autonomy. As before, the underlying conceptions of reason and of morality will be the ultimate target. And pursuing them will carry us deep into questions about the very nature of mind and world.

5. THE ETHICS OF AUTONOMY

First, some historical background that will help to explain the shape that Kant's own ethics of autonomy took in the end. Despite his reading of Rousseau, Kant seems to have been keen to find an argument to justify the

---

²³ Jean-Jacques Rousseau, *Oeuvres complètes* (Paris: Gallimard, 1969), vol. IV, p. 600. For more on Rousseau's views, see fn 30.
²⁴ Kant, *Gesammelte Schriften*, Akademie-Ausgabe (Berlin: de Gruyter, 1902–), vol. XX, p. 44.

authority of the moral law, and early on one in particular captured his attention, taking the certainty of our freedom as its premise. Traces of this argument appear, for example, at the beginning of Chapter 3 of his *Grundlegung zur Metaphysik der Sitten* (1785).[25] In taking our judgments to be based on reasons, we assume – so the argument ran – that they are not the product of impulses stemming from our place in the natural order of cause and effect. The exercise of theoretical reason presupposes a freedom that is the ability to detach ourselves from given circumstances and to shape our thinking by our own lights. If, then, we must regard ourselves as free in the judgments we make as rational beings, there can be no grounds for denying that we are similarly free in the exercise of practical reason – that is, in the actions we do for what appear to be good reasons. (Dismissing such freedom as illusory would equally impugn the freedom we attribute to ourselves as thinking beings and thus the supposed rationality of that very claim.) Now the freedom we attribute to ourselves in these two domains consists in abiding by reasons, and just as a reason for belief must be one we hold to be equally valid for other rational thinkers, so a reason for action must be one we assume that all other rational agents would endorse. Any general policy (or "maxim") I adopt for my conduct must therefore be able to serve as "a universal law" binding on every rational being as such. The authority of the moral law would thus follow from our conception of ourselves as rational and free beings.

Kant eventually despaired of this argument, and his qualms sprang chiefly from its inability to rule out the possibility that reasoning about what to think or do might itself derive from the natural order of cause and effect, in which case freedom would be an illusion. (Rightly or wrongly, he considered all compatibilist reconciliations of freedom and necessity a "wretched subterfuge," tantamount to denying freedom.) The sole basis on which we can assure ourselves of our freedom is the thought that otherwise we could not comply with those categorical obligations that are ours what-ever the course of experience has made of us. It followed that freedom can be a certainty only if we already regard ourselves as moral beings.[26]

---

[25] Kant, *Gesammelte Schriften*, vol. IV, pp. 446–453. There are two classic essays by Dieter Henrich devoted to Kant's interest in this argument and to his eventual abandonment of it, in the doctrine of the "fact of reason": "Der Begriff der sittlichen Einsicht und Kants Lehre vom Faktum der Vernunft" (in Henrich et al. [ed.], *Die Gegenwart der Griechen im neueren Denken*, Tübingen: Mohr, 1960, pp. 77–115) and "Die Deduktion des Sittengesetzes" (in A. Schwan [ed.], *Denken im Schatten des Nihilismus*, Darmstadt: Wissenschaftliche Buchgesellschaft, 1975, pp. 55–112). See, too, Karl Ameriks, *Interpreting Kant's Critiques* (Oxford: Oxford University Press, 2003), Chapters 6 and 9.

[26] As a matter of fact, there is no reason to privilege morality in this regard. In reasoning about what to believe, we must also take ourselves to be subject to categorically binding norms (that is, rules of reasoning) and must also suppose ourselves endowed with a will able to comply with them. For this criticism of Kant, see Chapter 2 ("Back to Kant? No Way"), §3.

This turnaround occurs with the *Kritik der praktischen Vernunft* (1788), and it shows us Kant moving nearer to the insight encountered much earlier in Rousseau's *Emile*: morality draws its credentials from itself, and not from external considerations.

Kant formulated his new position by introducing the notion of "a fact of reason" (*ein Faktum der Vernunft*). The acknowledged authority of moral claims is a *fact* in that we "cannot reason it out (*herausvernünfteln*) of already available deliverances of reason, such as the consciousness of freedom (for this is not antecedently given)." Yet it counts as a fact *of reason* in that these claims are perceived as providing us reasons for action.[27] The truth to which Kant was inching closer was, so I would say, the idea that moral value is *sui generis*, intelligible only in its own terms. Unfortunately, however, he never really embraced it. Recall that he gave up on the project of justifying the authority of the moral law, not because he had come to believe that the very project was wrong-headed but because he felt unable to establish the certainty of our freedom, which was to serve as the premise for that justification. It is therefore not surprising that he continued to regard moral value as fully intelligible only in terms that reach beyond morality itself and invoke a conception of ourselves as free beings.

Kant's new position was that though freedom, as the ability to stand back from the pressure of given desires and beliefs and shape our conduct in accord with reasons, cannot serve to establish or *justify* the authority of moral claims, it does offer the best *explanation* of their authority. That is, freedom alone, if rightly understood, can render intelligible how it is that moral claims can be binding on us, even though such an account must be far too speculative to produce anything like a validation of morality. As he put it in the preface to the Second Critique, freedom forms the *ratio essendi*, not the *ratio cognoscendi*, of the moral law (the latter being itself the *ratio cognoscendi* of freedom, the sole grounds on which we can know ourselves to be free).[28] How exactly is freedom held to make sense of the authority of morality? The distinctive feature of Kant's account is that it explains that authority in terms of the ability reason supposedly has to prescribe rules to itself. Freedom entails thinking and acting in accord with reasons, but nothing in the world, Kant maintained, can count as a reason unless it acquires that status in virtue of some principle that our reason, precisely because it cannot take its bearings from the world, has therefore to have imposed upon itself. The upshot is the familiar refrain of Kantian philosophy: freedom consists essentially in *autonomy* or self-legislation, and the authority of the moral law, like that of all the principles that reason employs, can only be understood as an authority of reason's

---

[27] Kant, *Kritik der praktischen Vernunft*, in *Gesammelte Schriften*, vol. V, p. 31. Other references to the "fact of reason" occur on pp. 43, 47, 55, 91–92.

[28] Kant, *Kritik der praktischen Vernunft*, p. 4.

own devising. Whatever the domain, "reason has insight only into that which it produces after a plan of its own."[29]

In claiming that reason's autonomy cannot serve as a basis for justifying the authority of morality, the Kant of the Second Critique differs importantly from the many contemporary neo-Kantians who look to it for just this purpose; I shall examine one example in §6. He had not moved any closer, however, to the sort of position I have been advocating. True, he now held that moral philosophy ought to focus on defending what we already know in our conscience to be true, dismantling the confusions and preconceptions – some of them perennial, others merely fashionable – that impel us to look outside morality for reasons to accept the authority of its claims. That conception resembles the negative task of moral philosophy I described in the previous section. But his reasons for adopting it had nothing to do, unfortunately, with recognizing that ultimately morality speaks for itself. He was forced into this position because the deeper terms in which he thought the authority of morality was alone intelligible could not be securely established within the bounds of our experience. And thus when he turned to the positive task – in itself perfectly legitimate – of trying to understand (if not justify) how it is that morality proves authoritative for our conduct, his explanation took the form of tracing its authority back to an allegedly ulterior source: reason's ability to legislate for itself.[30]

---

[29] Kant, *Kritik der reinen Vernunft*, preface to the second (1787) edition, Bxiii. For Kant, reason is autonomous, not just in the moral domain, but in the theoretical domain as well. See Chapter 2, §3. That Kant means by "autonomy" what the etymology of the term implies – namely, reason's or the rational will's self-legislation – is abundantly clear from the *Grundlegung zur Metaphysik der Sitten* (pp. 431–433), as is the fact that such legislation (*Gesetzgebung*) – as this term implies in turn – makes reason the author (*Urheberin*) of its principles – that is, the source of their authority (p. 448). I believe that Kant was on the right track in holding that we are free to the extent that we are moved by reasons, and not by other sorts of causes. He went astray in going on to declare that, reasons themselves having to be self-legislated, freedom is essentially "autonomy."

[30] Rousseau has seemed to many to have anticipated Kant when declaring in *Du Contrat social* (I.8) that morality is the freedom that consists in "obedience to the law one has prescribed oneself" ("*l'obéissance à la loi qu'on s'est prescrite est liberté*"). Yet the two were actually far apart. As I have indicated, the Rousseau of the *Emile* held that morality speaks with its own authority. What he meant by "prescribing oneself a law" in that passage is the attempt to give systematic form to moral principles that are understood to have an independent validity. It corresponds to the *droit naturel raisonné* that in the first version of the *Contrat social* (the so-called *Manuscrit de Genève*) is said to rest on the *droit naturel proprement dit* (*Oeuvres complètes*, Paris: Gallimard, 1964, vol. III, p. 329). It was with this in mind that Rousseau could say in the *Lettres écrites de la Montagne* (*Oeuvres*, p. 807) that the social contract (which is the self-prescribed law at issue in that passage) may not violate the natural law ("*les Lois naturelles*"). For a comprehensive interpretation of Rousseau that shows how his theory of the social contract remains subordinate to the moral principles of natural law, see Robert Derathé, *Jean-Jacques Rousseau et la science politique de son temps* (Paris: Vrin, 2nd ed., 1979), pp. 151–171.

The theory of reason as autonomy will not work, however, and the cause of its failure indicates why morality's authority in particular cannot be explained as Kant proposed. In demonstrating where the theory goes wrong, I shall not plunge into the intricacies of Kant's own argumentation. Kant philology is an unending affair, and it is easy to lose sight of the whole when embroiled in the particulars. I want instead to lay out in general terms the nature of the mistake as well as the motivations that lead Kant, along with much of modern philosophy, down this path.

Let me state again, very abstractly, the view in question. No fact in the world – no experimental finding, no distress in another person – forms in and of itself a reason for belief or action, Kant declared. It is we who decide, tacitly or reflectively, what weight the facts of experience will have for us, and we do so in virtue of general principles – rules for evidence, moral convictions – by which we guide our thought and behavior. Whether we are right to bestow on certain facts the status of being reasons depends, therefore, on the worth of the principles on which we rely. These principles need to be ones which our reason can endorse. (Clearly Kant was not imagining that autonomy consists in taking up whatever principles we please.) Yet it appears already settled that we cannot rely on anything in the world to validate them. Their validation can only come from within reason itself, which consequently endows all principles or "laws" of thought and action with the authority they possess. Reason, Kant concluded, must be understood as self-legislating or "autonomous": in endorsing principles, it does not so much recognize as establish their right to regulate our conduct.

The trouble is that this conception, however venerable it has become, makes little sense upon closer inspection. It talks of reason, or as Kant liked to say, the "rational will," as though it were an agent (a legislator), yet reason is not an agent but rather a faculty that we, who are agents, exercise more or less well. To exercise the faculty of reason is to engage in reasoning, to adduce considerations we see as reasons in order to conclude that we should believe this or do that. All that it can mean to say that reason endorses some principle is that we have found good reasons to accept the principle. Contrary to Kant, reason is not therefore essentially autonomous or self-legislating, since it operates by way of responding to reasons. Reason, as I suggested before, involves a *receptivity to reasons.* Though we may determine by appealing to principles that particular phenomena give us reason to think and act in certain ways, the principles themselves count as rational only if there are reasons recommending their adoption.

Is it not, one might rejoin, always up to us whether we will be swayed by such reasons? Certainly we cannot be moved by reasons unless we grasp their force and can hold ourselves responsible to them by judging when need be how well we are complying with them. Responsiveness to reasons is not a blind passivity. Yet the sort of uptake it requires does not consist in our endowing them with authority but rather in acknowledging the authority they possess. So, too, we sometimes do ask ourselves whether the reasons that appear to favor a principle are truly compelling, but this sort of reflection involves discovering what further reasons there may be to accept the initial argument for the principle. In the end, reasoning always requires responding to reasons, basing conclusions on reasons we suppose that we have discerned, not legislated. Incidentally, this truth points up a related error in Kant's thinking – namely, the belief that our judgments about reasons always take shape through the mediation of principles. Some reasons we must acknowledge directly, if only to have grounds to espouse the principles that are ours. I suspect that Kant held as firmly as he did to the supremacy of principles because he saw in it an expression of the autonomy of reason.

In some cases, to be sure, finding reasons that favor a principle consists not so much in recognizing that the principle is valid as in conferring on it a validity it does not possess on its own. Thus do governments or con- stitutions stipulate what shall be the voting procedures in force, just as a scientific community determines what shall count as the acceptable margin of experimental error. Laws and standards of this sort are indeed the work of "autonomous" reason, but manifestly the reasons for adopting them do not likewise derive from reason's self-legislation. Our grounds for imposing them on ourselves are, moreover, exceptional in that they cite the need, given our other commitments, to set up rules where none existed before. Generally, and certainly when fundamental matters are at stake, reasoning about what principles to accept is not like this at all. Instead we are concerned to discover how it is in fact that we ought to think and act. Self-legislated principles play only a limited role in our life, and the idea of autonomy is doomed to fall short of providing a complete account of the "normativity" that structures all our experience.

In this light, there can be little prospect that the idea of autonomy should be able to explain the specific authority of morality. Some moral precepts we do institute for ourselves, as when we decide, knowing our weaknesses, that we must keep our borrowing to a minimum. But we legislate such rules for ourselves because of our deeper moral convictions (we believe that debts ought to be repaid), and these principles appear to have a very different kind of rationale. Their authority does not stem from expediency, as should now be evident. And if they are embraced for their moral worth, which Kant himself was after all assuming, the reasons we have for endorsing them (it is unfair to take advantage of another's trust, say) are reasons for thinking we are bound by them, not reasons for making them binding when otherwise they would not be. The conclusion is inescapable: our reason does not constitute, it acknowledges the authority of moral claims, since it involves heeding the reasons there are to regard them as valid.

I hasten to add that this critique of the notion of autonomy is not meant to impugn the far less ambitious ideas with which the term has often come to be associated. Sometimes moral "autonomy" means the capacity we have to grasp and to do what is right regardless of the threats or rewards that a higher power, human or divine, may hold over us – as when St. Paul said of the Gentiles that they were a "law unto themselves" (*Letter to the Romans* 2:14).[31] Sometimes individual "autonomy" denotes our right or ability to think for ourselves, instead of yielding to custom or coercion. Such was the theme of Kant's famous essay, "*Was ist Aufklärung?*" though in this text, tellingly, he never used the word itself. (In his vocabulary, it was reserved for the idea of self-legislation.) Both these meanings of the term concern a person's relations to others, and my aim here is not to oppose this usage or the views thereby expressed. But "autonomy" in the sense that Kant pioneered and that shapes the philosophical tradition he has inspired bears on a very different kind of problematic – namely, reason's relation to the authority of the principles by which it operates. Partisans of those other conceptions must ultimately tackle this question too, and they need not end up agreeing with Kant; indeed, I think the only coherent way for them to defend their ideals is to recognize that reason consists in being responsive to reasons. It is, then, the idea of reason as self-legislation that is the target of my critique.

The objections I have raised are hardly recondite, but instead rather obvious. So an explanation is needed for why this concept of autonomy does not cease to prove attractive. I do not think it is hard to find. Deep philosophical pressures pushed Kant, and continue to push modern philosophy as a whole, in this direction – pressures so strong that no other alternative can seem remotely plausible. One way or another, it is thought, despite the problems encountered by this or that version of the doctrine, reason has to be autonomous or self-legislating, if it is to exist at all. The source of this conviction is the *naturalistic* picture of the world that dominates modern thought, and that sees the world (or as Kant would caution, the world of experience) as ultimately nothing more than the matter in motion that, along with our thoughts and feelings (if minds are not themselves further matter in motion), make up the object of the natural sciences.[32] The world so understood is normatively mute, barren of

---

[31] In *The Invention of Autonomy* (Cambridge: Cambridge University Press, 1998), J. B. Schneewind helpfully distinguishes this idea of "self-governance" from the strict Kantian concept of autonomy.

[32] "Naturalism" is a term with more than one meaning, and I shall mean by it only this ontological thesis about what sorts of things (the objects of modern natural science) can be said truly to exist. This is the sense in which, I believe, "naturalism" has played a central role in shaping the agenda of modern philosophy, a sense according to which, in J. L. Mackie's famous words (*Ethics: Inventing Right and Wrong*, Penguin: Harmondsworth, 1977, p. 40), the idea of the world as containing "intrinsically prescriptive entities or features of some kind" is "metaphysically queer."

any guidance as to how we are to conduct ourselves. For there to be such things as reasons for thought and action, reason must therefore introduce them into the world from without, by way of imposing principles of its own devising on the neutral face of nature. Certainly the contrary view of reason as responsive to reasons looks impossible to house within a naturalistic worldview, where "*le silence éternel de ces espaces infinis*"[33] contains nothing inherently normative to which we might regard ourselves as responding. Reason, it seems, just has to be autonomous, if not in its individual, then in its collective employment. Whence the persistent refusal to face squarely the fact that every theory of autonomy must come up short: no principle can count as rational unless there exist reasons that recommend its acceptance.

"The ethics of autonomy is the only one consistent with the metaphysics of the modern world."[34] This statement by Christine Korsgaard expresses perfectly the basis of the conviction that there is no alternative to the Kantian notion of self-legislative reason. Yet it also serves to remind us that the naturalistic picture of the world is indeed a metaphysics, and not a theorem of modern natural science itself. Perhaps the incoherence of the idea of autonomy indicates how we might break the hold of the naturalistic worldview and look more favorably on the contrary idea of reason as a responsiveness to reasons. In §7, I shall outline what shape this different "metaphysics" would take. But first I want to examine in detail Korsgaard's own version of an ethics of autonomy.

6. REFLECTION AND REASONS

Korsgaard's book, *The Sources of Normativity*, has the merit of being one of the few sustained efforts in contemporary philosophy to vindicate the Kantian concept of autonomy. The "source of the normativity of moral claims," the basis of the authority they have for us, lies in their being "laws of the agent's own will."[35] It is important to note, however, one important respect in which her approach differs from that of Kant in the Second Critique. In her hands, autonomy or reason's self-legislation is designed to be an answer to what she calls "the normative question," which asks "what *justifies* the claims that morality makes on us."[36] It serves, therefore, not only to explain the authority of moral claims but also to show why it is that

---

[33] Pascal, *Pensées* §201 (Lafuma). Modern naturalism often sounds the same note as Pascal's Jansenism, which was indeed one of its forbears, insinuating that a world marked by God's absence is a world emptied of all normative distinctions, as though they could only form part of the fabric of reality if they had been instituted by God. In this regard, autonomy serves as a God-surrogate, and the way forward, in my view, is to get past the notion that reasons, to exist, must be an artifact of someone's devising – if not God's, then ours.

[34] Korsgaard, *The Sources of Normativity*, p. 5.

[35] *Ibid*, p. 19. See also p. 104.

[36] *Ibid*, pp. 9–10.

we ought to conform to them.[37] The reasons for this difference are plain enough. The notion of autonomy can assume this further role because Korsgaard, unlike Kant, does not hold that the sort of freedom it expresses must be empirically unconditioned, independent of the natural order of cause and effect. On the contrary, she is happy to regard our bestowing of normative significance on things in the world as an ability we exercise in virtue of being the kind of animals that we are. Kant, it will be recalled, only abandoned his own attempts to justify the authority of morality because he despaired of ever being able to know that we are free. Korsgaard feels freer to take on the task.

In this spirit, she gives considerable attention to defining the exact meaning of the normative question. Though it may assume in particular circumstances the form of asking, "Is this action really obligatory?" that phrase is potentially ambiguous, as it might suggest that we want to know whether the action is in fact morally required. The question at issue is one that asks instead whether we have any reason to comply with moral requirements. Korsgaard accuses Prichard – quite unjustly, as I noted before (§1) – of confusing these two questions. True, Prichard maintained that when we are moved to ask "Why should I be moral?" the only solution is to review the reasons why the action before us is morally right. But he was not thereby running together the question of morality's authority with the very different question about whether the moral predicate "right" has been correctly applied. He meant that there is no other way to see why we should heed the demands of morality than to attend more closely to what they involve. They cannot be justified in terms other than those of morality itself.

On just this score, of course, Korsgaard disagrees. The "normative question," at least as she understands it, asks that morality's claims be vindicated from a standpoint we supposedly occupy external to morality itself. If she fails to perceive the real nature of her disagreement with Prichard, no doubt it is because the kind of position he effectively held seems to her to miss altogether the force of the normative question. For he believed, as I do, that moral reasons are *sui generis*, an irreducible domain of value into which we cannot reason ourselves from the outside, but which we can only acknowledge. And considering such a view under the heading of "substantive moral realism," Korsgaard complains that it "refuses to answer the normative question. It is a way of saying that it cannot [or need not] be done."[38] She dismisses moral realism on two counts. It cannot be squared with "the

---

[37] *The Sources of Normativity* never mentions the doctrine of the "fact of reason," in which Kant expressed his ultimate conviction that the authority of the moral law does not admit of justification. In *Creating the Kingdom of Ends* (Cambridge: Cambridge University Press, 1996), Korsgaard does discuss this doctrine, but only interpretively, and without relating it to the present issue.

[38] Korsgaard, *The Sources of Normativity*, p. 39.

metaphysics of the modern world," and it confuses the practical with the theoretical attitude: it wrongly construes normative concepts in general as meant to describe aspects of the world, when actually their role is to guide us as we "figure out what to believe and what to do."[39]

I shall return to Korsgaard's grounds for rejecting moral realism. But, first, let us look more closely at why she believes that the authority of morality stands in need of the sort of justification she seeks. As she observes, the question "Why should I do the moral thing?" arises when moral claims prove particularly onerous, given our other interests. Like most in the philosophical tradition, however, she turns this situation of inner conflict, where we find ourselves torn between existing commitments, into a situation where we must determine whether we should be committed to morality at all. This move, as I emphasized earlier (§1), changes the character of that situation quite a lot, and no more in this case than in others is it an innocent reformulation. Driving it is always some prior conception of the nature of reason and of morality too. In §§ 2–3, I brought out (and criticized) the presuppositions that have impelled Hobbesians – from Hobbes to Gauthier – to regard the authority of morality as having to have an external rationale: an instrumental conception of reason and the view of morality as a cooperative scheme for mutual advantage. Korsgaard's conception of "the normative question" draws on different but equally dubious ideas about the nature of reason and morality, ideas characteristic of the Kantian tradition as a whole.

We have already met the underlying idea of reason – namely, the conviction that reason must be self-legislating to be real at all. But morality, too, is understood in a certain light: it is seen as essentially a matter of what *each of us owes himself* as a free and rational being. Thus Kant himself wrote that respect for the moral law comes down ultimately to respect for our own "personality,"

the freedom and independence from the mechanism of nature [that is] a capacity of a being that is subject to ... pure practical laws given by its own reason ... This idea of personality awakens respect; it places before our eyes the sublimity of our own nature.[40]

And as Korsgaard summarizes her eventual solution to the normative question, echoing Kant in her own idiom,

If you value anything at all ... you must value your humanity as an end in itself ... If you are to have any practical identity at all, you must acknowledge

---

[39] *Ibid*, p. 46. See also pp. 37, 44, 47.

[40] Kant, *Kritik der praktischen Vernunft*, p. 87. See, too, the *Metaphysik der Sitten*, at the beginning of Part One of the Doctrine of Virtue (*Tugendlehre*), where Kant argues that duties to others rest on the fundamental duty we have to ourselves, which is to exercise our rational nature (*Gesammelte Schriften*, vol. VI, pp. 417–418).

yourself to have moral identity.... and this identity like any other carries with it obligations.[41]

It is not difficult to grasp how these two assumptions about reason and morality go naturally together. If principles of conduct draw their authority from reason's legislating for itself, and not from its responding to the reasons there are, then the allegiance we owe to the claims of morality has to stem from a respect we feel for our own powers of rationality. So long as it has not been shown that morality arises from our being true to ourselves as rational beings, a question (Korsgaard's "normative question") must hang over the bindingness of its claims.

I have already indicated why the notion of reason as autonomous proves incoherent. The allied notion of morality looks no more promising. Is not morality at its heart a matter of what we owe to others rather than to ourselves? Whence derives the reason to help another – from his distress, or from our sense of our own worth? Think back to the biblical saying that sums up so well what morality truly requires. If we are to love our neighbor as ourselves, then the interest we take in how he fares must be as direct, as pure of ulterior purposes, as the interest we readily take in how well we ourselves fare. Hobbesians miss this truth insofar as they hold that our concern for another's good must, if rational, figure in the efficient pursuit of those interests that happen to be ours. Kantians miss this truth as well, since they trace our moral concern for another back to what they regard as our supreme interest – namely, the affirmation of our own rational freedom. Recognizing the moral point of view for what it is really means, in contrast, learning to see the reason to do well by others as a reason that speaks for itself.

To better appreciate these points, let us now turn to the line of reasoning by which Korsgaard believes the claims of morality are to be legitimated. For her argument fails, and cannot but fail, given its assumptions about reason and morality. Once we correct their defects, the apparent need for this sort of justification will in fact disappear.

The argument of *The Sources of Normativity* revolves around the idea of a *practical identity*. Whenever we deliberate about what to do, we weigh our given desires and interests by reference to principles telling us how we ought to conduct ourselves, principles expressing some conception we

---

[41] Korsgaard, *The Sources of Normativity*, p. 125. Rainer Forst has nicely shown how this assumption about the nature of morality shapes the views that both Kant and Korsgaard have of its authority. See Forst's "Moralische Autonomie und Autonomie der Moral," *Deutsche Zeitschrift für Philosophie*, vol. 52 (2004), no. 4, pp. 179–197, especially pp. 189–191. Forst rejects the realistic view of reasons that I propose as an antidote, claiming that this sort of metaphysics is incompatible with our "finitude" (p. 196). I do not believe, however, that my view denies the historicity of human reason, if that is what "finitude" comes to. See Chapter 1, "History and Truth."

have of how it is worth living. All of us rely on numerous such "practical identities," looking (let us say) at some decisions as a university professor, at others as a long-distance runner, and at still others as a spouse and parent. And one such identity may be our conception of ourselves as moral beings. What would it be to deliberate from this perspective? It is not enough, Korsgaard claims, to say that we would then attend to the obligations and human goods before us – in short, to the moral reasons favoring one course of action over another. For whence our conviction that moral duties and values really exist? One might reply that we need only consider our situation impartially, setting aside our personal interests, to make out the moral reasons it gives us to do one thing rather than another. Yet such is the language of that "substantive moral realism" that we have noted her grounds for rejecting. To say that reasons of any type, be they moral or otherwise, are there to be acknowledged entails postulating the existence of intrinsically normative entities, which can have no place in the modern worldview; besides, talk about reasons is not descriptive in intent anyway, but rather practical and action-guiding.

The proper outlook, in Korsgaard's view, is the one that gives her book its title. Normativity has its source in the reflective structure of our consciousness.[42] We can stand back from our impulses and ask whether we ought to follow them, and reflection's way of approving some desire lies in announcing that we "have a reason" to act accordingly. It is we who introduce reasons into the world:

> The normative word 'reason' refers to a kind of reflective success.... Reasons exist because we need them, and we need them because of the structure of reflective consciousness.[43]

People who declare that there are reasons for a particular action are not really reporting a discovery, Korsgaard insists. They are simply expressing their confidence that they ought to act in that way, a confidence that stems from their allegiance to some practical identity and its principles for determining which desires are worth acting on.[44] If the question arises whether that confidence is rational, there can, once again, be no looking to the world for reasons to ratify it. The only way to deal with such a question is by the process she calls "*reflective endorsement*."

In this regard, Korsgaard invokes not just Kant, but also Hume and Bernard Williams as models. I shall leave aside the historical commentary,

---

[42] See Korsgaard, *The Sources of Normativity*, pp. 103–104, 122.

[43] *Ibid*, pp. 93, 96. She calls her own view sometimes, confusingly, "procedural moral realism," and sometimes, following Rawls, "constructivism". For a critique of Rawls' constructivism, see Chapter 4.

[44] "The realist's belief in the existence of normative entities is not based on any discovery. It is based on his *confidence* that his beliefs and desires are normative" (*ibid*, p. 48). See also pp. 40f, 91.

however, and focus on how she actually portrays the process. The gist of her account is that determining whether to accept some conception of how to live consists, not in showing that the values it embodies really exist, but in reflecting whether we can coherently endorse them in the light of the needs and interests that make up who we are. The aim is practical rather than theoretical: we consider not whether the conception is true but whether we would live more flourishing lives if we made it our own. So we must proceed, whatever be the normative identity under scrutiny, including the moral point of view itself. This is the sense, she argues, in which our will is essentially autonomous: the principles of conduct we thus ratify amount to laws we give ourselves.[45] We can, of course, fail to exercise the autonomy that is the mark of reason; that is what happens when we blindly follow a principle, without critically assessing it.

Thus we meet Korsgaard's version of the Kantian idea of autonomy. And the fundamental difficulty with this account ought accordingly to be plain. How can reflective endorsement work if not by responding to reasons? Presumably the needs and interests in whose light we evaluate some conception of how to live stem from other identities already in place that, so she must be assuming, could similarly be made an object of reflection, should the necessity arise. I shall let this last point pass, for the sake of argument. But how can we decide whether to endorse that conception except by figuring out *what reasons there are* to conclude that, given our other convictions, we will be the better for making it our own? Reasons are not the output of reflective success, since success in reflecting is measured by how well we respond to reasons.[46] Korsgaard's notion of reflective endorsement is a variant of the ever-popular idea that having a reason to do something means no more than that one would want to do it if one were rational, and the trouble is that being rational cannot be understood except as the ability to think and act in accord with reasons. In short, there cannot be a "source" of normativity in the sense Korsgaard seeks: the existence of reasons cannot be traced back to some operation of the mind not itself presupposing a responsiveness to reasons.

I am by no means disputing the idea that reasons are essentially action-guiding. To think that we have a reason for some endeavor is indeed to be thereby disposed, all other things being equal, to pursue it. Yet, at the

---

[45] *Ibid*, pp. 98, 105f

[46] To put the point in Korsgaard's own terminology, the "procedural moral realism" she champions, and which holds that "there are answers to moral questions *because* there are correct procedures for arriving at them," reduces to the "substantive moral realism" she deplores, to the view that "there are correct procedures for answering moral questions *because* there are moral truths or facts which exist independently of those procedures, and which those procedures track" (ibid, p. 36). For what can make the proceduralist's procedure (for example, reflective endorsement) "correct" – in its application or indeed in its very adoption – if not that it answers appropriately to the reasons there are?

same time, we are moved in this way because we believe we have found good reason to do the action in question. Something is therefore clearly amiss in the dichotomy that Korsgaard erects between the practical and theoretical, the action-guiding and the descriptive, and I will return to this problem at the end (§8). For now, I want to underscore the fact that realism about reasons is inescapable, if reasoning is to make any sense at all. And I note this fact right away, as it explains the ultimate flaw in the way she believes the normative question about morality is to be answered.

Let us consider then her answer. Every practical identity, she holds, expresses a principle of conduct that, if reflectively endorsed, is a law we give ourselves. Autonomy in this broad sense does not presuppose any allegiance to morality. On the contrary, it defines the external standpoint from which we are to be reasoned into the moral point of view. Korsgaard's key move is to note that if we had no practical identities at all, we would be directionless, unable to see any reason to do some things rather than others. Each of us, therefore, in addition to pursuing the things our various practical identities recommend, can also see a reason to value our very reliance on such identities. Indeed, we all acknowledge this reason, if only implicitly, since otherwise we would not feel moved, as we do, to reflect on the merits of our various identities, revising them when necessary, in order to live better than we otherwise would.[47] Reasons, however, always derive from identities (we might call this "Korsgaard's axiom," the essence of her Kantian anti-realism about reasons), and the present case is no exception. The reason we see to prize the having of practical identities flows from an even more fundamental identity of ours – namely, our affirmation of our humanity, of what makes us human, which is to shape our conduct by principles and reflection:

This reason for conforming to your particular practical identities is ... a reason that springs from your humanity itself, from your identity as simply a human being... You must value your own humanity, if you are to value anything at all.[48]

This "transcendental argument," as she calls it, shows that we cannot help but value our own humanity, if we value anything at all. Yet we will not have entered the perspective of morality until we likewise value the

---

[47] Korsgaard does not make this point outright. But it must underlie her assertion, never really explained, that "part of the normative force of those reasons [deriving from our particular practical identities] springs from the value we place on ourselves as human beings who need such identities" (*ibid*, p. 121). Conceptions of how it is worth living involve caring about the worth of those conceptions themselves, reflecting on them if need be, and their value includes among other things their ability to give direction to our lives.

[48] *Ibid*, pp. 121, 123. For statements of the axiom in question, see p. 123: "If you had no normative conception of your identity, you could have no reasons for action," and p. 246: "In my view, a reason derives its normative force for an agent from a perspective provided by her identification with a principle of choice."

humanity of others. What secures this further conclusion? Korsgaard's strategy is to lean on the fact that the reasons we have to value our own humanity are in their very nature *public* reasons. It is not that our reason to value our own gives us an instrumental reason to value that of others, nor is it that we can infer from our having a reason to value ours that we must therefore honor the equally good reasons that others have to value theirs. In both these lines of argument, reasons are understood as essentially private, as being in the first instance reasons that a single individual has. But reasons, she declares, are not like that at all. Saying that I have a reason to do a certain thing is tantamount to saying that anyone has that reason who finds himself in similar circumstances. To have a reason for an action means that the action is justified, not merely that it strikes me as being so, and the action cannot be in fact justified unless it is the case that anyone ought to act that way, given the same premises that recommend the action in my own case. Consequently, the reason I have to value my own humanity just is, she concludes, a reason to value humanity wherever it appears.[49]

Now Korsgaard is right about the public nature of reasons. Every reason for action or belief, so I would put it, is essentially universal in scope (though it may apply only if specific conditions obtain). All the same, this argument fails, and does so on a number of scores. To begin with, though it is true that the reason I have to value my humanity is the very reason others have to value theirs, nothing has been done to show that this reason entails that each of us ought to value the humanity of our fellows. The publicity of reasons is not enough, despite Korsgaard's assurances to the contrary, to disarm the criticism that Bernard Williams famously made of neo-Kantian attempts to justify morality.[50] His objection went as follows: the reason each rational agent has to value his own humanity can become a reason each has to value the humanity of others, only if each has abstracted from the fact that his humanity is his own and is considering its value impersonally – but that means, only if the moral point of view has already been adopted. Reasons may be necessarily universal in scope, applying to all if they apply to any, but they need not be impersonal in the object they recommend. Korsgaard's argument, as stated, falls short because it begs the question.

Let us imagine, however, that this gap is filled. Korsgaard might have appealed, for example, not to the publicity of reasons, but to the idea that I cannot have reason to value my own humanity merely because it is mine: I must suppose that humanity itself is valuable if I am to have any grounds for taking relish in the fact that this particular instance of it belongs to me.

---

[49] The argument spans pp. 133–145 of *The Sources of Normativity*.

[50] See Bernard Williams, *Ethics and the Limits of Philosophy* (Cambridge, MA: Harvard University Press, 1985), pp. 60–63, and Korsgaard, *The Sources of Normativity*, p. 134.

That seems right.[51] But now we come upon two further and more fundamental defects in her way of answering the normative question about morality.

First, what business can Korsgaard have to talk here as she does about *reasons to value* humanity, be it my own or that of others? Recall that her "transcendental argument" was that I must value my own humanity if I am to see the reason I evidently do, given my commitment to reflecting on their worth, to prize the very having of particular identities. Here, as elsewhere, she was proceeding according to the anti-realist axiom that reasons derive from identities: the reasons I take there to be merely express the principles I espouse in adhering to certain conceptions of how to live. The argument did not therefore show, if understood on her terms, that I have reason to value my humanity, only that I must in fact value it if I am thus committed to reflectively monitoring my more particular self-conceptions. Korsgaard might well reply, in keeping with the tenor of certain passages, that if I value my own and others' humanity, then I must regard it as valuable.[52] Whence her license to talk about the reason I have to value it. Yet that inference, though valid, depends on the very realism about reasons she rejects: valuing something indeed makes no sense unless I perceive it to be valuable – unless, that is, I perceive some reason to value it. Korsgaard has no right to any such move, since her position is that reasons always flow from our self-conceptions and never serve ultimately to ground them. She can talk about the reasons my deepest sense of how to live (valuing humanity) gives me to care about my more particular identities, but she has no basis for assuming that if I must value my own humanity to prize them as I do, I must have a reason to value it.

In introducing the idea that we see a reason to value our own humanity, and as a result that of everyone generally, a reason to which we must thus understand ourselves to be responsive at the deepest level of our being, Korsgaard has violated the terms of her own position. The inconsistency in which she has landed was inevitable, however. For as noted before I took up the details of her argument: reasons cannot be equated with the deliverances of reflection, since reflection's success is measured by how well it answers to the reasons there are. Her underlying mistake is the Kantian credo that reason operates, not by responding to reasons, but by determining through its own legislation what facts in the world shall count as reasons.

---

[51] This is in fact the analysis of "agent-relative reasons" presented in Korsgaard's essay "The Reasons We Share" in *Creating the Kingdom of Ends*, pp. 275–310, and referred to at p. 136 (fn) of *The Sources of Normativity* as "a slightly different approach" to her intended conclusion.

[52] So she assumes on pp. 123–4 of *Sources of Normativity*, before going on to argue that if we must find our own humanity valuable, it must therefore actually be valuable.

Korsgaard insists that reason's self-legislation should not be understood as our choosing to impose certain principles on ourselves that we might just as well choose not to impose. Rules of that sort are "external" to the activities they govern, as when we decide that a series of chess matches should be open only to people in our neighborhood, in contrast to other rules, such as those regulating the movements of the pieces, which are "constitutive" of the very activity of chess playing. Fundamental principles of thought and action are, she claims, constitutive in this sense: if we do not adhere to them, we will have failed to really think or act at all or at least in any intelligible fashion.[53] Some of the examples she gives – that contradictions are to be avoided, or that to will the end is to will the necessary means – are, I agree (see Chapter 9, §5), constitutive of coherent thought and action, though I doubt that any moral principles can be shown to be of this group. Still, constitutive principles of this sort are not ones whose authority we ourselves create, as though they became binding only through our initiating the activities they inhabit. For what it is to think and act is to guide ourselves by such principles, to recognize the authority that they antecedently possess and to which we must conform if we are to think or do anything coherent. There is no way round the fact that reason makes sense only as a responsiveness to reasons.

The point is confirmed if we look at the way Korsgaard, once she has taken to talking of a reason to value humanity, seeks to protect her position against any realist slippage. While this reason is public like reasons generally, it is not therefore "objective," not part of the objective world, as a "substantive moral realist" would hold, but is to be viewed instead as "shareable."[54] This contrast comes to naught, however. That reasons are "public" means that any reason I have is in itself a reason that others have as well. *A fortiori*, such a reason obtains independently of my or any particular person's believing that it does. Moreover, its being shareable can surely not consist in its simply being a reason everyone may come to endorse. The sense in which it counts as shareable must be that everyone would believe that it obtains, if they were reasoning correctly. Therefore, only because reasons are objective, valid in themselves, can they be shareable in the way Korsgaard must have in mind.

But there is still more – the second fundamental defect I mentioned earlier. Let us grant that we do not merely value our humanity, but see a reason to do so. This is the conclusion that Korsgaard wants (though to

---

[53] *Ibid.*, pp, 234–7 This thesis is developed at length in Korsgaard's John Locke Lectures of 2002, entitled "Self-Constitution," at present available on her website (http://www.people. fas.harvard.edu/~korsgaar), and soon to be published. Despite their great interest, I stand by the objection I go on to make that constitutive principles, if of a fundamental character, cannot be understood as ones that reason legislates for itself.

[54] *Ibid.*, p. 135.

which she has no right, given her anti-realism about reasons) since only then can she argue that we must see a reason, supposedly the very same reason, to value the humanity of others and treat them with the respect their humanity demands – to occupy, in other words, the moral point of view. Even then, her argument will not succeed. It will not provide a way of reasoning anyone into an acceptance of morality. It will not constitute an answer to "the normative question." For though I cannot regard my own humanity as valuable simply because it is mine, but must see humanity itself as valuable wherever it exists, it does not follow that I thereby have reason to value *equally* the humanity of others. I can still suppose that the mineness of my own counts for something, and indeed for a whole lot more than that of others. Despite all the revisions, the argument fails to usher in the moral point of view. The sole way for me truly to acknowledge the authority of morality is, without any detour through my own good, to focus at the outset on the defining value of moral thinking – namely, the fact that another's good is in itself a reason for action on my part.

Not only then must the Kantian conception of reason as autonomy be abandoned, but also the project of finding a justification for morality in terms other than those of morality itself. The Kantian conception of morality too is a distortion. Morality is not ultimately a set of obligations each of us owes ourselves as a rational or reflective being, such that (as Korsgaard phrases that conception) "to value yourself just as a human being is to have moral identity."[55] Our moral identity consists not in valuing our own humanity and thereby determining that we ought to value that of others, but in recognizing directly the reason there is to value humanity in whatever person it may happen to appear. It is a reason to love our neighbor in no less an immediate fashion than we are naturally moved to care about ourselves.

The flaws in Korsgaard's attempt to answer "the normative question" about morality mirror the failures of Kantian thinking in general. The conception of reason as self-legislating is at heart incoherent, and every attempt to have it serve as the basis for justifying the authority of morality ends up violating its own strictures, as well as creating a skewed image of morality itself. The *ethics of autonomy* needs to be jettisoned, and in its stead belongs what I have called the *autonomy of morality* – by which I mean, obviously enough, not that morality is self-legislating (that would be nonsensical), but that morality forms an autonomous, irreducible domain of value, into which we cannot reason ourselves from without, but which we must simply acknowledge.

---

[55] *Ibid*, p. 121. On p. 134, there are in fact glimmerings of the contrary and proper view that morality is fundamentally a matter of what we owe to others.

7. RECONCEIVING THE WORLD

Earlier I emphasized the essentially negative import of what the analysis of Hobbesian views had achieved. In part it involved diagnosis: the claims of morality cannot but appear to require an external rationale, once reason is understood as the efficient pursuit of one's own interests and morality itself as a system for mutual advantage. And in part it was critique: not only is this conception of morality morally unacceptable, but no justification relying on an instrumental conception of reason holds any promise of success. I noted how reason and morality might be differently understood, and in a way that eliminates the search for a way to reason us into the moral point of view. We can rightly feel ourselves bound to take an interest in another's good independently of any interests of our own. But the diagnosis and the critique did not prove that this is so. They only opened up the space for considering the possibility seriously.

My analysis of the Kantian approach has the same limitations. It has established that the attempt to trace the authority of morality back to the autonomy of reason cannot succeed, and that it comes to grief because of the notions of reason and morality on which it relies. No more than in the first case is this negative result negligible. The Hobbesian and Kantian traditions form the principal strands of modern moral philosophy. Still, I have produced no argument to establish that moral reasons for action carry their own intrinsic authority. As I mentioned before, it is hard to envision what such an argument would look like, if morality must indeed speak for itself. As with the value of prudence, there is in the end no other way to grasp its importance, once the obstructions created by contrary theories have been cleared away, than to reflect more closely on what morality involves. We have to just see that another's good is in itself a reason for action on our part.

It does not follow, however, that moral philosophy can have no positive ambitions, only the chore of dispelling illusions. On the contrary, there remains at the very least the need to understand what must be true about mind and world if, as the autonomy of morality implies, reason consists in a receptivity to reasons. We have to figure out, in other words, how to get beyond the metaphysics of naturalism that shapes so much of modern thought. To this task I now turn. My discussion will proceed at a rather abstract level, with only occasional reference to the particularities of moral thinking.[56] The abstractness is necessary since, as we have learned, the way the authority of morality is understood depends on one's idea of the very

---

[56] The following section draws upon the "normative" theory of mind and self developed in my two books, *Les pratiques du moi* (Paris: Presses Universitaires de France, 2004) and (with Alain Renaut) *Débat sur l' éthique. Idéalisme ou réalisme* (Paris: Grasset, 2004). See, too, Chapter 3 of the present book.

nature of reason. The conception that animates the Kantian tradition reaches deep (far deeper than the Hobbesian conception, which is more concerned with what reasons there are than with what it is to be a reason). To counter the hold of that conception, which, moreover, extends well beyond the Kantian fold, we must develop an alternative metaphysics.

Let us begin by returning to a broad subject touched on before. What is the goal of reflection? What are we seeking when we deliberate about what to believe or do? Clearly we do not deliberate for the pure pleasure of doing so, but in response to some problem that has arisen in the course of experience. Things have not turned out as we expected, or we no longer know how to go on in the path we were following. This means, first of all, that deliberation is always situated: only in the light of our existing beliefs can we so much as identify the problem, and only by leaning upon those elements that remain unproblematic can we set about finding a solution. But it also means that deliberation aims at discovering something we do not already possess – namely, an answer to the doubts that have given rise to it. It is often said, and rightly so, that we do not deliberate about what is not in our power; it is equally true that we do not deliberate about matters where the way to go is already plain. Now what are we trying to discover, if not the reasons there may be to adopt some belief or course of action that will put an end to the difficulty in which we find ourselves? And what can discovering such reasons amount to if not learning what we did not know before? Reflection in these circumstances is a cognitive enterprise, directed toward the acquisition of knowledge, and the object of the enquiry consists in reasons for belief and action.

Yet here we meet the thorny question, metaphysically speaking: what exactly are reasons? The proper answer, I believe, is that reasons are essentially normative in character and cannot therefore be equated with any features of the natural world, physical or psychological, though they certainly depend on the natural facts being as they are. I discussed these matters in Chapter 3, but now I will push the analysis further.

Consider then, first, why it is that a reason cannot consist in a physical state of affairs. We may certainly say, for example, that the cold, or the fact that it is cold, is a reason to wear a coat. But, strictly speaking, our reason to do so is not the cold itself but rather a certain relation that the cold bears to our possibilities of action. After all, one might agree that it is cold outside, yet dispute that this fact gives a reason to put on a coat. Only insofar as the cold justifies or counts in favor of wearing a coat does it take on the status of a reason, and this status – the relation of *counting in favor of* – is not a physical quality of the cold.[57] It is a *normative* attribute. "The cold

---

[57] Though rightly denying that the reason in such cases is the belief in the physical fact, both Joseph Raz in *Practical Reason and Norms* (Oxford: Oxford University Press, 1975, 2nd ed. 1999), Chapter 1, and Rüdiger Bittner in *Doing Things for Reasons* (Oxford: Oxford

is a reason to wear a coat" means the same as "given the cold, I *ought* to wear a coat." To be sure, other things may count in favor of not wearing a coat. As a rule, reasons are in themselves *pro tanto*, as are the "ought"s to which they correspond, and only if they are not outweighed by contrary considerations do they indicate what we overall have reason or ought to do. The point is that, whether *pro tanto* or decisive, reasons are not identical with the physical facts that may give rise to them.

Similarly, the reasons people have to believe or do one thing or another are not the same as any psychological state in which they find themselves. In this, I oppose the widespread idea that a reason is a particular combination of belief and desire. My reason to wear a coat, many say, consists in my belief that it is cold conjoined with my desire to keep warm.[58] But that sounds very odd. It may be true that I would not have such a reason unless I indeed wanted to keep warm, so that in this respect the reason is conditional, binding only insofar as I have a desire to keep warm. Yet it does not consist in this desire as such, but rather in the fact that the desire counts in favor of putting on a coat. After all, I might have the desire and still no reason to wear a coat, if the weather is actually quite warm. Moreover, what makes it true that the desire favors that action is not my belief that the weather is cold (as though the reason were constituted by that belief conjoined in an appropriate way with the desire). The reason to wear a coat depends in no way on my believing that it is cold. It is the fact that it is cold that gives rise to the reason. For if you learned that the weather has just turned mild, you would inform me that I really have no reason to fetch my coat, even though clearly I still believe that it is cold. A reason is the possible object of a belief and not itself a mental state.

Some philosophers maintain that the only reasons we have are those we would come to grasp were we to deliberate soundly on the basis of our present beliefs and desires. The reasons we can be said to have are always, they claim, in this sense "internal" to our existing motivations.[59] The thesis is untenable since reasons for belief and action can, and sometimes must, impress themselves on us by means other than deliberation. Even though we may be unable to make them out by reasoning from where we stand, we can come to grasp them by other means, and not just by the sort of conversion experiences where we suddenly see the world in an entirely

---

University Press, 2001) propose identifying it with the physical fact itself. This approach cannot do justice to the essentially normative character of reasons (which, oddly, Bittner himself denies) – that is, to the equivalence between "A has a reason to X" and "A ought to X." Whence my claim that reasons are neither psychological nor physical in nature.

[58] The classic statement of this view is Donald Davidson, "Actions, Reasons, and Causes" (1963), reprinted in his collection, *Essays on Actions and Events* (Oxford: Oxford University Press, 1980), pp. 3–19.

[59] Bernard Williams, "Internal and External Reasons," in *Moral Luck* (Cambridge: Cambridge University Press, 1981), pp. 101–113. See, Chapter 3, §3, of the present book.

new light. There is the more ordinary process of training, and it is no doubt by being coached and disciplined by others, rather than by deliberating, that we learn to appreciate the value of certain basic ways of comporting ourselves. That is indeed the case with morality. Throughout this chapter, I have argued that we cannot reason ourselves into the moral point of view from the outside, and so to that extent I am an "externalist." However, externalism here amounts to what ought really to be a platitude. It is not by deliberation, but instead by training, that we come to see in other people's good a reason for action on our part (though once we have acquired a sense of the moral point of view, moral reasons will count as "internal").

But let us return to the topic at hand. As I indicated in Chapter 3 (§3), "internal" reasons – despite what the term may suggest – are not anything "in" the mind. When we conclude that our present convictions give us a reason to believe this or to do that, we do not think we have discovered a fact about our own psychology. For the reason does not derive from our having those convictions, but from what those convictions are about. Just as it is the evidence itself, and not our believing it, that justifies us in accepting a scientific theory, so it is the cold, and not our belief in it, that gives us a reason to wear a coat. And note again that the reasons cannot be the physical facts themselves, but rather their relation to our possibilities, their counting in favor of a certain conclusion. For we may lack reason to proceed as we do, despite the truth of the grounds we cite, if the facts they adduce do not really support our decision.

Another distinction sometimes drawn is between "motivating" reasons, invoked to explain a person's action, and "normative" reasons, whose role would be to justify it – between the reasons that moved him to wear a coat and the reasons that might have warranted wearing one.[60] And so it might seem that motivating reasons at least are psychological states of the agent, for how else could they cause him to act? Yet there are not really two different kinds of reasons. When we talk about the reasons for a person's acting as he does as though they were psychological states, we are employing a bit of shorthand. We are referring, strictly speaking, to his regarding certain things as reasons since in such cases only this attitude of his, and not the actual existence of those reasons, is relevant to the sort of explanation we seek. But the reasons he believes there to be (not necessarily by way of explicit or reflective belief, of course) are the reasons that appear to him to justify what he does. So-called motivational reasons, understood as psychological states, are therefore a person's view of the normative reasons he has. And in some cases, there actually being such reasons, independent of his psychology, plays a vital role in the sort of

---

[60] See, for example, Michael Smith, *The Moral Problem* (Oxford: Blackwell, 1994), pp. 94ff.

explanation we seek for his action – as when we want to find out whether he did the right thing for the right reason.

It is, then, their essentially normative character that stands in the way of identifying reasons with any physical or psychological facts, and it follows that they can form no real part of the world as naturalistically conceived. I am not alone in this view. The naturalistic metaphysics I oppose generally thinks the same. The Kantian theory of autonomy sets out from precisely this premise, as it then goes on to declare – and here is where we part ways – that reasons must therefore enter the world from without, being no more than the significance that we ourselves bestow, in the light of our self-imposed principles, on the value-neutral facts of experience. Kant was not the first to head down this path. The idea that reasons are of our own authorship is as old as the triumph of the naturalistic worldview in the seventeenth century. It appears already in germ, for example, in Pufendorf's thesis that

the way in which moral entities are produced can scarcely be better expressed than by the word *imposition*. For they do not arise out of the intrinsic nature of the physical properties of things, but they are superadded, at the will of intelligent entities, to things already existent and physically complete.[61]

And its appeal extends today well beyond the Kantian tradition. It inspires the many versions of contemporary "expressivism" that construe normative judgments (having the form "A has a reason to X"), not as statements aiming to describe correctly the reasons there are, but as simply the expression of one's preference that people, oneself included, conduct themselves in certain ways even should they wish not to do so.[62]

This conception has no basis for limiting itself to morality alone. If it applies to moral reasons, it must also apply, not just to reasons for action more generally, but to reasons of every sort, including reasons for belief. Pufendorf did not grasp this implication, holding that God was "entitled" as creator to institute the basic rules of moral right and wrong. But Kant certainly did. And present-day expressivists usually appear willing to admit it as well.[63] They tend, however, to make things easier for themselves by focusing nonetheless on morality alone. For though we may perhaps convince

---

[61] Samuel Pufendorf, *De jure naturae et gentium* (1688), I.1.iv.

[62] This common ground comes out, for example, in Korsgaard's admission (*The Sources of Normativity*, pp. 164f) that her Kantianism is fundamentally of a piece with Pufendorf's view that all moral distinctions derive from a legislator, and in the considerable sympathy shown by Allan Gibbard, whose book *Wise Choices, Apt Feelings* (Cambridge, MA: Harvard University Press, 1990) is the best exemplar of expressivism, with Korsgaard's view of moral reasoning (see his review essay, "Morality as Consistency in Living," *Ethics* 110 (1999), pp. 140–164).

[63] I am thinking here, not just of Gibbard, but also of Simon Blackburn, as in his book *Ruling Passions* (Oxford: Clarendon Press, 1998), pp. 51–59.

ourselves that moral distinctions are our own creation, the conception proves far more difficult to swallow when stated in its properly universal form.

Can we really suppose, for instance, that the canons by which we judge a scientific theory to be worthy of acceptance – its fit with experimental data, its coherence with existing doctrine, its performance on severe tests – have only the authority we give them? If we hold that there is good reason to adhere to these principles, are we only expressing our endorsement of a norm to the effect that one ought to abide by them whether one happens to want to or not, which is the way that an expressivist such as Gibbard proposes to explain the difference between a principle's validity and its mere acceptance?[64] Or do we not instead endorse such a norm precisely because we believe that the principles in question are valid? Is it not the perceived validity of the principles that explains our endorsement of the norm requiring adherence to them, and not the other way around? Reasoning proceeds by being responsive to reasons, a fact whose most straightforward explanation is that reasons are a reality we discover, not an artifact of our ways of thinking. That is why stories of how reasons come to be instituted by us so often fall back in the end upon ways of talking that violate their own strictures – as happens when Korsgaard arrives at the basis of morality and finds herself obliged to invoke a reason to value humanity. Determined expressivists may succeed in avoiding such lapses, going even so far as to assure us that in claiming we all have good reason to accept expressivism they are simply expressing their conviction that we ought to do so whether we want to or not. That position may be consistent. Yet is it persuasive? What has happened to the idea that rational argument consists in pointing out to others the reasons they have to change their minds, not in merely voicing one's own convictions? No doubt philosophy is always engaged in reinterpreting our everyday understandings. Sometimes, however, the determination to hold on to a theory whatever the cost ends up twisting beyond recognition our sense of what it is to think and to act. That is what has happened with naturalism's denial of the reality of reasons.

Thus I believe we must take the other fork in the road. If reasons can form no part of the ontology of the world as naturalistically conceived, then it is the metaphysics of naturalism that needs to be rejected. Reasons, too, belong to the fabric of reality. They are not, to be sure, some sort of independent entities, hovering alongside the more down-to-earth things we see and feel. Reasons consist in a certain *relation* – the relation of *counting in favor of* – that features of the natural world, the physical and psychological facts that make it up, bear to our possibilities of thought and action. Yet relations of this sort also constitute facts – *normative facts* having to do with what we ought to believe or do, and normative facts also figure in the world, now understood more broadly as the totality of what exists.

---

[64] Gibbard, *Wise Choices, Apt Feelings*, pp. 164–166. Similarly, Blackburn, *op. cit.*, p. 67.

Reasons, being essentially normative in character, cannot be equated with anything in nature. But at the same time, they manifestly depend on the physical and psychological facts being as they are. Equally clearly, they depend on our having possibilities of thought and action. In this sense, reasons exist only because we do, too, though this does not mean that they amount to the significance we bestow upon those facts. That one thing counts in favor of another is a relation (a normative relation) that in general we discover, not establish. So while I believe this conception of reasons may rightly be called "platonistic," that term should not suggest that they dwell in some Platonic heaven, unsullied by the contingencies of the world here below. The point is that reasons have one thing important in common with Plato's Forms. They constitute an intrinsically normative order of reality, irreducible to physical or psychological fact. (Obviously, unlike the Forms they are neither paradigms nor universals.)[65]

8. RECONCEIVING THE MIND

Despite my assurances, this position will no doubt strike many as a piece of metaphysical extravagance, and calling it "platonistic" will scarcely dispel the impression. To counter such a concern, I shall sketch a view of the mind that should make more palatable this realism about reasons, a view that breaks with the different picture that has long given aid and comfort to the naturalistic conception of the world. So far, the theme has been the activity of reflection. Let us now look more broadly at the very nature of the beliefs and desires that are the stuff of the mind. Though they do not make up the whole of our mental life, they certainly stand at its center. And in their case, too, responsiveness to reasons will turn out to play the defining role.

What is a belief? It is not a feeling or the particular vivacity with which some idea presents itself to our attention. Nor is it the act of assenting to a proposition, since no such act is continually going on as we remain of a certain belief, or occurs every time we do something on its basis. Assent may be the means by which we acquire a belief, but belief itself is not a mental event. Instead, it is dispositional in nature. And yet a belief is not

---

[65] The view of reasons I am putting forward resembles the account that T. M. Scanlon presents in *What We Owe to Each Other* (Cambridge, MA: Harvard University Press, 1998), Chapter 1, and particularly "the belief interpretation of judgments about reasons" that he favors, though as should be plain, I do not think, as he does, that its metaphysical implications can be neutralized (pp. 55–64, and also his APA Presidential Address, "Metaphysics and Morals," in *Proceedings and Addresses of the American Philosophical Association*, 77 (2), November 2003, pp. 7–22). See, too, Derek Parfit, "Reasons and Motivation" (*Proceedings of the Aristotelian Society*, suppl. vol. 71 [1997], pp. 99–130), whose position is also close to the view defended here. For more on what this "platonism" involves, as well as on some of the difficulties it faces, see Chapter 3.

merely a disposition to endorse the proposition that is its object, or to behave in certain ways in various circumstances. The solubility of salt means no more than its tendency to dissolve in water at a certain rate, a capacity that specific conditions serve to actualize. But belief has a special relation, distinctive of the mind in general, to the phenomena that are, as it were, its actualization. The behavior that counts as an expression of a belief must be such that the belief would have shown the individual in question *a reason* to act as he did. There is no other basis on which to specify the effect the belief has on his behavior, in fact no other basis on which to attribute to him that very belief. In explaining a person's movement toward the refrigerator by saying he believes he will find there what he wants to eat, we are supposing that the belief makes this action appear reasonable in his eyes. If other things we knew about him would make such a belief irrelevant – if we learned, for example, that he had already eaten quite a lot – the explanation would lose its plausibility; perhaps he walked toward the appliance because it was making a strange sound. Naturally a person may act contrary to some of his beliefs; but we would have no grounds to think they were his, unless they made sense of his behavior in other regards. In short, belief is a disposition having an essentially normative dimension. If we attribute to a person certain beliefs on the assumption that they would have given him reason to act as he did, that is because belief by its nature aims at being responsive to reasons.

A similar conclusion holds for the case of desires, even if they sometimes are more like transient events than dispositions. We attribute certain desires to a person in order to render his behavior intelligible, to show how he saw reason to act as he did. Desires, too, possess this sort of normative relation to the actions they inspire, and not merely because they motivate only in conjunction with the person's beliefs, but more deeply because their very content is bound up with belief: the desire to take a walk, for example, assumes that a stroll would benefit one's health or prove pleasant in some way. In general, a desire portrays its object as a thing there is reason to want – in other words, as something that is good. Naturally a person may refuse to act on a desire, regarding it even as a sort of alien force. Nonetheless, if he has the desire, something must appear to count in favor of pursuing its object, at least in a certain respect or to a certain extent. Desires too are therefore essentially responsive to reasons, no less than beliefs. By virtue of the good they perceive in their objects, they push us to act in accord with what there appears thereby reason to do.[66]

---

[66] In company with a long tradition, I hold therefore that the object of desire always appears *sub specie boni*, and does so, moreover, not because perceived goodness is simply a projection of desire, but because desire is a response to perceived goodness, to the reasons that appear to recommend the object. Some have recently criticized this point of departure (most notably David Velleman in "The Guise of the Good," reprinted in his

Beliefs and desires can certainly be said to *represent* states of affairs as being, respectively, real or desirable. This representational aspect, however, is in the service of a prescriptive role, which is to orient our thought and action. That may seem obvious with regard to desire. Yet it is no less true in the case of belief. A belief functions as a standing directive, committing us to proceed in accord with its presumed truth, to respond to the reasons for thought and action we thereby acquire. If belief amounted merely to holding a certain fact to be true, it could not in itself dispose us to heed the reasons that fact gives us to think and act in certain ways. In principle, it would thus be possible to adopt a belief without ever intending to conduct ourselves in accord with it. Anyone operating in this fashion, however, would hardly count as believing what he says he does. In reality, beliefs represent so as to fix a basis for determining what we thereby have reason to do. Like desires, they embody *commitments*, and though we may fail (as we often do) or even refuse to follow through on them, the very fact of failure or refusal signifies that we have gone contrary to where we were otherwise headed.

It should now be clear that the view of the mind I have been sketching stands opposed to a very different model that has shaped much of modern philosophy and that does take representation to be basic. I mean, of course, the "way of ideas" that came to dominance in the seventeenth century. Many of the greatest thinkers in the past century – from Heidegger and Dewey to Rorty and Davidson – have also challenged its sway. I will not try here to situate my position with respect to theirs. My aim is to indicate why correcting the representationalist model in the way I propose should make it easier to accept a realism about reasons (a project those thinkers certainly did not share). For observe how tailor-made that model is for the naturalistic conception of the world. The mind's fundamental relation to the world is held to be one of representing, to be, as it were, a mirror of nature. Primarily, so it is said, we picture to ourselves how things are in the world, and only then determine on this basis what we will do as a result. First we are spectators, and only then agents. The notion that making out the way things are is not as such to commit ourselves to thinking and acting along certain

---

book *The Possibility of Practical Reason*, Oxford: Clarendon Press, 2000, pp. 99–122), but I find their arguments unconvincing. Certainly we may desire something we take to be bad, and even say with Milton's Satan, "Evil be thou my Good" (*Paradise Lost* IV.110). Yet we can do so only because in some respect the object also appears to us as good. Thus Satan aims his desire at evil because he regards full-scale rebellion against God's goodness as his only chance to shake off "the debt immense of endless gratitude" (IV.52) and to make himself into his own creature: "Better to reign in Hell than serve in Heaven" (I.263). It is not to blunt Satan's horns, as Velleman supposes (p. 119), to hold that he must see some good in dedicating himself to evil, even though in other respects he must – to be Satan – understand his course to be indeed evil. For his sin is his pride, a love of freedom so inordinate that he sacrifices to it every other claim on his allegiance.

lines can appear to make sense, if the way things are is held to be normatively mute. What else could reasons be if not the significance we attach to
the things we survey as they stand before our mind?

As I have suggested, the fatal error in this model is not so much the
assumption that the mind represents or frames "ideas" as the claim that
representing constitutes its core activity. Certainly desire is poorly understood if conceived as fundamentally a representation of what is desirable.
But belief too is misconceived by this model. If representing were basic,
then belief would entail no more than holding an idea to be true. Following
through on the idea's implications, however imperfectly, would have to
derive from some additional operation of the mind – from a decision, the
application of a method, or a process of habituation, as various proponents
of the representationalist model have held. Belief would not of itself dispose
us to conduct ourselves in accord with what we take to be its truth. Yet such
a view is patently wrong. Beliefs, as Peirce famously insisted, are "rules for
action."[67] If they represent, it is in order to indicate what we thereby have
reason to think and do.

Belief and desire, properly conceived, show themselves then to be in
their very essence responsive to reasons. I am not referring just to our
having perhaps reasons to believe and desire what we do.[68] I mean that
beliefs and desires are the mental states they are in virtue of how they move
us to heed the reasons they point to. We are not spectators first and agents
second. To picture the way things are is in and of itself to gear ourselves to
think and act accordingly. Every idea we have, however insignificant,
projects us along a path through, in Wilfrid Sellars' phrase, "the space of
reasons."[69] The world that forms the object of our thought and action is
a world in which from the very start some things are seen as counting in
favor of others, a world that is not normatively mute, but exhibits reasons
for this or that. The naturalistic worldview is therefore a view it looks
impossible ever really to take up. The world in modern times may have
become disenchanted, "*entzaubert*" as Max Weber famously said. Yet all that
this disenchantment can mean is that something of value, perhaps of
immeasurable value – all trace of the sacred – has disappeared from our
horizons. It cannot mean that the world has come to seem barren of every
sign as to how it is that we should proceed. After all, those who deny that

---

[67] C.S. Peirce, "How to Make Our Ideas Clear" (1878).

[68] For a fine account of how beliefs are responsive to reasons in this regard, see Joseph Raz,
"When We Are Ourselves," in *Engaging Reason* (Oxford: Oxford University Press, 1999),
pp. 5–21.

[69] Wilfrid Sellars, *Science, Perception, and Reality* (London: Routledge & Kegan Paul, 1963), p.
169. It may be objected that the propositional content of a belief, as distinct from belief in
its truth, is a mere representation. I doubt that this view is tenable. The content itself can
be determined only inferentially. See Robert Brandom, *Making It Explicit* (Cambridge, MA:
Harvard University Press, 1994), a book to which my debts in this section should be clear.

the world holds any trace of the divine presumably believe that they see good reason to embrace this conclusion.

In laying out this alternative view of the mind, I have focused on the nature of belief and desire. But my assumption has not been that all the items of our mental life fall into one or the other of these categories. The two were chosen only because of their centrality. And the choice was certainly not dictated by an adherence to the widespread notion that beliefs alone cannot move us to act, but motivate only in company with some desire. On the contrary, this so-called belief/desire theory of motivation forms another of the apparent truisms whose speciousness should now be plain. If belief is inherently responsive to reasons, then it is very far from being motivationally inert. To believe that p is in itself to be moved to comport ourselves in accord with the presumed truth of p. That is what is happening, after all, when we form conclusions on the basis of what we already believe. Being disposed to draw appropriate inferences is part of believing. To suppose that it requires in addition the desire to reason from our beliefs is to reduce belief itself to a mere holding to be true. If I believe that the cat is on the mat, am I not led by that very belief to conclude that my neighbor is mistaken when he says that it is outside on the lawn? Drawing conclusions figures among the things we do, and it is our given beliefs unaccompanied by desire that move us to do it, by virtue of indicating what else we have reason to believe.

What then about a belief that I ought not just to think but also to act in a certain way? Sometimes, to be sure, desire is essential to action, as when we act in order to get something we happen to want and the belief tells us the best way of attaining it. But consider the belief that I ought to treat my neighbor fairly. Ordinarily I do not seem to have to have as well a desire to do so, in order to act accordingly. The belief alone suffices. Expressivists will object, of course, that it is not strictly speaking a belief at all, but instead a preference on my part to act in a certain way, a preference that itself embodies a desire. A well-known argument going back to Hume has appeared to many expressivists to clinch the issue in their favor: while moral judgments do generally incline us at least to act on their basis, beliefs alone have no motivating force, and therefore moral judgments cannot really be vehicles of belief. But the second premise of that argument we now know to be false. Belief is not motivationally inert. Our beliefs can move us to decide what else to believe. Why can beliefs not also move us to decide how to act? Convictions that present themselves as beliefs, that aim like beliefs to get things right about their object, as our moral convictions do, cannot be denied the status of beliefs solely because they prove able to motivate.[70]

---

[70] Adherents of the belief/desire theory of motivation commonly invoke a difference between belief and desire with regard to "direction of fit": whereas desires aim to make things fit them, beliefs aim at fitting themselves to the way things are, which is why, they claim, belief alone cannot motivate. The supposed distinction cannot survive the spectator conception of

The truth of the matter is that beliefs move us depending on the sorts of reasons they point us to. Certainly they do so, as a rule, only in conjunction with our other commitments, but these need not involve any independent desires; they may consist entirely of other beliefs. Seeing the cat lying on the mat will move us to conclude that our neighbor is wrong (if we trust our ability to recognize the cat more than his). Seeing the boy lying injured on the mat will move us to take steps to help him (if we also believe we ought to help those in distress). But beliefs whose very object is the reasons we have to think and act in certain ways, "*normative beliefs*" we may call them – like the moral belief just mentioned ("we ought to help those in distress"), though beliefs about what counts as good evidence for a scientific theory are no different – bear their motivational force on their face. That is why partisans of the belief/desire account of motivation must be keen to deny that convictions of this sort are really beliefs at all. Their basis for doing so, however, makes a mockery of belief in general.

In reality, the notion that belief has in itself no effect on the will is part and parcel of that model of the mind that makes representation funda-mental and that finds a ready ally in the naturalistic picture of the world. If believing that p meant merely holding p to be true, then it would indeed not be such as to dispose us to do anything in particular, and this would seem to be all the more obvious if p itself – the content of the belief – could only be some physical or psychological fact, not anything normative in character. Our beliefs would simply display the world as it is, and the impulse to intervene in the world (or even to draw any further inferences about the way things are) would have to come from another quarter – namely, from our desires. The spectator conception of belief is patently untenable, however, and so too the account of motivation it inspires.

Once we appreciate the error involved, we will be able to explode yet another supposed truism that typifies the intellectual complex in which that account has its home, the complex formed by the representationalist view of the mind and the naturalist view of the world. I mean the con-ventional dichotomy between the theoretical and the practical attitude. In the former, it is said, we describe the world as it is, mapping it out, whereas in the latter, we determine what to do. Because reasons are essentially action-guiding, figuring out what reasons we have cannot consist in dis-covering some further fact about the way things are. Earlier (§6) we found Korsgaard making just such a claim. Now we can appreciate why it is wrong. Theory and practice are entwined from the start, in that the beliefs that represent things as they are commit us at the same time to heed the way some things count in favor of others. Normative beliefs about the

belief it epitomizes. For an extended critique of the Humean argument, see my book, *The Morals of Modernity* (Cambridge: Cambridge University Press, 1996), Chapter 5 ("Moral Knowledge").

reasons for thought and action we have only bring to the fore the interweaving of the theoretical and the practical that constitutes all our thinking. They make explicit the inseparability of figuring out how things are and determining what to do.

To consider our convictions about the reasons we have as beliefs answerable to an independent reality is not to reduce them to merely theoretical claims, as though further reasons would then be necessary to determine whether they ought to be applied in practice, a consequence that entails an infinite regress. Korsgaard raises this complaint against the realist conception of reasons, arguing that our judgments about reasons cannot therefore be fundamentally a matter of knowledge. If one supposes that reasons exist independently of the mind so that being rational consists in conforming our conduct to them, one fails to explain how reasons "get a grip" on us and can only fall back on the useless expedient of postulating some further "reason to be rational."[71] However, this objection rests on the flawed assumption that belief or knowledge has to be applied if it is to shape our conduct. All beliefs, normative or not, dispose us in and of themselves to act in accord with the reasons they point us to. They are at once theoretical in content and practical in import. The "application" of knowledge, where the term signifies that the beliefs are one thing and their utilization another, normally takes place only in special contexts, where we bring our beliefs to bear on subjects they are not directly concerned with (as when the laws of physics are applied to the building of bridges).

Reason just is our responsiveness to reasons.[72] It underlies all our beliefs and desires inasmuch as they involve being disposed, however imperfectly, to conduct ourselves in accord with the presumed truth or value of what we believe or desire. Reasons have a grip on us because our beliefs and desires do. When, therefore, we reflect and form beliefs about the reasons we have, there should be no mystery why we care about them or are moved to heed them. To believe that we have a reason to do such-and-such is to stand committed to think and act in accord with what that truth entails.

---

[71] See Korsgaard, "Realism and Constructivism in Twentieth-Century Moral Philosophy," in Robert Audi (ed.), *Philosophy in America at the Turn of the Century* (APA Centennial Supplement, *Journal of Philosophical Research*, 2003), pp. 99–122 (pp. 110ff), and "The Normativity of Instrumental Reason," in Garrett Cullity and Berys Gaut (eds.), *Ethics and Practical Reason* (Oxford: Clarendon Press, 1997), pp. 215–254 (pp. 240ff.).

[72] Korsgaard complains that "to define rationality in terms of reasons" leads to "a purely definitional account of rationality and can tell us nothing substantive about what function or power of the human mind rationality is" ("The Normativity of Instrumental Reason," p. 243). But that is not right. Capacities are understood in terms of the way they are exercised and thus in terms of their characteristic subject-matter. Rationality is the capacity to reason, and reasoning consists in responding to reasons.

Such then is, in outline, the conception of mind and world that ought to replace the naturalism and representationalism so dominant in our day. Its cogency does not rest solely on its ability to make sense of the idea that morality speaks for itself. It offers, I have urged, a better account of the shape of our experience as a whole. All the same, it does not show that there are indeed reasons to take an interest in another's good, irrespective of what our own interests may be. Recognizing that reason is best understood as a receptivity to reasons does not by itself tell us what reasons for belief and action there actually are. True, we could not enter into the moral point of view if we did not have the remarkable capacity that appears to set us off from all the other animals, the capacity that consists in being able to stand back from our own person and to see ourselves as but one among many. But it is not that this power of self-detachment provides a basis for reasoning ourselves into the moral point of view. It doesn't. Nothing does. In the end, we must simply reflect on whether our neighbor's good, quite apart from our own, has a claim on our attention.

PART III

POLITICAL PRINCIPLES

6

The Moral Basis of Political Liberalism

1. INTRODUCTION

The exchange of essays between John Rawls and Jürgen Habermas, published in 1995 by *The Journal of Philosophy*, was an important and long-awaited event.[1] The two greatest political philosophers of our time had turned to comment directly on each other's conceptions of political legitimacy and social justice, the nature of citizenship, and the goals of political argument. We learned what Rawls and Habermas each thought, rightly or wrongly, are the strengths and weaknesses of the other's philosophy. On the whole, Habermas sought to accentuate their differences, while Rawls, though noting significant disagreements, tried to underscore the common elements in their positions. I believe that in reality the two thinkers are far closer to one another than Habermas realized, but that their proximity is not of the sort that Rawls imagined. In my view, their fundamental point of convergence consists in a common failing.

Each of them aims to reconceive the core principles of liberal democracy in a "freestanding" or "autonomous" fashion, dispensing with the divisive ethical or religious underpinnings of the past and regarding them instead as having a strictly political basis in their acceptability to the citizens whom they are to bind. This project, the project of "political liberalism," is one I share.[2] Yet in pursuing it, Rawls and Habermas both lose sight of the moral assumptions that inspire this project and that therefore underlie the common ground on which the principles of liberal democracy are to rest, even when standing free from any general philosophy of man. Reasonable

---

[1] Jürgen Habermas, "Reconciliation through the Public Use of Reason: Remarks on John Rawls' Political Liberalism," pp. 109–131, and John Rawls, "Reply to Habermas," pp. 132–180, in *The Journal of Philosophy* (March 1995), XCII (3). Subsequent references to these two essays will be given in the text by page number without a preceding abbreviation.

[2] See my essay, "Political Liberalism," in *The Morals of Modernity* (Cambridge: Cambridge University Press, 1996), Chapter 6.

agreement among citizens cannot serve as the ultimate source of political authority, as both Rawls and Habermas suppose, since it draws upon a principle of respect for persons whose validity must be understood as antecedent to the democratic will.

Early in his book *Political Liberalism*, Rawls formulates his position in terms with which I have no quarrel, and since they capture well the motivations we share, I shall begin with the line of argument they embody.[3] A political conception is freestanding, he declares, if it looks only to the principles that should govern the political life of society. It does not present itself as applying to the political realm a comprehensive doctrine about the human good. Nothing, of course, prevents such a political conception from being integrated into a broader ethical, religious, or metaphysical view of the world. Indeed, Rawls believes that it cannot be fully justified unless it forms a common part or "overlapping consensus" of the different visions of the human good that figure prominently in our society. For only then can citizens see reason to endorse it given everything they happen to believe about the way they should live. But at the same time, the basic principles of political association must be such that they can be framed and legitimated without appeal to any particular comprehensive standpoint.

I agree, as I have said, that the defining ideals of liberal democracy ought to be freestanding in this sense. For liberal thought is best understood as responding to an essential ingredient of our modern self-understanding. On the fundamental questions of human life, we have come to expect that reasonable people tend naturally to disagree with one another. During the religious wars of the sixteenth and seventeenth centuries, many people came to the painful realization that even with the best will in the world they would continue to differ about the nature and demands of the true faith. Since then, this insight has widened in scope. In a free and open discussion about human flourishing and the nature of the good, it seems that the more we talk, the more we disagree (sometimes even with ourselves). On these matters, being reasonable – by which I mean thinking and conversing in good faith and applying, as best as we can, the general capacities of reason that pertain to every domain of inquiry – tends not to produce agreement but to lead to controversy. Taking this experience to heart, liberal thinkers have concluded that political association should no longer undertake to express and foster a conception of the ultimate ends of human existence. Instead, it must seek its principles in a minimal morality, which reasonable people can share despite their expectably divergent religious and ethical convictions. Only so can the political world,

---

[3] John Rawls, *Political Liberalism* (Columbia University Press: New York, 1993), p. 12. Subsequent references to this book will be given in the text, with the page number preceded by the abbreviation "PL."

governed as it must be by coercive rules, sanctioned by state power, come to more than merely the rule of force. Only so can it enjoy the sort of transparency in which citizens recognize the political principles that bind them as the expression of their own convictions.

Central though it is to modern experience, the phenomenon of reasonable disagreement is not easy to explain. It runs contrary to one of the deepest preconceptions of our philosophical tradition. Why should reason, on questions of supreme importance, work not to bring us together but instead drive us apart? Historical contingencies surely play an important role. We are the inheritors of a great many different cultural traditions and find ourselves caught up in increasingly complex forms of the division of labor, so that it is not surprising we end up diverging in our sense of what is important in life. No doubt too, the liberal practices of toleration and public debate have themselves encouraged social and cultural heterogeneity, multiplying the very circumstances to which they respond.

But we might also wonder whether reason does not naturally breed discord on difficult questions. If earlier societies often spoke with a single voice about the higher things, does not this apparent unanimity reflect the limits they placed on open discussion? Perhaps the tendency of reasonable people to differ on these matters stems from the fact, as "value pluralists" such as Isaiah Berlin have claimed, that the human good consists, not in one, but in many different ultimate ends, irreducible to any common measure, resistant to any definitive ranking, and likely to come into conflict with one another. Value pluralism is not the same thing as the expectation of reasonable disagreement, as it is itself a doctrine about the nature of the good, but it may well explain why such disagreement easily occurs.[4] And if the modern sciences display, by contrast, a striking convergence of opinion about complicated matters, perhaps this is because they subject the observation of nature to forms of reasoning that, based on controlled experiment and measurement, make agreement all the more likely – focusing, in other words, on one way of approaching nature to the exclusion of others that are also valuable but far less able to produce settled results.[5]

---

[4] On the difference between the two, see my book, *The Morals of Modernity*, Chapter 7. For the view that the truth of value pluralism serves to explain the existence of reasonable disagreement, see George Crowder, *Liberalism and Value Pluralism* (London: Continuum, 2002), and William Galston, *Liberal Pluralism* (Cambridge: Cambridge University Press, 2002).

[5] Contrary to Galston (*op. cit.* p. 47), this point, which I have made before (*The Morals of Modernity*, p. 171), does not deny that the modern natural sciences "have managed to get on the track of truth." The idea is rather that there is a plurality of values that inquiry into nature could pursue, and that science today is geared to discovering certain sorts of truths (those that allow it to be a cumulative enterprise) as opposed to others. See "History and Truth," Chapter 1, §2, in the present book.

Explaining the prevalence of reasonable disagreement about the human good is necessarily a speculative endeavor, and we do not need to have a satisfactory explanation in order to recognize the phenomenon and expect that it will endure. Indeed, value pluralism is itself the sort of philosophical view about which reasonable people are bound to be divided. It may well be correct (I count myself among its adherents), but certainly many religious and philosophical doctrines, having their own plausibility, will continue to oppose it, seeing the human good as fundamentally a matter of a single and ultimate end, such as serving God, exercising reason, or enjoying pleasure. If liberalism's hope is to devise a form of political life that people can find grounds to endorse despite doctrinal differences of this sort, then it would do well not to make value pluralism one of its cardinal premises.[6]

However, realizing this hope is not an easy matter. On the contrary, the liberal ideal requires that the very notion of political order be reconceived. Political institutions have always aimed at restraining the struggle for advantage and the violence of emotion in order to achieve a common good. In the past, however, this common good was typically understood as involving a comprehensive vision of human purposes, a vision that belonged to a society's most treasured knowledge, interpreted and propagated by a clerisy (often a priestly class) and sanctioned by state authority. As the appreciation of reasonable disagreement has grown, the fundamental tasks of politics have come to appear more complex. No longer are interest and passion alone the chief objects of concern, for the proliferation of reasonable views of the good life constitutes a political problem in its own right. Though people may be looking to their own interest or may be carried away by the passions of conviction when they wish to impose on others their conception of the good, they may also be moved by the disinterested desire to see their fellows live in the light of the truth they themselves have come to love. It has become a distinctively modern question to ask on what basis reasonable people, divided by the things they hold most dear, can nonetheless live together in political community. Now the common good must be understood as a way of life that makes possible the pursuit of different and conflicting conceptions of human flourishing.

It is important to note that in referring as I have to "reasonableness," I do not mean what Rawls himself did by this term. He generally meant by it the

---

[6] Crowder (op. cit. p. 170) claims that since "value pluralism is the best explanation for reasonable disagreement about the good...reasonable disagreement therefore presupposes value pluralism." But this is not so at all. Recognizing the existence of a phenomenon does not entail having to accept a certain explanation of it, even if that explanation is the best available, since there may be various doubts about its own truth or coherence, as is certainly the case with the doctrine of value pluralism. We should not always make "the inference to the best explanation." Despite Galston's and Crowder's arguments, I therefore continue to hold, as I argued in *The Morals of Modernity* (Chapter 7), that liberalism should not base itself on the controversial doctrine of value pluralism.

moral commitment to seek and to abide by fair principles of cooperation, particularly in view of the extent to which people tend naturally to disagree in their comprehensive conceptions of human flourishing; thus he distinguished the "reasonable" from the "rational," the latter designating the intelligent pursuit of one's own ends, apart from considerations of fairness (PL, pp. 48–58). Throughout this chapter as in previous writings,[7] I use the term more abstractly, to mean the free and open exercise of the basic capacities of reason. "Reasonable" people according to my usage are therefore "rational," though they may also be "reasonable" in Rawls' sense if they are concerned to reason about how best to be fair (though their commitment to fairness will not follow from being reasonable alone, a point to which I return in §9). It follows that "reasonableness" for Rawls denotes a moral response to the predicament, the profusion of differing views about the human good, that arises as a result of the more inclusive disposition I call being "reasonable."

In itself, this difference is merely terminological. I do not deny that only in virtue of certain moral commitments can liberalism give the weight it does to what I have called the "phenomenon of reasonable disagreement." On the contrary, such is the very theme I pursue in this chapter. Yet it must also be said that they do not come through very distinctly in the use of so broad a term as "reasonableness" (whence the different meaning I have given it). Nor is it therefore accidental that Rawls, as I contend, fails to grasp the real nature and import of the moral assumptions that drive his project. To have an inkling of their significance, one need only consider the following.

Political liberalism requires focusing on what reasonable people can still share, despite their differences about the makeup of the human good. But surely we would badly misunderstand its nature if we supposed its guiding principles to consist simply in whatever might turn out to be common ground among reasonable people otherwise divided by their convictions. More fundamental than the political principles on which they will agree is the very commitment to organize political life along these lines, to seek principles that can be the object of reasonable agreement. This commitment forms the moral core of liberal thought, and it embodies, I believe, a principle of respect for persons.[8] Such is the main result I want to

---

[7] See *The Morals of Modernity*, Chapters 6 and 7.

[8] Despite its philosophical salience, this moral commitment does not, I should add, provide a sufficient basis for a liberal political order. It cannot explain why people who hold this commitment should think of themselves as "a people," bound together in a common political destiny that distinguishes them from others. At the same time, this further and more particular element in their self-understanding need not embody some distinctive, substantial conception of the human good. It can consist – as in modern liberal democracies it typically does – in a shared historical experience, particularly the memory of past conflicts that were fueled by the effort to impose faiths or other comprehensive ideals on one another. I cannot pursue this important point here, but for a bit more detail, see my *Morals of Modernity*, pp. 141–144.

establish as I look at the famous exchange between Rawls and Habermas and at the central question of their debate: what exactly is involved in the demand that political association have a freestanding basis, independent of the ongoing disputes about the nature of the human good?

2. CLASSICAL AND POLITICAL LIBERALISM

First, however, some historical background. We need to keep in mind the reasons why this question has come to have so great an importance for liberal thought today.

From John Locke's time to our own, liberal thinkers have often presented their political philosophy in terms of a full-scale individualism, urging a critical detachment toward inherited forms of belief and cultural traditions. This is not surprising. Individualism has formed a pervasive current in our culture. It grows out of basic features of modern society, particularly the market institutions of a capitalist economy. It has also drawn upon the sense that reasonable disagreement is an ever-present possibility, as people have concluded that they must therefore work out for themselves their conception of the human good. And so it has seemed to comprise as well the basis on which the terms of our collective existence should be defined. Such was the approach taken by the classical liberalism of Locke, Immanuel Kant, and J. S. Mill, who argued that the principles of political life should forego appeal to ideals of the good so as thereby to express the individualist spirit that ought to shape the whole of our lives. Classical liberals differed, of course, in important ways concerning the precise nature of the individualism they embraced. But they agreed on the fundamental idea that our allegiance to any substantial view of the good – to any concrete way of life involving a specific structure of purposes, significances, and activities (such as a life shaped by certain cultural traditions, or devoted to a particular religion) – should always be contingent and revisable on reflection. Such forms of life can be truly valuable, they believed, only if we understand them as ones we choose, or would choose, from a position of critical reflection. And, most importantly, they were at one in defending their political principles within the framework of this general philosophy of individualism. Our status as political subjects or citizens should be independent of whatever view of the human good we affirm, because in that way political principles respect – as Locke, Kant, and Mill would have said – the fallibilist, autonomous, or experimental attitude that we as persons should maintain at the deepest level of our self-understanding.

Things have not stayed so simple, however. Individualist views have themselves become an object of reasonable disagreement. Especially in the wake of the Romantic movement, there has arisen a new sense of the significance of belonging, an appreciation of tradition to which the premium that individualism places upon critical reflection appears to embody a kind of moral blindness.[9] In reality, a distanced and questioning attitude toward inherited ways is one value among others. To give it supreme authority may therefore block recognition of much else that is also of value. Thus it has been held that we can share in the good that some ways of life offer only if we do not think of our allegiance to them as elective, as a matter of decision, but regard it instead as constitutive of what we hold to be valuable, as rooted in a feeling of belonging. The importance of common customs, ties of place and language, and religious faith can lie in their shaping the very understanding of value on the basis of which we make the choices that we do. At the very least, is it not difficult to imagine our deepest moral commitments as ones we choose or would choose to affirm as the result of critically examining their merits? To stand back in reflection from them is tantamount to occupying a point of view in which we must lack the necessary resources for any sort of moral deliberation.[10] Ought they not to be understood, therefore, as the inherited basis of our moral thinking, rather than as objects of choice themselves?

The praise of belonging, though often presenting its critique of individualism as an opposition to the Enlightenment, does not really involve a reversion to pre-modern modes of thought. The forms of life with which it encourages identification were seldom tradition-minded themselves, seeking instead their legitimation in some transcendent source such as the voice of Reason or the will of God. Paradoxical as it may sound, traditionalism is a modern innovation, and for that reason we can expect it to prove an abiding feature of our culture. Today, despite the enormous influence they continue to wield, individualist modes of thought have become eminently controversial. No doubt they have always been contested, but now their philosophical difficulties are open to view. However we settle to our own satisfaction the merits of individualism and the sense of tradition as conceptions of the good and the right, we cannot deny that on this question reasonable people continue to disagree.

Here, then, liberalism faces a new challenge. Should it keep its classical commitment to an individualist view of life? Or, taking instead its bearings from that modern experience of reasonable disagreement to which it has been a response, should it seek a reformulation of its self-understanding that can accommodate both sides to this new area of controversy? The second

---

[9] For a more detailed account of this Romantic theme, see my book, *The Romantic Legacy* (Columbia University Press: New York, 1996), Chapter 2, as well as *The Morals of Modernity*, pp. 127–134.

[10] The point was already made by the great skeptic, Pierre Bayle, at the end of the seventeenth century, in something like a proleptic critique of the Enlightenment. See "Takiddin," Remarque A, in his *Dictionnaire historique et critique*, as well as my article, "Pierre Bayle," in M. Canto-Sperber (ed.), *Dictionnaire d' éthique et de philosophie morale* (Paris: PUF, 1996), pp. 133–137.

path is the one pursued by political liberalism, as both Rawls and I understand it. The aim is to fix the principles of political association in terms independent, not just of religious convictions and substantive notions of the good life, but of comprehensive moral conceptions as well to the extent that, espousing individualist ideals or rejecting them, they have become an object of reasonable disagreement in their own right. So understood, political liberalism does not represent a radical departure from the motivations of its classical forebears. The underlying continuity is the focus on the disharmony of reason, and the differences stem from experience, as we have learned how pervasive this phenomenon actually is. There may not therefore be much of a puzzle as to why political liberalism did not emerge earlier. It took the Romantic critique of individualism and its absorption into our culture to make plain how controversial reasonable people can find the overall moral vision to which classical liberalism has appealed.[11]

3. POLITICAL LEGITIMACY AND MORAL RESPECT

Historical experience provides the impetus for liberalism to shed its individualist philosophy of man. Nonetheless, in assuming the form of what Rawls called a freestanding political conception, liberal doctrine is heeding more than just the widening scope of reasonable disagreement. As I have maintained, it must also be drawing upon certain moral convictions, which imply that this is the proper route to take. After all, we may intelligibly ask why liberalism's response to this controversy should be a reformulation of its principles. Why should liberalism become "political" in the sense that Rawls and I intend? Why should liberal thinkers not instead dig in their heels and, observing correctly that no political conception can accommodate every point of view, maintain that liberalism stands or falls with a general commitment to individualism? The answer must be that the essential convictions of liberal thought lie at a more fundamental moral level. So it needs to be made plain what these convictions are.

Rawls once remarked that liberalism seeks the form of a freestanding political ideal because it "applies the principle of toleration to philosophy itself." His point was that, since its goal is a conception of justice to which reasonable people can agree, this conception must "be, as far as possible, independent of the opposing and conflicting philosophical and religious doctrines that citizens affirm" (PL, pp. 9–10). In other words, the reason why liberalism must abandon its classical appeal to an overall individualism and become a strictly political doctrine is that basic political principles should be suitably acceptable to those whom they are to bind. This idea Rawls came to call "*the liberal principle of legitimacy*": "Our exercise of political power is fully

---

[11] In giving such weight to this historical perspective, I may differ from Rawls, who found puzzling the late development of political liberalism. See his "Reply to Habermas," p. 133n.

proper," he explained, "only when it is exercised in accordance with a constitution the essentials of which all citizens as free and equal may reasonably be expected to endorse in the light of principles and ideals acceptable to their common human reason" (PL, p. 137; see, too, pp. 139–140, 143, 217, 225–226). This principle (subject to some refinement) does give voice, I agree, to the abiding moral heart of liberal thought.[12] Yet I do not think that Rawls brought out as clearly as he ought to have the nature of this moral foundation and the precise position it occupies in political liberalism.

To see better what the liberal principle of legitimacy involves, let us ask why we believe, if we do, that the fundamental terms of political life should be the object of reasonable agreement. In fact, answering this question will prove essential to determining what reasonable agreement should mean in this context. Do we accept the liberal principle of legitimacy because we think that, in general, people are bound only by moral rules they could not reasonably reject?[13] Whether ultimately correct or not, this view of morality as a whole is far too controversial for the present purpose. Too many good arguments seem to count against it. One might well object, for instance, that as an explanation of the grounds of moral obligation it looks circular. Can we really find reasons to accept the fundamental rules of morality that do not turn on the fact that it is simply wrong not to observe them? Is it not then their rightness that explains why they are not to be reasonably rejected, and not the reverse?[14] Moreover, views of this sort seem difficult to detach from the broader moral ideal of individual autonomy or self-determination toward which political liberalism must strive to be neutral. In any case, general conceptions of moral obligation are not, at least directly, the source of our conviction that political principles must be able to meet with the reasonable agreement of the citizens they are to govern.

That conviction reflects instead the distinctive feature of political principles that sets them apart from the other moral rules to which we may believe people are subject.[15] Moral principles fall into two groups. With

---

[12] Along with Rawls, I also believe that this principle serves chiefly to define the basic, constitutional structure of a society. Within that structure, decisions of policy can sometimes legitimately be made according to less demanding rules, such as majority-voting, in which indeed appeals to controversial ideals of the good may be appropriate.

[13] Such a conception of morality is presented by T. M. Scanlon in *What We Owe to Each Other* (Cambridge, MA: Harvard University Press, 1998).

[14] For further thoughts along these lines, see Chapter 5, "The Autonomy of Morality."

[15] Bernard Williams complained that "political philosophy is not applied moral philosophy, which is what in our culture it is often taken to be" (Williams, *In the Beginning Was the Deed*, Princeton: Princeton University Press, 2005, p. 77). I agree with the essence of this complaint, though I think it is poorly expressed. One ought rather to say that in our political thinking we should not draw on the full moral truth as we see it. We need instead to focus on what distinguishes the political realm from the other areas of social life – namely, the public exercise of power (as Williams went on to say). Nonetheless, we must at the same time ask ourselves what moral principles ought to regulate the use of coercion.

some we believe people can be rightly forced to comply, but others we do not regard as valid objects of enforcement, whatever disapproval or even outrage we may feel when they are violated. The first group alone has the status of political principles. For an association is political insofar as it relies upon what it claims to be the legitimate use of force to secure compliance with its rules.[16] It is this coercive character of political principles that we have in mind when we hold with the assurance that we do, and whatever our allegiance to the general ideal of judging people only by rules they could find acceptable, that such principles must be the object of reasonable agreement. Our belief is that only so can the use of force to implement these principles be justified. This, incidentally, is why political liberalism, though aiming to be a strictly political conception, does not imagine that the political domain forms a prepackaged sector of society, its boundaries marked out in advance.[17] It is we who decide what will count as "political," depending on what elements of social behavior we think should be subject to coercion.

With these last remarks Rawls himself would have concurred, for at one point he noted that the liberal idea of legitimacy rests on the fact that political power is coercive power (PL, p. 139). However, our analysis of this core liberal commitment must go deeper still. We need to make clear why it is that the validity of coercive principles should depend upon reasonable agreement.

I believe that the source of this conviction is a principle of *respect for persons*. Let me explain.[18] Observe first that the use or threat of force cannot be deemed wrong in itself, for then political association would be impossible. What we must regard as improper is to seek compliance by force alone, without requiring reasonable agreement about the rules to be enforced. Now an essential feature of persons is that they are beings capable of thinking and acting on the basis of reasons.[19] If we try to bring

[16] Here I follow Max Weber, *Wirtschaft und Gesellschaft* (Tübingen: Mohr, 1972), I.1. §17 (p. 29).

[17] Habermas makes this criticism of Rawls' political liberalism, wrongly it seems to me, in "Reconciliation through the Public Use of Reason," p. 129.

[18] Here I rely on the argument laid out in *The Morals of Modernity*, pp. 136–141. In insisting on the foundational role of equal respect in a liberal political philosophy, I am obviously much indebted to the writings of Ronald Dworkin, who has consistently argued a similar point ever since his article of 1973 on Rawls' *A Theory of Justice* (reprinted as Chapter 6, "Justice and Rights," in his *Taking Rights Seriously* (Cambridge, MA: Harvard University Press, 1978). I have tried, however, to be more specific than he about exactly what sense of "respect" is involved, connecting it in particular with the fact that political principles are essentially coercive in character.

[19] This feature is a necessary, though not a sufficient, condition for being a person. I agree with Harry Frankfurt ("Freedom of the Will and the Concept of the Person," in his book, *The Importance of What We Care About*, Cambridge: Cambridge University Press, 1988, pp. 11–25) that to be a person also requires being able to take second-order evaluative attitudes toward our beliefs and desires. And yet, exercising this capacity for reflection itself involves

about conformity to a rule of conduct solely by the threat of force, we will be treating persons merely as means, as objects of coercion, and not also as ends, engaging directly their distinctive capacity as persons. True, they cannot be moved by threats except by seeing good reason to fear what we may do if they do not comply. But we will be appealing to their ability to act on reasons simply in order to achieve the goals of compliance – the establishment of public order, perhaps also the reformation of people's character. We will not be engaging their distinctive capacity as persons in the same way we engage our own, making the acceptability of the principle depend on their reason just as we believe it draws upon our own. Thus, to respect others as persons in their own right when coercion is at stake is to require that political principles be as justifiable to them as they presumably are to us.

This is certainly not the only sense that the notion of respect can be given.[20] Nor is it all that we might understand by respect in a comprehensive moral theory. But it is the principle that stands at the basis of a liberal conception of political life. Though it obviously owes a lot to Kant's views about respect and treating persons as ends, never merely as means, it has a more specific scope (namely, the institution of coercive principles) and avoids the many peculiarities of Kantian ethics as a whole.

4. RAWLS' AMBIGUITIES

Liberalism, conceived as a strictly political doctrine, rests then on this moral foundation of respect for persons. I will formulate the principle of equal respect more carefully over the course of this section, but one crucial point should already be clear. Political liberalism forms a freestanding conception in regard to comprehensive moral visions of the human good, but it cannot coherently claim to be freestanding in relation to morality altogether. In particular, we would be wrong to suppose that the principle of respect has the political significance it does because reasonable people share a commitment to it. On the contrary, the idea of respect is what directs us to seek the principles of our political life in the area of reasonable agreement. Respect for persons lies at the heart of political liberalism, not because looking for common ground we find it there, but because it is what impels us to look for common ground at all.

---

responding to reasons, since otherwise such evaluation can make no sense. For some more detail, see my book, *Les pratiques du moi* (Paris: PUF, 2004), pp. 135–137.

[20] Thus, as William Galston points out (*Liberal Purposes*, Cambridge: Cambridge University Press, 1991, p. 109), we respect a person in a different sense when explaining to him fully our reasons for the principle by which we judge his conduct, whether or not he can appreciate those reasons. I do not mean to settle what respect "really" means, for it really means a great many different things. My concern is with what it ought to mean when figuring at the foundations of liberal thought.

From this there follows a very important result. As citizens of a political association organized in accord with the liberal principle of legitimacy, we cannot regard the norm of respect as having the same sort of validity as the constitutional principles by which we live. Those principles are legitimate in virtue of being the object of reasonable agreement, and thus their authority is taken to derive from our collective will as citizens. Or at least this is how they are viewed for political purposes (for when we refer to our global visions of the good, we may also attribute to them a deeper justification). But even in our capacity simply as citizens, relying solely on the commitments we share as members of a political community, we cannot take this view of the principle of respect. It must instead be understood as having a deeper kind of validity. Certainly it is a political principle, since its requirement that the terms of political life be reasonably acceptable to all is itself something to be enforced. But unlike the other political principles it serves to ground, it does not count as valid by virtue of being an object of reasonable consensus. Respect for persons must be considered as a norm binding on us independent of our will as citizens, enjoying a moral authority that we have not fashioned ourselves. For only on its basis can we account for why we are moved to give our political existence the consensual shape it is meant to have.

It is at this point that the inadequacies of Rawls' understanding of political liberalism come clearly into view. From the beginning, Rawls showed great reluctance to focus explicitly on the principle of respect that lies at the basis of liberal thought. In the final pages of *A Theory of Justice*, he argued that the notion of respect, meaning so many different things, is not "a suitable basis for arriving at" liberal principles of justice; its relevant meaning must instead be fixed by those principles themselves.[21] That is true. Yet it does not alter the fact that respect for persons, once circumscribed in this way (as I have indeed done), forms the basis for making sense of why those principles must be binding on us. There is, after all, a distinction between the order of knowledge and the order of explanation, as when we use observable phenomena to determine the nature of microscopic particles, which are then regarded as explaining the occurrence of those very phenomena. And so in the case of political liberalism, we may have to rely on givens such as the liberal idea of legitimacy to determine the appropriate sense of "respect." But the principle thus delimited forms nonetheless the moral foundation of the doctrine as a whole – a foundation whose authority must be understood as antecedent to the collective will of the citizens.

Skirting any close discussion of the principle of respect, Rawls never clearly acknowledged the special status it must enjoy. To be sure, he thought of his political liberalism as a "moral conception" (PL, p. 11n). In holding

---

[21] Rawls, *A Theory of Justice* (Cambridge, MA: Harvard University Press, 1971), p. 586.

that liberal principles should be formulated as a strictly political conception, he did not mean to suggest any contrast between the political and the moral, as though liberal doctrine did not form a normative conception, as it manifestly does, consisting in certain ideals, standards, and values. But was he willing to admit that, as citizens reasoning from the standpoint of this political conception, we must acknowledge a moral authority higher than the political principles we give ourselves?

No unambiguous answer is available. About the liberal principle of legitimacy, Rawls said that it has the same basis as his two principles of justice: it would be chosen in what he called the "original position," being indeed bound up in those very two principles (PL, pp. 137n, 225–6). In other words, he seemed to regard that principle of legitimacy as one whose validity, at least from the political point of view, depends on our collective will as citizens, whereas I have been arguing for just the opposite conclusion. And yet Rawls also noted that the original position, which is but a device for representing the basis on which we understand ourselves as choosing or imposing on ourselves political principles, incorporates certain values in the conditions under which such a choice is to be imagined taking place, values that are thus not themselves the object of choice (for example, PL, p. 103). Though we do not, Rawls stipulated, imagine the parties choosing in the original position as endowed with any moral sensibility (they are merely "rational," engaged in the efficient pursuit of their ends), the fact that we place certain conditions on their choice – they are to be supposed ignorant of their own talents or conception of the good life, for example – reflects a moral commitment of our own – namely, a commitment to what he called "reasonableness," the readiness to seek fair principles of cooperation (PL, p. 305). Political principles apparently have then a moral basis that we cannot conceive as rooted like them in our political will. Moreover, Rawls described this moral commitment of reasonableness as embodying the resolve to propose political norms justifiable to all (PL, pp. 49, 50). But this brings us right back to the liberal principle of legitimacy. That principle therefore cannot have the same status as the two principles of justice. And, as it expresses in effect the idea of respect for persons, Rawls ought then to have agreed that this idea must have for citizens a moral authority independent of their political will.

Yet Rawls never said so explicitly. On the contrary, his stated view was that because of its freestanding character political liberalism is "doctrinally autonomous" (PL, pp. 98–99). At least in our role as citizens, if not according to our comprehensive views, we are to regard our political principles as deriving their validity from our political will. These principles cannot, he held, be understood as "moral requirements externally imposed" (PL, p. 98). This phrase might mean more than one thing, however. If it means that basic political principles are not to be imposed upon a citizenry by some external agency – by an enlightened monarch, for example – then I agree.[22] But if instead it means that citizens should not regard their political principles as drawing upon moral requirements whose validity is external to their collective will, then I believe that here Rawls went wrong. Political liberalism makes sense only in the light of an acknowledgement of such a higher moral authority.

In fact, the idea of respect plays this foundational role in several ways. It forms, as we have seen, the basis for believing that political principles should be the object of reasonable agreement. But, in addition, it serves to define the very nature of the agreement to be sought. To explain, I observe that consensus in this case is clearly a normative notion if only because it refers to reasonable instead of simply actual assent. Political life is to be based on principles that citizens, despite their various moral, religious, and metaphysical beliefs, can see reason to accept, exercising (as I have said) the basic capacities of reason applicable to any domain of inquiry.[23] But reasonableness (so understood) is not the sole standard governing the sort of consensus in question. Because the idea of respect directs us to look for common ground in the first place, it should be understood as a further condition that acceptable principles must satisfy. In other words, the terms of political association are to be judged by reference to what citizens would accept, were they reasonable as well as committed to the principle of equal respect for persons. The basic terms need not be rationally acceptable to everyone given his present thinking, certainly not to bandits or religious fanatics, for instance. No political conception can fail to exclude some. From the liberal point of view, the basic rules of political life must be justifiable to people willing to comport themselves rationally and fairly. (We may say that they must be justifiable to bandits and fanatics, too, on the assumption that such persons were different enough from what they are actually like to be reasonable and committed to respecting others.) The notion of agreement to which political liberalism appeals is therefore an idealization. It comes into play only within the bounds set by these two norms – the one epistemic, the other moral.

Nothing in this conclusion departs from Rawls' own deepest commitments. Indeed, his liberal principle of legitimacy ties consensus to precisely the two norms just mentioned, when it refers to what citizens in the light of "their common human reason" may be "reasonably expected to endorse." (Recall that his notion of the reasonable – unlike mine – has a moral content that effectively implies the principle of respect.) Yet he

---

[22] In this connection, see Rawls, "Reply to Habermas," pp. 162–163.

[23] The reasonable so understood does not entail uncritical deference to common sense and to the formal fallacies of reasoning it may harbor. Contrary to Gerald Gaus (*Justificatory Liberalism*, New York/Oxford: Oxford University Press, 1996, pp. 3–5, 131–136), political liberalism as I conceive it (or, I believe, as Rawls did as well) is not "populist" in this sense.

unfortunately failed to make as clear as he should have the moral foundations of this idea of consensus.[24]

Let me then formulate as precisely as possible the moral principle of respect for persons that lies at the basis of political liberalism: the basic rules of political association, being coercive in nature, ought to be such that all citizens who are to be subject to them must be able to see reason to endorse them, on the assumption (perhaps counterfactual) that they are committed to basing political association on rules that can meet with the rational agreement of all.

5. WHAT HABERMAS AND RAWLS SHARE

Jürgen Habermas, too, has aimed to develop a self-standing or, as he says, "autonomous" conception of the guiding principles of modern democracy. The most systematic exposition of his theory appears in the book *Faktizität und Geltung*, translated into English as *Between Facts and Norms*.[25] There, Habermas carefully distinguishes his democratic ideal from communitarian claims to the effect that today, as in the past, our political life needs to orient itself around a common vision of the human good. In this regard, he shares the outlook of political liberalism. But he also rejects what he calls the liberal idea that individual rights set limits to the exercise of democratic self-rule. Liberal thinkers err, Habermas believes, in holding political association accountable to moral norms supposedly given in advance, since they thereby fail to heed the intellectual conditions of our time. In an age where religious and metaphysical worldviews have lost their authority, we can have reason to consider ourselves subject to political principles only if we are able at the same time to see ourselves as the authors of these principles:

> Without religious or metaphysical support, the coercive law designed for legal behavior can preserve its socially integrative force only insofar as the *addressees* (*Adressaten*) of legal norms may at the same time understand themselves, in their collectivity, as the rational *authors* (*Urheber*) of those norms. (BFN, p. 33; FG, pp. 51–52)

In Habermas' view, this kind of collective autonomy (to be distinguished, obviously, from the ideal of individual autonomy, though the two are structurally similar) constitutes the source of the basic norms shaping

---

[24] For more on how the principle of equal respect for persons structures implicitly Rawls' political thought, see Chapter 8.

[25] Jürgen Habermas, *Faktizität und Geltung: Beiträge zur Diskurstheorie des Rechts und des demokratischen Rechtsstaates* (Suhrkamp: Frankfurt, 1992), p. 13; English translation by William Rehg: *Between Facts and Norms* (Cambridge, MA: MIT Press, 1996), p. xlii. Subsequent references to this work will be given in the text, with "FG" preceding the page in the German original and "BFN" the corresponding page in the translation. In quotations, I have changed the English translation as I saw fit.

political association. We miss the true character of the principles of modern democracy, he claims, if we adhere to the "classical" or premodern notion of a normative hierarchy whose pinnacle is occupied by independent moral principles to which political association must defer (FG, p. 137; BFN, p. 106, 449). By subordinating democratic self-rule to an ensemble of individual rights, liberal thought continues to rely on this outdated "natural law" model. We must be resolutely modern, recognizing that political principles have their basis only in the autonomous will of citizens who are the full authors of the rules that bind them.

Habermas often describes his position as one in which fundamental individual rights, no longer serving to check democratic self-rule, turn out to be "co-original" (*gleichursprünglich*) with it (FG, pp. 135, 155, 161; BFN, pp. 104, 122, 127). In other words, the modern and ancient ideals of liberty, as those two principles have come to be called (since Benjamin Constant's famous essay), are not so heterogeneous in their basis or thus so liable to conflict as commonly supposed.[26] Sometimes he appears to mean by this claim that the two mutually support one another. Just as self-government can serve to protect individual rights, so these rights themselves provide the necessary means for the exercise of popular sovereignty – the right to free expression, for example, making available the wide range of information and points of view which are essential to wise political decisions (FG, pp. 155, 161; BFN, pp. 122, 127–128).

But, in introducing the idea of "co-originality," Habermas has clearly a deeper point in mind as well. It is that the two principles have a common origin, and that source turns out to be none other than the idea of autonomy by which a political community is to give itself shape. As a result, and despite his talk of mutual implication, Habermas unmistakably makes democratic self-rule, in its essence (the addressees of the law must at the same time be understood as its authors) if not in its particular institutional forms, a principle prior in status to that of individual rights. The claim that rights and self-rule are "co-original" is therefore misleading, given what is assumed to be the only plausible origin of political norms in the modern age. In reality, popular sovereignty functions for Habermas as the ultimate basis on which our political life should be organized, and thus as the true source of individual rights, their ultimate justification lying in the way they embody the principle of self-rule (cf. FG, pp. 134–135; BFN, p. 104).[27] His reason is plain: only so can we escape what he sees as the outmoded hierarchical model according to which the principles of political

---

[26] See Jürgen Habermas, *Die Einbeziehung des Anderen* (Frankfurt: Suhrkamp, 1996), p. 298, and B. Constant, "De la liberté des modernes comparée à celle des anciens," in *De la liberté chez les modernes* (Paris: Livre de Poche, 1980), pp. 493–515.

[27] Habermas continues today to hold this position. See, most recently, Habermas, *Zwischen Naturalismus und Religion* (Frankfurt: Suhrkamp, 2005), pp. 85–86.

association draw upon independently given moral norms. (I come back to the details of Habermas' argument in §8.)

A striking similarity thus emerges between Habermas' conception of "autonomy" and Rawls' demand that political principles be "freestanding." Indeed, as I have remarked, Rawls called his freestanding political conception "doctrinally autonomous" and explained this term in much the same way. A political conception is autonomous, he wrote, if "the political values of justice and public reason (expressed by their principles) are not simply represented as moral requirements externally imposed" (PL, p. 98). In their companion essays in *The Journal of Philosophy*, both philosophers underscored this common view (pp. 127, 150).

But it is also obvious that Habermas' idea of political autonomy is the very notion I have criticized in my discussion of Rawls. Political association, so we have seen him claim, must not be understood as drawing its principles from a moral source superior to its collective will. Yet this conception fares no better in his hands than it does in Rawls'. Habermas, too, misses the moral basis that supports the democratic ideal of self-rule. To make clear where precisely his mistake lies, I shall first look at some points of dispute between the two philosophers, since in their debate they both noted important differences in their handling of this common idea. Rawls rejected the manner in which Habermas arrives at his conception of political autonomy. Habermas, in turn, charged that Rawls strayed from a consistent development of such a conception. Understanding these points of divergence will put us in a better position to see why, contrary to them both, modern democracy rests upon independent moral foundations.

6. METAPHYSICS AND POLITICS

As Rawls observed (pp. 135–138), political autonomy in Habermas' eyes stems from a broader philosophical position described as "*post-metaphysical*." In our time, Habermas declares, metaphysical theories asserting the existence of entities that are neither physical nor psychological in nature ("ideal entities," he calls them), as well as religious conceptions that see the world as the work of God and the vehicle of providence, have lost their plausibility. His point is not simply that they no longer hold sway over society as a whole, having become the object of apparently unending controversy. For Habermas, the age of metaphysical and religious worldviews is over in the deeper sense that, properly speaking, rational belief in their truth is no longer possible. Reason itself, he believes, now presents itself as essentially finite, fallible, procedural, and oriented toward intersubjective agreement. It consists in thinking or acting on the basis of reasons we take to be valid, not because we imagine them to be guaranteed by an objective order of the world, but because we suppose that they would command the assent of others under appropriately ideal conditions. We are to locate the norms of reason, no longer in an ideal realm independent of us, but instead in the idealizations we necessarily make in speaking with one another.[28] A battery of philosophical arguments, assembled under the title of "*discourse theory*," is meant to bring out the necessity of this post-metaphysical shift in our conception of reason and to explain the idealized form of discussion (*Diskurs*) to which reason thus refers.

For Habermas, the idea of political autonomy derives from this general philosophical standpoint. We are to establish the terms of political association by applying the general account of reason just summarized to the fundamental task of politics, which is to determine the scope of the rule of law. Once reason can invoke no higher authority than agreement under ideal conditions, the principles of conduct that are to bind us, in the political realm as elsewhere, must be such that we can see ourselves to be their source, their authors. That is the meaning of the passage I quoted at the beginning of §5.

From this approach, Rawls took his distance, and rightly so. It has the significant disadvantage that it appeals to a comprehensive vision of man's place in the world and the nature of reason's authority. Habermas' post-metaphysical point of view shares, as Rawls noted, the ambition of Hegel's logic in providing "a philosophical analysis of the presuppositions of rational discourse . . . which includes within itself all the allegedly substantial elements of religious and metaphysical doctrines" (p. 137). These doctrines will scarcely recognize, much less accept, the form into which they are thus translated, for it is one in which, as Habermas remarks, "worldviews are measured more by the authenticity of the life styles they shape than by the truth of the statements they admit" (p. 126). His idea of post-metaphysical reason can therefore be expected to provoke controversies of precisely the sort that we must look beyond, so Rawls insisted (and I agree), if we are to discover acceptable terms of political association. After all, the notion of ideal discussion to which Habermas appeals is far from self-explanatory, and the transcendent interpretation he favors, defining ideal conditions as he does by reference, not to the ("local") standards of belief we currently have reason to espouse, but to the best standards we ever could have (FG, pp. 30–31, 36, 202, 566; BFN, pp. 15, 20, 163–164), is neither the only possibility nor one likely to strike many people as itself anything short of metaphysical.

In point of fact, the vitality or obsolescence of metaphysical and religious worldviews is an issue on which reasonable people tend naturally to

---

[28] There is a succinct and lucid account of this line of thought in FG, pp. 24–37; BFN, pp. 9–21. See also Habermas, *Nachmetaphysisches Denken* (Frankfurt: Suhrkamp, 1988). In recent years, he has been concerned to distinguish "post-metaphysical" thought, not just from religious views and metaphysical theories postulating an objective rational order in the world, but also from reductionistic forms of scientific naturalism, which deny the reality of our ability to think and act on the basis of reasons. See Habermas, *Zwischen Naturalismus und Religion*.

disagree. True, none of these conceptions can today prove to be authoritative for society as a whole. Yet to go further and say, as Habermas does,
that they can no longer figure as objects of rational belief, but only as life
styles, means adopting a position that itself is party to these disputes.
Habermas has misidentified the feature of modern experience that is
crucially relevant to the basis of political association. The decisive element
is not the waning of metaphysical and religious worldviews (though that
has occurred). It is instead the recognition that such worldviews, as well as
the recurrent post-metaphysical efforts to make do without them, have
shown themselves to be enduringly controversial.

Indeed, it seems to me that Habermas' conception of post-metaphysical
reason goes wrong in two important respects.[29] First, our conception of the
world must have room for ideal entities, for only if there exist such things as
reasons (which are themselves neither physical nor psychological in
character), can there be such a thing as normative knowledge – knowledge
of how we ought to act, but also more fundamentally knowledge of how we
ought to think. Second, the notion of ideal discussion cannot really form
a substantial part of the theory of justified belief. We may say, if we wish, that
justified beliefs are ones to which we assume that all would agree in an
"ideal" discussion. Yet ideal conditions of this sort, if we can attach any
effective meaning to them, must be understood as embodying our best
standards of warranted belief, and so we might as well say, more directly,
that the beliefs are justified if they satisfy these standards. True, Habermas'
account of justified belief typically invokes the notion of ideal discussion in
a way that resists such elimination, insofar as he imagines it transcending
any reliance on our current standards of justification. But, as a result, it loses
all discernible content.

I want to emphasize, however, that the main point in the present context is not whether Habermas' conception of reason is correct, but
whether it can serve as an appropriate basis for establishing the terms of
our political life. These two questions must be distinguished, once we are
convinced that political association turns crucially on finding principles
reasonable people can accept despite their disagreements about the fundamental questions of human existence. In seeking a solution to this
political problem, we cannot call upon all that we ourselves may reasonably
believe to be true about such matters. Habermas gives little attention to
the difference between these two perspectives. That, no doubt, is why he
runs them together. The result is an account of the foundations of political
life that, whatever its interest, and whatever the ultimate validity of the

---

[29] I have developed this critique of Habermas at some length in "Der Zwang des besseren
Arguments," in L. Wingert and K. Günther (eds.), *Die Öffentlichkeit der Vernunft und die Vernunft
der Öffentlichkeit. Festschrift für Jürgen Habermas* (Frankfurt: Suhrkamp, 2001), pp. 106–125. For
an exposition of the thesis underlying the first criticism, see, Chapters 3 and 5.

conception of reason on which it relies, is destined to remain an object of reasonable disagreement. In this regard, Habermas' political theory falls short of what is needed.

7. HABERMAS' IDEAL OF POLITICAL AUTONOMY

Habermas himself located elsewhere the crucial difference between himself and Rawls with regard to the notion of political autonomy. In his view, Rawls failed to adhere consistently to the idea, since his theory of justice maintains the liberal assumption of individual rights existing prior to democratic self-rule and delimiting its scope. This backsliding, he charged in *The Journal of Philosophy* exchange, arises from the "two-stage character of his theory" (p. 128). While Rawls' idea of the original position, in which rational parties choose principles of justice, captures something like collective autonomy, it is used to justify a model of the just society in which "liberal rights...constrain democratic self-legislation" (pp. 128–129). Citizens will then be unable to "reignite the radical democratic embers of the original position in the civic life of their society" (p. 128).

Behind this objection there may lie, as Rawls suspected (p. 160), some sympathy with the quixotic idea (once famously voiced by Thomas Jefferson) that every generation should give itself its own constitution, unfettered by the past decisions of those now dead. But I believe that the gist of Habermas' complaint has little to do with a call for permanent revolution. It concerns instead the understanding we should have of the basis of our political association. His view is that citizens must be able to see all their political principles, even those establishing individual rights, as rooted in their autonomous political will. Such a self-understanding is blocked by a conception that gives these rights, as he believes Rawls' theory does, a status prior to the democratic process. This is the point at which, so he claims, liberalism and his own theory of radical democracy part ways.

How convincing is Habermas' criticism? I think that what he termed an "inconsistency" is really what I have called an "ambiguity." Habermas objected that Rawls failed to carry through consistently an autonomous or freestanding conception of political life. But another way to put the point would be to say, as I have argued, that Rawls' idea of a freestanding political conception was ambiguous. Sometimes he denied, and sometimes he effectively admitted, that his strictly political doctrine rests on a moral principle of equal respect. To the extent that he acknowledged the foundational role of this principle (and as I noted in §4, it shapes the original position itself), his understanding of a freestanding political conception did not correspond to Habermas' notion of autonomy, which excludes this sort of normative hierarchy. In any case, it is clear that Habermas and I appraise quite differently the tensions at work in Rawls' thought.

But there is a further complication. Habermas' own political theory does not hold consistently to the conditions he assigns to the notion of autonomy. In fact, his conception of political autonomy makes sense only on the assumption that self-rule rests on an underlying, moral norm of respect. Nor is that astonishing. For only if it draws on such a moral basis can popular sovereignty take the form of a democratic ideal we would want to prize. Moreover, this moral foundation involves, contrary to Habermas' stated intention, an idea of individual rights that precedes and defines the exercise of self-rule. In the end, therefore, the sharp opposition he constructs between liberalism and his own conception of radical democracy, and thus the criticism he makes of Rawls, lose their rationale. Habermas, I believe, misunderstands himself. It is to developing these points that I now turn.

To begin, let us examine more closely the way Habermas understands political autonomy. In explaining how the autonomy characteristic of modern democracy must proceed without relying upon any antecedent moral norms, Habermas appeals to what he calls "*discourse principle D*":

Just those action norms are valid to which all possibly affected persons could agree as participants in rational discourses (*Diskursen*). (BFN, p. 107; FG, p. 138)

Democracy has its basis in the collective autonomy of its citizens, Habermas declares, because in determining the principles by which they will govern themselves, they defer to no pre-given norms other than just this principle D. "Nothing is given prior to (*vorgegeben*) the citizens' practice of self-determination (*Selbstbestimmungspraxis*) other than the discourse principle" (BFN, pp. 127–128; FG, p. 161). In contrast to liberal theories, which appeal to antecedent moral norms (in the form of individual rights) in order to limit the scope of self-rule, radical democracy, as Habermas conceives it, looks to no higher authority than its own self-legislative activity as governed by principle D. Rights guaranteeing individual freedoms (such as speech and assembly) have their basis, he claims, in the application of the principle to the very form of a legal system, whereas the rights of political participation serve to make possible the institutionalization of this sort of self-rule (FG, pp. 154–162; BFN, pp. 121–128).[30]

Now, my concern lies, not with the details of this "logical genesis of rights," but with the status of D itself. It is crucial for Habermas' conception of radical democracy, as he makes clear (FG, p. 138; BFN, p. 107), that principle D possess no moral content of its own.[31] Morality and democracy, he holds, involve distinct and equally basic applications of principle D, the difference consisting in whether the principle is to shape the interactions between human beings as such or is to take a legal form binding for

---

[30] See also Habermas, *Die Einbeziehung des Anderen*, pp. 299–301.

[31] As Habermas observes (FG, p. 140; BFN, p. 108), this thesis of *Faktizität und Geltung* represents a departure from his earlier writings. I think it was a wrong move.

a specific political community. Certainly there is a significant overlap between the norms thus generated in these two domains. But in Habermas' view, this does not change the fact that the terms of political life find their justification solely in the autonomous will of the citizens, as expressed according to principle D, and not in any moral principles that citizens must recognize as setting limits to their will.

This is the point, however, where Habermas displays an incomplete understanding of his very devotion to democratic self-rule. Observe that the idea of popular sovereignty may itself take different forms, depending on how the popular will is supposedly determined and given authoritative expression. Even modern dictatorships, since unlike pre-modern monarchies they disclaim dynastic or divine legitimacy, are a phenomenon of the democratic age: they too draw their authority from the will of the people, as they choose to understand it.[32] When conceived as heeding a principle such as D, popular sovereignty assumes a form that is recognizable precisely by its moral character, for all that Habermas may protest to the contrary. In his view, D has "normative" content without constituting a moral principle (FG, p. 138; BFN, p. 107). Yet surely that is a feeble distinction. D has unmistakably moral content, and we can bring it to light by asking the simple question: Why should we believe, as this principle requires, that norms of action must be rationally acceptable to all whom they are to bind? Whence the authority of principle D itself?

8. DEMOCRACY AND LIBERALISM

Habermas himself never provides an adequate answer to this question. He suggests that such a principle is inevitable once we realize that in our age metaphysical and religious conceptions, characteristically inclined to invoke principles of conduct of which we are not the source, have lost their rational warrant. But this response will not work on a variety of counts. As I have already indicated, it is rash to imagine that reason today stands uncontroversially opposed to belief in the truth of metaphysical or religious worldviews. A more accurate diagnosis of our situation is that such visions can no longer enjoy reasonable agreement within society as a whole. We might well take this fact to entail that metaphysical and religious conceptions should not figure among the principles that bind us together politically. But note that such a conclusion is valid, only if we already accept some principle such as D; it cannot serve to justify that principle. Observe further that if we refuse a political role to metaphysical and religious worldviews on some other grounds – because, for example,

---

[32] This point was rightly made, however disingenuously for his own purposes, by Carl Schmitt, *The Crisis of Parliamentary Democracy* (Cambridge, MA: MIT Press, 1985), p. 28. (German original: *Die geistesgeschichtliche Lage des heutigen Parlamentarismus*, 1923 and 1926).

we believe, as Habermas does, that they can no longer be rationally held to be true – we will not thereby have reason to adopt principle D. Why should we not suppose that without appeal to such ultimate truths the problem of political association is insoluble? Or why should we not organize our political life around some principle other than D, such as the maximization of the general welfare?

Sometimes Habermas claims that the principle enjoys a privileged status because it inheres in the very idea of discussing with others the norms to which our actions should conform, such discussion forming the only resource on which we can all draw in an age of controversy.[33] This suggestion continues Habermas' longstanding interest in basing morality on a "universal pragmatics." I doubt, however, that so much can be gotten for so little. D is too substantial a principle, precisely because of its significant moral content, to be implicit in the mere idea of practical discussion.

A good way to see this is to reflect that, taken as a general principle applicable to every domain of our dealings with others, D is not even obviously correct. Of course, the very meaning of D is obscure so long as the notion of "rational discourse" is left unexplained, and Habermas' own wish to understand that notion in abstraction from any specific standards of belief does not help. But however we explicate the idea of rational agreement, principle D in its general form faces the sort of objection I mentioned in §3. That is, many people may hold that we should not judge others by rules that on due consideration they would not themselves accept, but many, too, believe the opposite. They are convinced that certain fundamental norms of conduct, possessing an objective validity, can serve as a basis for judging others, whether or not they meet with their assent. I myself subscribe to this latter view. But what should be clear is that the general (that is, domain-unspecific) validity of a principle such as D is a matter on which reasonable people can disagree. And equally plain is the fact that this disagreement turns on different moral convictions about the conditions under which we may judge others morally and no doubt too on different appreciations of the moral ideal of individual autonomy. This suffices to show that contrary to Habermas D, taken as a general principle, has a moral content and a controversial one at that.

But let us go further and look at D in the specifically political role it is supposed to play. Recall a point made earlier. Norms of conduct are of two kinds – norms we invoke solely to judge the conduct of others and norms we believe should be backed up by the threat and use of force to ensure compliance. So let us consider principle D as applied simply to norms of the second kind – that is, to *political* principles. Now its complexion is rather different. It need not be rejected by someone who believes that in

---

[33] Habermas, *Die Einbeziehung des Anderen*, pp. 58–59.

some areas of life we may rightly judge others by reference to norms they do not themselves see reason to accept. It requires only that the principles of our political life, by nature coercive, be rationally transparent to those whom they are to bind. In this limited, political form, D thus amounts to the conviction that Rawls called the "*liberal principle of legitimacy.*" Yet now we see that Habermas cannot rightly regard D as independent of any antecedent moral commitments. For, as I have argued, the liberal principle of legitimacy embodies a moral principle of respect for persons. This moral foundation is what gives D the political authority it enjoys. Habermas' conception of democracy fails then to be autonomous in the absolute way he desires. The idea that political association should be organized around some principle such as D rests on a prior allegiance to the moral principle of equal respect.

The sort of normative hierarchy that Habermas dismisses as pre-modern shapes in fact his own thinking. Self-government, so far as it admits only those political principles on which all can reasonably agree, draws upon an independent moral basis.[34] We cannot regard respect for one another as just one more political principle among others whose validity derives from our political will. On the contrary, this principle justifies the ideal of self-government and defines for us what it means. Reasonable agreement must in this context be understood (as I argued in §4) as circumscribed by the moral principle of respect. Comprehensive moral views of the ends of human existence being eminently controversial, our political life cannot seek its basis in them. About this point Habermas is right. But we cannot suppose, as he does, that our political life should be similarly freestanding or autonomous with regard to morality altogether. Citizens can understand themselves as the collective author of their political principles only if they see themselves as already bound by the demands of respect for persons.

This moral principle refers, moreover, to an individual right, even if one more fundamental than the political rights that usually figure among explicit constitutional guarantees. Every person has the right, it claims, to be bound only by political principles whose justification he can rationally accept.[35] As a result, Habermas' position comes down to one in which, contrary to his own account, an individual right sets limits to democratic self-rule, determining as it does the sort of expression of the popular will that shall count as democratic. The familiar constitutional rights of free-expression, property, and political participation, though no doubt serving to secure the goal of democratic self-rule, also have an independent

---

[34] This, I would say, is the abiding truth in the idea of "natural law."

[35] This fundamental right one can nicely formulate in German as the *Recht auf Rechtfertigung* ("the right to justification"). See Rainer Forst, *Das Recht auf Rechtfertigung* (Frankfurt: Suhrkamp, 2007).

rationale. They draw upon that most fundamental of individual rights, which is the right to equal respect.[36]

In the Postscript to the English translation of *Faktizität und Geltung*, Habermas has replied to an earlier version of this criticism.[37] To understand the normative basis of modern democracy, he argues, we must distinguish "the horizontal sociation of citizens," in which they constitute their collective will and in so doing mutually accord rights to one another, from the subsequent step, in which they set up rights to protect individuals from the political power so constituted. Therefore, individual rights against the state "are not *originary* but rather emerge from a transformation of individual liberties that were at first *reciprocally* granted" (BFN, p. 457) – that is, established in the very formation of their collective will.

I am not sure how neatly these two steps can be distinguished from one another, but I shall let that go. My concern lies with the first step. Observe that Habermas himself describes the "horizontal sociation," which he holds to be foundational, as a process in which citizens "recognizing one another as equals, mutually accord rights to one another" (*ibid.*). Whence, I ask, comes their recognition of one another as equals? As Habermas' very words imply, this is not a commitment they acquire in virtue of such association, but rather one that defines the sort of association they understand themselves to be forming. This commitment amounts in fact to precisely what I have been calling the "principle of respect." And that principle embodies an individual right – a right requiring that the terms of political association to be developed be as transparent to one's own reason as to that of others. Such a right does not arise through being mutually granted by citizens as they form their collective will. It has an independent authority that individuals must acknowledge if they are to form a democratic will in the way Habermas envisions.

I see no reason, therefore, to change my conclusion that Habermas' notion of radical democracy is not really so radical that it differs materially from the idea of liberal democracy to which he imagines himself opposed. Failing to note the moral basis of his own commitment to democratic self-rule, he misses the fact that he too assumes, if only implicitly, the antecedent validity of individual rights.

---

[36] Another way to put this criticism would be to say that Habermas' "logical genesis of rights," aiming to derive individual rights from the application of principle D to the idea of a legal system, is *circular*: D itself embodies a fundamental individual right. Some adherents of Habermas' approach endorse this circularity as a virtue (for example, Ingeborg Maus, "Popular Sovereignty and Liberal Rights," pp. 89–128 in R. von Schomberg and K. Baynes, eds., *Discourse and Democracy*, Albany: SUNY Press, 2002). I do not believe that the cause of clarity is thereby advanced.

[37] I first presented this criticism in a review of *Faktizität und Geltung*, "Die Wurzeln radikaler Demokratie," *Deutsche Zeitschrift für Philosophie* 41 (1993), pp. 321–7. I developed it further in Chapter 10 of *Morals of Modernity*.

9. FREEDOM AND MORALITY

Modern democracy is government by self-rule, animated by the ideal that the basic rules of political life are legitimate only if those whom they are to bind can all reasonably endorse them. But we misunderstand the nature of the democratic ideal, I have insisted, if we suppose that for it the collective will of the citizens constitutes the ultimate source of authority. Looking more closely at the notion of the collective will employed, we see that it is conceived in moral terms. Popular sovereignty can be understood as manifesting itself through reasonable agreement, only if it is assumed to be heeding the obligation of respect for persons. Democracy is thus a moral conception, and not just in the trivial sense that the principles and values by which a democratic people organize their political life are recognizably moral in character. More profoundly, democracy involves commitment to a moral principle that citizens must see as binding on them independently of their democratic will. Respect for persons is what gives their democratic will the normative shape it has.

I have claimed that Habermas misses this moral basis of modern democracy and that Rawls, too, though recognizing it in part, failed to bring it out as distinctly as he should have done.[38] My point, as I hope is plain, is not to reject the project of working out a conception of liberal democracy that is politically freestanding. That project I share. But its moral presuppositions need to be made explicit. Why, we may ask, should there be such reluctance to admit these assumptions? One reason is not far to seek. Liberal thinkers who continue to sympathize with earlier individualist versions of liberal democracy do not hesitate to expound the moral foundations of this ideal as they see them.[39] But both Habermas and Rawls, in their different ways, aim to work out a political conception that does not depend upon comprehensive moral views, especially individualist ones, about the ends of life. In the effort to devise a political conception that is thus freestanding, it is only too easy to slide over the moral commitments that propel this very enterprise.

True, the principle of respect does not express or entail a comprehensive moral philosophy. It has its place in a great many otherwise disparate ideas of the human good. Particularly significant is the fact that it can

---

[38] Because Rawls did not bring out clearly enough the role of the principle of respect, Habermas could charge (wrongly) that he made the reasonable agreement or "overlapping consensus" standing at the heart of a liberal political order depend simply on a fortuitous convergence among citizens' different conceptions of the human good. (See Habermas, *Die Einbeziehung des Anderen*, pp. 105–111.) Habermas is right that citizens need to have a normative standpoint they can endorse in common, though, as I have explained, I do not believe he has identified it properly.

[39] This is how Jeremy Waldron proceeds in *Liberal Rights* (Cambridge University Press: Cambridge, 1993), pp. 56–57, 163–168.

figure in those conceptions (see §2) that refuse to accord supreme value to critical reflection and call instead upon forms of moral allegiance that are rooted in a sentiment of belonging. We may feel that our deepest commitments are constitutive rather than elective, fashioning our very sense of the persons we are and the choices we can understand ourselves as making, and at the same time believe that political principles, relying as they do upon coercion, must be reasonably acceptable to all whom they are to bind, even those who differ with us on the relative importance of critical reflection. There exist, of course, conceptions of the human good that reject such a principle of respect for persons. No doubt many of them also desire to limit critical reflection, preaching obedience to traditional, often religious, authorities. But these two views do not go necessarily together. In fact, individualist views too, when they exalt the will to power of creative individuals and heap contempt upon the bulk of mankind, can prove to be just as illiberal. A reverence for tradition is not inherently hostile to liberal ideals any more than the cultivation of individuality is intrinsically friendly to them.

It also therefore bears noting that reasonable people, exercising the basic capacities of reason and conversing with others in good faith, are not obliged on this basis alone to believe that the use of force should remain within the bounds of consensus. Being reasonable (in my sense of the term) does not entail the principle of respect for persons. Though the moral basis of liberal democracy stands free of any comprehensive conception of the good, its claims are not such that everyone is in a position to see reason to endorse them. In this sense, their reach cannot count as universal. The term "universal" has in fact two distinct meanings, which unfortunately are often confused with one another. Principles may be regarded as binding on everyone, independent of time and place, but *universal bindingness* does not necessarily entail *universal justifiability*: to grasp the reasons for their validity, we may have to have had a certain history and gone through certain experiences.[40] Just this, I believe, is the situation with the principle of equal respect, along with the view of political life it inspires. It has a universal validity, but there is no reason to suppose that all reasonable persons must find grounds to agree. That is why, despite my continual reference to moral foundations, nothing I have said in this chapter is "foundationalist" in an objectionable sense; there have been no appeals to the *a priori* or the rationally indubitable, but instead an acknowledgement of historical contingency.

Today, commitment to the principle of equal respect may have become so much a matter of second nature that, like Habermas and Rawls, we fail to recognize or mention it. We may simply look through it, as we reflect upon the constitutional rules a democratic people should give themselves

---

[40] For more on this distinction, see *The Morals of Modernity*, Chapter 2, §5.

to govern their political life. Or we may miss how much we continue to rely on it if instead we urge liberal thinkers to think less about laying down universal principles and more about recognizing the variety of ways in which people of different convictions can live together in a spirit of toleration.[41] Rightly recognizing that conceptions of justice, no less than ideas of the good life, are an abiding object of reasonable disagreement, we may think that legislatures should often play a greater role than judicial review as practiced by unelected courts in deciding disputed questions about individual rights. Yet even then, the moral authority that legislatures are thought to enjoy derives from the way the rule of majority-decision accords an equal respect to legislators when they vote and to citizens when they elect them.[42] In reality, equal respect defines the specific moral "we" we have come to be in the democratic world, even as we remain divided by important differences about other fundamental matters. Self-understanding, here as elsewhere, requires that we turn our mind to what lies so close to us as to go unseen. Then we can comprehend why this moral outlook, transparent though it may be to us, is not universally available and has met indeed with sincere rejection from others. For many people even today, as certainly through most of human history, a proper understanding of man's place in the world requires that the terms of political life be in the first instance pleasing to God, whether or not they are rationally acceptable to those whom they are to bind.

Yet I wonder whether there is not another reason why Habermas and Rawls do not make explicit the moral basis of their conceptions of liberal democracy. Perhaps in their case, as certainly in the case of others, another contemporary ideal has come to stand in the way of seeing our deepest commitments for what they are. In our time, freedom of self-determination, as both an individual and a collective value, enjoys a tremendous prestige. It commands so ready an allegiance that all other values can seem of subordinate importance. Individuals can be bound, it is said, only by the rules they give themselves. So, too, we continually hear that citizens, in their collective capacity as members of a political community, are to determine themselves the principles by which they will live.[43] I doubt that morality in general can

[41] As an example, see John Gray, *Two Faces of Liberalism*, New York: New Press, 2000.

[42] Thus, Jeremy Waldron, in underscoring the "dignity" of legislation and arguing that it constitutes a better response than judicial review to our enduring disagreements about the right as well as the good, finds himself obliged to acknowledge that majority rule draws in just this way on a fundamental principle of equal respect for persons. See his book, *Law and Disagreement* (Oxford: Oxford University Press, 1999), pp. 107–114.

[43] See Habermas, *Die Einbeziehung des Anderen*, p. 301: "Menschenrechte mögen moralisch noch so gut begründet werden können, sie dürfen aber einem Souverän [here, the democratic will, C.L.] nicht paternalistisch übergestülpt werden. Die Idee der rechtlichen Autonomie der Bürger verlangt ja, dass sich die Adressaten des Rechts zugleich als dessen Autoren verstehen können. Dieser Idee widerspräche es, wenn der demokratische

make much sense if its roots are sought in freedom as a supreme value.[44] I am certain, as I have argued here, that our commitment to democracy or political self-determination cannot be understood except by appeal to a higher moral authority, which is the obligation to respect one another as persons.

Verfassungsgesetzgeber die Menschenrechte als so etwas wie moralische Tatsachen schon vorfinden würde, um sie nur noch zu positivieren." (Translation: "However morally well grounded human rights may be, they ought not to be imposed paternalistically upon a sovereign [here, the democratic will, C.L.]. For the idea of the juridical autonomy of citizens requires that the addressees of the law be able to be understood at the same time as the authors of the law. It would contradict this idea if democratic constitutional legislation were to encounter human rights as a set of moral facts, which it had then simply to turn into positive law."

[44] See Chapter 5.

7

The Meanings of Political Freedom

"Give me liberty or give me death!" cried Patrick Henry. "Live free or die" declare the license plates of the state of New Hampshire. Plainly, people care a lot about freedom. It has indeed been one of the cardinal ideals of modern political thought, and not only in America. Yet what political freedom means and why it should matter are far from clear. Freedom seems to be an essentially contested concept.[1]

In this chapter, I focus on a conception of political freedom that has recently undergone a notable revival, having its roots in what is known as the "classical republican tradition." My aim is to explain its meaning and assumptions, and to show why it has proven to be so attractive a conception. But I shall not claim that it constitutes the correct account of political liberty, nor shall I reject it in the name of some alternative theory. For one of the points I want most to establish is that it is a mistake to suppose that any one conception can rightly be said to capture the true essence of individual freedom. That is because freedom is a value that we can understand only by reference to other values, and depending on what other human goods we place at the center of our attention, we will arrive at different understandings of what freedom means and why we should care about it. Following this line of argument through to the end, I shall argue that freedom should not be viewed, as it so often is, as our most fundamental political value.

Recent years have witnessed a remarkable surge of interest in classical republicanism. Among the different currents in this republican revival, the most important, I believe, traces its lineage back through Machiavelli and his *Discorsi sopra la prima deca di Tito Livio* to the political thought of ancient Rome. It has been the subject of a series of important historical studies by

---

[1] The kind of freedom discussed in this chapter is political and social freedom, having to do with a person's relations to other persons and institutions. In the first two parts of this book, I often had occasion to discuss the nature of freedom in its relation to reason. I hope one day to develop a general theory of freedom to unite these two domains in an illuminating way.

Quentin Skinner,[2] and in the Anglo-American world it has found its most ambitious theoretician in Philip Pettit. The republican model of political life has received at his hands the sort of detailed exposition it has never in fact enjoyed before. His book, *Republicanism. A Theory of Freedom and Government,* is a landmark work.[3]

Despite some areas of disagreement, Skinner and Pettit have essentially the same vision of what is of enduring importance in the republican tradition – namely, its understanding of freedom. In this conception, they are joined by two other contemporary neo-republicans, Maurizio Viroli and, in France, Jean-Fabien Spitz.[4] Though their neo-republican writings represent an invaluable contribution, they do not succeed – no single theory can, I have suggested – in defining what political freedom really means. They also go wrong in their oddly antagonistic relation to modern liberalism, for the republican principles they champion only make sense within a discernibly liberal framework. Since Pettit has been the most systematic thinker in the group, I lay out the neo-republican argument largely in the terms that he has fashioned. But at times I develop it further in my own way. This is a sign of how great, if not unlimited, is the extent of my agreement.

1. THREE CONCEPTS OF LIBERTY

At the center of the neo-republican enterprise is a conception of political liberty that Pettit and the others call "non-domination." According to this view, we are free to the extent that we do not find ourselves under the domination of others, subject to their will and thus vulnerable to how they may choose to use their power. The conception goes back to Roman law, in which a free person is one who, unlike a slave, does not find himself *in potestate domini.* But in the republican tradition of the sixteenth through eighteenth centuries, its meaning broadened into a comprehensive political ideal. "Liberty," wrote Algernon Sidney, the great republican thinker executed for treason in 1683, "solely consists in an independency upon the will of another."[5] "La liberté," wrote Rousseau, "consiste moins à faire sa volonté qu' à n' être pas soumis à celle d'autrui."[6]

---

[2] See, in particular, Skinner, *Liberty Before Liberalism* (Cambridge: Cambridge University Press, 1998).

[3] Pettit, *Republicanism. A Theory of Freedom and Government* (1st ed. published in 1997; 2nd ed. with Postscript; Cambridge: Cambridge University Press, 1999).

[4] The central statements of their views are Viroli, *Republicanism* (Italian original 1999; New York: Hill and Wang, 2002), and Spitz, *La liberté politique* (Paris: PUF, 1995).

[5] Sidney, *Discourses concerning Government* (first published 1698; ed. by T.G. West, Indianapolis: Liberty Fund, 1996), p. 17.

[6] Rousseau, *Lettres écrites de la montagne* (1764), in Rousseau, *Oeuvres complètes* (Paris: Gallimard, 1964), vol. 3, p. 841: "Liberty consists less in doing one's own will than in not being subject to the will of others."

This notion of freedom, as we may begin by noting, refers to a *condition* in which we may find ourselves – namely, the condition where we are not living under the thumb of another. It does not denote the *exercise* of a capacity, and so not in particular the control that an individual or community exercises over the shape of its own existence. Another way to put this contrast lies with the categories deployed by Isaiah Berlin in his classic essay of 1958, "Two Concepts of Liberty."[7] The idea of freedom as non-domination forms a *negative*, not a *positive* conception. In general, identifying freedom with a condition entails equating it with the absence or non-occurrence of those factors – in the present case, living at the mercy of another's will – that are regarded as significantly diminishing our possibilities. Negative conceptions say nothing about what we are to do with the possibilities at our disposal – thus nothing, for example, about how we are to live in the absence of domination. Positive conceptions, by contrast, measure freedom not by the extent of the possibilities open to us, but by the degree of self-mastery or control we effectively exercise over our actions and circumstances. We are free, they claim, to the extent that we rule ourselves, individually or collectively, shaping our lives in accord with our own best aspirations instead of being driven by forces from without.

Clearly, freedom as non-domination does not coincide with rational autonomy or democratic self-government. It refers to a condition in which we may choose to go one way or another, not to some activity by which we supposedly realize our true nature or give expression to our higher self, which are the sorts of views to which positive conceptions of freedom typically lead.[8] To be free from the domination of a master does not mean being the master of ourselves, since it is a condition we may enjoy in a variety of ways – as much by letting ourselves be carried away by passion (sometimes a good thing, but a perilous affair when living at the mercy of the powerful) as by bringing ourselves under the rule of our own reason.

It would certainly be wrong to suppose that positive conceptions of freedom have no political importance, and I shall shortly return to just this point (§§2 and 3). But they fail to capture, I could not agree more, the basic (if not the sole) dimension of what we value as freedom in this domain. The primary sense in which people are free, politically speaking, consists in the

---

[7] Reprinted in Berlin, *Four Essays on Liberty* (Oxford: Oxford University Press, 1969), pp. 118–172. I am also drawing here on the distinction Charles Taylor introduced between "opportunity-concepts" and "exercise-concepts" of freedom in his essay, "What's Wrong with Negative Liberty?" in his *Philosophical Papers* (Cambridge: Cambridge University Press, 1985), vol. II, pp. 211–229.

[8] "Autonomy" is a term with many different senses. Sometimes it denotes a condition or status – for example, an individual's ability or right to decide some matter for himself, in which case it coincides with freedom from interference or domination. The exercise-concept of autonomy to which I shall be referring reflects Kant's usage and means an individual's actually living in accord with a "law" of conduct he gives himself.

character and extent of the possibilities that lie open to them, including the choice, if they so please, to devote their lives to participating in democratic self-government or to living "autonomously" in accord with a rational plan of their own devising.[9] The freedom that consists in self-rule must draw its value from the way it safeguards this most fundamental kind of freedom.

Nonetheless, freedom as non-domination differs crucially from the understanding of negative freedom that Berlin himself advocated. In fact, one of Pettit's most important contributions lies precisely in having broadened our conceptual repertoire. Negative freedom as Berlin conceived of it is the domain of action where individuals can do as they may want without interference at the hands of others – interference itself being understood broadly to include, not just the actual preventing of a course of action (for example, by imprisonment), but also such acts of coercion as threats or the affixing of penalties that make the pursuit of a certain alternative more costly. It corresponds, so he claimed, to what Benjamin Constant (in his celebrated lecture of 1819) called "the liberty of the moderns" in contrast to "the liberty of the ancients," which meant participation in political self-rule. Whether this interpretation of Constant is correct is a question I shall return to (§4). For now, let us note that Berlin was certainly at one with thinkers such as Hobbes and Bentham in viewing individual freedom as the absence of actual obstacles. "A Free-Man," Hobbes declared, "is he, that in those things, which by his strength and wit he is able to do, is not hindered to do what he has a will to do," and Berlin explicitly endorsed this definition.[10] To be sure, Berlin cautioned that a person's freedom should not be equated with the absence of impediments *to the fulfillment of his desires*. Such a definition would too easily allow someone to increase his freedom merely by extinguishing his unsatisfied desires. The obstacles relevant for judging the extent of a person's negative liberty ought rather to be conceived as obstacles to his *possibilities*, as roadblocks standing in the way of the courses of action that he might choose to pursue.[11]

---

[9] For doubts about the worth of this latter ideal, however, see Chapter 10, "The Idea of a Life Plan."

[10] Hobbes, *Leviathan* (Harmondsworth: Penguin, 1968), Part II, ch. 21, para. 2; Berlin, *op. cit.*, p. 123, fn. 2. See also *Leviathan*, Part I, ch. 14, para. 2, where Hobbes claims that "by LIBERTY is understood, according to the proper signification of the word, the absence of external impediments." For Bentham's understanding of freedom, see his treatise *Of Laws in General* (ed. H. L. A. Hart, London: Athlone, 1970), p. 253: "Liberty then is of two or even more sorts, according to the number of quarters from whence coercion, which it is the absence of, may come." See also his letter to John Lind of 1776, quoted by Pettit in *Republicanism*, p. 44. There Bentham writes of his discovery that "the idea of liberty imported nothing in it that was positive: that it was merely a negative one: and that accordingly I defined it 'the absence of restraint.'"

[11] Berlin, *op. cit.*, p. 139. See also the Introduction in the same volume, pp. xxxviii–xxxix. John Gray puts this point well by remarking that for Berlin, in contrast to Hobbes and Bentham, negative freedom consists, not in the unobstructed pursuit of one's desire, but

Berlin did not waver, however, in defining negative freedom by reference to actual interference, even when it is our possibilities that are thereby limited. As a result, people count as free in this sense, even when others could encroach upon their choices (present or possible) and yet decide not to do so. Negative freedom, Berlin once remarked, is not compromised by a despotic regime, so long as the despot happens to be benevolent and chooses to pursue an indulgent policy toward his population. Reserving all political power to himself, such a ruler may otherwise leave his subjects a large measure of freedom to pursue their various projects as they please.[12]

Yet surely it is wrong, Pettit objects (and rightly so), to hold that people are then free, inasmuch as they pursue their projects at the mercy of a prince who, well-disposed for the moment, can always change his mind and policies. Similarly, workers are not free if, to have a job at all and earn enough to survive, they have no choice but to work for a single employer who, well-meaning though he may be, can at any time shut up shop or move his enterprise elsewhere. Freedom really entails an absence of both actual and possible interference at the hands of others.

Or, more exactly, Pettit adds, it consists in being exempt from all such *arbitrary* interference, "arbitrary" in the sense of not being responsive to the interests of those who are its object, but reflecting instead the interests of those exercising the interference.[13] For suppose that we inhabit a society governed in accord with just laws: we will not have thereby escaped interference, actual or possible, in our affairs. Even then, the state must attach penalties to certain courses of action and stand ready to punish infractions of the laws. But such conditions, involving no element of arbitrary interference, mark a qualitative difference. Just laws do not amount to the exchange of one form of domination for another, as though their purpose were to offer us a greater net balance of freedom over constraint than we would otherwise have if living under despotic rule or under no rule at all (in a "state of nature"). Domination itself has come to an end when the authority of just laws, which are responsive to the interests of all, replaces the will of particular individuals.

Freedom as the absence of domination differs therefore in two respects from any view such as Berlin's that equates negative freedom with the absence of actual obstacles.[14] On the one hand, domination can occur without any actual interference. Our freedom is abridged by the simple fact that we depend on the goodwill of others, since their power to meddle

in "the capacity for choice among ... options that is unimpeded by others." Behind Berlin's conception stands the idea of 'self-creation through choice-making.' See Gray, *Isaiah Berlin* (Princeton: Princeton University Press, 1996), pp. 15–21.

[12] Berlin, *op. cit.*, p. 129: "It is perfectly conceivable that a liberal-minded despot would allow his subjects a large measure of personal freedom."

[13] Pettit, *Republicanism*, p. 55.

[14] *Ibid*, pp. 22ff.

in our lives can be so great that, even if they choose not to exercise it, we find ourselves obliged to anticipate their possible actions, modify our plans, and curry their favor. On the other hand, not every act or threat of interference comes from a dominating power. If just laws serve to check the arbitrary will of others, their impact on our conduct and the prohibitions they impose do not amount in themselves to a reduction in our freedom. By doing away with our vulnerability, they bring into existence a realm of freedom that we would not otherwise have.

It is on this latter score that the two "negative" conceptions of freedom differ most tellingly. For Hobbes and Bentham and those who follow in their footsteps, every law as such must diminish our freedom, even if its objective is to prevent the greater loss of freedom that would ensue if it did not exist. Berlin himself made the point explicitly. "Law is always a 'fetter,'" he wrote, "even if it protects you from being bound in chains that are heavier than those of the law." Similarly, "every law seems to me to curtail *some* liberty, although it may be a means to increasing another."[15] On this view, civil freedom, the liberty we enjoy within political society, becomes the silence of the law, since all law is in itself a constraint, and liberty begins where law ends. As Hobbes wrote,

The Liberty of a Subject lyeth therefore only in those things, which in regulating their actions, the Sovereign hath praetermitted.

Or again:

Liberties ... depend on the silence of the law. In cases where the Sovereign has prescribed no rule, there the Subject hath the liberty to do, or forbeare, according to his own discretion.[16]

According to the republican conception, by contrast, law and liberty do not stand intrinsically opposed. The exact character of their relationship depends on the substance of the laws in question. To the extent that just laws deliver us from the relations of domination in which we would otherwise find ourselves, they make up freedom's condition of possibility, not its antithesis.[17] Here is the way that Machiavelli summed up the point:

Only the name of freedom is extolled by the ministers of license, who are the men of the people, and by the ministers of servitude, who are the nobles, neither of them desiring to be subject either to the laws or to men. But when it happens ... that by

---

[15] Berlin, *op. cit.*, pp. 123 (fn.), xlix (fn.).

[16] Hobbes, *Leviathan*, Part II, ch. 21, paras. 6 and 18. In the second of these passages, Hobbes is talking in fact about those "other liberties" of the subject besides that in virtue of which he may refuse without injustice to obey any explicit command of the Sovereign not to defend his own person. This latter freedom, he maintains, is the one natural freedom that can never be surrendered upon entering civil society.

[17] Pettit, *op. cit.*, p. 35; Viroli, *op. cit.*, p. 9.

the good fortune of a city there rises in it a wise, good, and powerful citizen by whom laws are ordered by which these humors of the nobles and the men of the people are quieted or restrained so that they cannot do evil, then that city can be called free.[18]

This difference between the two conceptions of negative freedom leads in turn to another in their attitudes toward the state. If every law in and of itself supposedly diminishes our freedom, then the state as the source and enforcer of the laws will always have the appearance of a threat to liberty, a necessary evil to be accepted only to prevent a greater harm. Partisans of this view who are also champions of individual freedom (in other words, Berlin rather than Hobbes) will therefore show a constant concern to *limit* the state, to keep its power within bounds so that the damage it does is outweighed by the benefits it affords. But if the law has instead the status of a precondition for freedom, so too does the state, and a prime worry can then be that the state is not *powerful enough* to curtail the relations of domination that make individual freedom impossible. Behind the republican conviction that the state is a liberating force there stands, in fact, a very plausible picture of social life: the natural course of events is such as to produce concentrations of power and deep inequalities, and only the state has the means, in the form of just laws, to free the individual from their tyranny. Individual freedom is not first and foremost a good to be secured against the incursions of government; it is no less threatened by the forces of civil society. (In this regard, the socialist tradition carried forward a central concern of republican thought.)

Law cannot, of course, aim at abolishing every relation of domination. Some ways in which people find themselves exposed to the arbitrary will of others are relatively insignificant, and the limited resources of the state need to be focused on graver injustices. Moreover, not every relationship that entails living at the mercy of another's good intentions should be considered a relation of domination. It would be wrong-headed, for instance, to think of love as a form of domination, since the vulnerability it creates is in fact a human good, making possible an intimacy and devotion without which our lives would be the poorer. So the law's target must be relations of personal dependence that are essentially harmful to those who find themselves caught up in them. And, finally, it goes without saying that the state must not acquire so much power to intervene that it becomes itself a behemoth of domination. In all these regards, we need to remember that the legal regulation of human affairs has to weigh costs along with benefits and that freedom, however conceived, is not the only good to be considered.

[18] Machiavelli, *Istorie fiorentine*, IV.1.

2. FREEDOM AND SELF-GOVERNMENT

In the light of these initial observations, it should be plain that the idea of freedom as non-domination, distinct though it is from the "positive" conception of freedom as autonomy, provides nonetheless a ready rationale for the institution of democratic self-rule.[19] Universal suffrage and the widespread participation of citizens in political life offer the best guarantee that the laws will be just, instead of serving particular interests and private concentrations of power. For those who see the essence of freedom as the absence of interference, there exists no such internal connection between liberty and democracy or self-rule. For them, as we have seen, extensive freedom may coexist with government by the few. Berlin was displaying an admirable consistency when he declared that "freedom in [my] sense is not, at any rate logically, connected with democracy or self-government."[20] He was drawing the same implication from the notion of freedom as non-interference that Hobbes did when observing in a famous passage of the *Leviathan* (directed explicitly against the republican writers of his time):

There is written on the Turrets of the city of Lucca in great characters at this day, the world LIBERTAS; yet no man can thence inferre, that a particular man has more Libertie ... there, than in Constantinople. Whether a Commonwealth be Monarchicall, or Popular, the Freedome is still the same.[21]

For Hobbes, as for Berlin, freedom depends on the absence of actual interference, whatever may be the source of the limits on conduct represented by the law.

Once freedom is understood as the absence of domination, it takes on a more intimate relation to the idea of democracy than thinkers of such an outlook would allow. Popular self-rule then appears as an indispensable means to the creation of the just laws that make for the very possibility of liberty. That was James Harrington's point, when the seventeenth-century republican writer quipped in response to the passage just quoted from Hobbes, "The mountain hath brought forth, and we have a little equivocation." Hobbes had missed, as he explained, the all-important difference between liberty "from" and liberty "by" the laws.[22]

Yet, at the same time, we need to keep in mind that such a conception does not go so far as to equate freedom with the exercise of self-government. The kind of republican theory that it inspires – Pettit calls it "neo-Roman" (not

---

[19] See Pettit, *op. cit.*, pp. 8, 183ff.
[20] Berlin, *op. cit.*, pp. 129–130.
[21] Hobbes, *Leviathan*, Part II, ch. 21, para. 8.
[22] Harrington, *The Commonwealth of Oceana (1656) and A System of Politics*, ed. J. G. A. Pocock (Cambridge: Cambridge University Press, 1992), p. 20.

least because its early-modern exponents drew so often upon Machiavelli's *Discorsi*)[23] – has therefore quite a different shape from another strand of political thought that also styles itself "republican," but that takes its bearings from a positive notion of freedom. This other version of republican thought Pettit appropriately calls "neo-Athenian," and he finds it exemplified by writers such as Hannah Arendt and Michael Sandel, the former of whom certainly liked to invoke a highly idealized view of the Greek *polis* and express an unqualified admiration for "the liberty of the ancients." Such thinkers identify freedom with self-rule because they conceive of political life, in which common purposes are discussed, decided, and acted upon, as the primary domain in which the virtues are exercised and the human good achieved.

    Other names too might be added to Pettit's list of contemporary "neo-Athenians." One would be J. G. A. Pocock, though I hasten to add that I mean, not so much Pocock the historian whose admirable book, *The Machiavellian Moment*, helped to spark the rediscovery of the republican writers of early-modern Europe, as rather Pocock in his own theorizing moments. The key text is his essay of 1981, "Virtues, Rights, and Manners." There, Pocock asserts that the republican idea of freedom was at bottom the "positive" notion of participating in the activity of self-rule since it drew on the civic-humanist conviction that "*homo* is naturally a citizen and most fully himself in a *vivere civile*."[24] During the course of the seventeenth and eighteenth centuries, Pocock argues, this republican conception was shoved aside by a "jurisprudential" paradigm that viewed freedom as merely the ability to pursue one's own affairs unimpeded by others. The language of *virtue* gave way to the language of *rights*, as the focus of attention shifted from the relations in which people stand to one another, sharing in the construction of their common life, to the relations in which they stand to things (that is, to property), secure from interference on the part of others, and conceiving on that basis their mutual dealings.

---

[23] Pettit introduced the distinction between neo-Athenian and neo-Roman versions of the republican tradition in his essay, "Reworking Sandel's Republicanism," *The Journal of Philosophy* (vol. XCV, no. 2, February 1998), pp. 73–96. Pettit's distinction corresponds closely to the one Rawls drew between "civic humanism" and "classical republicanism" (Rawls, *Political Liberalism*, New York: Columbia University Press, 1996, pp. 205–206). Like Rawls – but unlike Pettit – I do not believe that the latter stands opposed to liberal thought, properly understood; indeed, it relies essentially upon distinctively liberal principles (see §5).

[24] Pocock, *Virtue, Commerce, and History* (Cambridge: Cambridge University Press, 1985), p. 39. On pp. 40–41, he describes the republican notion of freedom in terms more apt to suggest that it meant the absence of domination, though still calling it a 'positive conception' and identifying its value with its making possible this political realization of the human good: "The republican vocabulary ... contended that *homo*, the *animale politicum*, was so constituted that his nature was completed only in a *vita activa* practiced in a *vivere civile*, and that *libertas* consisted in freedom from restraints upon the practice of such a life."

Pocock's historical thesis has an alluring simplicity, yet it is too simple to be the whole truth. The increasing importance of rights in early modern thought did not reflect solely a concern for the protection and disposability of property. On the contrary, the notion of rights – particularly those of conscience and free association – recommended itself also as a way to order directly the relations between people in light of their deep and abiding disagreements with regard to the nature of the human good. The language of fundamental rights was a modern development, not merely because it served "bourgeois" interests but also because it aimed to put an end to the Wars of Religion and provide the new basis of a common life. Not by accident, it played a significant role even in the thought of seventeenth century thinkers who, taking Machiavelli's *Discorsi* as their inspiration, must surely count as "republican," but whose republicanism differs markedly from Pocock's in that they defined liberty as not living at the mercy of another's will, and did so not least with an eye to that form of domination that springs from according some single but contested vision of the human good a favored status in the political community. Algernon Sidney is a perfect case in point.[25] Like other figures in the "neo-Athenian" current, Pocock sees in the virtues of active citizenship the essence of the human good. Whence his conviction that sharing in the exercise of self-rule represents the core meaning of freedom.

For the different pattern of republican thought that Pettit champions, the primary task of self-government is to make possible a free society, freedom itself consisting first and foremost in an individual's being able, out of the shadow of the arbitrary will of others, to pursue his good as he understands it.[26] Freedom understood as the absence of domination remains, therefore, a negative conception, referring to a condition of which citizens may make use in various ways, even if its existence depends on their also being free in a positive sense, taking part in the process of self-rule. This is a clear sign, incidentally, that the neo-Roman conception cannot really be the basis of a theoretical alternative to modern liberalism: it serves as a natural buttress to the cardinal liberal principle that holds that our standing as free and equal citizens ought to stand free from controversial ideals of the human good. But for now, I want to underscore

---

[25] See A. C. Houston, *Algernon Sidney and the Republican Heritage in England and America* (Princeton: Princeton University Press, 1991). To the extent that early modern notions of rights remained housed within theories of natural law whose fundamental concept was that of duty (rights being understood as powers to fulfill one's duties and as entitlements to be treated by others in accord with theirs), no great distance separated this current of thought from the republican devotion to civic virtue. See Knud Haakonssen, *Natural Law and Moral Philosophy: From Grotius to the Scottish Enlightenment* (Cambridge: Cambridge University Press, 1996), pp. 326–327.

[26] Skinner takes this view as well (*op. cit.* p. 74, fn. 38), as does Viroli (*op. cit*, pp. 11, 42, 49).

the fact that, for Pettit and his allies, democracy's relation to freedom is that of an essential means, not a privileged expression.

Clearly this view too must insist on the importance of participation in political life. Yet in contrast to the neo-Athenian model, it does not enthrone civic virtue as the very heart and soul of the moral life. There is accordingly no risk that the republican ideal will become (as ever since the French Revolution it has sometimes seemed) an insatiable demand for ever more "virtue" from the citizenry. Civic virtue will comprise those specific qualities that citizens must possess if the substitution of the authority of law for personal dependence is to be achieved. They need to respect the law for its own sake, instead of seeking to circumvent it or adhering to it solely out of a fear of sanctions. They should also feel moved to voice their needs and concerns in the public life of the community, since otherwise the law is likely to become an instrument of particular interests. And they must practice a constant vigilance, staying on the lookout for excessive concentrations of power, which will never cease to be a danger.[27]

These traits of character are far from spontaneous. They require fostering, and are no doubt considerably weakened today by the countless pressures encouraging a consumerist approach to social life, in which each person seeks to make the best bargain for himself instead of working with others to tame the powers, particularly economic, that set the terms for their calculations. But the key theoretical point is that civic virtue so defined is a specifically political virtue, necessary for the securing of a society without domination. Its role is to make possible the pursuit of different visions of the good life, and not to define the human good itself.

In sum, freedom from domination depends, in a way that freedom from interference does not, on there being in place specific sorts of institutions and traits of character – the rule of law, democratic self-government, civic virtue – if it is to be a reality. Yet these preconditions still leave significantly open the range of different conceptions of the good life to which citizens may devote themselves.

3. FREEDOM AND PLURALISM

The republican conception of freedom as the absence of domination has many attractive features. It would be unwise, however, to conclude that non-domination constitutes the true meaning of political freedom. A number of distinct values, none of them negligible, have each taken the name of freedom, and our concern ought to be not to settle which of them really captures its essence, but to recognize the differences between these

---

[27] On these three basic elements of civic virtue, see Pettit, *Republicanism*, pp. 246ff. and "Reworking Sandel's Republicanism," pp. 81, 87–89.

ideals, chart their motivations and interconnections, and determine the conditions under which one or the other of them may be at stake or prove to be of greater importance.

Berlin's own writings on freedom, despite their inadequacies, display just this virtue. He had no intention of arguing that negative liberty (as he understood it) forms the whole of freedom or that the conception of freedom as self-rule ought to be rejected.[28] His concerns were quite different. He did believe that though the negative idea of freedom as the absence of interference had often been invoked to license the creation of inhuman conditions, particularly in the economic realm, the misuse of the positive idea had historically gone much further and had turned that notion of freedom into a synonym of tyranny, proclaiming the individual's "higher self" to be the Nation or the Party. But his primary aim was to articulate the sort of political framework that would best accommodate his deepest theoretical conviction – namely, the "value pluralism" according to which there exists an irreducible and conflicting plurality of human goods. This doctrine shaped his thinking about freedom in two ways: not only did he prize negative liberty precisely because it enables people to pursue their diverse ideals of the good life; but liberty itself, he rightly recognized, has given rise to different yet justifiable understandings.[29]

A similarly pluralistic outlook does not inform the neo-republican discussions of freedom. Certainly, freedom from domination represents an essential value, and its contours differ significantly from those of non-interference and self-rule. There are, moreover, cogent reasons for attributing to this republican ideal a more fundamental role in our political life than the other two ideas of freedom. Democratic self-government draws its chief rationale from the need to do away with relations of domination, and ceasing to live at the mercy of powerful individuals and interests is of far greater moment than simply living unobstructed by others. None of this, however, is reason to conclude, as Pettit does, that the absence of domination constitutes the whole of freedom. The absence of interference, the ability to act as we wish, is also one of the things we rightly mean by "freedom," and its abridgement, even for the sake of a greater good, must often count as an undeniable loss. Some laws, however just they may be (one need only think of tax codes, for instance), require us to give up some of our freedom to do as we would like, which we may reasonably regret having to surrender, even if we regard them as having been

---

[28] See Berlin, *Four Essays on Liberty*, p. xlvii: "'Positive' liberty ... is a valid universal goal. I do not know why I should have been held to doubt this, or, for that matter, the further proposition, that democratic self-government is a fundamental human need, something valuable in itself, whether or not it clashes with the claims of negative liberty."

[29] Berlin, *op. cit.*, p. lviii (fn.): "I am not offering a blanket endorsement of the 'negative' concept as opposed to its 'positive' twin brother, since this would itself constitute precisely the kind of intolerant monism against which the entire argument is directed."

legitimately enacted and as being for the best. Or, again, suppose that two possible laws each equally limit the influence of powerful interests, yet diverge in how much they permit interference with the daily lives of citizens: ought we not to prefer the less intrusive one, and for the reason that the absence of interference, all other things being equal, is something of value? By arguing as he does that non-domination is the correct view of political liberty, Pettit seems committed to denying – to my mind, wrongly – that acting unimpeded by others is itself a form of freedom as well as a good in its own right, even if one of secondary importance.

Other contemporary republican theorists proceed in a similarly monistic fashion. Though Skinner differs a bit from Pettit on the nature of freedom, he too fails – one might say, for the opposite reason – to recognize that the idea of freedom is in reality the site of a number of competing human goods. In his opinion, the neo-Roman line of thought stretching from Machiavelli through the English commonwealth men of the seventeenth century measured a person's freedom by the "absence of constraint," constraint meaning (here his point of disagreement with Pettit) both interference and domination.[30] Perhaps certain writers did engage in so expansive a way of thinking. But, if so, they were not thereby deploying any single coherent notion of freedom, as Skinner appears to assume. Non-interference and non-domination give rise to contrary conceptions of freedom, which are destined to conflict, as the opposing views they imply about the relation between freedom and law suffice to show.

In a number of writings subsequent to the publication of *Republicanism*, including the 1999 postscript, Pettit has inched his way closer to recognizing that "freedom" is the name of a number of distinct values, none of them insignificant, although they may prove to be of different moment. Sometimes, for instance, he observes that interference as such constitutes a "secondary evil." Yet to the extent that he also phrases this point by saying that interference counts as a "secondary offence against freedom,"[31] he falls back into a unitary conception of freedom, just as he did in the book itself when he described the non-arbitrary interference permitted by just laws as making people, if not "unfree" (as domination does), then "non-free" all the same.[32] The truth he half-glimpses but never acknowledges is that "freedom" in this context actually denotes two different values, equally real, though of unequal importance. After all, the person who, living by another's leave, then meets with actual interference

---

[30] Skinner, *op. cit.*, pp. 82–84.

[31] Compare Pettit, *Republicanism*, pp. 301–302, and his essay, "Keeping Republican Freedom Simple," *Political Theory* 30 (3), June 2002 (pp. 339–356), pp. 342. 347.

[32] Pettit, *Republicanism*, pp. 26, 76, 94. As he also put it there, the interference that just laws may entail acts to "condition," though not to "compromise," the freedom that consists in the absence of domination. Yet how exactly do they "condition" it if not by limiting the individual's freedom (freedom as absence of interference) to do as he pleases?

from that quarter, has not only had to reckon with two blows against his freedom, but has also seen his freedom compromised in two quite different regards.

Another, very interesting sign of Pettit's lack of clarity on these matters is his repeated disclaimer of "any Rousseauesque paradox to the effect that submission to the law is a form of self-emancipation."[33] The only reason he can have to imagine that such a claim is paradoxical is that he is attending, despite himself, to the idea of freedom as non-interference. For, in reality, the supposed paradox is no paradox at all, and the feeling that it is one comes from failing to acknowledge that freedom means different things and to keep in mind the difference between them. To the extent that freedom is understood as the absence of domination, just laws form its precondition, and therefore forcing the recalcitrant individual to comply with them does indeed mean forcing him to be free – free, that is, in the sense of sharing in a system by which he, along with others, will no longer live at the mercy of the eminent and powerful. There is nothing paradoxical in Rousseau, that paradigmatic republican thinker, having said of such a person, "on le forcera d'être libre," since the notion of freedom as non-domination sometimes requires nothing less, as Rousseau himself immediately explained (*Du contrat social* I.7):

Car telle est la condition qui donnant chaque citoyen à la Patrie le garantit de toute dépendance personnelle.

Any sense of paradox comes from confusing the absence of domination with the absence of interference, as though Rousseau were supposing, incoherently indeed, that the coercion (that is, interference) involved in forcing a person to obey the law means liberating that person from coercion.[34]

Nor is there anything morally suspect in the notion that one may have to compel people to be free, so long as it is clearly understood that the sense of freedom at issue is the freedom that consists in not being subject to the arbitrary will of others, and that such compulsion does abridge a person's freedom in another and no less real sense – namely, by interfering with his ability to do as he wants. Rousseau, it is true, refused to acknowledge the latter (he called it "natural freedom") as a real good, at least in the social world, and thus he blinded himself to the costs that the pursuit of republican or "civil" freedom may well entail.[35] But once we

---

[33] Pettit, *Republicanism*, p. 302, and "Keeping Republican Freedom Simple," pp. 346ff.

[34] Viroli and Spitz, by contrast, are admirably clear about why Rousseau's famous statement involves no paradox. See Viroli, *Jean-Jacques Rousseau and the 'Well-ordered Society'* (Cambridge: Cambridge University Press, 1988), pp. 150ff, and Spitz, *La liberté politique*, pp. 139, 173f., 407ff.

[35] See Rousseau, *Du contrat social* I.8.

recognize that the ideal of freedom is essentially pluralistic, encompassing a number of different values, we will not only have avoided a dangerous inflexibility in Rousseau's thought; we will also be able to accept without misgiving that obedience to the law can be in itself one form of freedom, even if not the only one.

Why does the idea of freedom exhibit this sort of complexity? That is a large and difficult question, but I venture the following hypothesis. It is that we cannot really make sense of what we mean by political freedom except by reference to other human goods, and more than one kind of good can prove relevant.

We no doubt begin with a vague notion of individual freedom as the absence of constraint. Yet that is only a starting point. Not every psychological and social structuring of our activities can count as a constraint if the idea of freedom is to have any real content or represent anything worth having; some rules and institutions must be regarded as preconditions of freedom, not as abridgements of it. How could grammar, for instance, constitute a curtailment of our freedom, when without it intelligible speech and thought would not even be possible? A viable notion of freedom depends on distinguishing between *harmful constraints* and *enabling conditions*, and clearly such a distinction embodies some prior understanding of the human good, and one that refers to more than just freedom itself. The trouble, however, is that different values lend themselves to the drawing of such a distinction and, as a result, distinct and conflicting conceptions of freedom can emerge. If we consider the good that lies in making things our own by investing our labor in them, then laws that interfere with that activity – tax laws, for example – will seem an unwelcome constraint. If we attend instead to the good that consists in being able to look others in the eye as our equals, then a system of just laws will appear, not as a constraint, but as the very basis of our freedom. It is a mistake to assume that only one kind of good can serve to specify the range of possibilities whose absence would represent a restriction of freedom, even when our concern is to define, not freedom generally, but freedom as a political value.

True, political freedom cannot plausibly be construed as simply license, with doing anything we please, such as taking another person's possessions simply because we want them. The laws forbidding theft do not cut into the freedom we care about from a political point of view. Political freedom refers to those liberties that citizens may possess compatibly with being members of a political association and with the basic purposes that any such association must set itself, such as the protection of property. Thus, making things our own by investing our labor in them constitutes a political liberty only insofar as it respects the property rights of others. Nonetheless, one ought not to go further and argue, as Ronald Dworkin has done, that political freedom can only mean those liberties that citizens may rightfully claim to have, taking into account all that social justice requires.[36] Dworkin leans on this argument in order to maintain that liberty and equality (the latter the core concern of justice) cannot really come into conflict with one another if they are correctly understood, contrary to what pluralists such as Berlin have held. But such a position is surely wrong. Conflicts of this sort do arise, and the reason is that political freedom itself is caught up in the pluralism of values: even within the bounds of political society, other human goods matter besides justice alone, and they may yield a different way of marking out the conditions that make freedom possible, in contrast to the constraints that reduce its extent. Think, once again, of the good that consists in making things our own by investing our labor in them. Viewed from this angle, the demands of social justice will look like limits on our freedom of acquisition, even assuming a regard for the property rights of others, since tax laws apply to the wealth and income that, antecedent to taxation, are taken to be ours by law. (At the same time as we recognize this cost to our liberty, we may also, of course, endorse the justice of having thus to give up part of what we own.)

Freedom, therefore, is unintelligible except by reference to other human goods, and it takes a different shape depending on the standpoint we adopt. I have developed this point in the language of value pluralism, assuming that the goods giving rise to the different conceptions of freedom form an irreducible plurality. I think that is true. But as I observed in the previous chapter, pluralism is itself an eminently controversial doctrine, and for that reason ought not to figure among the defining principles of a liberal political order. At that fundamental level, the aim should be to focus on a core morality that reasonable people can share, despite their abiding differences on difficult issues such as the truth of pluralism. Indeed, there the cardinal value will not be freedom at all, but rather (as I explain in §5) the equal respect that citizens owe one another. Nonetheless, questions about the proper understanding of freedom are still bound to arise within such a framework, and then the conclusions of the present section will be pertinent. They can, moreover, be rephrased so as not to rely on the truth of pluralism. Even if the various human goods in terms of which political freedom can be conceived draw upon a single, ultimate source of value, the differences between the resulting conceptions will not disappear and none of them will be able to count as the only one valid. And certainly it will remain the case that freedom, however

---

[36] R. Dworkin, *Sovereign Virtue* (Cambridge, MA: Harvard University Press, 2000), Chapter 3, and particularly his direct attack on Berlin in "Do Liberal Values Conflict?" in R. Dworkin et al. (eds.), *The Legacy of Isaiah Berlin* (New York: New York Review Books, 2001), pp. 73–90. I am indebted to Bernard Williams' critique of Dworkin in "From Freedom to Liberty: The Construction of a Political Value" (B. Williams, *In the Beginning Was the Deed*, Princeton: Princeton University Press, 2005, Chapter 7), even though I do not follow his argument in every particular.

conceived, has to be understood by reference to other values. Toward the end of this chapter, I will have more to say about the moral principles that serve to shape the neo-republican idea of freedom as non-domination.

4. REPUBLICAN VS. LIBERAL

I come now to another matter of theoretical consequence on which I believe that contemporary republican thinkers – I mean Pettit, Skinner, Viroli, and Spitz – go astray. I have already noted it a number of times. It is the opposition they are all keen to proclaim between their conception of freedom and the modern liberal tradition. According to them, liberal thinkers have uniformly adhered to the principle that freedom means non-interference. "Liberalism," so Pettit writes, "has been associated over the two hundred years of its development, and in most of its influential varieties, with the negative conception of freedom as the absence of interference, and with the assumption that there is nothing inherently oppressive about some people having dominating power over others, provided they do not exercise that power and are not likely to exercise it."[37] When liberals have wanted to criticize relations of domination, such as poverty or job insecurity – social conditions in which no interference may actually take place – they have therefore had to fall back, he says, on other values such as equality or the satisfaction of basic needs. The republican conception of freedom, by contrast, is held to be of sufficient substance that it can serve all by itself as the basis of a cogent ideal of social justice. It represents, in his view, "the supreme political value."[38] In sum, Pettit presents his republicanism as a full-scale alternative to the liberal understanding of political life.

Skinner too likes to play off the republican doctrine of freedom as non-domination against an entity called "liberalism" and identified with the view of freedom as simply the absence of interference.[39] So does Spitz.[40] And though Viroli begins his own principal account by declaring his opposition to "the conventional view ... that republicanism is an alternative to liberalism," he turns out to mean merely that liberalism, once again equated with the notion of freedom as non-interference, represents an "impoverished" version of republican thought.[41] All four writers agree therefore that on the central question of freedom republican and liberal thought stand dramatically opposed.

[37] Pettit, *Republicanism*, pp. 8–9. He continues to hold to this conception of liberalism in his 1999 Postscript to the book, p. 298.
[38] *Ibid.*, pp. 80–81.
[39] Skinner, *op. cit.*, pp. x, 113.
[40] Spitz, *La liberté politique*, pp. 50f.
[41] Viroli, *op. cit.*, pp. 6, 10, 43, 61.

Despite their unanimity, I find this pattern of argument importantly mistaken for two distinct reasons. Here, as elsewhere, Pettit shows himself to be the most systematic thinker in the group, and I shall explain my dissatisfaction by reference to his account. First, it is not right to suppose that the liberal tradition displays a monolithic allegiance to the notion of freedom as non-interference. The evidence that Pettit adduces to defend this interpretive thesis is partial and misleading. But in addition, the exposition he goes on to give of his own republican theory does not really make of non-domination the supreme political value, and the source of this failure is significant. For he finds himself obliged to appeal to recognizably liberal principles in order to define the precise content of his republican conception of freedom. In the end, Pettit belongs to the very liberal tradition that he imagines he has transcended. I shall begin with the first point, reserving the second to the next section.

It is indisputable that some liberal thinkers fit the picture that Pettit draws of the liberal point of view. Isaiah Berlin is a perfect example. Distinguishing two grand conceptions of freedom, the absence of interference and autonomy, Berlin held that democratic self-government is a good only so far as it remains subordinate to a respect for individual rights. For this reason, liberalism tended to signify for him a political vision whose fundamental commitment is to the negative conception of freedom as non-interference. Nonetheless, the fact that this conception found its first detailed exposition in Hobbes' writings ought to give us pause. The Hobbesian theory of the state scarcely looks like a liberal philosophy.

Of course, one might reply that Hobbes, though no liberal himself, furnished some tools – among them an idea of freedom – that later thinkers were able to exploit in constructing a model of the open society that can properly be called "liberal." Freedom understood as the absence of interference was in fact later taken up by Bentham, who stands at the source of an important current of liberal thought. In the nineteenth century, its most eminent representative was John Stuart Mill, who argued that "the only freedom which deserves the name is that of pursuing our own good in our own way" and who therefore conceived of law, which like "all restraint, *qua* restraint, is an evil," as a necessary limit on individual freedom so that "we do not attempt to deprive others of theirs."[42] For the classical utilitarians, all law as such represents a reduction in one's freedom, even if it serves to prevent the even greater degree of interference that would occur in its absence. This idea of freedom has obviously had its followers among liberal thinkers in the twentieth century as well.

But the question is whether liberalism as a whole coincides with this line of thought. One signal difficulty is that John Locke, incontestably a founding father of the liberal tradition, took great pains in his political

---

[42] Mill, *On Liberty*, Chapter 1, paragraph 13, and Chapter 5, paragraph 4.

writings to reject the equating of law with a limit on freedom. Distinguishing sharply between "liberty" and "license,"

Although this [state of nature] be a state of Liberty, yet it is not a state of License ... The State of Nature has a Law of Nature to govern it (*Second Treatise*, §6),

Locke insisted on the role played by law in the very constitution of freedom. Such a view is, as we have seen, a corollary of the republican concern with non-domination. And Locke's asseverations in §57 of the *Second Treatise of Government* could not have been bettered by any avowedly republican theorist:

Law in its true notion is not so much the limitation as the direction of a free and intelligent agent to his proper interest ... The end of law is not to abolish or restrain, but to preserve and enlarge freedom ... Where there is no law, there is no freedom.

Pettit deals with this problem by placing Locke among the republicans.[43] But that is a desperate remedy. Something must be amiss in a definition of liberalism that accommodates Hobbes but excludes Locke. The way out of this impasse is obvious, and it is to admit that the liberal tradition is not all of a piece. On the one hand, we do often find an identification of freedom with the absence of interference, perhaps most explicitly in utilitarian thought. (In this as in other regards, Bentham and John Austin were close students of Hobbes.) Yet, on the other, a great many thinkers whom it would be hard to classify as anything but "liberal" have rejected an essential opposition between freedom and law. In their eyes, freedom seems therefore to have meant something very much like the absence of domination.

As another example, let us take Benjamin Constant and his famous evocation of "the liberty of the moderns." Pettit follows Berlin in regarding Constant as an illustrious advocate of the fundamental value of non-interference.[44] But how did Constant himself portray modern liberty? Here is what he said:

C'est le droit de *n'être soumis qu'aux lois*, de ne *pouvoir* ni être arrêté, ni détenu, ni mis à mort, ni maltraité d'aucune manière, par l'effet de la *volonté arbitraire* d'un ou de plusieurs individus.

[It is the right to be *subject only to the laws*, such that one *cannot* be arrested, detained, executed, or mistreated in any way by virtue of the *arbitrary will* of one or more individuals.][45]

---

[43] Pettit, *Republicanism*, p. 40, and "Reworking Sandel's Republicanism," pp. 84–85.

[44] Pettit, *Republicanism*, pp. 18, 27, 50; Berlin, *Four Essays on Liberty*, pp. xlvi, 124. For doubts similar to mine about whether this is a correct characterization of Constant's views, see Alain Boyer, "De l'actualité des anciens républicains," in *Cahiers de philosophie de l'Université de Caen* 34 (2000), pp. 37–58.

[45] Constant, "De la liberté des Anciens comparée à celle des Modernes," in *De la liberté chez les modernes* (Paris: Pluriel, 1980), pp. 494–495 (emphasis added). I have amended Biancamaria Fontana's translation in Constant, *Political Writings* (Cambridge: Cambridge University Press, 1988, p. 310), because unfortunately it fails to preserve the key terms I have underscored.

Freedom thus defined certainly differs from the collective exercise of sovereignty – that is, from the liberty of the ancients in Constant's terminology. But does it therefore amount to the freedom of non-interference? I have emphasized the phrases indicating that for Constant "modern liberty" consists in being subject to the *law* and not to the *arbitrary will* of another, and that its opposite is not merely actual interference in the harmful ways mentioned, but also the *possibility* of such mistreatment. The passage seems so clear an expression of the republican idea of freedom as the absence of domination that one might think it had been taken from the pages of Pettit's own book.

Naturally we cannot be sure of Constant's intention, since he did not differentiate between the two negative conceptions of freedom – absence of interference, absence of domination – and so never formally rejected the one in favor of the other. But precisely in this respect, Pettit's true achievement comes into view. He is the first to have analyzed in a systematic way the difference between these two conceptions. His work has put us in a position to appreciate some of the crucial obscurities and disagreements surrounding the notion of freedom within the liberal tradition itself. Not only ought we to recognize, as I have suggested, the existence within that tradition of two quite distinct lines of thought about freedom, one characteristic of utilitarianism, the other attuned to the unity of freedom and law, but we should also expect that single thinkers may sometimes be drawn in the one direction and sometimes in the other. A fine example is Locke himself. Though in his political writings he readily declared (like a good republican) that "freedom is not a liberty for every man to do what he lists," he seconded the Hobbesian definition in the *Essay concerning Human Understanding*: "freedom [consists] in our being able to act or not to act, according as we shall choose or will."[46] Now that the lineaments of the republican ideal of freedom are clearly in view, the proper task would therefore be to devote ourselves to a more careful articulation of liberal principles. Yet this is not, unfortunately, the spirit in which Pettit presents his republican theory of government. Instead, he has chosen to set up a grand opposition between liberal and republican thought. Understanding is not thereby advanced.

Consider, as a final example, Pettit's attempt to draw John Rawls too within the maw of his critique of liberalism. Rawls' idea of the "priority of liberty," the principle that "liberty can be restricted only for the sake of liberty," serves as Pettit's chief evidence for placing him among those who hold that we are free to the extent that we escape interference from others.[47] On Pettit's telling, that principle expresses the characteristic view of Hobbes and

---

[46] Locke, *Second Treatise* §57 and *Essay concerning Human Understanding* II.xxi.27.

[47] Rawls, *A Theory of Justice* (Cambridge, MA: Harvard University Press, 1971), pp. 244, 302; Pettit, *Republicanism*, p. 50.

Bentham, for whom law, even when just, constitutes a restriction of freedom to be accepted only because its absence would entail an even greater loss of freedom. This interpretation misses, however, the real meaning of Rawls' principle. The import of that principle is to require that liberty (or more exactly, the scheme of equal basic liberties)[48] never be compromised in order to promote some other good such as a fairer organization of the economic conditions in society. Rawls invoked the "priority of liberty" with the aim of underscoring the subordinate importance to be assigned to his second main principle of justice, "the difference principle," whose domain includes the distribution of income and wealth. Consequently, this position resembles that of Pettit himself when he argues that existing relations of domination should be tolerated only if they happen to constitute the best means for promoting non-domination overall.[49]

Pettit's argument for aligning Rawls with the Hobbesian theory of freedom is unpersuasive. That does not mean, of course, that we should abandon the idea of figuring out whether Rawls conceived of liberty as the absence of interference or as the absence of domination. Nonetheless, I believe not only that there emerges no clear-cut answer to this question, but also that we should not be surprised to come up with none. Only as a result of Pettit's own work has it become possible to formulate precisely the distinction between these two conceptions and to grasp their different implications. One might well expect that Rawls sometimes leaned toward the one, and sometimes toward the other.

In fact, just this fluctuation is what we find when looking at Rawls' writings in the light of our preceding remarks. His general definition of liberty undeniably speaks the language of non-interference:

This or that person (or persons) is free (or not free) from this or that constraint (or set of constraints) to do (or not to do) so and so.... Persons are at liberty to do something when they are free from certain constraints either to do it or not to do it and when their doing it or not doing it is protected from interference by other persons.[50]

Yet many of the things that Rawls went on to say about political liberty show an affinity with the republican conviction that freedom consists in the absence of domination. The freedom he made the object of his first

---

[48] As Rawls wisely made more explicit in his later writings, what is important from a political point of view is not liberty in the abstract, but instead that set of basic liberties that citizens require in order to develop and exercise their sense of justice and their ability to pursue a conception of the good, what he calls their two key "moral powers." See the clarification in his *Justice as Fairness: A Restatement* (Cambridge, MA: Harvard University Press, 2001), pp. 44–45. Yet even if liberty is in this way a "list-concept," there remains the question of how liberty itself is being understood.

[49] Pettit, *op. cit.*, p. 102.

[50] Rawls, *A Theory of Justice*, p. 202.

principle of justice counts as a value only to the extent that it embodies an equal freedom for all, a scheme of basic liberties that each person enjoys compatibly with a similar scheme for everyone else. Why regard equality as essential to freedom? Were non-interference the only concern, then citizens ought not to worry about some people having a more extensive set of basic liberties than theirs, provided that they themselves are able to pursue unobstructed their individual purposes. If equal liberty forms the paramount principle, the point must be that people should be free, not only from undue interference by others, but also from the unfair influence or domination of others, when such essential matters as religious conscience, association, and political voice are at stake.[51]

Another reason for thinking that Rawls did not really equate freedom with the absence of actual obstacles is his evident reluctance to regard law as in itself an abridgement of liberty. "Whether men are free," he wrote,

is determined by the rights and duties established by the major institutions of society. Liberty is a certain pattern of social forms.[52]

Note that in this statement the fundamental laws of society are described as determining whether citizens are free at all. Law is very far from appearing as an abridgement of freedom designed to prevent a still greater loss of liberty. No devotee of the Hobbesian conception of freedom could have penned those words.

But, again, my aim is not to suggest that in his heart of hearts Rawls adhered to the republican conception. A well-defined distinction between the two views of freedom was not available when he wrote *A Theory of Justice* or *Political Liberalism*. Nothing impelled him to take a stand one way or the other. Here then lies Pettit's real contribution. His work forces us to be more explicit than before about what we mean when we say that freedom is "freedom from."

What we should not do, however, is to seek in the republican ideal of freedom the makings of a non-liberal theory of political association. Pettit himself imagines that he stands outside the liberal framework. In reality he does not, and this will become clear as we examine more closely the way he proposes to understand freedom as the absence of domination.

---

[51] Pettit himself (*op. cit.*, p. 111) notes that the value of equal liberty makes most sense when freedom is understood as absence of domination.

[52] Rawls, *op. cit.*, p. 63. See also p. 202, right in the middle of the passage I cited earlier as showing his allegiance to the idea of freedom as non-interference: "Liberty is a certain structure of institutions, a certain system of public rules defining rights and duties." In the later postscript to *Republicanism* (p. 301, fn.), Pettit admits that passages like this suggest an understanding of freedom as non-domination. Still, he discounts them as not shaping Rawls' theory "in any distinctive way." I indicated in the previous note why that verdict is unfair: Rawls' "equal liberty" principle, which plays so central a role in his theory, makes most sense when liberty is understood as the absence of domination.

5. DOMINATION AND RESPECT

So far, little has been said about the nature of domination itself, the concept that occupies so central a place in the neo-republican thought of Pettit, Skinner, Viroli, and Spitz. Pettit holds, as I have indicated, that we are free from domination to the extent that we do not find ourselves subject to the arbitrary will of others. What, however, does this proposition mean exactly?

Pettit's analysis of domination distinguishes three components.[53] An individual A is dominated by another (individual or group of individuals) B to the extent that

(1) B has the capacity to interfere,
(2) on an arbitrary basis, and
(3) in certain choices that A is in a position to make.

The first condition involves one important difficulty, which I shall begin by discussing. But clearly condition (2) must be our main focus. The term "arbitrary" cries out for explanation, and one might imagine a number of very different ways of spelling out its meaning. As we explore Pettit's own way of defining it, the essential relation between republican freedom and liberal principles will come into view.

First, however, what can it mean to say, in accord with condition (1), that in dominating another a person has a *capacity* to interfere arbitrarily? For the time being, let us understand by "arbitrary" interference the sort that a system of just laws is intended to prevent. We may then say, broadly speaking, that people have the capacity in question when they are able to interfere, when they have the means at their disposal to obstruct the possibilities of others, even should they choose not in fact to intervene. The puzzle, however, is whether such a capacity is really eliminated by a system of just laws, as on Pettit's analysis it must be, if domination is to cease. Do such laws actually end or even diminish people's ability to interfere at will, or do they rather make it more costly for them to do so, in virtue of the sanctions involved?[54]

In many cases, the law can do no more than the latter – namely, deter. Sometimes offenders can be stopped in the act, and sometimes the law can bring a situation back to the *status quo ante*, by restitution or compensation. But seldom can the law undertake to eliminate the ability itself that some people have, as a result of their position, wealth, or talents, to interfere

---

[53] Pettit, *Republicanism*, p. 52.
[54] This important objection is raised by Gerald Gaus, "Backwards into the Future: Neorepublicanism as a Postsocialist Critique of Market Society," *Social Philosophy & Policy*, 20 (1) [2003, pp. 59–91], pp. 69–73. The following four paragraphs attempt to answer the objection.

arbitrarily in the first place. Anti-monopoly legislation, which takes away resources, and laws protecting unions, which equalize bargaining power, are the exception. As a rule, law can serve only to discourage people from taking advantage of the power differentials they possess. Pettit's condition (1) therefore needs to be modified, if just laws are to be seen as putting an end to domination, even in cases where the capacity to interfere arbitrarily remains unchanged.

At this point, it is useful to explain more carefully than before why good intentions are no substitute for just laws. Why is there not similarly an absence of domination when those in a position to interfere at will in the lives of others would never think of doing so because they are kindly and well-disposed? The reason cannot be that the chances of their nonetheless deciding to interfere are greater than the likelihood that they might do so were the deterrent force of the law in place. In some cases, the difference in the odds would be negligible. The explanation, I believe, lies in what a system of just laws represents, in contrast to individual cases of goodwill – namely, a public commitment that all can acknowledge, and that ideally all do, to hold in check any ability they may have to interfere arbitrarily with one another. We do not cease to live at the mercy of others, be the chances of their obstructing our choices ever so low, if we rely solely on their virtue. For in that case, it is still only by their leave that we live unimpeded. We need to take our fate out of the hands of particular persons and entrust it to an impersonal, collective agency. Such is the function of the law. Only when laws, not individuals, guarantee our status as free and equal citizens does personal dependence come to an end, so that we can look one another in the eye. Only then – when the rule of law has replaced the rule of persons – are we free to pursue our own goals without worrying that we must win or keep the goodwill of the powerful.

Just laws would fail to have any force, of course, if they did not include penalties against possible infractions. Yet sanctions are important, not simply because they deter but also because, as part of the law, they too express, in a particularly emphatic form, the common resolve to abolish dependence on the personal will of others. Indeed, as I mentioned at the end of §2, laws along with legal sanctions are unlikely to be just unless made by and for citizens who respect the law for its own sake – that is, for what it represents.

In this light, condition (1) in the definition of domination should therefore be amended to read, let us say:

(1')   B has a capacity to interfere that is not subject to public penalties sufficient to discourage its exercise.

But I also wish to underscore the point that a society free of the most egregious forms of domination is one in which citizens regard themselves as standing in a public relation of basic equality with one another, a relation they can all jointly acknowledge. This result will assume an even greater significance when we explore the meaning of condition (2) in Pettit's definition, and to this topic I now turn.

The state has the capacity to interfere in the affairs of its citizens. But provided that the basis of its interference is not arbitrary, it does not count – so the republican believes – as exercising a power of domination. How then ought the key term "arbitrary" to be defined?

Pettit's answer is that the basis for possible interference is not arbitrary if it leads to interference aimed at "tracking" or promoting the interests, or more exactly the politically relevant, the common and collectively actionable interests, of the individuals who are its object.[55] For instance (this is Pettit's example), it is in the common interest that each citizen pay his taxes, so that even if I do not want to pay my own, the coercion that the government may employ to force my payment does not constitute an arbitrary interference. Yet how should the common interests of the citizens be ascertained? Is it a matter of the interests that they themselves avow? Or is it instead a matter of their "real" interests, of which they may have only an imperfect grasp?

Pettit embraces the first alternative, in a suitably flexible form. Which interests state power can pursue on a non-arbitrary basis is a matter that in the end only the deliberation of the citizens themselves can settle.[56] Though legislative bodies and officials decide government policy, their decisions must always be open to contestation in the back-and-forth of public discussion. This position is undeniably attractive. Yet it gives rise to a further question – namely, what are the rules that ought to govern this collective deliberation among citizens? In the absence of appropriate principles to structure their deliberation, there will be no result, or the outcome will have no claim to being fair and just.

This point is not lost on Pettit himself, who proceeds to lay down two conditions that political deliberation must satisfy if it is to constitute the ultimate court of appeal for determining which interests the state ought to promote.[57] First, citizens should rely solely on "conceptual distinctions and inferential patterns which no one in the community has a serious reason to reject." And, second, the fundamental notions on which they do rely must nonetheless be substantial enough to permit an adequate articulation of their various grievances and goals. These two conditions clearly have a normative content. What, then, is the underlying value they express? I do not think it is hard to discern, though Pettit himself never acknowledges its presence. If laws, to be just, must ultimately be justifiable in ways that no citizens have good reason to reject, the reason is that otherwise citizens would not be accorded the sort of *respect* they deserve.

---

[55] Pettit, *Republicanism*, pp. 55, 287.
[56] *Ibid*, pp. 56, 63.
[57] *Ibid.*, pp. 131ff.

Respect, of course, has many different meanings. Only one is relevant here – namely, respect for persons (in contrast, say, to respect for their views), and it is moreover a sense of respect that reflects the specific character of the political realm. Politics is all about the legitimate use of force. Political principles, as I observed in the previous chapter (§3), are those moral principles with which we believe that people can rightly be forced to comply, if need be. And how should we understand the idea of persons? Again, there are many possibilities. But a core meaning is that persons are beings capable of thinking and acting on the basis of reasons. Now, making their conduct subject to possible coercion would amount to treating persons solely as means, to using their capacity of reason simply for the sake of ensuring public order, unless they too were able to endorse the rationale for imposing the principles in question. Only then could their reasons for compliance include, besides the fear of sanctions, the very considerations that count in favor of instituting those principles of political life.

This idea, as we might say, of treating persons as ends, not simply as means, is often associated with Kant. But note that the form invoked here can be separated from the peculiarities of his ethical theory. The present focus is not on moral principles as a whole, but instead on that subset consisting in political principles, whose hallmark is their coercive nature. The relevant sense of treating people as means and as ends can therefore be understood more narrowly and far less controversially. The reasons that force or the threat of force give us to act in certain ways assume that the principles involved are already in place, and so they exploit our ability to act for reasons in order to achieve an ulterior end – for instance, the benefits (particularly, the sense of security) our compliance will afford everyone else. Our capacity for reason is by contrast valued for its own sake, and in this sense treated with respect, only when it too is taken to determine the very legitimacy of the principles with which compliance is demanded – only when the principles are as justifiable to us as they presumably appear to those who have instituted them.[58]

It is then this political principle of respect for persons that constitutes the deepest stratum in Pettit's republican theory. It guides the determination of the interests that non-arbitrary – that is, just – laws ought to promote. And if such interests form part of the definition of what is to count as the absence of domination, then Pettit is hardly right to assert that the republican notion of freedom can serve as the supreme political value. We are not in a position to figure out whether domination is present, either in society at large or in the operations of the state, unless we rely upon the principle of respect for persons.

---

[58] For more on this notion of respect, see Chapter 6 as well as "Respect for Persons," *The Hedgehog Review*, vol. 7, no. 2 (summer 2005), pp. 66–76.

But there is more. For what is this very principle if not, as I also argued in the preceding chapter, the defining value of the modern liberal tradition? It is the ideal that political association must embody a sort of rational transparency for each of its members, the use of coercion having to be justifiable to all those who are to be subject to it. From this standpoint there derives the characteristically liberal conviction that the state must remain neutral with regard to the comprehensive ideals of the human good on which citizens tend naturally to disagree. Two points of detail should be noted in passing, since they are discussed more thoroughly elsewhere (Chapter 6, §4, and Chapter 8, §3). First, the liberal principle of respect applies in the first instance to the fundamental terms of political association and not to particular laws as such. Legislation remains legitimate despite the continuing disagreement of those citizens who opposed it so long as the constitutional framework of political ideals and procedures in accord with which it was enacted is one they have reason to endorse; in this derivative sense, if not in and of themselves, such laws do express their political will. And, second, if the principle of respect requires that the basic terms of political life be the object of reasonable agreement among all, then only insofar as citizens are assumed – in some cases, this may be counterfactually – to accept that very principle. Serving as it does to justify the need for agreement, respect for persons has to be understood as a moral constraint on what shall count as appropriate agreement. But for present purposes, the essential thing to observe is that since Pettit himself implicitly accords this conception of respect a foundational importance, in defining domination as he does, his republican model does not really stand in opposition to the essentials of liberalism. Its true adversary is that utilitarian stand of liberal thought that reduces freedom to the absence of interference.

A recurrent theme in Pettit's book is that contestability counts for more than consent in his ideal republic.[59] Only if citizens are prepared to challenge the government's decisions can they make sure that it will not slip into the arbitrary exercise of its prerogatives, advancing its own particular interests and catering to the concerns of the powerful, as it can so easily do. There is good sense in this observation, and actual consent, shaped as it generally is by a motley of pressures, ought indeed to be an object of suspicion. But Pettit goes too far when he asserts that "once a contestatory democracy is in place, then of course everything is up for grabs."[60] Not everything can be subject to revision, if contestation is to mean anything like what he himself has in mind. Not the principle of respect for persons that serves to delimit the very idea of arbitrary power, animates therefore the appropriate spirit of contestation, and gives in effect his republican ideal its recognizably liberal character.

[59] Pettit, *Republicanism*, pp. ix, 63, 184ff.
[60] Ibid., p. 201.

No doubt there exist other ways to define what counts as the power of "arbitrary" interference than the path Pettit has adopted. According to some of them, an individual's reason has no real bearing on whether domination is present. We are truly free – so some may suppose – and no longer subject to the arbitrary will of another when we place ourselves under the authority of God or the Nation, whatever our own reason may say. One might therefore be "republican" without being liberal. But that is manifestly not the kind of republicanism that Pettit envisions, nor the kind, I presume, that other contemporary neo-republican thinkers would wish to espouse.

Earlier in this section, as I was amending the definition of "domination," I argued that a society devoted to ending domination must require of its citizens that they have a shared commitment to this ideal. For only a system of just laws, as the public expression of that commitment, can truly eliminate relations of personal dependence. We can now see that this commitment finds its natural home within a vision of political life defined by the liberal principle of respect for persons. The basic terms of political association must be ones that all can affirm together (given that principle as a guiding premise), in a common or "public" point of view that embodies the fundamental relation of equality in which they understand themselves as standing to one another as citizens.[61] The republican ideal of replacing personal dependence with the rule of law becomes fully intelligible only within a liberal framework.

This brings me to a final point. If any value has a claim to constituting the foundation of the sort of political order that republican and liberal thinkers can be at one in seeking, it is not freedom in any of its senses, but rather the idea of respect for persons. Powerful currents in our culture push against a recognition of this fact. Freedom, in all its various meanings, is continually invoked as forming the ultimate framework for all our moral thinking. The only obligations individuals can truly be said to have, so we hear, are those that under suitably ideal conditions they would find reason to impose upon themselves. So, too, a democratic people is thought to be one in which free and equal citizens in their collective capacity determine for themselves the principles by which they will live. These self-descriptions do not go deep enough, however. They blind us to the true structure of our moral and political world, as I have shown in Chapters 5 and 6. The freedom we prize, as I have more particularly argued here (§3), is always a freedom shaped by other moral principles, principles whose authority must therefore be understood as binding on us independently of our own will, individual or collective. Political freedom, if it is to have a shape that we today would welcome, must take its bearings from the obligation to respect one another as persons.

---

[61] For more details, see Chapter 8.

8

Public Reason

One of the dominant themes in John Rawls' later philosophy is the idea of public reason. It does not signify simply one political value among others. In his view, public reason envelops all the different elements that make up the fabric of a constitutional democracy:

> The idea of public reason specifies at the deepest level the basic moral and political values that are to determine a constitutional democratic government's relation to its citizens and their relation to one another. In short, it concerns how the political relation is to be understood.[1]

Clearly the idea of public reason therefore means more than just that the principles of political association ought to be an object of public knowledge. It has to do with the very basis on which collectively binding decisions are to be established. We exercise public reason, Rawls believed, when we bring our own reason into accord with the reason of others so as to develop a common point of view for settling the terms of our political life. The conception of justice by which we live is then a conception we endorse, not for the different reasons we may each discover, and not simply for reasons we happen to share, but instead for reasons that count for us because we can affirm together. In this undertaking is expressed that spirit of reciprocity that for Rawls makes up the foundation of a democratic society.

Public reason emerged as an explicit theme in Rawls' writings only after *A Theory of Justice*, with his turn to a "political liberalism" that seeks to work out a common ground on which people can stand together as free and equal citizens despite their profound ethical and religious differences. But

---

[1] John Rawls, *Collected Papers* (Cambridge, MA: Harvard University Press, 1999), p. 574. In this chapter, references to Rawls' writings will henceforth be generally given in the text and in accordance with the following abbreviations: *Collected Papers* (= CP), *A Theory of Justice* (= TJ) (Cambridge, MA: Harvard University Press, 1971); *Political Liberalism* (= PL) (New York: Columbia University Press, 2nd paperback edition, 1996), *Justice as Fairness: A Restatement* (= JF) (Cambridge, MA: Harvard University Press, 2001).

the concept itself always lay at the heart of his philosophy. It ran through his first book under the name of "publicity" and played in this form an indispensable part in the theory of justice as fairness. The very notion of fairness, so central to Rawls' thought, denotes that mutual acknowledgement of principles that public reason demands and that constitutes the real import of the language of social contract that, for better or worse, he used to articulate his conception of justice.

Rawls' later writings about public reason outline a complex model of deliberative democracy, as it is often called today,[2] and I shall examine his account closely in §§3–4. But I begin by laying bare its roots in his earlier idea of publicity. Thus we shall see how deep and formative a role the concept of public reason always played in his thinking. This chapter is therefore largely interpretive, devoted in no small part to removing some of the common misunderstandings of this dimension of Rawls' political philosophy. Yet my aim is also critical. I believe it imperative that we recognize more clearly than Rawls ever did himself the way his conceptions of public reason and fairness turn upon a fundamental principle of respect for persons. In Chapter 6, I pointed out how the "political liberalism" he developed (like the one I too have put forward) depends essentially on this principle. In the present chapter, I shall be driving home once again its cardinal importance, and doing so will lead me to correct his account of public reason in some specific though quite important regards.

1. PUBLICITY IN *A THEORY OF JUSTICE*

Readers of *A Theory of Justice* ought to wonder more than they do about the contractarian form in which Rawls presented his theory of justice as fairness. Even in the introductory chapter of the book, he does little to explain the need to think about justice in terms of a contract. His notion of an "original position" is meant, like "the state of nature" in the social contract tradition, to describe a situation in which free and rational beings determine the principles that will regulate their common life together. Yet, as Rawls admitted (more forthrightly than earlier contract theorists), this initial situation has never existed and never will. The "original position" is a condition in which we imagine choosing principles of justice, not one in which as real people we ever find ourselves, nor one that we should endeavor to bring about, as in some grand constitutional convention. Something needs to be said therefore about the reasons to think of principles of justice as the result of an agreement that in fact we never make.

[2] For a theory of deliberative democracy building on Rawls' work, see Joshua Cohen, "Democracy and Liberty," in Jon Elster (ed.), *Deliberative Democracy* (Cambridge: Cambridge University Press, 1998), pp. 185–231.

In one passage, Rawls remarked that to understand fair principles of justice as the object of agreement among free and rational persons entails seeing that "the theory of justice is a part, perhaps the most significant part, of the theory of rational choice" (TJ, p. 16). This formulation wrongly suggests that fairness derives from the rational pursuit of individual advantage, when in reality it forms an irreducibly moral notion – a fact that Rawls himself would have been the last to deny. Though the parties in the original position are described as deliberating in accord with the principles of rational choice, the conditions imposed upon their choice (for instance, the "veil of ignorance" that denies them knowledge of their social position, their natural talents, and their comprehensive ideal of the human good) constitute moral limits on the sorts of information it would be fair to utilize. The facts about themselves of which they are imagined to be ignorant correspond, he held, to considerations that we ourselves would consider inappropriate to invoke when arguing for a particular conception of social justice. Later, Rawls introduced a distinction between two capacities of reason – the "rational" and the "reasonable" – that are reflected in these two distinct elements of the original position, and he disclaimed any attempt to derive the reasonable, or the disposition to seek fair terms of cooperation, from the rational (PL, pp. 48–53). Still, our question remains: What useful purpose is served by the idea of an original contract, morally defined though it is, if it refers to an agreement that is never really made?

One could well argue that the structure of Rawls' theory would have been clearer had he not made use of this idea. In an insightful review of *A Theory of Justice*, Ronald Dworkin observed many years ago that a hypothetical contract, being strictly speaking no contract at all, can have no binding force on people who never actually agreed to it, even if they would have done so had they found themselves in certain circumstances. It is, moreover, an idle notion. To claim that certain principles are valid because they would be the object of rational agreement is, he observed, a roundabout way of saying that they are valid because there is reason to accept what they assert. The two principles of justice championed by Rawls – the liberty principle (a scheme of equal basic liberties) and the difference principle (the arrangement of social and economic inequalities, in keeping with the fair equality of opportunity, so as to be to the greatest benefit of the least advantaged members of society) – have their real basis, according to Dworkin, in the fundamental right to equal concern and respect which they express.[3]

---

[3] Ronald Dworkin, *Taking Rights Seriously* (Cambridge, MA: Harvard University Press, 1978), Chapter 6 ("Justice and Rights," originally published 1973). Rawls replied to the criticism in CP, pp. 400–401n, as well as in JF, p. 17, claiming in the latter passage, interestingly though far too briefly, that the idea of a contract, as a "device of representation" serves to bring out "what we regard – here and now – as acceptable restrictions on the reasons on the basis of which the parties ... may properly put forward certain principles of political justice and reject others." As will become clear, I believe that the point of the contract metaphor is

This skepticism about contractarian terminology has my sympathy, and I agree that a principle of respect for persons undergirds Rawls' theory of justice.[4] But though the idea of an original contract is, as Rawls would later say, just a "device of representation" (PL, p. 24), we need to attend to all the aspects of justice that it serves to represent. In fact, conceiving of the principles of justice as the object of a (hypothetical) rational agreement comes to more than saying that each individual concerned has reason to accept them. The language of contract also points to the good in each individual finding that reason in the reason that others have to accept them as well. This good lies at the core of the ideal that Rawls called "publicity," and a virtue of the idea of contract, as he noted (TJ, p. 16), is that it gives expression to this ideal.

The point is that just as the validity of a contract does not turn solely on the terms agreed to, but also on the fact of agreement, so justice must consist in more than the proper distribution of rights and assets. Principles of justice, Rawls believed, should also be such that each of us affirms them in light of the fact that others affirm them too. In general, as we may say to fix terms, the justice of a social arrangement is judged, not merely by the *distributive scheme* it embodies, but also by the *basis of its authority* over those whom it binds. (Certainly, institutions cannot count as just if, however much they may benefit their members, their authority derives from the will of a despot, however benevolent.) Thus the idea of a contract serves to express an important claim about the basis on which a system of justice should rest: not only should it be such that each of us has reason to endorse it, but our reason for accepting it should also turn on others having reason to endorse it too. This is the core of the idea of *publicity*, which Rawls placed at the foundations of his theory of justice. When a conception of justice enjoys this kind of common support, it figures in our thinking, as he said a public conception will do (TJ, pp. 55f, 133), much as though it had indeed been the result of an agreement: we will feel bound by it because we see that others too have reason to feel themselves similarly bound by it. Even though no formal act of agreement is needed for us to base our reasons on those of others, a "just so" story about a hypothetical contract helps to highlight this public dimension of justice.

The contractarian metaphor, however dispensable, has then the merit of combining in a single image two essential conditions that the principles of justice should satisfy – their justifiability to reason and their publicity. Together these two conditions define Rawls' ideal of a "well-ordered" society, which advances the good of its members in accord with a public

---

indeed to underscore an essential feature of the reasons on which political principles should rest.

[4] See Chapters 4, 6, §§ 3–4, and 7, § 5. I have tried to be more specific than Dworkin about what is the pertinent notion of respect.

conception of justice. It is "a society in which (1) everyone accepts and knows that the others accept the same principles of justice, and (2) the basic social institutions generally satisfy and are generally known to satisfy these principles" (TJ, p. 5). Justice would not be all that it should be without this shared affirmation.

It is therefore unfortunate that Rawls did not adequately explain in *A Theory of Justice* why publicity represents so preeminent a value. As a rule, the "publicity condition" enters the discussion from the side, as though merely a further desideratum that the principles of justice should possess. It receives no extended treatment of its own, and so one can easily overlook how central it is to Rawls' very idea of justice. Regrettably, too, Rawls' statements about publicity in this book generally equate it with public knowledge, as though it entailed only that citizens know the operative principles of justice and one another's reasons for accepting them. The work he expects from it shows, however, that he had something more ambitious in mind. Publicity really amounts to the demand that the reasons each person has to endorse the principles be reasons the person sees others to have to endorse them as well. It requires that the principles of justice be grounded in a shared point of view. We can grasp the true import of the concept if we follow the role it plays in *A Theory of Justice*. Publicity shapes the ideal of a well-ordered society, as we have seen. But it also acts as a crucial premise in the so-called stability argument for the two principles of justice. To that I now turn.

Other things being equal, a conception of justice is better, Rawls pointed out, the more stable it is, generating its own support so as to outweigh the contrary motives to which our narrower interests may give rise. Citizens living under the institutional arrangements it recommends should tend to acquire thereby a standing commitment to its principles. Stability obtains "when the public recognition of its realization by the social system tends to bring about the corresponding sense of justice" (TJ, pp. 177; also 454). And thus he was immediately able to reject those indirect forms of utilitarianism that encourage people to act on non-utilitarian motives so that thereby the general happiness may be most efficiently maximized. Such a manipulative system would fail even to be an object of public knowledge (TJ, p. 181). Yet he then went on to invoke publicity in a deeper sense as he argued that utility, even if understood as the explicit charter of society, would prove to be unstable, since its cult of efficiency inevitably places too great a strain on individual self-esteem (TJ §§ 29, 69–77). Principles of justice centered on the maximization of average utility are unlikely to generate their own support, since they accord poorly with the facts of moral psychology. For how can they inspire the allegiance of those who are asked to give up their life prospects for the greater good of all? Only by calling upon improbable reservoirs of sympathetic identification with others and with the social whole can utilitarians hope that such a system of justice will endure. The situation is quite different with Rawls' own conception. The liberty principle secures the fundamental inviolability of each individual, and the difference principle ensures that everyone benefits from social cooperation. Together these two principles define a system of justice whose operation is more likely to engage the support of all, even of those who fare worst. Unlike utilitarianism, they exemplify the idea of "reciprocity" (TJ, p. 14), an idea rather undeveloped in *A Theory of Justice*, but lying at the center of *Political Liberalism* and its doctrine of public reason.

Now, this stability argument relies in fact on the inner meaning of publicity, though to see it we must look at the argument somewhat differently than Rawls did himself. One might suppose that it requires principles of justice to be public simply so that everyone may know that they are in force and see what their institutions stand for. However, more must be involved. For stability is said to obtain when the "public recognition of [their] realization," hence the knowledge that others too affirm these principles, fosters everyone's conviction that they are valid and worthy of support. Unfortunately, Rawls did not fully explain why people might be moved to espouse certain principles by the fact that others espouse them as well. Indeed, he presented this argument in terms of the good that each person will discern in the liberty and difference principles from his own point of view – their guarantee of individual inviolability and their assurance that all will benefit from social cooperation (TJ, pp. 177ff.). But the stability argument has to be different in character. It has to show that each person can find reason to embrace these principles in the fact that others embrace them too. It therefore needs to indicate the good that the public affirmation of the principles embodies.

Halfway through his account of the argument, Rawls took up a line of thought that suggests what that good is. "The public recognition of the two principles," he wrote (TJ, p. 178), "gives greater support to men's self-respect and this in turn increases the effectiveness of social cooperation." Respect is indeed the good in question. But note that Rawls' statement asserts not so much that the principles express respect as that their public recognition does so. Thus, the self-respect each person finds confirmed in them has to be part of a mutual respect that their common affirmation displays. Though Rawls is not as clear on this matter as one might wish, his discussion of "the natural duty of respect," both here and later in the book, entails that the good of mutual respect lies in there being a shared basis for the determination of principles of justice. We respect others as ends in themselves, he held, when in regard to their claims and interests we act on reasons that we are prepared to explain to them in the light of mutually acceptable principles (TJ, pp. 179, 337–8). We try to see things as they do, taking our bearings from a point of view that we can all endorse together. Respect for persons implies allegiance to principles that we affirm in the light of others having a reason, indeed the same reason, to affirm them too.

Naturally, respect can mean many things, but in the sense just mentioned it constitutes the true nature of the publicity condition. When citizens adopt certain principles of justice for reasons they understand one another to acknowledge, their joint endorsement of the principles amounts to showing one another respect. Their grounds for embracing them do not lie solely in their own, but in a shared point of view. The mutual respect demonstrated by their allegiance to this common basis is then a good that they can regard themselves as having achieved, and that is why the scheme of justice gains in stability. Such a society illustrates Rawls' claim that "a desirable feature of a conception of justice is that it should publicly express men's respect for one another" (TJ, p. 179). What the publicity requirement really comes to, therefore, is that each person's adherence to the principles of justice should turn on reasons that he also understands others to have for affirming them as well. This point remains largely implicit in *A Theory of Justice*, but in several essays published shortly afterwards Rawls spelled it out in detail (see §2).

Once its full meaning is laid bare, we can better understand why Rawls should have attached so great a value to the ideal of publicity. Only principles of justice that citizens affirm on a common basis are ones by which they can show one another respect as persons. The idea that political community should rest upon this sort of mutual respect belongs to the heart of Rawls' philosophy. It underlies one of the most telling ways he had of contrasting his view of justice as fairness with utilitarian conceptions (TJ, pp. 23–27, 187–190). "Utilitarianism," he observed, "does not take seriously the distinction between persons." Utilitarians propose that we adopt for society as a whole a form of practical reasoning appropriate for the single individual: just as the prudent person evaluates his possibilities with an eye to achieving the most good overall, accepting some losses for the sake of a greater gain, so a just society regards persons as different lines for an allocation of benefits and burdens that will maximize the net balance of satisfaction as judged by a sympathetic observer. To heed the separateness of persons, by contrast, is to seek principles that they can freely acknowledge before one another – principles, that is, that each can see that others have the same reasons to endorse as he. This mutual acknowledgement of principles is the very essence of what Rawls meant by fairness as a conception of justice, though he brought it out better in his earlier and foundational essay "Justice as Fairness" (1958) than in the book, which cloaks it in the language of an original contract. "A practice is just or fair," he wrote in that essay,

when it satisfies the principles which those who participate in it could propose to one another for mutual acceptance ... Persons engaged in a just, or fair, practice can face one another openly and support their respective positions, should they appear questionable, by reference to principles which it is reasonable to expect each to accept.[5]

[5] Rawls, "Justice as Fairness," CP, p. 59 (see also p. 70). Contrast the less perspicuous, contractarian presentation of the idea of fairness in TJ, p. 11.

The idea of fairness explains the value of publicity, and it embodies in turn what Rawls himself called the natural duty of respect.

One reason for Rawls' reluctance to present his theory in these terms may well have been the many different meanings "respect" can have. At the end of *A Theory of Justice* (TJ, pp. 585–6), he declared that he had not derived the principles of justice from respect for persons because the very notion of respect calls for interpretation, which only a conception of justice can provide. The hermeneutic point is well taken. But it does not rule out the possibility that respect, in a specific sense we grasp perhaps only in the light of his theory as a whole, is a value on which that theory rests. And so, as Rawls went on to admit, respect for persons plays two roles in his conception of justice. It shapes the two principles themselves with their emphasis upon the inviolability of the individual. It also figures in the demand that persons be treated "in ways that they can see to be justified." That is the role of respect that underlies the ideal of publicity.

2. FROM PUBLICITY TO PUBLIC REASON

In several essays published after *A Theory of Justice*, the notion of publicity received more systematic attention, and not by accident. Its greater prominence reflects the new direction in Rawls' thought that led to *Political Liberalism*. It gradually grew into a full-fledged doctrine of "public reason." A sign of how essential to political life he always considered the construction of a shared point of view is that in following this transformation we see emerge all the characteristic themes of his later philosophy.

For instance, Rawls acknowledged more clearly that the importance of publicity in a well-ordered society is not simply a matter of its principles of justice being known to all. They should also be principles that citizens affirm on the basis of a shared rationale. Such is the intent of the distinction introduced in his *Dewey Lectures* (1980) (CP, pp. 324–326) and contemporaneous writings (CP, pp. 293) between three "degrees" or "levels" of publicity.[6] A conception of justice satisfies the "full" publicity condition when its acceptance is not only an object of public knowledge, and not only based upon beliefs to which everyone can assent, but also thereby justified in a manner that all can embrace. In *A Theory of Justice*, Rawls had generally used the term "publicity" in a sense equivalent to the first of these levels, the other two being tacitly at work in the way the stability argument capitalized upon public knowledge of the operative conception of justice. Now the virtue that principles of justice have in being affirmable from a common point of view was made part of the very idea of publicity. Principles public in this strong sense should be our goal, he argued (CP, p. 325), because a well-ordered society rests upon fair

---

[6] This material is taken up again in PL, pp. 66ff, and in JF, p. 121.

terms of cooperation to which free and equal persons could agree. Thus, also for the first time, Rawls connected publicity directly (and not just via the metaphor of contract) to the ideal of fairness, so that its centrality to his conception of justice comes through more perspicuously than before.

Rawls also offered a further argument for the full publicity condition (CP, pp. 325–326). Principles of justice should draw on common ground because they apply to institutions having a deep and durable effect on people's lives. This transparency in which people can acknowledge before one another the basis of their common life is "a precondition of freedom." Plainly, however, it was essentially political freedom that Rawls had in mind, for moral principles outside the domain of justice need not, he added, be public in this strong sense, even though their effects on adherents and others alike can be equally profound. Why did Rawls thus limit the scope of the publicity condition? One tacit reason may well have been that political principles differ from other moral principles in virtue of being enforceable when necessary, and that coercion, because of its irresistibility, differs so significantly from other forms of social influence that it ought to be grounded in consensus. As I indicated in Chapter 6 (§§ 3–4), Rawls came to take just this position in *Political Liberalism*, despite never being inclined to lay out the idea of respect for persons on which it rests.

But another reason for the limitation was presented explicitly in the *Dewey Lectures* (CP, p. 326). Moral notions distinct from the principles of justice often belong to religious, philosophical, or ethical doctrines on which people in modern societies are unlikely to agree, even as they can find a shared basis for settling questions of political justice. Publicity aims at a freedom of self-determination that citizens can exercise together despite their abiding disagreements. To enjoy this identity-in-difference, they must observe therefore a certain self-discipline, bringing to their deliberations about issues of justice only those convictions that can form part of a common point of view. "In public questions," Rawls wrote, "ways of reasoning and rules of evidence for reaching true general beliefs that help settle whether institutions are just should be of a kind that everyone can recognize" (CP, p. 326). Here is a first statement of the theory of public reason, formulated in response to the doctrinal diversity that will be the chief preoccupation of his emerging political liberalism.

In the transitional essays of the 1980s, Rawls often described this public form of reasoning in terms of a distinction between justification and proof.[7] Justification is not merely "valid argument from listed premises." Instead, it "is addressed to others who disagree with us, and therefore it must always proceed from some consensus, that is, from premises that we and others publicly recognize as true" (CP, p. 394; also pp. 426–427).

---

[7] The distinction goes back to *A Theory of Justice* (TJ, pp. 580–581). It also reappears in the late essay "The Idea of Public Reason Revisited" (1997), CP, p. 594.

The contrast was overdrawn, since justification can take many forms, depending on the purpose at hand; sometimes it only consists in showing people how our assertion follows from our own beliefs. But the point Rawls had in mind is obvious. In a well-ordered society, citizens do not determine basic matters of justice by announcing to one another the conclusions they each have derived from their own first principles and then resorting to some further mechanism, such as bargaining or majority voting, to resolve the ensuing conflicts. They reason from what they understand to be a common point of view; their aim is to adjudicate disagreements by argument. As we have seen, a public life founded on mutually acknowledged principles is precisely what fairness entails.

This idea of consensus underlies the different notion of an "overlapping consensus," which made its appearance in his writings of this period.[8] Principles of justice, he argued, ought to be the object of an overlapping consensus among citizens otherwise divided by their comprehensive ethical, religious, and philosophical doctrines. Rawls' point has often been misunderstood. Many have supposed that he meant to abandon the claim that his theory of justice is true or correct. If the nature of justice is to be defined by reference to what a society's members happen to agree upon, how can there be any room to argue that current opinion is wrong? And why should we believe that in these matters there is much of substance that people agree upon at all? However, our earlier discussion of publicity explains why these worries are ill-conceived. The basic sense in which principles of justice ought to be the object of consensus is that each person should have both sound and identical reasons to embrace them, for only then does their publicity give expression to mutual respect. Consensus so understood is therefore hardly identical to the extent of actual agreement about justice that obtains in a society. Yet an important question is whether this shared perspective, rooted as it must be in reasons that citizens can acknowledge only by abstracting from their divergent visions of the human good, nonetheless coheres with the comprehensive conceptions to which they are attached. Only if the consensus shaping their public reasoning about justice forms an overlapping consensus, a common element in their otherwise different points of view, is the structure of their political life likely to endure. The notion of overlapping consensus serves therefore to connect a conception of justice already arrived at, and already marked by a more fundamental kind of consensus, to the question of its stability.

---

[8] See "Justice as Fairness: Political not Metaphysical" (1985), CP, p. 390, and the two subsequent essays that explore the notion in detail, "The Idea of an Overlapping Consensus" (1987; CP, pp. 421–448) and "The Domain of the Political and Overlapping Consensus" (1989; CP, pp. 473–496), reworked to form Chapter IV of *Political Liberalism*. The term with a somewhat different sense appears in TJ, p. 388, whereas the concept itself is at work at TJ, pp. 220–221.

Rawls himself spoke in this regard of two "stages" in his theory of justice as fairness (PL, pp. 64, 140ff.). In the first stage the theory aims to describe fair terms of cooperation among citizens, while in the second it considers whether such principles can prove stable. The notion of overlapping consensus comes into play only at this subsequent stage. Clearly principles of justice are not being fixed by appeal to the common denominator of existing opinion. At the same time, we should not overlook the idea of consensus that does figure in the initial determination of these principles. Publicity requires that they draw upon reasons that all can acknowledge. As Rawls observed (PL, p. 64), public reason is a value that even the first stage of his argument seeks to honor.

Overlapping consensus became a central notion for Rawls in the 1980s as he realized how much broader is the range of moral outlooks congruent with a commitment to justice as fairness than he had assumed. He also became far more alert than before to the fact that people, in their comprehensive philosophical and religious conceptions of the human good, have a natural tendency to diverge, not because of prejudice or inadvertence, but because of what he called "the burdens of reason" (CP, pp. 475–478) or later "the burdens of judgment" (PL, pp. 54–58). The complexity of the evidence, the necessity of weighing together different sorts of considerations, the need for judgment in applying key evaluative concepts, the variety of life-experiences in modern society – all these factors conspire to make agreement about the nature of the good life improbable. To be sure, some comprehensive ideals deny the importance of fair terms of social cooperation, and their adherents cannot be expected to endorse Rawls' two principles of justice. But there remain a great many different ethical and religious ideals that share a commitment to fairness. Their proliferation Rawls called "reasonable pluralism" (PL, pp. 36, 63f.), since by reasonableness he meant, as I have noted (§1), precisely such a commitment.[9] Reasonable pluralism is the condition we should expect to thrive under free institutions where, in the absence of state power enforcing any particular doctrine, the burdens of judgment naturally drive people's thinking in different directions. The principles of justice that citizens embrace from a sense of fairness can therefore prove stable only if they cohere with the various elements of this diversity.

A *Theory of Justice* did not itself approach the problem of stability in this pluralist spirit. Part III of that book laid out a single ethical conception, based on regarding an individual's good as the object of a rational plan of life,

---

[9] "Pluralism" can be a misleading term in this context if it suggests the sort of ethical conception made famous by Isaiah Berlin. Berlin's pluralism is a positive doctrine according to which there are many ultimate, irreducible, and sometimes incompatible ends of life. The pluralism Rawls has in mind might be better described as the existence of reasonable disagreement about the nature of the human good (Berlin's value-pluralism being one of the views in dispute). For more on this distinction, see my book *The Morals of Modernity* (Cambridge: Cambridge University Press, 1996), Chapter 7 ("Pluralism and Reasonable Disagreement").

in the light of which the citizens of a well-ordered society would be moved to act justly. Moreover, this conception, often in so many words but sometimes explicitly (TJ, p. 572), displayed the hallmarks of the Kantian ideal of individual autonomy, according to which all our principles of conduct (not just those of justice) should be ones that free and equal rational beings would choose under the ideal conditions of an original position. Such a strategy embodied too narrow a view of the possibilities.[10] Indeed, the multiplication of reasonable views of the human good is something a modern constitutional democracy is bound to encourage, and thus Rawls' initial solution of the stability problem was caught in an internal contradiction. The way out, he came to see, lies in recognizing that in a free society, many disparate comprehensive views of life can still overlap in a public understanding of justice.

It was by taking to heart the fact of reasonable pluralism, and seeing the error in his earlier solution of the stability problem, that Rawls went on to develop his new theory of "political liberalism" (PL, p. xlii). In the classical liberalisms of Kant and Mill, the account of justice had been presented as part of an all-encompassing moral philosophy, and *A Theory of Justice* followed their lead. Yet in fact neither the moral ideal of individual autonomy nor an experimental attitude toward life is an essential ingredient in the rationale for his conception of justice as fairness. What is necessary, Rawls announced in the first essay marking this turn in his thought, is "to apply the principle of toleration to philosophy itself."[11] Justice as fairness, along with the reasons making up the public understanding of its basis, should be regarded as a "freestanding" conception, which people can embrace who see a greater value in tradition and belonging than the Kantian and Millian philosophies allow.

Political liberalism is not "political" in the sense that, forsaking principled argument, it reduces justice to a compromise among given interests or to the common denominator of existing opinion (CP, p. 491). That should now be plain. But it does seek principles of political association that citizens have reason to affirm together despite the religious and philosophical disagreements setting them apart. Moreover, their reasons for embracing the principles must not spring simply from their different perspectives, but must also draw upon a common point of view. Only so, as we have seen, can these principles represent fair terms of cooperation that express mutual respect. The shared understanding of principles of justice must therefore be at once reasoned and neutral with regard to the comprehensive conceptions of the good on which citizens disagree. Obviously it is no small task to work out the character which this common language should have. In the essays of

[10] For my own doubts about the idea of a rational plan of life and about the ideal of autonomy, see, respectively, Chapters 10 and 5.
[11] "Justice as Fairness: Political not Metaphysical" (1985), CP, p. 388. See also PL, p. 10.

the 1980s and then in *Political Liberalism*, the "full publicity condition" was expanded into a detailed and sophisticated account of "public reason." The idea of public reason had its roots in the notion of publicity employed in *A Theory of Justice*, but Rawls' new concerns moved this theme from the periphery to the center of his attention.

3. THE DOMAIN OF PUBLIC REASON

Rawls gave the idea of public reason two extended treatments. The first occurred in *Political Liberalism*, chiefly in Chapter VI, and the second in an essay of 1997, "The Idea of Public Reason Revisited." I shall center my account around the first, while noting the significant revisions presented in the later essay.

Public reason, Rawls wrote (PL, p. 217), is an ideal of democratic citizenship, a "duty of civility," which governs the way in which citizens should deliberate together about the fundamental questions of their political life. In seeking to draw up fair terms of cooperation, they should reason from premises they can all acknowledge. As a rule, the exercise of public reason will not mobilize their full thinking about the problems before them, since their comprehensive conceptions of the good and the right are also bound to entail distinctive views about aspects having nothing to do with what justice itself requires. On these matters they may find themselves in deep and irresolvable disagreement. But such differences are set aside when citizens committed to fairness decide questions having to do with the basic structure of society, questions that in Rawls' view concern both "constitutional essentials" (the general form of government and the fundamental rights of citizens) and the core issues of social and economic justice (PL, pp. 227–230). Similarly, people may well continue to understand these decisions in the light of their various comprehensive doctrines. The demand is only that they see the need for a common perspective and be able and ready to justify their decisions within its terms (PL, pp. 241–243).

Why, one might ask, should the domain of public reason be limited to these fundamentals, instead of extending to all the political decisions a community must make? Rawls never gave a clear-cut answer to this question. At one point, he suggested that the restriction might eventually be lifted: the sense in focusing on fundamentals would be that if the demands of public reason cannot be shown to hold in this case, they will scarcely admit of a broader application.[12] But he then ended this all-too-brief treatment of the issue with the intimation that citizens might sometimes be right to settle these further issues in a more particularist spirit:

---

[12] Here, Rawls' thinking came close to the all-embracing view of deliberative democracy defended in Amy Gutmann and Dennis Thompson, *Democracy and Disagreement* (Cambridge, MA: Harvard University Press, 1996), pp. 34–49.

It is usually highly desirable to settle [all] political questions by invoking the values of public reason. Yet this may not always be so. (PL, p.215; see also JF, pp. 41, 91.)

Regrettably, he gave no example of what he had in mind. One possibility, however, is the present system in the Canadian province of Quebec, which guarantees basic rights for all while giving special protection and support to the use of the French language, despite the existence of a sizable Anglophone minority.[13] Insofar as the laws embodying these cultural policies issue from democratically elected legislatures and do not compromise the equal standing of all citizens, as enshrined in the fundamental rights that historical experience has shown to be essential to this equality (such as the right to free association and the right to organize politically so as to change such laws, but not, say, the "right" to commercial signs or public schools in the language of one's choice), I do not myself see a difficulty. The principle of equal respect, which underlies the idea of public reason, defines the basic relationship in which citizens should stand to one another as they go on to pursue various goals as a political community. These goals must remain compatible with the essential rights of citizens and be adopted in accord with democratic procedures, but they need not be ones that everyone must be understood as having reason to endorse.

Another question is whether the discipline of public reason applies to every kind of political deliberation in which citizens may engage, or only to those deliberations that form part of the official process for arriving at binding decisions that will have the force of law. Certainly when citizens take part in decision-making, by voting in elections or exercising public office as legislators and officials, Rawls held that they must base their decisions (again, where matters of basic justice are involved) upon reasoning rooted in a point of view which all can share. Thus, the U.S. Supreme Court, charged as it is with settling questions of constitutional principle, counts as an exemplary organ of public reason (PL, pp. 231ff.). He also emphasized that in "the background culture" – as members of the particular associations (churches, universities, and professional groups) making up civil society and as adherents of different philosophical and religious conceptions – citizens may discuss among themselves political questions, even of a fundamental sort, according to their own "non-public reasons" (PL, p. 14; CP, p. 576). Political debate rightly shows a greater mix of voices in areas of society other than the circumscribed realm of public reason, and it would be wrong to suppose that Rawls' theory of public reason was meant to encompass the "public sphere" in this broader sense, which was the topic for example of

---

[13] Quebec is the model for the less "procedural," more "communitarian" form of liberalism favored by Charles Taylor, as in "The Politics of Recognition," pp. 242–248, in *Philosophical Arguments* (Cambridge, MA: Harvard University Press, 1995). It is not obviously at odds with Rawls' doctrine of public reason.

a widely influential study by Jürgen Habermas.[14] Much misdirected criticism has arisen from this confusion.

But to return to our question, can citizens or particular associations address their comprehensive conclusions about political issues, not only to like-minded souls, but to everyone in the community whatever their persuasion? Can the Catholic bishops, for example, direct their religiously inspired arguments for regarding abortion as murder to believers and non-believers alike? Or does the ideal of public reason require that citizens participating in the political debates of society as a whole hold back and speak only in the regimented terms it provides, even if they are engaged not in making binding decisions, but only in the back and forth of argument? Should they reserve their full-scale views for intramural use?

It may seem that Rawls believed they should. For neither in *Political Liberalism* nor in "The Idea of Public Reason Revisited" did he note the difference between two forms of public debate – *open discussion*, where people argue with one another in the light of the whole truth as they see it, and *decision-making*, where they deliberate as participants in some organ of government about which option should be made legally binding. To say, as he did, that public reason concerns the "kinds of reasons [citizens] may reasonably give one another when fundamental political questions are at stake" (CP. p. 574) fails to discriminate between the two. Yet the distinction is plain and important, and unfortunately Rawls never gave it its due. He did acknowledge the value of what he called "declaration," in which citizens make known to one another their comprehensive understandings of the right and the good (CP, p. 594; PL, p. 249). But in this case, he had in mind only their showing one another how their conceptions support the common viewpoint of public reason. Such exchanges certainly promote mutual trust, as he observed, but they are not the same as a free and open discussion of political questions.

Moreover, several passages in *Political Liberalism* place "political advocacy in the public forum" (PL, pp. 215, 252) among the activities regulated by public reason. Many have therefore taken Rawls to have claimed that all political debate in society at large, at least when it bears on fundamentals, should not depart from the common ground that citizens share.[15] Such

---

[14] Jürgen Habermas, *Strukturwandel der Öffentlichkeit* (Darmstadt: Luchterhand, 1962). Rawls noted this terminological difference with Habermas at PL, pp. l, 382. Behind Habermas' usage stands Kant's famous appeal in the essay "Was ist Aufklärung?" to the "public use of reason" (*der öffentliche Gebrauch der Vernunft*), in which "a man of learning addresses the entire reading public." Oddly, what Kant called "the private use of reason … which a person may make in a particular *civil* post or office with which he has been entrusted" (Kant, *Political Writings*, ed. H. Reiss, Cambridge: Cambridge University Press, 1977, p. 55) is the form of argument that Rawls intended his rules of "public reason" to cover.

[15] Two examples are Michael Sandel in his review of *Political Liberalism* (originally published in the *Harvard Law Review*, vol. 107, no. 7 (May 1994), and reprinted in his book, *Public*

a view would be unappealing for a number of reasons. First, it is essential for us to know the different convictions our fellow citizens hold about controversial issues, and not only in order to be reassured that they can nonetheless find in them reasons to embrace a common standpoint for political decisions. We also gain a firmer appreciation of the value of that standpoint, seeing how without it so much would tend to drive us apart. Second, unbridled public discussion has the obvious virtue that through it we may come to change our mind. We can find ourselves persuaded by the way some initially unattractive opinion is defended. We can also be impelled to think through more carefully than before our own comprehensive commitments. In fact, the community as a whole may be moved to give a deeper or more nuanced articulation to the common principles by which it orders its political life.[16] And, third, an essential part of many religious views of life is that their adherents ought to do their best to persuade others too to heed the vital truths about the human good they believe they have seen. Coercion must be impermissible, of course. But ruling out a free and open exchange of views seems unjustly discriminatory. It would be an unacceptable abridgement of the free exercise of religion if the Catholic bishops were to feel inhibited from doing their religious duty and trying to convince the citizenry as a whole that abortion is morally wrong.

It should be observed, however, that a straitjacketed view of political debate does not follow from the justification that Rawls himself presented for the ideal of public reason. Its basis, he wrote, is "the liberal principle of legitimacy," which holds that "our exercise of political power is proper and hence justifiable only when it is exercised in accordance with a constitution the essentials of which all citizens may reasonably be expected to endorse in the light of principles and ideals acceptable to them as reasonable and rational" (PL, p. 217). This principle captures the thesis advanced in his earlier writings – namely, that the terms of political association must form part of a public consensus because of their essentially coercive character. And that thesis in turn, as I mentioned before (§1), gives expression to a specific value of respect for persons that underlies his political thought as a whole, including both his cardinal ideal of fairness as well as what he called, rather misleadingly (see Chapter 6 of the present book), the "freestanding" conception of justice essential to his political liberalism. Rawls unfortunately never gave this underlying norm of respect the systematic attention it deserves. Had he done so, it would

Philosophy ([Cambridge, MA: Harvard University Press, 2005], see particularly pp. 239ff) and Nicholas Wolterstorff in Wolterstorff and Robert Audi, *Religion in the Public Square* (Lanham: Rowman & Littlefield, 1997), pp. 67–120. Wolterstorff continually runs together "deciding" and "debating" political questions both in his critique of Rawls and in the position of "no restraint on religious reasons" that he himself advocates.

[16] For reflections along these lines, see Jeremy Waldron, "Religious Contributions in Public Deliberation," *San Diego Law Review*, vol. 30, no. 4 (fall 1993), pp. 817–848.

have become plain that the ideal of public reason, based as it is upon this norm, as embodied in "the liberal principle of legitimacy," really should govern only the reasoning by which citizens – as voters, legislators, officials, or judges – take part in political decisions (about fundamentals) that will be backed up by coercion and therefore have the force of law. Rightly conceived, it does not thwart the uninhibited political discussions that are the mark of a vigorous democracy. We can argue with one another about political issues in the name of our different visions of the human good while also recognizing that, when the moment comes for a legally binding decision, we must take our bearings from a common point of view.

Rawls never put things in quite this way, so one cannot be sure that he would actually have agreed. But it is what the logic of his position entails. By "political advocacy in the public forum" perhaps he meant (as the context suggests) only the terms in which a candidate for office seeks support, and indeed political campaigns, no less than the votes they solicit, should adhere to the canon of public reason when constitutional essentials and basic matters of economic justice are at stake. In general, clarity would have been better served had Rawls given a more complete picture of the different kinds of political discussion that have a place in a constitutional democracy. He tended to contrast the "background culture" with what he called the "public political culture" (PL, pp. 13–14) or the "public political forum" (CP, pp. 575–576). Though he defined these latter terms as referring to the institutions in which citizens or their representatives authoritatively settle fundamental questions of justice, the terms themselves suggest a wider range of political discussion where the rules of public reason do not rightfully apply. Indeed, I shall indicate in the next section one instance where Rawls himself seems to have been misled by this terminology.

One point should now be clear, however. Public reason, as Rawls conceived it, cannot be equated with "secular reason." Many people think of liberalism as an essentially secular conception that aims to keep religion out of the public square. We have now seen two respects in which that would be a misleading characterization of the sort of political liberalism that Rawls developed. The public reason in which citizens are to hammer out the terms of their political association must forego appeal to all comprehensive ideals of the human good, whether religious or secular. It therefore places no greater burden on those for whom their life's meaning turns upon their relation to God. Moreover, and on this score I have sought to refine Rawls' own argument, public reason in this sense applies to a limited domain only, where citizens decide upon the basic principles of their political life, as opposed to debating with one another the import of these measures in the light of the whole truth as they see it. The public square, in its usual meaning, refers to all the arenas and media in which citizens come together to discuss issues of common concern, and there religious convictions need not remain silent.

Now that we have delimited the proper domain of public reason, we may look at some more specific questions that arise.

4. AIMS AND EXCEPTIONS

Public reason amounts to a demanding form of self-discipline that the citizens of a liberal democracy are called upon to exercise. Many questions of an ethical or religious character, immensely important though they may be to people's self-understanding, will have to be set aside if they are to determine the political principles by which they will live, for such questions cannot receive any commonly acceptable answer. We need to keep in mind, however, the rationale for this enterprise. It would be wrong to suppose that for Rawls issues are to be removed from the political agenda just because there exists widespread disagreement about their solution. Public reason does not demand the blanket avoidance of deep-seated conflict, as though its highest value were civil peace. On the contrary, public reason embodies the ideal of fairness, and so questions having to do with the fair terms of social cooperation – in other words, matters of basic justice – belong on a society's program of political deliberation, however disputed they may be. Rawls could not have been more explicit on this score (PL, p. 151). It is hard to see, therefore, how he would have been obliged, as some have strangely charged,[17] to side with Stephen Douglas in the famous Lincoln–Douglas debates of 1858 and regard the issue of slavery as too controversial to be the object of political decision.

Slavery and its abolition constitute one of the formative experiences in American political life. To regard civil war as the worst of political evils and to suppose that differences should always be papered over by a *modus vivendi* is not a view likely to impress any American thinker, though Europeans of a Hobbesian persuasion sometimes endorse it. One of the benchmarks, not just of Rawls' conception of public reason, but of his political philosophy as a whole, was that basic justice takes precedence over civil peace or, perhaps better put, that it is a precondition for any civil peace worthy of the name. However, the American abolitionists, along with the more recent civil rights movement, also inspired a more specific feature of his theory of public reason. William Ellery Channing argued for the emancipation of the slaves just as Martin Luther King, Jr. argued against racial segregation by appealing to the belief that all human beings are equally God's creatures. Clearly they did not do so simply to indicate where they stood personally and to persuade others to share their faith.

---

[17] Notably Michael Sandel, in his review of *Political Liberalism*, op. cit., pp. 227–230; see also his *Democracy's Discontent* (Cambridge, MA: Harvard University Press, 1996), pp. 21–23. Rawls pointed out the unfoundedness of this charge in "The Idea of Public Reason Revisited" (CP, pp. 609–610).

Their aim was to encourage others to act on this religious view as they went about actually deciding those questions in their capacities as voters, legislators, officials, and judges. (Note that I have underscored the involvement of both forms of public debate, which Rawls' own depiction of these movements unfortunately does not distinguish.) Did Channing and King therefore overstep the bounds of public reason? On a straightforward understanding of that concept, they did. But this "*exclusive*" interpretation is not, Rawls argued (PL, 247–254), the only or even the proper way to think about public reason.

In a well-ordered society, where all citizens affirm together just principles of social cooperation, no one would need in public debate to look outside this common point of view to settle what justice requires. But the situation is different when a society is deeply at odds with itself about constitutional essentials. Then there exists no generally accepted language of public reason. In such cases, Rawls held, citizens may base their decisions upon comprehensive views that are themselves unlikely ever to form part of public reason, provided they believe or could have believed that thereby the ideal of public reason would be strengthened in the long run (PL. pp. 247, 251). Such is the "*inclusive*" interpretation of public reason presented in the first edition of *Political Liberalism* (1993). Subsequently, however, he modified this account, though not so as to switch to the opposite, "exclusive" position. Rather, he concluded that the conditions imposed on the appeal to comprehensive views needed to be relaxed even further. Instead of holding that citizens may reach beyond public reason only when their aim is to steer a profoundly unjust society toward greater justice, Rawls decided that citizens may call upon their full convictions at any time. The sole qualification is what he termed "the proviso": "in due course public reasons, given by a reasonable political conception, [must be] presented sufficient to support whatever the comprehensive doctrines are introduced to support" (PL, pp. li–lii). This "*wide*" view of public reason was introduced in "The Idea of Public Reason Revisited" (CP, pp. 584, 591–592). In the introduction to the second edition of his book (1996) he declared it to be his final and considered position.

I am not convinced that this change was for the better, at least in the form in which Rawls presented it. To begin with, one cannot help but worry about the vagueness of the proviso. On whom does the obligation fall to satisfy it and to provide the necessary public reasons? And how is the phrase "in due course" to be defined? Rawls conceded the existence of these difficulties, adding that no hard-and-fast rules but only "good sense and understanding" (CP, p. 592) can serve to handle them. That is fine, if the proviso is truly necessary. But it is unclear what advantages favor this more permissive conception in the first place. What need would there be in a well-ordered society to abandon the constraints of public reason? Rawls' answer was that in invoking their comprehensive views subject to the proviso, citizens make known how their ethical and religious convictions entail commitment to a common idea of justice. As a result, others will feel more secure in their own commitment, and stability will be enhanced, a boon even in the best of circumstances (CP, pp. 592–593; PL, p. lii).

Certainly, mutual reassurance of this sort is important. But does it have a part to play in the process by which citizens arrive at legally binding decisions in a well-ordered society? When fair principles of justice are acknowledged by all, why should citizens ever cast their nets more widely to establish how a remaining question of constitutional essentials should be authoritatively settled? It cannot be because they have found they disagree or because they feel uncertain about how the question is to be decided in accord with political reason. For, as we shall see, Rawls believed (and correctly so) that even then citizens should continue to heed the voice of public reason as each of them best understands it. In truth, showing one another the different routes by which they nonetheless converge on a shared conception of justice is beside the point when citizens are engaged in authoritatively *deciding* what principles governing the basic structure of society shall have the force of law. Their business then is to see how best they can implement the common ground they occupy together. Mutual reassurance does, however, have a place in the different sort of public debate that I have called *open discussion.* Indeed, Rawls may well have been led to his "wide" conception by the wish to make room for the freewheeling arguments about political issues that belong to the public life of a vigorous democracy. According to his own terminology, such arguments belong to what he called "the background culture." In permitting them to figure in the "public political culture" (subject to the proviso), Rawls was misled, I believe, by what that latter term suggests, as opposed to the way he had himself defined it. In situations where citizens decide upon the basic principles of their political association, the canons of public reason necessarily apply, at least in a well-ordered society, and basing one's decisions then upon divisive ideas of the human good must always be inappropriate.

The earlier, "inclusive" conception, which allows departures from public reason only when its most elementary ingredients are in great dispute, appears therefore to be the better position. It is important, however, not to exaggerate the rigor of its demands. In determining the fundamental principles by which they will live together, citizens in a well-ordered society ought indeed to choose those principles alone that they all can see reason to endorse. But they need not block from their minds the way their own comprehensive views about human flourishing may favor those principles; they need not even abstain from invoking those views, to themselves or to others, when such decisions are to be made. The requirement is that they do so only if they also acknowledge that the political authority of the principles in question rests solely upon their having a public justification,

acceptable to all. Citizens need not forget who they are or pretend to be
without their particular allegiances. At the same time, they must in fact act
as citizens.

So much for the question of how strictly the discipline of public reason
applies. Another question concerns how much it should aim to accomplish
within its sphere. Ideally it should set its sights on settling all matters of
fundamental justice, for they make up its appointed domain. A political
conception of justice, as Rawls says, should aim to be complete. Yet
situations arise where citizens, reasoning as best they can from the common ground they endorse as free and equal persons, find that they cannot
achieve reasonable agreement on an important issue of justice. The right
response may be to put off its resolution, not so much to avoid conflict as
to allow more time for reflection and experience to shape deliberation.
Suspending judgment can promote democracy.[18] Sometimes, however,
a decision cannot be postponed. It would be wrong, Rawls argued (PL,
pp. lvf., 240f.), for citizens then to suppose that, public reason having
failed to settle the issue, they may resort to considerations farther afield,
borrowed from those parts of their comprehensive views on which there is
no overlapping consensus.[19] Standoffs requiring a decision are indeed to
be handled by a vote, but a vote carried out in the spirit of public reason.
On this score, I am in full accord. Citizens should follow their best sense of
what public reason entails, despite the disagreement about what that is and
despite the uncertainty they may therefore feel in their own mind. And so,
where possible, they should also seek to minimize their differences by
giving extra weight to points of convergence (PL, p. 217).[20]

In fact, disagreements within the realm of public reason are only to be
expected (PL, pp. xlix, liif., lvi), since its common point of view, rightly
conceived, is not defined by any one political conception of justice – not
even by the liberty and difference principles in Rawls' own theory of justice.
This feature of his position has not been widely noted. It first appeared
in "The Idea of an Overlapping Consensus" (CP, p. 427), and after *Political
Liberalism* he returned to it in "The Idea of Public Reason Revisited" (CP,
pp. 581, 583, 605f.):

The content of public reason is given by a family of political conceptions of justice,
and not by a single one. There are many liberalisms and related views, and therefore

---

[18] This is one of the themes in the "judicial minimalism" of Cass Sunstein, *One Case at a Time*
(Cambridge, MA: Harvard University Press, 1999). For Rawls' sympathy with Sunstein's
approach, see CP, p. 618.

[19] For the contrary view, see Kent Greenawalt, *Religious Convictions and Political Choice* (New
York: Oxford University Press, 1988), and *Private Consciences and Public Reasons* (New York:
Oxford University Press, 1995).

[20] Here, Rawls alludes to the "principles of accommodation" advocated by Gutmann and
Thompson. See their book, *Democracy and Disagreement*, pp. 79–91.

many forms of public reason specified by a family of reasonable political conceptions. Of these, justice as fairness, whatever its merits, is but one. (CP, p. 581)

Rawls never gave this point the detailed treatment it deserves. But the thesis is exceptionally important. It represented his way of dealing with the fact, often adduced as a point (though wrongly) against his political liberalism, that justice, no less than the good life, has been an enduring object of dispute, even within liberal societies.[21] It also marked a significant innovation in his thinking since, as we have seen, "publicity" and then "public reason" were notions first worked out as part of his account of the two principles of justice. In the end, they came to be understood in a less partisan fashion.

Public reason, Rawls argued, must be able to welcome a family of liberal conceptions of justice, the essential conditions of a "liberal" conception being that it specify certain basic rights, liberties, and opportunities; that it assign a special priority to these elements of a constitutional regime; and that it aim to provide citizens with the means to make effective use of their freedoms (PL, pp. xlviii, 6, 223; CP, pp. 581–2). These are broad conditions, and citizens may make use of their political traditions and theoretical imagination to flesh them out in various ways.[22] Opposing views are likely to arise, and it is the sign of a vibrant democracy that controversies of this sort should go on and that individuals and social movements should be able to challenge the reigning interpretation of justice – not just in open debate, but also in political decision-making. Utilitarians, opposed though they must be to Rawls' own principles of justice and wedded instead to the ideal of efficiency, can still conclude that the general happiness is maximized by a scheme of justice satisfying these three conditions.

In their exercise of public reason, citizens may therefore appeal to the different perspectives making up this family of liberal conceptions. Rawls did not explain how they can do so while still heeding the demands of public reason. But it is not difficult to figure out how they have to proceed. In deciding some disputed issue, they must invoke their own views about justice in a form that does not exceed the bounds of the common point of view they share with their fellow citizens. This means that they must present them as ways of formulating more concretely the three conditions constitutive of a liberal outlook. Of course, their different conceptions of justice will also transcend this public rationale, which explains why they are likely to produce contrary interpretations of those basic, but very general principles embraced by all. Yet such disputes revolve around the proper

---

[21] See, for example, Jeremy Waldron, *Law and Disagreement* (Oxford: Oxford University Press, 1999), especially Chapter 7.

[22] Societies as a whole may also interpret these conditions differently and still remain essentially liberal in character, as I remarked before in connection with Quebec. See §3 at fn. 13.

understanding of this common point of view and do not call into question the authority of public reason. As Rawls remarked in this context (PL, pp. xliv, xlix, li; CP, pp. 574, 581), citizens espousing different conceptions of justice have to share a commitment to reciprocity if public reason is to be possible: they must view one another as free and equal citizens and be prepared to offer one another terms of cooperation that all have good reason to affirm. This standard, of course, is tantamount to what Rawls meant by fairness, and fairness, as we have seen, forms the core of the ideal of public reason.

Yet precisely when we see this defining feature of public reason for what it is, we may wonder whether Rawls' wish to accommodate a family of liberal conceptions can really be as generous as he supposed. On the one hand, his own two principles of justice are claimed to embody one possible view among others that citizens may invoke as they settle basic questions about constitutional essentials and about social and economic inequalities. But on the other, the very exercise of public reason must embody a commitment to fairness. Does not public reason effectively exclude appeal to any idea of justice that does not, unlike Rawls', view the distribution of rights and resources as a matter of arranging fair terms of social cooperation? Must not utilitarians, for example, find themselves debarred from speaking their minds? Believing that justice is to be achieved by institutions promoting the greatest net balance of satisfaction, they may well find reason to agree to the three broad principles characteristic of a liberal society. But if they must reason about how to give content to these principles in accord with the ideal of fairness, are they not being expected to switch philosophical allegiances and give up their distinctive way of thinking?

In reality, Rawls' latitudinarian vision of public reason is not the sham that it might seem at first glance. Recall the distinction I mentioned earlier (§1) between a *scheme of distributive justice* and *the basis of its authority* – that is, the nature of the reasons (for Rawls, essentially public reasons) that individuals can have for adhering to its principles. As I explained at the end of that section, his theory of justice aims to handle both these matters by means of the single notion of fairness (and the principle of respect for persons which it embodies). And thus this theory – as we can see now, all the more appropriately entitled "justice as fairness" – has a special standing among the liberal conceptions consonant with public reason. In it, as Rawls himself observed (PL, p. 225), "the guidelines of inquiry of public reason ... have the same basis as the substantial principles of justice." But nothing prevents other members of the group from treating these two topics by separate means. It is not, for example, incoherent to consider questions of distributive justice as ultimately questions of efficiency, while admitting that principles of justice, to have the force of law, must satisfy the criteria of public reason. Still, utilitarians who hold such a position will have to give their philosophical doctrine an "indirect" form: they will have to support as the public basis for affirming principles of justice a viewpoint (fairness) different from the one they themselves occupy when judging the ultimate reasons for any moral principles. No doubt Rawls continued to think (as in *A Theory of Justice*) that indirect utilitarianism is therefore inferior to his own liberty and difference principles of justice. But he admitted that it can belong to the overlapping consensus of a liberal society and thus take part in the discourse of public reason (CP, pp. 433–434). Indeed, he welcomed this fact, given the prominent place of utilitarian thought in the democratic tradition.

5. CONCLUSION

The loosening of the link between the ideal of public reason and Rawls's own two principles of justice, the increased recognition that controversy is an inescapable part of public reason, was one of the most interesting developments in his final writings. Clearly it involves many complexities, perhaps difficulties too, that have yet to be explored. Yet the key point to keep in mind is that these changes took place within a continuing allegiance to the guiding idea of fairness. If Rawls acknowledged that citizens may rightly interpret the core principles of a liberal society in different ways, he also insisted that they must remain united in their commitment to work out these differences within the terms of public reason. The disagreements that mark their deliberations must embody at the same time the fundamental sort of respect for one another which the idea of fairness requires.

As I indicated at the outset (§1), fairness and respect are notions that shaped Rawls' thought at the deepest level. Nowhere did he subject them to sustained analysis in their own right. Rather, they were deployed in a variety of ways, sometimes (as with fairness) in the metaphor of the social contract, sometimes (as with respect) more implicitly than otherwise, and sometimes in the guise of cognate notions such as reasonableness and reciprocity. But we will not understand his thought aright unless we trace their ramifications and perceive the overall conception they define. Fairness and respect inspired the social ideal to which his philosophical work sought to give systematic expression, an image of society that the early essay, "Justice as Fairness," evoked as the "mutual acknowledgement of principles by free persons" (CP, p. 59). According to this vision, the essential question is not so much the total good achieved as the relations in which people stand to one another as members of a collective undertaking. To borrow a phrase from the German Idealist tradition, we may say that for Rawls the just society was, first and foremost, a matter of "mutual recognition."

Public reason is the practice in which citizens make this vision a reality. Though an implicit theme already in *A Theory of Justice*, the idea of public reason assumed its true dimensions only in the "political liberalism" that Rawls went on to fashion in his later work. It stands at the heart of a philosophy devoted to exploring the meaning of fairness for political life.

PART IV

TRUTH AND CHANCE

9

Nietzsche and the Will to Truth

1. PIOUS AND FREE SPIRITS

In Book Five of *The Gay Science*, Nietzsche proudly placed himself among "the fearless ones" (*die Furchtlosen*), determined as he was to explain "to what extent even we are still pious."[1] One final form of piety has yet to be challenged, he declared, despite the Enlightenment's campaign against religious and metaphysical illusion, and indeed because of that movement's very success. It is the belief in the unconditional value of truth. Nietzsche wanted us to understand, of course, that he alone was the really fearless thinker. For only he dared to ask, "Why truth? Why not rather untruth?"

One mark of a philosopher's importance is to have seen the need to ask fundamental questions where others have proceeded with unquestioning assurance. Nietzsche was right that far too few have wondered why we should care about truth as we apparently do, holding our thought and action accountable to the way things are, by contrast with the way we might wish they were. Posing deep questions was one part of what made him a radical thinker. The other was his habit of going on to answer them in ways that sought to overthrow our ordinary self-understanding. To my mind, many of the recent Anglo-American commentaries on Nietzsche wrongly try to domesticate his thought, to make it presentable by likening

---

[1] Nietzsche, *The Gay Science* (*Die fröhliche Wissenschaft*), §344. As a rule, I shall refer to Nietzsche's writings by section numbers or chapter titles, and the translations given will be mine, though I have leaned on some published ones. There are two exceptions. One is the *Nachlass*, which I cite by referring to the page numbers in Karl Schlechta's edition of Nietzsche, *Werke in drei Bänden* (Munich: Hanser, 1966), and to the sections numbers in the English translation, *The Will to Power*, by Walter Kaufmann and R. J. Hollingdale (New York: Vintage, 1967). The other is *The Genealogy of Morals*, to which I refer often, and in citing which I add the page numbers from the English edition by Maudemarie Clark and Alan J. Swensen (Indianapolis: Hackett, 1998), though I have occasionally corrected their translation.

it to familiar philosophical options, whereas Nietzsche's aim was revolutionary, to shatter the most basic assumptions of the philosophical tradition. By his own self-description, he "philosophized with a hammer."[2] That was certainly the case in his critique of the "will to truth." Nietzsche believed that, once certain philosophical idols have been smashed, we should indeed be able to consider pursuing untruth rather than truth. I think that we have more to gain by following Nietzsche's thought on this subject through to the end, instead of holding back out of a wish to keep it within safe bounds. Some of his conclusions are indeed untenable, if not incoherent. But thereby the real and complex nature of our relation to truth will come more clearly into view.

In the passage I have cited, Nietzsche begins by noting that one of the chief elements in the scientific ethic is that the scientist's personal convictions are irrelevant, so far as the acceptance or rejection of hypotheses is concerned. Science – by which he means of course, not just the natural sciences, but all systematic and apparently disinterested inquiry (*Wissenschaft*, in the broad German sense of the term) – is an organized form of skepticism. It holds itself subject to the "police of mistrust."[3] However, things are not so simple, he insists, since science must always operate on the basis of presuppositions, and its deepest assumption is that truth "is necessary" (*noth tue*): "in relation to it everything else has only secondary value." Whence, Nietzsche asks, this will to truth? Why should we not rather deceive and let ourselves be deceived?

This passage of *The Gay Science* (§344) marked a crucial moment in the development of Nietzsche's thought. As part of Book Five ("We Fearless Ones"), it was written between the end of October 1886 and the spring of 1887, and first appeared in that book's second edition (1887), five years after the first. It took up a question already broached, though only briefly, in a work that had been published in the interim – namely, *Beyond Good and Evil* (1886). "Given that we want truth," he wrote there while surveying "the prejudices of philosophers," "*why not rather* untruth?"[4] And the passage provided the basic materials for the treatment Nietzsche gave of the will to truth in the last of his great published works, *The Genealogy of Morals*, written in July and August 1887 and published at the end of that year.

In the *Genealogy*, the will to truth stands at the center of the concluding sections (III. 23–28), where Nietzsche examines the role that the ascetic ideal has played in the development of modern science. Devotion to truth

---

[2] *Ecce Homo* (1889), "*Götzendämmerung. Wie man mit dem Hammer philosophiert.*"

[3] As he also makes clear in *The Genealogy of Morals* (III.23–24), Nietzsche is referring to the ideals of modern science (broadly construed), not to its reality, since it has in large part become, he believes, a business like any other, in which personal ambition and routine have replaced an all-consuming will to truth.

[4] Nietzsche, *Jenseits von Gut und Böse*, I.1: "Gesetzt, wir wollen Wahrheit, *warum nicht lieber Unwahrheit?*"

is not, he argues, merely one expression among others of the ascetic denial of life and its profusion of competing desires and interests. It is "that [ascetic] ideal itself in its strictest, most spiritual formulation, completely and utterly esoteric, stripped of all outworks, thus not so much its remnant (*Rest*) as its *core* (*Kern*)" (III.27, 116) – and so if the vantage point from which the errors of the old religious ideals are to be laid bare, then also the very heart and soul of the religious mentality. In Book Five of *The Gay Science*, Nietzsche had sketched his fantasy of the "free spirit" in the following terms: "a delight and power of self-determination (*Selbstbestim-mung*), a *freedom* of the will, in which the spirit takes leave of all faith or belief (*Glauben*) and every wish for certainty, practiced as it is in maintaining itself on light ropes and possibilities and dancing even beside abysses" (§347). But he now insists that free spirits are not really free so long as they still *believe* in truth – that is, so long as they remain driven by an "unconditional will to truth" (III.24, 109). For how can they really be self-determining if they suppose that truth is a value demanding their unqualified respect? If we hold that truth must prevail over every other sort of consideration, that it can never be compromised for the sake of some other end, and that we must follow it wherever it leads, then are we not still pious? Does not truth represent a final holy of holies, whose authority we remain afraid to challenge? Nietzsche's suspicion is that "we too still take our fire from that great fire that was ignited by a thousand-year-old belief, that belief of Christians, which was also Plato's belief, that God is truth, that truth is *divine*" (III.24, 110).

Thus Nietzsche now proclaims that he at least is prepared to question the authority of the will to truth. "Just look," he urges, after referring back to §344 of *The Gay Science*, "at the earliest and the most recent philosophies: all of them lack a consciousness of the extent to which the will to truth first needs a justification, here there is a gap in every philosophy" (III.24, 110). To be sure, his aim was not to fill this gap. In his view, the unconditional will to truth cannot be justified. He wanted instead to bring to our attention the blind spot in all philosophy until now, so that we might then understand ourselves to be free to create an altogether new order of values. His goal was to show why we should not *overestimate* truth. We must learn to regard it in the same way we are able to assess our other values, weighing its advantages and drawbacks (III.25, 111).

2. TRUTH AND MORALITY

In the *Genealogy of Morals*, Nietzsche leans heavily on the analysis he gave in Book Five of *The Gay Science* of the will to truth. So let us begin by looking at the key passage (§344) in that earlier work.

There he had asserted that insofar as we hold ourselves uncompro-misingly committed to truth, we stand in effect upon "moral ground" (*dem*

Boden der Moral). The stance we are adopting involves, he claimed, not so much a wish for our own good ("I do not want to let myself be deceived") as the idea of a duty under which we believe we stand ("I will not deceive," not even myself"). Later, in §3, I shall discuss in detail the significance Nietzsche attached to this distinction, which continues to play a decisive role in the *Genealogy*. But here is the gist of what he meant. Morality consists in a body of obligations that we supposedly owe to each and every person and that purport to be binding on us, whatever our other interests may be, and yet, he claimed, it is an illusion to suppose that there are any objective requirements of this sort. Now the will to truth displays all the formal features of a moral commitment. It exalts truth as requiring our steadfast devotion, and imposes on us the obligation to respect its demands, whatever may be our other desires, so that in cases of conflict we must be prepared to place truth above every other consideration. That is why *The Gay Science* describes the will to truth as at bottom a moral phenomenon, and thus similarly founded upon an illusion.

In the *Genealogy*, Nietzsche does take, in one respect, a somewhat different approach to the will to truth. The change comes about because he has become convinced in the meantime that the essence of morality lies in its being an "ascetic ideal" of life. Accordingly, he now asserts that the will to truth too must be an expression of that ideal.

What exactly did Nietzsche mean by an ascetic attitude toward life, of which morality is held to constitute one example among others? Asceticism signifies self-denial, of course. But Nietzsche understood such an attitude in very broad terms, including under it more than just a dedication to monkish virtues. In general, the ascetic outlook is for him an approach to life centered about a supreme and never fully achievable goal, to which we feel obligated to devote all our energies, foregoing our other possibilities as required. Ascetic ideals organize our lives into a pattern, relating all our experience and action to an overarching and constantly demanding purpose. They thereby bestow, as Nietzsche says, a meaning on suffering itself (III.28), since they allow us to see in it the price of our struggle or a sign that we have not exerted ourselves enough (III.15). The moral view of the world is one such form of self-discipline, and the will to truth, so he now claims, is another. It too embodies an ascetic attitude toward life, inasmuch as it represents truth as a goal commanding our unconditional allegiance even if it is never to be attained fully and definitively. Such has been the spirit of the philosophical tradition, and it continues to animate modern science, which, always ready to put apparent certainties into question and pursuing ever more fundamental and systematic explanations of things, will never reach anything like a definitive picture of the truth.

Even though the most illuminating way to analyze the will to truth now appears to consist in treating it as an expression of the ascetic outlook, Nietzsche still insists on the intimate relation it bears to the idea of moral obligation. The *Genealogy* (III.27, 116–117) quotes approvingly a long passage from §357 of Book Five of *The Gay Science*, which argued that the modern passion to expose the illusions of Christian dogma and to replace them with the scientific worldview stems from the very ethic of truthfulness (*Wahrhaftigkeit*), of "intellectual cleanliness at any price," that belongs at the heart of Christian morality. That ethic, he continues, needs to direct its energies toward itself, so that the question can at last be squarely faced, "*What does all will to truth mean?*" Still, we will be best able to get to the bottom of this question, once we realize that

What *compels* us to this unconditional will to truth is the *belief in the ascetic ideal itself* . . . . It is the belief in a *metaphysical* value, a value *in itself of truth* as it is established and guaranteed by that [ascetic] ideal alone (it stands and falls with that ideal)" (III.24, 109–110).

For then it becomes apparent, so Nietzsche declares, that behind the will to truth, as behind the ascetic attitude in general, there stands a fundamental aversion (*Widerwille*) to life (III.28, 118). Ascetic ideals embody a refusal to accept life on its own terms. What he takes these terms to be I shall explain at length later on (§5), though as I have already indicated, the leading idea is that value is something that we – that is, the forces of life at work in us – create rather than discover.

Nietzsche's ultimate aim is also clear. He longs for a way out of the ascetic outlook. And to that end, so he feels, nothing is more important than that the will to truth be dismantled, its inner motivations analyzed, and its apparent authority dissolved:

From the moment belief in the god of the ascetic ideal is negated, *there is a new problem*: that of the *value* of truth. – The will to truth is in need of a critique – let us thus define our own task – the value of truth is for once to be experimentally *called into question*. (III.24, 110)

The will to truth, particularly as it has taken shape in modern scientific consciousness, represents the ascetic ideal in its purest and "noblest form" (III.23, 107). What surer way, then, to break free from the ascetic attitude toward life in general than to expose the illusions still at work in the will to truth? "What meaning would *our* entire being have," so Nietzsche describes his present point of departure, "if not this, that in us this will to truth has come to a consciousness of itself *as a problem?*" (III.27, 117).

3. DECEPTION AND SELF-DECEPTION

In all these passages, Nietzsche was raising one of the deepest of philosophical questions. Why should truth appear so essential, so ineluctable a concern, that we can barely imagine a life in which we did not guide ourselves by what we held to be true? Whence this drive to dwell in the light of the truth, instead of opting for untruth and self-deception? Oddly, philosophy has tended to skirt the question of truth's authority, concentrating instead on the nature of truth or on the conditions under which our beliefs can be justified as true.[5] Why should we care about truth at all? It is all to Nietzsche's credit that he sought to tackle this neglected, but surely crucial question head-on. Yet I do not think that he truly appreciated its depth. Ultimately, his treatment remained superficial, and this failure was not accidental. At fault, as I shall explain, was his underlying conception of the nature of value in general, his so-called perspectivism.

Nietzsche also failed to distinguish clearly between two distinct things that he ran together under the term "the will to truth," and the difference between them needs to be noted at the outset, at least briefly, before we go any further. One is the *pursuit of truth as a goal*, or the determination to seek out the truth on matters about which we feel ourselves unacceptably ignorant or about which we suspect that we are mistaken or deluded.[6] This endeavor can take a highly systematic form, as in the modern scientific ethic to which Nietzsche so often refers, and that aims at ever deeper and more comprehensive explanations of the phenomena in some given domain of inquiry. But naturally it is at work in everyday life as well. Distinct from the pursuit of truth, however, is *respect for truth as a standard* – that is, the recognition that we should believe only that which we see to be true. When analyzing the will to truth in any detail, Nietzsche focuses on this latter and far more basic sort of commitment, despite the fact that he generally introduces his misgivings about the will to truth by referring to "*die moderne Wissenschaft*" as its exemplary embodiment. The crucial question, he then goes on to declare, is why truth rather than untruth and self-deception should serve as the rule for what we believe.

The difference between truth as a goal and truth as a standard ought to be plain enough at first glance, though I shall have more to say about it as I proceed. In particular, I shall argue that, in addition to their difference in content, the two may also diverge in the strength of the claims they make

---

[5] A recent and notable exception is Bernard Williams, *Truth and Truthfulness* (Princeton: Princeton University Press, 2002). Our ways of dealing with this question are so fundamentally opposed, however, that it may not be useful to discuss specific points of disagreement or convergence (though see fn 11 below). Williams pursued a broadly "naturalistic" approach, seeking to show how our allegiance to truth and to normative principles of thought and action in general can be understood in terms of more basic human interests (see. pp. 22–27). As my critique of Nietzsche will show, I do not believe that the naturalistic program can work. In the end, our normative attitudes only make sense by reference to an independent order of norms or reasons governing how we ought to think and act.

[6] Actually, the "search after truth" comprises two distinct goals, acquiring truths and avoiding error, but I will leave aside here this complication. See my essay, "Descartes and Skepticism," in Stephen Gaukroger (ed.), *The Blackwell Guide to Descartes' Meditations* (Oxford: Blackwell, 2005), pp. 17–29.

upon our thinking. A fundamental allegiance to truth as a standard of belief is a norm essential to what it is to be a thinking being, and in this regard quite different from truth taken as a goal. The will to truth understood in this sense, if not in the other, cannot be considered, as Nietzsche wants to do, as an option we might forego in favor of "untruth" instead.

With these preliminaries behind us, let us now look at the actual analysis he proposes of the will to truth. The best starting place is once again §344 of *The Gay Science*, for in the *Genealogy* itself (III.24, 110) he refers the reader back to this earlier text for the necessary details. That section begins with the statement that there seem to be two possible ways one might try to explain the will to truth. Is it the will not to deceive, or is it the will not to let ourselves be deceived? "Note," Nietzsche urges, "that the reasons for the former lie in a completely different area (*Bereich*) than those for the latter." We have already seen what he has in mind: the will not to deceive is an essentially moral phenomenon. But let us now look more closely at his argument (and observe that it deals exclusively with the will to truth in the elementary sense of truth regarded as the standard of all belief). The first option, "I will not deceive," if construed as meaning the same as "I will not in general deceive, and thus not even myself," is what lies at the heart of the unconditional will to truth, he argues. When we assume that we ought never to deceive – neither others nor ourselves (since we are but one person among others), we are supposing that we stand under an absolute obligation. That is why Nietzsche declares that "here we stand upon moral ground." And precisely because, so he continues, life "aims at semblance, i.e. error, deception, simulation, blinding, self-blinding," this immovable obligation to truthfulness shares in the ascetic attitude toward life, which runs through all morality.

But what about the other outlook, expressed in the phrase, "I will not let myself be deceived"? Nietzsche is convinced that the reasons to adopt this standpoint toward experience, if it is considered in its own right, unencumbered by any association with the resolve never to deceive anyone, have nothing to do with the notion of duty. "One does not want to let oneself be deceived," he assures us, "because one assumes it is harmful, dangerous, disastrous to be deceived," A judgment of this sort is based on prudence and, because it involves a calculation of utilities, it does not refer to any unconditional obligation. After all, one might calculate that in some circumstances life would go better with a little bit of self-deception, and as I have said, that is very much Nietzsche's opinion. Semblance and deception belong to the essence of life, so that "truth *and* untruth ... [are] both useful," he claims. If we were to look at the possibility of letting ourselves be deceived on its own terms, it would never occur to us to think that truth represents an unqualified duty, and we would never suppose that "truth is more important than anything else." So long as prudence, and not morality, calls the tune, there can be no such thing as the unconditional will to truth.

Precisely in his treatment of this last question, however, Nietzsche makes his fundamental mistake. He assumes that if we do not want to let ourselves be deceived, our decision must be based on the foreseeable disadvantages of self-deception. Our reflections supposedly take the following path: "It could prove harmful if I deceive myself or let myself be deceived; therefore it is best if I follow the truth." From this point of view, truth would be one possible consideration among others, which we may honor or set aside, depending on our given interests. An attachment to truth is not, however, so extrinsic to thought as Nietzsche imagines. On the contrary, thought is ultimately unintelligible unless it involves a basic directedness toward truth. This necessary relation between thought and truth has moreover very much the form of an *obligation* – if not a moral, then a rational obligation. For how can we possibly think anything at all, without feeling that we *ought* to respect, in some regards at least, the truth as we already conceive it? Even when we let our minds wander and dream about how the world might look, had it not turned out the way it actually did, we cannot escape having to draw our bearings from knowledge we already have. Otherwise, we would not have the slightest idea of what are the things we are fantasizing about, or of how they would behave as we imagine them endowed with different properties or situated in different circumstances.

4. TRUTH AND THOUGHT

But let me formulate my objection a bit more narrowly so that it applies to the case of self-deception, which Nietzsche finds so appealing. No doubt we sometimes willingly deceive ourselves. We persuade ourselves to believe an idea that is flattering to our interests despite the fact that the truth lies manifestly on the other side. It should be noticed, however, that self-deception never takes place under its own name. We cannot deceive ourselves while fully aware that self-deception is what we are engaged in. Like a gifted story teller, we have to fool ourselves into taking the fantasy to be true. And what does this fact show if not that it is impossible to believe something without believing it to be true? Naturally we can pretend to believe what we continue to regard as false. But that is cynicism, and cynics are those who do not really believe what they say that they believe.

In order to grasp the point more fully, let us look at what it means in general to believe something. The belief that some proposition p is the case – that the cat is on the mat, for example – does not consist in the content of the belief, the thought of the cat being on the mat, standing before the mind in some especially vivid way. Belief is a disposition, a tendency of the mind by which we are moved to think and act in ways appropriate to the proposition believed. In particular, it is a disposition inescapably bound up with the idea of truth. Believing entails holding to be true, and in more than a purely contemplative sense, for the aim of belief is not merely to represent to us the way things are. To believe that p is to stand committed to conducting ourselves in accord with the presumed truth of p. Anyone declaring that he believes the cat is on the mat but who then adds that he has no intention of acting accordingly, or who behaves with total indifference to the obvious implications of that belief, walking across the mat as though nothing were there, would hardly count as actually believing it. Belief is therefore a disposition of mind whose directedness toward truth is normative in character. To believe that p means being obligated to think and act in accord with the presumed truth of p, so that when our further thoughts and actions depart from what the belief would require, we are rightly said to have *failed* to proceed as we *should have done*.

All the greater then must be the failure to respect the obligation to truth inherent in all belief, if we take ourselves to believe something that at the same time we regard as false. Because the function of belief is to orient us in the world – a belief, said Peirce, is a "rule for action"[7] – we would be undermining its very purpose, were we to pull away the basis on which it serves to guide us – namely, by denying the presumed truth of the thing believed. So direct a violation of the normativity of belief amounts to *incoherence*. That is why, as G. E. Moore famously observed, it is self-defeating or paradoxical to say "It is not raining, but I believe that it is raining," even though the two conjuncts, "It is not raining" and "I believe that it is raining" could both be true, and even though the sentence "It is not raining, but John believes that it is raining" is not paradoxical in the least.[8] To assert a proposition, such as "It is not raining," is to assert it as true, and to believe it is to be committed to its truth, so that making a statement of that paradoxical sort is effectively to contradict ourselves.

Certainly truth has the status of a value when we regard it as a mistake not to respect the presumed truth of our beliefs and what it entails for our conduct. But truth is not an optional value. It makes no sense to ask, "Why not untruth instead?" – as though we had two options before us, between which we were to choose as we please. As John Donne once wrote,

> Though truth and falsehood be
> Near twins, yet truth a little elder is.[9]

Without a fundamental directedness and obligation toward truth, belief is unintelligible, and without a reliance on belief, thought itself – be it ever so imaginative or fantastical – becomes impossible. In *Beyond Good and Evil*

---

[7] See C. S. Peirce, "How to Make Our Ideas Clear" (1878), in Peirce, *Selected Writings*, ed. P. Wiener (New York: Dover, 1958), p. 121.

[8] G. E. Moore, "A Reply to My Critics," in P. A. Schilpp (ed.), *The Philosophy of G. E. Moore* (Evanston: Northwestern University Press, 1942), p. 541.

[9] Donne, *Satires* III ("Kind pity chokes my spleen"), 72–73.

(I.4), there occurs a claim that underlies the *Genealogy's* critique of the will to truth as well:

The falseness of a judgment is for us not necessarily an objection to a judgment; in this respect our new language sounds perhaps strangest. The question is to what extent the judgment is life-promoting, life-preserving.

But this way of talking is not just strange and disconcerting. It is incoherent. The falseness of a judgment is so conclusive a mark against it that we cannot decide to endorse it nonetheless except by talking ourselves into regarding it as true.[10]

The fact that belief aims essentially at truth has rightly been seen as explaining why we cannot believe anything at will. For if we could, then we would be able to choose to believe what at the same time we regard as false, and that is impossible (unless we first talk ourselves into supposing that it is true).[11] Indeed, our inability to believe at will extends even further. We cannot decide to believe what at the same time we see no *reason* to think may be true – such as the proposition that the number of stars is even rather than odd (unless again we trick ourselves into thinking that there is some such reason). This fact shows that belief necessarily aims, not simply at truth, but at truth as supported by reasons. And yet, one might now object, how can this inherent truth-directedness of belief also be regarded as normative in character, as involving an obligation to respect truth? Must not what we ought to do be something that we can fail to do?

This objection falls away, however, once we recognize that belief is in its very nature a normative state. The inability to believe at will is not a

---

[10] At one point in the *Nachlass*, Nietzsche appears to recognize that all belief involves an obligation toward truth, but only in order to declare that obligation optional after all, appealing to his "perspectivist" critique of the notion of truth (on the incoherence of which, see §5 of this chapter):

What is a *belief*? How does it originate? Every belief is a *holding-something-to-be-true*. The most extreme form of nihilism would be the insight that *every* belief, every holding-something-to-be-true, is necessarily false because there simply is no *true world*. Thus: a *perspectival appearance* whose origin lies in us (insofar as we continually *need* a narrower, abbreviated, simplified world).
– That it is the measure of strength to what extent we can admit to ourselves, without perishing, the merely *apparent* character, the necessity of lies.
To this extent, nihilism, as the denial of a truthful world, of being, might be a *divine way of thinking* (*Werke* vol. III, 555; *The Will to Power* §15, translation modified. Kaufmann dates the passage to Spring–Fall 1887).

[11] See the classic essay by Bernard Williams, "Deciding to Believe," in his *Problems of the Self* (Cambridge: Cambridge University Press, 1973), pp. 136–151, as well as his *Truth and Truthfulness*, pp. 79–83. It is not clear to me whether Williams thought of the inability to believe at will as a psychological or normative impossibility (for the distinction, see the next paragraph).

psychological incapacity (as though, try as we might, we cannot manage to pull it off, just as we cannot form the mental image of a chiliagon). It is a logical matter, a direct implication of the normative commitments essential for a state of mind to count as a belief. Believing at will is impossible in the sense of being contrary to what belief as such requires. To believe is to hold ourselves accountable to the supposed truth of what we believe, and the normative character of all believing shows itself unmistakably whenever we come upon some reason to think that what we believe may be false. For that very discovery impels us to think that we ought to do something about the situation, if only to forget about what we have discovered. Certainly we can fail to respect truth in our beliefs as we ought to do. We may, for example, be too distracted to realize that other things we know show that some belief of ours is false, or perhaps we are blocking such evidence from our minds in an effort to delude ourselves that the world is otherwise. The point is that we cannot knowingly disregard truth as the standard that our beliefs must respect, for then we will not qualify as actually believing these things; we will only be saying or pretending to do so.[12]

With this, I come to the heart of my complaint: Nietzsche does not realize that thought in general is possible only in virtue of its being bound by norms, truth as a standard of belief belonging inescapably among them. Thus it is that he fails to see that the concept of obligation must also figure in the answer to the question, "Why not let ourselves be deceived?" He could not have been more wrong in claiming that an unconditional "ought" only comes into play with the universal principle, "One ought never to deceive anyone, not even oneself." Certainly a demand of this latter sort would form part of morality, if valid. But nothing in the preceding remarks serves to justify a universal prohibition against lying. As a matter of fact, any categorical rule of that sort is morally unacceptable. We have no overriding duty to tell the truth. Benjamin Constant was surely right to argue against Kant that sometimes we ought to lie in order to protect the lives of others.[13] But the moral "ought" is not the only kind of "ought" – this is the key point. There also exist obligations of thought, belonging to what is rightly called the ethics of belief, to which we must consider ourselves to be subject, in order to be able to think coherently at all.

---

[12] As Jonathan Adler rightly insists in his book, *Belief's Own Ethics* (Cambridge, MA: MIT Press, 2002), the ethics of belief, governing how we ought to form our beliefs, is rooted in the very nature of belief, and particularly in our inability to believe at will. For Adler, the key point is that if we ought only to believe what we take ourselves to have good reason to regard as true, that is because we cannot – as a matter of "conceptual necessity" – do otherwise when fully aware of our epistemic circumstances. I would only add that the "conceptual necessity" involved is normative in character: all belief necessarily embodies a commitment to respect the truth of what is believed.

[13] See Kant's famous, or rather infamous, reply to Constant; "Über ein vermeintliches Recht, aus Menschenliebe zu lügen."

If the will to truth consists in believing only what we take to be true, then it is already at work in our relation to our own thinking, whatever may be the character of our relations to others.

5. PERSPECTIVISM

If Nietzsche analyzes so poorly the will to truth (again in the elementary sense under consideration), it is because he is wedded to a particular picture of the mind: on the one side there is thought, and on the other side, values. To be sure, he never tires of asserting that we are in essence evaluating (*schätzend*) beings, always ranking the things of our experience in terms of "better" or 'worse," "noble" and "base," "good" and "evil." But when we do so, he assumes, the values we thereby express are ones that we have chosen to affirm, and in place of which we could have adopted others. The mind's relation to any particular value is contingent in nature. That is because, as Nietzsche even more basically assumes, our adherence to values is an expression of our will. We ourselves create the values we affirm, in the sense that the authority they exercise over our belief and action is one of our own making, even though our religious and philosophical traditions ("Christianity" and "Platonism," as he called them) have obscured from view our authorship and lent them an objectivity, an independence from our will, that they do not possess. Thus Zarathustra says:

Truly, men have given themselves all their good and evil. Truly, they did not receive it, they did not find it, it did not descend to them as a voice from heaven.... Evaluation is creation (*Schätzen ist Schaffen*).... Only through evaluation is there value (*Wert*).[14]

What Nietzsche fails to realize, however, is that thinking is in itself a norm-governed activity.[15] We cannot think without acknowledging the authority of certain basic obligations governing how it is that we ought to think. All thought aims, whatever its other ends, at a minimal level of intelligibility, defined by such requirements as the avoidance of self-contradiction. Whether we are trying to find out the way things are or simply fantasizing about how they might be, if we set about deliberately flouting these norms, talking about square circles, we will not really have managed to think anything at all. Sometimes, of course, we may knowingly posit a contradiction in order to show (by way of a *reductio ad absurdum* argument) that one of its components must be false. Yet, even then, the contradiction does not express any thought that we can think; rather, it is the object of our thought, in that we think about it that it is a contradiction and draw the appropriate consequences. Sometimes too we may inadvertently assert something that

[14] Nietzsche, *Also sprach Zarathustra*, Erster Teil, "Von tausend und einem Ziele."
[15] For more details, see my book, *Les pratiques du moi* (Paris: PUF, 2004), Chapter 4, as well as "The Autonomy of Morality," §8, Chapter 5 in the present book.

happens to be contradictory. We may suppose, for instance, that there exists a largest prime number. But not only can we attach no sense to that idea once we hold before our mind Euclid's proof of the contrary, we also realize that in asserting it we were not giving voice to any real thought at all, though we may have thought that we were.

Another such elementary obligation of thought is the allegiance to truth in matters of belief: believing something requires holding it to be true, and regarding a proposition as false entails, on pain of incoherence, viewing it as one that we ought not to believe. Some values are not essential to the very possibility of intelligible thought – moral values, for example. With regard to them, there is at least the logical space for imagining that they are our own creation, and the question has then to be settled in a substantive way by reflecting on our reasons for endorsing them: we must ask ourselves whether they would matter to us as they do, if we regarded them as possessing only the authority we choose to give them, and not as standing in judgment over our desires and decisions. I hope that others on reflection would agree that this is not so.[16] But the situation is, in any case, different with values such as truth. A commitment to truth cannot be understood as distinct from our thinking and thus as a possible object of choice, to which we might respond by saying, "No, untruth instead," The obligation to respect truth is inseparable from what it is to think at all.

The source of Nietzsche's mistake is therefore his conviction that our adherence to values is always an expression of the will. This conviction takes on systematic form in his concept of life and in the doctrine of "perspectivism" he built around it. In the passage cited earlier from *Beyond Good and Evil* (I.4), he claims that the crucial feature of any judgment is not really its truth, but rather its capacity for being "life-promoting and life-preserving." And in the next-to-last sentence of the *Genealogy of Morals*, he calls the ascetic ideal in general – and thus the will to truth in particular – "an aversion to life, a rebellion against the most fundamental presuppositions of life" (III.28, 118). What are these fundamental presuppositions? "*Perspective*," he declares in the Preface to *Beyond Good and Evil*, "[is] the basic condition of all life."

By "perspective," Nietzsche had more in mind than just the idea that we always view the world from some particular standpoint, drawing our premises from our historical context, social expectations, and various interests. That is no doubt so. But Nietzsche's interest lay first and foremost with the norms of thought and action that give the world as we see it its overall shape, defining what possibilities will count as justified or good. Perspectives differ in virtue of the norms by which they variously structure

---

[16] I do not believe that we can be reasoned into an acknowledgement of basic moral values from a standpoint outside the moral point of view itself. Morality has to speak for itself. See Chapter 5.

our experience. Yet they are all, he held, expressions of life. What then did he mean by "life"? Nietzsche never wavered in his answer to this question. "A living thing seeks above all to *discharge* its strength," he declared in *Beyond Good and Evil* (I.13); "life itself is will to power." All life is driven by the effort to gain power over its environment, and that is no less the case for beings like us, who consciously rank some things as more worthy than others and guide ourselves by norms of conduct that distinguish between right and wrong ways of proceeding. Perspectives serve to render the world hospitable to our needs and desires. The norms that structure them – and this is the core idea of Nietzsche's perspectivism, combining his conceptions of perspective and life – have their basis in our will. The sole authority they possess is the authority we ourselves bestow on them. As Zarathustra puts the thesis,

Man first implanted values into things in order to maintain himself – he created the meaning of things, a human meaning! Therefore he calls himself: "Man," that is, the evaluator (*der Schätzende*).[17]

This doctrine, we must remember, concerns more than just moral and ethical values. Nietzsche's perspectivism presents itself as an account of value as a whole, including the principles by which we regulate the formation of belief, in everyday life as in the sciences. As a result, it is not simply the *value* of truth that on this view is a matter of the will. The *nature* of truth must be so too. If by truth we mean the way the world is, but can say nothing about the way it is except on the basis of reasons for belief whose authority derives from our own will alone, then truth in the only sense it can have for us must be something we create, not discover. "There are no facts, only interpretations" is the handy maxim by which he summed up the position,[18] and in the next section I shall have occasion to discuss the extra difficulties he got into on that score.

The point for now is that it was his general picture of the mind's relation to value that kept Nietzsche from grasping the normative constitution of thought itself. Certainly he recognized that we typically see ourselves, in fundamental ways, as subject to norms that are not of our own making. But that is an illusion, he insisted, arising from the will's tendency to turn against itself for the sake of its own ends. We deny our authorship of the values we posit, representing them instead as objectively binding, independently of the will, precisely in order to enhance our power (though usually without making it explicit to ourselves). Dressing up our interests in the garb of obligatory norms serves to make our disapproval of rival values all the more imposing, and at the same time reassures us that our

[17] *Also sprach Zarathustra*, Erster Teil, "Von tausend und einem Ziele."
[18] Nietzsche, *Werke*, ed. K. Schlechta, vol. III, p. 903 (*The Will to Power*, §481, dated by Kaufmann to 1883–1888).

lives have a meaning, attuned to an enduring order of right and wrong. Such, for Nietzsche, is the origin of all ascetic ideals. We refuse to acknowledge the very forces of life that give rise to our values, and continue to do so even as we strip away one religious or metaphysical illusion after another in the name of our obligation to the cause of truth. "Naysaying" of this sort has become so much second nature, he believed, that he wondered at the end of *The Genealogy of Morals* (III.28) whether man has ever managed to escape the ascetic attitude, ever been able to give a wholehearted "yes" to the will and to life.

What would it be like to be really a free spirit, no longer a prisoner of the ascetic outlook? Nietzsche provided an answer in the statement of his intellectual mission that appears in the preface to the second edition of *The Birth of Tragedy*, "An Attempt at Self-Criticism" (*Versuch einer Selbstkritik*), written in 1886. The task, he proclaimed (§2), is "to see science from the viewpoint of the artist (*unter der Optik des Künstlers*), and art itself from that of life." We need to regard all our values, including the values of science – and that means above all the value of truth – as though they were in essence works of art, beautiful and moving, but having no grounding in the way things really are. And that means seeing our values as expressions of life's boundless creativity, fashioning itself a world (a "perspective") for the exercise of its powers. In the *Genealogy* (III.25, 111–112), Nietzsche refers explicitly to this text, written only a short time before. Science ought to appear as a "problem," he declares, insofar as it supposes itself bound by an objective duty toward truth, thereby becoming "the confederate" of the ascetic outlook. "Art, in which lying hallows itself, in which the will to deception has good conscience on its side, is much more fundamentally opposed to the ascetic ideal than is science."

And yet, for all the eloquence with which Nietzsche evokes its radical promise, this vision of freedom is incoherent. Our lives cannot possibly be ones of limitless self-creation, and not only because we are always shaped by outside forces that we cannot fully control. Thinking itself would be unintelligible without a respect for the demands of truth.[19]

6. TRUTH AS A GOAL

Deciding to challenge the will to truth in its most elementary sense, Nietzsche failed to appreciate that, without a basic allegiance to truth, belief and thus thinking in general would be unintelligible. This failure was doubly disappointing. For in directing his doubts at norms of thought that are in fact inescapable, he let himself be diverted from a more rewarding line of inquiry. The real object of his distrust was the will to

---

[19] For more on this incoherence in Nietzsche's perspectivism, see my book, *The Morals of Modernity*, Chapter 4 ("Nietzsche's Legacy").

truth in quite a different sense – namely, the single-minded pursuit of truth whatever the cost to our other interests. As I have mentioned, Nietzsche never properly differentiated between truth as a goal and truth as a standard. Had he recognized the distinction and focused his skepticism on the former alone, or more exactly on the notion that truth constitutes an always paramount goal, he would have been on surer ground. For we are not bound to pursue truth unconditionally, even if we are strictly required to believe only that which we take to be true and to conduct ourselves accordingly. Moreover, imagining that truth does form that sort of supreme end is, as he suspected, a perfect example of what can be called the "ascetic attitude toward life." Nietzsche's sweeping rejection of the very idea of unconditional obligation ("the worst of tastes, the taste for the unconditional" – *Beyond Good and Evil* II.31) led him to miss the opportunity to distinguish what place truth must and what place it need not occupy in the stance, however open-minded or relaxed, we take toward the world.

These points will become clearer, if we look once again, though this time more closely, at the difference between truth as a goal and truth as a standard. The pursuit of truth may simply consist in the determination to seek out knowledge on matters about which we would prefer not to be ignorant or about which we fear we may be mistaken. It can also involve more systematic modes of inquiry. No doubt Nietzsche first grew suspicious of the "will to truth" because of the peculiar sense of mission he remarked in two quite influential forms that the pursuit of truth has taken in modern times. One was the Enlightenment campaign against religious superstition and prejudice, and the other the modern scientific ethic with its ideal of a common enterprise of theory-building, hypothesis-testing, experimentation, and technological application, in which each generation builds on the results of its predecessors. They were the phenomena that moved him to complain in *The Gay Science* and the *Genealogy of Morals* that the self-styled "free spirits" of his age and enthusiasts of "modern science" were still prisoners of that ultimate piety of thought, that purest expression of the ascetic attitude toward life, that is the "Platonic-Christian" conviction that "truth is divine." Yet if there is any justification to Nietzsche's charge, it depends essentially on the will to truth meaning in this case the pursuit of truth as a goal. For the target of his criticism is the assumption that truth represents a goal of such immense value as to override all other possible ends.

Consider, by contrast, truth's role as the standard of belief. It has a very different character from the pursuit of truth as a goal. In believing something, we commit ourselves to thinking and acting in accord with the presumed truth of what we believe, but not to the pursuit of any particular sort of goal. Respect for truth, in this elementary sense, is an obligation that functions as a *side-constraint*: our ends, whatever they may be, depend on our beliefs – that is, on what we see reason to do given the presumed truth of the relevant beliefs, so that if we change our mind about their truth, we ought to modify our conduct accordingly. This "ought" is indeed unconditionally binding; there is no way we can escape its demands, belonging as it does to the essence of belief. Nonetheless, it does not by itself direct us to adopt any specific ends or to rank our ends in any specific manner.

The pursuit of truth as a goal is a very different matter, and particularly so in the case of the two phenomena that most occupied Nietzsche's attention – the Enlightenment crusade against religious illusion and the enterprise of modern science. And yet, the real object of his suspicion was not so much these projects in and of themselves but rather the self-understanding they have typically embodied, their exaltation of truth as an end to be pursued unconditionally, wherever it may lead and whatever the cost. What he found problematic, in short, was their hardening into ascetic ideals. After all, as it should go without saying, Nietzsche himself felt a deep loyalty to both these intellectual movements: his analysis of the mechanisms of resentment supposedly underlying Christian morality was meant, for example, to be at once an attack against one of the last redoubts of a dying God and an exercise in scientific psychology. But loyalty need not mean idolatry. One need not regard the pursuit of truth as a sacred duty, before which every other human concern must make way, even if historically – and this was Nietzsche's complaint – it has often taken such a form. The notion that "truth is divine," that we must seek "truth at any price,"[20] is the residual sort of intellectual piety that he believed we must overcome in order to be genuinely free spirits.

Several considerations, of unequal merit, fueled this verdict. One has to do with the *nature* of truth. We imagine, thought Nietzsche, that truth is an end commanding our unconditional devotion, because we suppose that the true itself, the goal of inquiry, consists in what is the case independently of any interests of our own. But if we have no way of determining truth except by norms of inquiry that are our own creation, based on our needs and aspirations, not norms we stand under an obligation to heed, then there can be no basis for believing that the pursuit of truth must always count for more than our other concerns. Anything we can mean by truth must be a "human, all too human" construct. Notoriously, of course, Nietzsche espoused just such an anthropocentric account of truth, and it provided him with one of his reasons to reject the unconditional will to truth. How convincing is it, however?

Take the version he propounded in an early essay of 1873, *Truth and Lie in the Non-moral Sense*, an essay that has been an inspiration to deconstructionist thinkers such as Paul de Man.[21] There he argued that

---

[20] *The Gay Science*, preface to the second edition (1887), §4.
[21] Paul de Man, *Allegories of Reading* (New Haven: Yale University Press, 1979), pp. 110–118.

all so-called truth is actually illusion, a reduction of the teeming chaos of reality into a more manageable form to suit our own interests – to serve, in other words, the will to power. This theory is manifestly self-refuting. Is it, for instance, itself merely a convenient fiction? And how can it presume to know, consistently with what it takes truth to be, that the world itself differs from what we make of it? Accordingly, some recent commentators have claimed that Nietzsche went on to develop a more sophisticated account of truth. His mature position, they maintain, is that there is no such thing as "the world in itself," only the world as conceived in the light of various human interests, and therefore nothing with which the latter might be contrasted as "illusory."[22]

I doubt that this gambit offers a way out of the difficulty. Though Nietzsche did come to reject explicitly the intelligibility of any reference to the way the world is in itself, he never gave up his perspectivism nor the conviction he based on it that truth, in the only meaning the term can have for us, is something we create, an expression of the will to power.[23] And there lies the rub. For what can it mean to say that we always conceive the world from the standpoint of certain interests and preoccupations, if not that the world itself exists quite apart from being so viewed and indeed from however we may choose to view it? There can be no such thing as "perspective" without an independent reality that is its object. We have already seen that Nietzsche's perspectivism is incoherent insofar as it denies the objectivity of value: it fails to recognize that thought, to be intelligible, must hold itself accountable to certain basic norms. Now we can see that it is also incoherent to the extent that it denies that there is a world distinct from our perspectives, a world in itself about which some things are true and others false. This fact shows, moreover, that we cannot understand (as the perspectivist would want us to do) the authority of the

---

[22] The key text invoked to support this interpretation is the conclusion of the section in the *Twilight of the Idols* entitled "How the 'True World' Finally Became a Fable": "With the true world we have also abolished the apparent one." This statement is taken to express Nietzsche's recognition that once we reject as unintelligible the idea of a metaphysically "true world" – the way the world really is, independent of any human perspective – there can be no basis for thinking that the world as we do picture it to ourselves is "apparent" or "illusory." See Maudemarie Clark, *Nietzsche on Truth and Philosophy* (Cambridge: Cambridge University Press, 1990), and for the connection between this view of truth and Nietzsche's critique of the unconditional will to truth, see Brian Leiter, *Nietzsche on Morality* (London: Routledge, 2002), Chapters 1 and 8.

[23] Here is a representative passage, taken from the *Nachlass*: "'Truth' is not therefore something that is there, that is to be found or discovered – but instead something *that is to be created* and that is the name of a *process*... It is a word for the 'will to power'" (*Werke*, vol. III, p. 541; *The Will to Power* §552, dated by Kaufmann to Spring-Fall 1887). And for evidence that even with an explicit denial of there being a world in itself Nietzsche was still capable of calling all supposed truth an illusion, see the contemporaneous passage from the *Nachlass* quoted in fn 10.

principles by which we evaluate claims to truth as being simply of our own making. For to rely on these principles for the justification of belief is to suppose that we have reason to think they help us capture what is non-perspectivally true. Their validity is something we must therefore believe we have discovered. Let me state the general point in a more epistemological idiom: though we always judge truth by our existing criteria, which might well have been different had our experience gone otherwise, we cannot make sense of this very predicament except by assuming that the truth itself we thereby seek transcends such contingencies of time and place.[24]

Nietzsche always adopted a debunking tone when taking up the topic of the nature of truth and of what we can possibly mean by it. The *Genealogy of Morals* is no exception.[25] This *parti pris* did not keep him from also invoking certain "truths" as settled or from extolling a "respect for facts," when it suited his purposes.[26] But the existence of such passages is no reason to suppose that his actual position on truth must therefore have been uncommonly subtle. The fact of the matter is that Nietzsche did not aspire to be a consistent thinker (why should he have done so, given his scorn for the notion of objective obligations, moral or intellectual?), and it is futile to try to make him into one.

This first line of argument was not the only source of his attack on the unconditional will to truth, and fortunately so. He also took a more promising tack, one that considered directly the *value* of truth. Why, he asked, should we suppose that knowing the truth will always enhance the prospects of human flourishing? It is a "fundamental insight," he declared

---

[24] For more details, see Chapter 1, "History and Truth." Defenders of Nietzsche's views sometimes liken them to Hilary Putnam's "internal realism," and if the latter is understood as claiming that "true" properly means "verifiable under ideal epistemic conditions," as opposed to "agreeing with the world as it is in itself" (the position dubbed "metaphysical realism"), then these criticisms extend to that position as well. For what, in the end, can make the conditions under which we appraise our beliefs "epistemically ideal" if not that they allow us to grasp what the world is like in itself? Anything less would be less than ideal. "Internal realism" turns out to entail "metaphysical realism," just as "perspective" implies the existence of an independent reality that it purports to disclose. To prevent misunderstanding, let me add that the metaphysical realism I claim to be ineluctable has no inner affinity with the idea that the world as it is in itself just is the world of physics, with no room for thoughts, feelings, and values. (That sort of reductionism seems to have been Putnam's own chief worry in these matters; see his *Realism with a Human Face*, Cambridge, MA: Harvard University Press, 1990, p. xi). On this last issue, see "The Autonomy of Morality," Chapter 5 in the present book, §7.

[25] In the *Genealogy* III.24 (109), he suggests that the "*essence* of all interpreting" consists in "doing violence, pressing into orderly form, abridging, omitting, padding, fabricating, falsifying," and this from a philosopher who famously declared, at roughly the same time (in a passage from the *Nachlass*), that "there are no facts, only interpretations" (see fn 18).

[26] See, for example, *The Antichrist* §59, where he contrasts Christian faith with the ancients' "sense for facts, the last-developed and most valuable of the senses."

in *Human, All too Human* (1878), that "there is no pre-established harmony between the furtherance of truth and the well-being of humanity" (§517). And the main charge the *Genealogy* (III.25, 111) brings against the will to truth is that it expresses an "overestimation" of truth. Sometimes his concern is that the very truth we discover might prove irreparably damaging to our confidence in other purposes that we hold dear. "It is quite possible," he declares in a *Nachlass* passage, "that the true constitution of things should be so hostile to the presuppositions of life, so opposed to them, that we would need appearance in order to be able to live."[27] Such a possibility is certainly intelligible, though acknowledging it does stand in some tension, I would note, with Nietzsche's insistence that truth itself is but another name for the will to power. In other passages, he points to the possible costs, not of the truth discovered, but of the activity of pursuing it. Knowledge is not the only good, and wisdom involves maintaining a certain balance among our different and often competing interests. Other goods too have a claim on our attention, even though following their call can mean knowing less than we otherwise would about the world or about ourselves. To make the search after truth always our paramount concern is in reality the mark of an uncivilized mind.

This criticism could not be more justified. Think, for instance, of how impoverished our lives would be if we felt always obliged to seek out the real motives behind some passion or enthusiasm of ours before letting ourselves be swept away. Objections of this sort to the will to truth form a constant refrain in Nietzsche's writings, from early unpublished writings such as *Philosophy in the Tragic Age of the Greeks* to a passage such as the following from the preface to the second edition of *The Gay Science* (§4):

> No, we have grown sick of this bad taste, this will to truth, to 'truth at any price', this youthful madness in the love of truth: we are too experienced, too serious, too jovial, too burned, too deep for that.... Oh, those Greeks! They knew how to *live*: what is needed for that is to stop bravely at the surface, the fold, the skin, to worship appearance, to believe in shapes, tones, words – in the whole Olympus of appearance! Those Greeks were superficial – *out of profundity!*"

A statement like this might seem to suggest a recognition that there exists an irreducible plurality of different human goods potentially in conflict with one another. Yet plainly Nietzsche was no "value-pluralist" in any fundamental sense. Like other monists, he too believed that every good is good insofar as it expresses or promotes a single ultimate end.[28] Of course, in his case, the master value was none of the traditional candidates – not pleasure

---

[27] Nietzsche, *Werke*, vol. III, p. 763 (*The Will to Power*, §583, dated by Kaufmann to March–June 1888). Whence the famous remark, "We have *art*, so that we may *not perish from truth*" (ibid. p. 832; *The Will to Power*, § 822, dated by Kaufmann at 1888).

[28] I have explored in some detail the nature of value pluralism in *The Morals of Modernity*, Chapter 7.

or reason, for example. It was freedom, as he understood it. His guiding conviction, as is all too clear, was that every value we affirm is one we ourselves set up in order to bend the world to our will. "Life itself is will to power" (*Beyond Good and Evil*, I.13), and were we finally to say "yes" to life, instead of positing our values as somehow objective, binding on us independently of our will, then we would rejoice in our own powers as the source of everything we hold to be valuable. All Nietzsche's own assertions about what is good and noble always appeal to a single benchmark – the freedom to create values that acknowledges no higher authority, the freedom he celebrated in his ideal of the "free spirit." The reason, he believed, why the pursuit of truth should sometimes yield to other concerns is that our ends draw their worth, their essentially relative worth, from the way they manifest or further our own protean creativity.

7. OVERCOMING THE ASCETIC ATTITUDE

Here as elsewhere, the perspectivist credo acted to distort his best insights. If only he had been content to point out that knowledge, even self-knowledge, is but one good among others, instead of making everything a matter of the self-assertion of the will! A sense of proportion was not, of course, what Nietzsche, philosophizing with a hammer, was inclined to display. Yet it would in fact have been the best frame of mind in which to think about what is fundamentally wrong with the ultimate target of his critique of the will to truth – namely, the ascetic attitude toward life.

In his view, the tendency to regard the pursuit of truth as unconditionally binding – again I distinguish, as he did not, between truth as a goal and truth as a standard – is not simply one more manifestation of the ascetic attitude toward life. It is the very epitome of that attitude. "What compels one to this unconditional will to truth is the belief in the ascetic ideal itself," he wrote (*Genealogy* III.24, 109–110). The will to truth is "that ideal itself in its strictest, most spiritual formulation ... not so much its remnant as its core" (III.27, 116). Though he never explained why there is this special connection, I do not think his reasoning is difficult to divine. If the ascetic outlook is "a rebellion against the fundamental presuppositions of all life," and life itself is essentially the creative positing of values, then this life-denying outlook consists at bottom in assuming that the ends worth pursuing have a validity independent of our will – that there exists, in short, a truth about what is right and good, a truth it is imperative for us to grasp. What then would be a purer expression of that outlook than to have one's ascetic goal be the very thing that gives to ascetic goals their apparent objectivity, to make truth itself one's supreme end?

Enough has already been said, however, to show what is amiss in Nietzsche's diagnosis of the ascetic attitude. It is his conception of life itself. Thinking beings like us, who are able to reflect upon the discriminations they make between what is valuable and what is not, cannot coherently understand the lives they lead except in terms of their being responsive to norms that are not of their own making. Truth as the standard of belief is no doubt the most basic of such norms, but it is not the only one. Earlier (§6) I noted how the principles by which we think truth-claims ought to be evaluated must also be understood as principles whose validity we have discovered, not instituted. We are essentially normative beings, and not because we are inescapably the authors of the norms by which we operate. Just the reverse: we live and move and have our being only within an order of reasons to which we hold ourselves accountable.[29]

If there is a widespread attitude toward existence that might properly be criticized as "ascetic," closing itself off to the true dynamic of life – and I join Nietzsche in thinking that there is – it is not the belief that our will is subject to demands whose authority over our conduct we do not ourselves establish. That conviction reflects the essence of the human condition. Accordingly, the alternative to the ascetic outlook does not lie, as Nietzsche held, in affirming our own will as the source of all value, and thus in substituting the spirit of play for an ethic of obligation. Disease and cure must be understood differently. The outlook that may properly be called ascetic and life-denying is instead the idea that life is such a serious business that it needs to be made the object of a disciplined and well thought-out plan. Either foresight and control or an existence at the mercy of chance and whim – approaching life in these dualistic terms is a mainstay of both the philosophical tradition and everyday thinking. Each of us, it is commonly assumed, ought to weigh together our capacities, circumstances, and interests in order to devise an overall conception of how we should live, a conception in which we must sacrifice some possibilities for the sake of those we deem more important and realistic. The world, of course, may always end up defeating a rational life plan of this sort, but even then, so it is supposed, we will have done our best and will have nothing in hindsight to reproach ourselves for, despite our regret at not having succeeded. We will have taken charge of our lives, to the extent that it lies in our power, instead of letting life simply happen to us, and so we will no longer feel "like a leaf in the wind, a plaything of nonsense" – as Nietzsche himself describes the great fear driving the ascetic attitude (*Genealogy* III.28, 118).

The error in this way of thinking has to do, not with how it may conceive of human goods, as objective and awaiting our discovery, but rather with how it understands that particular articulation of the good that constitutes our own good, the way we would be able to best live our life. Its assumption is that our own good is also something already settled, and thus the possible object of a plan, which we should formulate carefully, in order to

---

[29] See Chapter 5, §§ 7–8.

achieve it if we can. The essential truth about life, however, is that our good changes as we live, and as a result of moments of surprise and redirection that we could never have foreseen. To seek to bring our lives under the discipline of our own reason means making them less than they would otherwise be, closing ourselves off to unexpected goods. The life lived well is as much the life that befalls us as the life we fashion for ourselves. This truth has largely been missed by the philosophical tradition, and in the next chapter I set out to restore it to its full rights.

10

The Idea of a Life Plan

1. A PHILOSOPHICAL PREJUDICE

When philosophers take up the topic of how we ought best to live our lives, they tend to rely upon a certain understanding of the human good that is far more problematic than they suspect. Among philosophers both ancient and modern, the reigning view has been, in essence, that the life lived well is the life we have shaped ourselves, in accord with a rational plan of our own design. Life is too serious a matter, it is held, for us to let ourselves be the plaything of the forces at work outside us. We ought instead to take control of our existence so far as possible, weighing carefully our circumstances, abilities, and interests, in order to determine the makeup of our good as well as the most efficient means to achieve it.

This way of thinking seems to me deeply mistaken. The idea that life should be the object of a plan is false to the reality of the human condition. It misses the important truth that Proust, by contrast, discerned so well and made into one of the recurrent themes of that great meditation on disappointment and illumination, *A la recherche du temps perdu*: the happiness that life affords is not just the good we are already

---

[1] Marcel Proust, *Albertine disparue* (Paris: Gallimard/Folio, 1992), p. 83. "In exchange for what our imagination leads us to expect and which we vainly give ourselves so much trouble to try to discover, life gives us something which we were very far from imagining."

246

in a position to prize and pursue, but also the good that befalls us unexpectedly.[2]

Though philosophy on the whole has gone wrong in dealing with the most important question we may ask ourselves – the question of how we are to live our lives – its mistaken approach does not constitute an inevitable failure, as though the very nature of philosophy were to blame. For philosophy really has no essence beyond the goal, as Wilfrid Sellars famously said, of trying "to understand how things in the broadest possible sense of the term hang together in the broadest possible sense of the term."[3] It aims to work out a comprehensive view of the relation between mind and world, aspiration and reality, and this is a goal that may be taken to mean a great many different and incompatible things. Nonetheless, the mistake in question has been more than fortuitous. Philosophers fall prey to it once they transfer to the question of how we should live an interpretation of comprehensiveness that seems appropriate when dealing with the question of how things are. They assume that in this area, too, to understand how things hang together is to master them once and for all, to turn them into an object of foresight and control.

I should begin by explaining more closely what I regard as so deeply wrong-headed in the idea of a life plan. The mistake lies at its very core, in the attitude toward life it embodies. That attitude is the view that a life is something we are to lead and not something we should allow to happen to us. We flourish as human beings, it supposes, only if we direct our lives ourselves, instead of leaving them to be the hostage of chance and whim. If this is our outlook, then we should indeed seek to live in accord with some unified conception of our overall purposes and of the path to achieve them. In other words, we should devise for ourselves some "plan of life," at least in its broad strokes, if not fine-tuned in its smallest details. To the extent that we develop our plan in a rational way, giving due weight to our beliefs about what is valuable, our knowledge of our own abilities, and our sense of the possibilities the world provides, we will have determined the character of our good and the way to achieve it. A life plan need not be anything so absurd as the attempt to program from the outset the various milestones to be passed every five or ten years of one's life – college at twenty, consulting firm at thirty, married at thirty-five with two children (a boy and a girl) and complete happiness, a country house at forty, professional glory at fifty, and all of it capped off with a splendid retirement in Florida. Though such clichés are what the term might easily

---

[2] I first sketched these ideas in *The Romantic Legacy* (New York: Columbia University Press, 1996), p. 95, and have also developed them at length in a somewhat different way, in connection with the nature of our identity over time, in *Les pratiques du moi* (Paris: PUF, 2004), Chapter 7.

[3] Wilfrid Sellars, *Science, Perception, and Reality* (London: Routledge & Kegan Paul, 1963), p. 1

suggest in today's world, the basic idea looks a lot more reasonable. To live in accord with a rational plan of life is to pursue what we have discovered on careful reflection to constitute our true good, our best possibilities. To be sure, there can be no guarantee that our efforts will be crowned with success. But the attraction of the idea is that in living thus we will have done the best we could.

This conception of life may seem so sensible that one might wonder what could possibly be amiss. The rub, I am tempted to say, is that it is too sensible. Yet that would be the wrong way to formulate the objection. At question is what really defines a sensible attitude toward life. A clearer way to put my complaint is that this frame of mind embodies too great a timidity with regard to the power of experience to change what it is that makes life worth living. It supposes that we should take charge of our lives, bringing them under our rule as best we can. But in reality, the choice before us is not between leading a life and instead letting life happen to us. Neither of these extremes is conducive to a flourishing existence. The good life is a life that is not just led but met with as well, a life that is both self-directed and shaped from without. We miss an important aspect of what gives our life meaning when we imagine that our good can be the object of an all-embracing plan. Our lives go well, not only when we achieve the good we plan for, but also when unlooked-for goods happen to befall us. Think of Daniel Deronda. Had he not stumbled by chance upon Mordecai and found himself strangely enthralled by that visionary's conviction that he was the long-awaited disciple (the "prefigured friend"), Deronda's eventual discovery of his Jewish origins would never have assumed the meaning it did, never have propelled him to seek a national homeland for the Jews.[4]

In order to clarify my objection to the idea of a life plan, it will be helpful to run through some familiar doubts about planning that do not capture what I have in mind. The point is not, for instance, that some goods by their very nature elude the art of planning. It is, in any case, far from clear that this is really so. Spontaneity, for instance, may be a value that we cannot achieve at will. All the same, there exist indirect methods (putting ourselves in situations we know are likely to move us to act naturally and without reflecting) by which it can come within our reach. Nothing therefore stands in the way of having spontaneity figure among the ingredients of a suitably sophisticated plan of life.[5] So, too, with love. We cannot plan to fall in love, but there are certainly things we can choose to do, and to avoid doing, that will increase the likelihood of falling in love

---

[4] See, in particular, Chapter 69 of George Eliot, *Daniel Deronda*.

[5] As has been observed by the leading contemporary proponent of the idea of a life plan – John Rawls, *A Theory of Justice* (Cambridge, MA: Harvard University Press, 1971), p. 423. I discuss Rawls' views at length in §3.

and finding love in return. The trouble with the idea of a life plan is not the possibility that certain goods by their very nature defy pursuit by means of planning. It is that a life itself cannot properly be the object of a plan.

Yet if this is so, the mistake is not therefore a failure to recognize that the best-laid schemes of mice and men go oft awry. Certainly our plans, when put into practice, risk defeat at the hands of reality. And disappointment may seem inescapable when so complicated a matter as one's life as a whole is made the object of a plan. Many people have raised this sort of difficulty against the idea of choosing a way of life, none perhaps so movingly as Samuel Johnson in his novel, *Rasselas*. In this story, the young prince Rasselas, cloyed by his pampered existence in the Happy Valley, escapes to order to forge his own way in the world. His faith is that with experience will come the ability to make, as he says, the proper "choice of life." But Imlac, his tutor, tries to disabuse him of this hope. Our grasp of how the world is put together is too unreliable for any such choice to stand a real chance of success. "The causes of good and evil," Imlac insists,

are so various and uncertain, so often entangled with each other, so diversified by various relations, and so much subject to accidents which cannot be foreseen that he who would fix his condition upon incontestable reasons of preference, must live and die inquiring and deliberating .... Very few live by choice. Every man is placed in his present condition by causes which acted without his foresight, and with which he did not always willingly cooperate.[6]

There is considerable wisdom in these observations, but they do not really suffice to break the hold of the idea of a life plan. Tangled and unpredictable though the ways of the world may be, we can always set our sights on ends that seem minimally threatened by chance or misfortune. To choose our purposes so as to minimize the risk of being thwarted by reality has been in fact a frequent basis on which the philosophical tradition in question has elevated the life of virtue above the pursuit of more inconstant goods such as honor or wealth. True, this line of argument can ultimately lead to quite perverse results, such as the Stoic maxim that we should remain unmoved by the loss of those things (family, friends, political liberty) that do not depend on us. Moreover, the virtue whose possession is the source of the Stoic's pride is itself the fruit of circumstances, such as upbringing and associations, over which he can have little control. Probably no way of life can escape altogether the play of luck.[7] But the fragility of whatever good we may achieve is not the reason why the idea of a life plan is false to life.

The essential mistake lies at a more fundamental level. It has to do, not with the vulnerability of our plans, but rather with the drawbacks of

---

[6] Samuel Johnson, *Rasselas*, Chapter XVI.

[7] This is the theme of Martha Nussbaum's magnificent book, *The Fragility of Goodness* (Cambridge: Cambridge University Press, 1986).

planning itself. We close ourselves off to a significant dimension of the human good if we believe that our attitude toward life must be at bottom one of foresight and control, as the idea of a life plan entails. On the contrary, we live well when we are not simply active, but passive too. There is an openness to life's surprises, which it behooves us to maintain. For instead of being the mishap that sadly defeats our plans, the unexpected can turn out to be the windfall that discloses new vistas of meaning and forms of happiness that we least suspected or never imagined and that may change our lives and who we are in the most far-reaching ways. Sometimes we learn that we have been mistaken in the things we have hitherto valued. Sometimes instead we learn to appreciate human goods of which we had little understanding before, and making them our own is likely to alter the complexion of our other commitments as well. Revelations of this sort do not, moreover, always require some novel input from the world. As Proust portrayed so powerfully, memory can jolt us into seeing our past in an unaccustomed light and thus remind us of forgotten or neglected sources of happiness that no longer figure in our current self-understanding. In general, our good as we can conceive it at any given time mirrors the course of our lives up until then, and as life goes on and shows us new ways one may flourish and find meaning in the world, we learn to appreciate what before lay beyond our ken.

Plainly I am assuming that unexpected goods have a certain "objectivity." They are something we discover, whose value we could not appreciate in the light of all that we thought and felt before, but come to perceive only through the impress of the new or the unaccustomed. Some philosophers, of course, will regard such talk as a mere *façon de parler*, not to be taken seriously, since they are convinced that in general the good is but the projection of desire: to say that a thing is good, they hold, is to do no more than to express our desire for it, along perhaps with our desire that others too should similarly desire it. This is not the place to argue at length against all the different versions of subjectivism about the good. It will be helpful, however, to indicate their basic failing, which is their inability to make sense of the fact that whatever we hold to be good is something we believe we *ought* or *have reason* to desire. If the "objectivity" of good may be broadly understood as consisting in precisely this fact – that is, in the good being what we have reason to desire, then the difference between the idea of a life plan and the opposing view of life I propose will come into sharper focus. For both positions regard our good as something objective in the sense just mentioned. The claim that we should shape our lives around our best possibilities of flourishing can have no other basis (so that subjectivists who want to follow this line of thought have to find a way to mimic talk of an objective good). Where the two positions differ is over the relation between the constitution of our good and the very process of living itself.

First, however, goodness and desire: certainly they are intimately connected. Though a thing may be good for us without our desiring it, once we come to see it as good we cannot fail to want it. The perceived good is necessarily an object of desire. Yet subjectivist conceptions wrongly reverse the distinctive relation between goodness and desire. For every desire represents its object as desirable, as something there is a reason to pursue, either because we need it, or would satisfy our interests by having it, or would be exactly like those we esteem if we managed to acquire it. The notion of a "brute desire," an impulse that simply comes over us without any sense of its object being desirable, is a philosophical fiction. To appear worth desiring, however, is precisely what it means for something to present itself as "good." Desire therefore depends on perceived good, and not the other way around. Even when we desire a thing that we know we should avoid, acknowledging the better but following the worse (*video meliora proboque, deteriora sequor*), the worse must still appear good in some light or other: we must see some reason, however ill-considered, to think that we should make it ours. Our desires are responsive to what we take to be good, to what we see a reason to desire. The apparent goodness of the things we value cannot amount to a projection of our desires, since to regard the object as good is to think that, in some respect at least, we *ought* to desire it. How some good can count as "objective" should therefore be clear. It is something that there really is reason for us to pursue.[8]

Within the broad category of the objectively good there is an important distinction between the various forms of the human good in general and the particular elements of what make up our own individual good. Our own good – the best life of which we are capable – cannot encompass every kind of good there is. Each of us, at our best, can be but a fragment of humanity. What counts as our own good has to fit who we are and the range of possibilities that are specifically ours. It embraces, therefore, those goods that we ourselves have reason to pursue, given our circumstances, capacities, and fundamental interests.

Now it is precisely at this point that the mistake at the heart of the idea of a life plan becomes apparent. If we are to shape our lives in accord with a rational plan, we have to be able, at least in principle and presumably once we have reached a certain age, to make out the nature of our good in advance of actually going on to live our lives. Only if our good counts as already settled, can it be reasonable to suppose that we should make it the

---

[8] For a more detailed presentation of this argument, see my book, *Les pratiques du moi*, chapters 3 and 4, and for more on how desire is based in reasons, see Chapter 5 in the present book, §8. Subjectivist conceptions of the good often draw their inspiration from the naturalistic view of the world so prevalent in modern thought, according to which all that truly exists must be either physical or psychological, not normative, in character. In Chapter 5, §7, I showed why we must see the world as also containing reasons, and the present argument indicates how the good can thereby form part of the world.

object of a plan that will enable us to achieve it. Yet the very factors on which our good depends – our circumstances, capacities, and interests – are not given once and for all. They are caught up in the twists and turns of life, and as we thus change, sometimes in unforeseeable ways, our good too must change and may well take on a character we could not have expected.

The truth overlooked by the notion of a life plan is therefore not simply that every conception we devise of how we ought best to live our lives, reflecting as it must the limitations of our previous experience, is bound to fall short of what life has yet to teach us. That is certainly so. But an even deeper truth is at stake. Not solely our understanding of our good, but our good itself changes with time and in ways we are unable to foresee. The idea of a life plan assumes that our good is a matter already determined, so that our task must be to discern its makeup and then to devote our energies to securing it. In reality, our good only takes shape in the very course of living and as a result of how our life happens to go. Would we in fact want things to be any other way? Being surprised by a good of which we had no inkling is itself an invaluable element of what makes life worth living. Our lives would be the poorer if our happiness unfolded perfectly according to plan.

There is no denying, of course, that planning has an important role to play in our lives. What is wrong is to suppose that our life itself should be made the object of a plan. Philosophers are not alone in making this mistake. All of us, once chastened by the effects of folly or self-deception, can easily conclude that we should structure our lives around a conception of our good that truly reflects who we are, so that even if despite all our efforts we end up failing to achieve it, we will at least have nothing to reproach ourselves for. We will have done the very best we could.

Still, the very nature of philosophy does much to encourage the idea that to live well is to live in accord with a rational plan of life. That so many philosophers have gone down this path is not accidental. The idea is fostered by what I have called philosophy's characteristic ambition, which is to work out a comprehensive vision of mind and world, aspiration and reality. Just as philosophers try to make sense of the way things are by explaining how the different dimensions of our experience hang together, so they naturally seek an account of how we should live that assigns our various concerns their appropriate role and importance. In itself, the quest for a view of the whole is not ill-conceived. Nor does it suffice by itself to generate the idea of a life plan, though it is certainly responsible for the systematic character such a plan is thought to demand. What must also be believed is that the makeup of our good is already determined, so that living itself, if it is to go well, has to be answerable to it. Nothing in the nature of philosophy requires this belief. If our good is indeed such as I have suggested, changing over time in ways we cannot foresee and as much a result of living itself as a goal at which our lives should aim, then the proper attitude to take toward our existence as a whole is that we need to remain open to the unexpected goods that experience may bring.

There is, however, a natural temptation to carry over to the question of how we should live the specific type of comprehensive understanding that fits the question of how things are. The way things are is already settled, and thus grasping how they hang together means mastering their inter-connections and being able to say in a definitive fashion what each thing is and can become. If reason is equated with this kind of foresight and control, then our good, too, if it is to be an object of reason, will similarly have to be already settled in its character, and the business of living will then amount to doing our best to make it a reality. I suspect that such reasoning has been the source for philosophy's almost universal convic-tion, if expressed in different idioms, that to live well is to bring our lives under the rule of a rational plan of life. That is only speculation, of course. What I do believe is plain is the nature of the mistake itself – namely, the notion that the nature of our good exists in advance of living itself and of the unexpected turns our lives can take. In the next section, I will chart how widely and deeply philosophy has been committed to thinking along these lines.

2. ANCIENT ROOTS

In our day, the idea of a life plan is rightly associated with the systematic account that John Rawls presented in his great work, *A Theory of Justice.*[9] But the conviction that the good life is a life lived in accord with a rational plan goes back to the very beginnings of moral philosophy. It forms an essential part of what Socrates had in mind in his famous assertion that "the unexamined life is not worth living."[10] From Socrates to Rawls – the length of that span, uniting two philosophers otherwise so visibly different in their views, is a measure of how pervasive has been the outlook on life that is the target of my opposition. Let us look closely at that statement by which Socrates (or at any rate Plato's Socrates) set the terms for much of the philosophical tradition that followed him. As he and so many others have understood it, more than one significant assumption has been involved, and bringing out the import of the others it embodies will serve to make clear the specific role of the mistake that I have outlined and that leads Socrates, like so many others, to believe that the examined life would have to be the object of a unified plan.

That only the examined life can be worth living may seem little more than a truism. Yet this impression only shows how accustomed we have become to conceiving of the good life along the lines of the approach that

---

[9] See, in particular, §63 of John Rawls, *A Theory of Justice.*
[10] Plato, *Apology*, 38a: "*ho de anexetastos bios ou biotos anthropoi.*"

Socrates introduced. The claim is not so innocent as it may initially appear. The first, and most obvious, among its assumptions is the conviction that a life as a whole, and not simply this course of action or that trait of character, can become the object of ethical evaluation. This presupposition is not beyond question. Does an individual's life display enough internal cohesiveness that we can rightly ask whether, taken as a whole, it should count as successful or not? Some philosophers have said that every life reveals the "unity of a quest" or has the shape of some "fundamental project," but such talk is surely unrealistic. As a rule, our lives hang together to the extent they do in virtue of their involving a host of overlapping and intersecting goals and activities, and not because they express any single all-embracing purpose. Nonetheless, this sort of complexity is no reason to believe that a life as such cannot rightly be deemed good or bad, flourishing or stunted. For we cannot live our lives except by thinking about them in these comprehensively evaluative terms. However variegated the fabric of our lives may be, we still see them as our own and feel a stake in how they go. It is natural and reasonable to reflect on one's life as a whole and to wonder whether there may not be a better way to live than one does at present. Who among us has not had, or would want to give up, those moments when we pause to take stock of our interests and abilities in order to make out more clearly the kind of person we really want to be?

The second significant assumption underlying the Socratic maxim is more difficult. In reflecting on how best our lives as a whole ought to go, we ought, it is assumed, to get beyond the limitations of our present point of view. We should look at our lives from the outside, instead of from within the concerns that happen to occupy us at the moment. To be sure, it is in the present that we deliberate, and our premises can only come from our existing knowledge. Our goal, however, should be to regard our life as spread out before us, timelessly as it were, so as to give each of its moments equal consideration and to loosen enough the hold of our current preoccupations that we can work out the way our life should really go, as opposed to simply continuing along the path we are already traveling. Only then can we ascertain, as Plato's Socrates once again says, in what manner we ought to live our lives (*ontina tropon chre zen*).[11]

This assumption is more problematic than the first. In his own, often penetrating analysis of the presuppositions underlying the Socratic principle, Bernard Williams argued that this one involves a fundamental mistake about the powers of reflection.[12] We cannot transcend our present perspective in the way it imagines, and the belief that we can, so he went

---

[11] Plato, *Republic* 352d.
[12] Bernard Williams, *Ethics and the Limits of Philosophy* (Cambridge, MA: Harvard University Press, 1985), pp. 4, 19.

on to claim in other writings, is precisely the error that gives rise to the idea, to which he was as much opposed as I, that we ought to live our lives in accord with a rational plan of life. I shall have occasion later (§4) to look more closely at Williams' critique of the idea of a life plan. Here I want to explain why this second assumption is not really so questionable as one might think. Its implications turn out to be far less momentous, once its import is properly understood.

In general, all our thinking, whatever its subject, bears the mark of our time and place. The problems we confront, the resources we bring to bear, are rooted in the understanding of the world, ourselves included, that tradition and experience have happened to give us. All this is true. Yet we are not thereby cut off from the world itself. On the contrary, our finitude is itself our access to reality. In reasoning from our existing beliefs and interests, making revisions as we deem necessary, we are measuring our thinking against the way things really are. Whatever we find good reason to regard as true or valuable presents itself therefore as being so independently of our present perspective, and in this way we can justifiably claim to see beyond the confines of our time and place.[13] Thus, more particularly, our existing convictions provide us with standards for distinguishing between momentary and more enduring interests as well as with a sense of the overall trajectory of a human life and of the various possibilities of human flourishing that our society makes available. On their basis we can stand back from our current concerns and regard them as but some among the many that we may or will have, with no special weight simply because they happen to command our attention at the present time. We can examine our lives from a vantage point distinct from any particular moment within it.

The only hitch, we must remember, is that critical reflection of this sort always draws its bearings from the course of our previous experience. The standards we use to evaluate our present views are not a sham, for we can have good reason to think them reliable. Yet the grounds on which we believe them to be attuned to the truth depend on what we have so far been fortunate enough to learn about the world. Every timeless perspective is itself time-bound. We cannot rule out the likelihood that the future may disclose ways of living well that we are not yet in a position to envision (just as it may bring the stunning overthrow of a scientific theory that hitherto seemed impeccably well-confirmed). Ideally, we would keep this very realization before our minds as we reflect, acknowledging that our image of the good life is not immune to revision. I should point out, moreover, that the second assumption, if understood strictly, is also compatible with the recognition that our good itself, not merely our conception of it, is bound to change with time and in virtue of the ways that we ourselves change. For all

[13] See Chapter 1, "History and Truth."

that it says, our good might differ from the natural phenomena that are the object of scientific theorizing in not yet possessing a determinate character, only taking on a shape in the very process of living. This is of course the truth (the timeless truth) that, in my view, Socrates and so many others have missed. If Socrates' insistence on the examined life harbors, as I believe it does, a commitment to the idea of making one's life the object of a rational plan, then it must be in virtue of some further assumptions.

The crucial elements come into view once we note that Socrates expects a certain kind of result from the self-examination he extols. The answer to the question of "how we ought to live our lives" should constitute a practical guide to action. It should show us how we are to proceed in order to realize the possibilities constitutive of the best life we can lead. Our good, so it is assumed, will not turn out to be something essentially beyond our powers to secure, and that only the outside forces of luck and circumstance can bestow upon us. The life embodying our best possibilities is one that at least in principle, given sufficient knowledge and resolve, we are in a position to lead, to fashion for ourselves. That it is ultimately up to us whether our lives go well or not is the meaning of the Myth of Er with which Plato's *Republic* closes. According to this version of the reincarnation motif, souls in the afterworld as they are about to be reborn choose the sort of life that they then go on to live. Socrates explains the moral thus:

> Our chief concern should therefore be to put aside all other forms of knowledge, and seek and discern that which will show us how to perceive and find someone who will give us the knowledge and ability to tell a good life from a bad one and to always choose the better one so far as possible.[14]

Certainly Socrates does not suppose that we can come to control everything that happens to us. Whatever foresight and strength we may possess, we remain part of a larger world that moves according to its own laws. But the worth of the life that is ours, the qualities that distinguish a life lived well in circumstances not of our own choosing, does lie in our hands. Reflection about how we ought to live should therefore result in a conception of how we should proceed so as to secure our good.

This assumption rests in turn on a deeper one, which is none other than the decisive mistake that I have been tracking. Socrates presumes that the character of our good is something already settled, awaiting our discovery as we reflect on how we should live. Only because he supposes that our good does not itself change in virtue of how our life actually goes, but is fixed in advance by our basic interests, capacities, and circumstances, can he imagine that it lies in our power to achieve, if only we manage to discern its nature. It is then these latter two assumptions that commit Socrates to the idea that we should live in accord with a rational plan of

---

[14] Plato, *Republic* 618c.

life. Observe, once again, that the conviction that our good should be judged without unduly privileging our present concerns is not the crucial factor. Standing back from the press of our projects of the moment might give us, in fact, the room we need to appreciate how often in the past, and so no doubt in the future as well, the unexpected goods we bump into give meaning to our lives as much as the goals we choose to pursue. Socrates effectively excludes this possibility by assuming that in reflecting impartially on the nature of our good, we should be able to make out its complete character, at least in outline, and the means for attaining it, at least in principle.

Later thinkers may have been more hesitant in thinking that the good life could ever be completely the creature of our own efforts. Whereas Socrates appears ready to imagine that true happiness (*eudaimonia*) – that is, the happiness of the just person – would not be imperiled by a loss of good reputation among his fellows, his virtue remaining intact, Aristotle disagrees: external goods such as reputation, over which one's control can never be total, look to him to be essential prerequisites for living a life of value: if we are poorly thought of by others, we will never be entrusted with the tasks in which we can do the things that give our lives meaning.[15] Nonetheless, these two philosophers, like countless others, have been at one in believing that the character of our good is something already determined and that we can take steps to make its achievement more likely, if not certain. These twin assumptions are enough for the idea that we ought to live our lives in accord with a rational plan of life.

Lest it be thought that I am reading too much into Socrates' (or rather Plato's) understanding of what it is to live the examined life, recall the answer the *Republic* gives to the question of what such a life will turn out to be. It would be a life whose reigning spirit is justice (*dikaiosune*). By this is not meant simply the specific virtue the term usually signifies today, the respect we ought to show the rights of others while otherwise being free to pursue our own interests as we please. "Justice" for Plato designates a far broader ideal, in essence a general economy of the mind in which reason harmonizes our various desires and emotions so as to make us, it is claimed, the "masters and architects of ourselves" (*arxanta auton hautou kai kosmesanta*).[16] This statement is no passing remark. It expresses the ambition that lies at the heart of the Socratic demand for self-examination.

One might still complain that Plato's dialogues are not a reliable guide to the thinking of the historical Socrates, that the dialogue form should discourage counting as Plato's own convictions the opinions voiced by the character Socrates, and that interpreting Plato's myths is a notoriously difficult affair. None of these worries is altogether unfounded. There can

[15] Cf. Plato, *Republic* 361cd, 612c, with Aristotle, *Nicomachean Ethics* 1099a31–b8.
[16] Plato, *Republic* 443d.

be no dispute, however, about the unswerving allegiance that other ancient philosophers displayed to the idea that the only life worth living is one lived in accord with a rational plan. Consider, for example, the words with which Aristotle begins his discussion of the good life in the *Eudemian Ethics*:

Everyone who can live according to his own choice should adopt some goal for the good life (*tina skopon tou kalos zen thesthai*), be it honor or reputation or wealth or culture – a goal that he will keep in view in all his actions. (For not to have ordered one's life in relation to some end is a sign of extreme folly). Therefore, before all else, he should settle in his own mind, neither hastily nor carelessly, in which of our concerns living well consists, and what are the things which make it possible for human beings.[17]

One could not hope for a clearer formulation of the view that the good life depends on organizing our existence around a plan, choosing all our actions with a view to making possible the overall goal we have set ourselves. For Aristotle, as John Cooper has rightly observed, "it is repugnant … to our idea of what it is for a human being to flourish, to allow that anyone is flourishing except insofar as he has taken charge of his own life."[18] Either planning or folly – that is the alternative Aristotle presents. Since the choice is clear, or so it seems to him, our business must be to figure out what is the plan of life that reason recommends, a question that in this ethical treatise, as in his others, Aristotle goes on to answer.

I will not run through all the different thinkers, from ancient to modern times, who have endorsed the assumption that the good life is one that relies upon a rational plan.[19] In some regards, such a survey would be very useful. It would make plain how extensive the commitment to this assumption has been; it might also serve to bring out some significant differences of emphasis among those who have embraced it. However, my interest lies principally in the essential error in the notion of a life plan. To see most clearly where it lies, we can do no better than to examine Rawls' development of the idea in *A Theory of Justice*. It is philosophically the most elaborate account there is, and one that still enjoys considerable authority in our time.[20]

---

[17] Aristotle, *Eudemian Ethics* I.2 (1214b 7–13).

[18] John M. Cooper, *Reason and Human Good in Aristotle* (Cambridge, MA: Harvard University Press, 1975), p. 125.

[19] For the elements of a bibliography, see John Finnis, *Natural Law and Natural Rights* (Oxford: Oxford University Press, 1980), pp. 129–130.

[20] I shall be examining Rawls' notion of a rational life plan as an overall ethical ideal, which is the form it assumes in *A Theory of Justice*, though in order to serve a political theory of justice. In later writings (*Political Liberalism* [New York: Columbia University Press, 1993], pp. 176–77, fn), Rawls declared that this notion, along with the associated theory of goodness as rationality, is best understood as simply part of a political conception, without any broader implications: for political purposes, citizens are to be viewed as pursuing,

3. THE RAWLSIAN CONCEPTION

Rawls models his account on some striking formulations in the lectures on ethics that Josiah Royce published in 1908 under the title of *The Philosophy of Loyalty*. "A person, an individual self," Royce declared, "may be defined as a human life lived according to a plan."[21] Royce's point was that our sense of who we are and what we stand for consists in our goals and the interconnections among them. "The answer to the question, 'Who are you?' really begins in earnest," he wrote, "when a man mentions his calling, and so actually sets out upon the definition of his purposes and of the way in which these purposes get expressed in his life."

There is certainly something right about the view that Royce puts forward. The question is whether it goes deep enough. Our self-understanding, and thus our conception of our good may well find expression in our aims. But rooted as they are in our past experience, do they not sometimes involve the memory of those moments of sudden illumination, those discoveries of an unexpected good, that have befallen us despite our best thought-out goals at the time? If this is so, then our good cannot be defined by reference to the purposes we can see reason to pursue prior to actually having come to participate in certain forms of living well. It will have been shaped at least in part by that sort of bafflement of our existing aims that forces us to embrace new purposes we could not have foreseen, and thus to define anew our idea of who we are.

Rawls, however, holds that our good is founded on what we can see antecedently, in advance of living itself, that we have reason to adopt as a way of life. Like Royce, he moves directly from our self-understanding's being bound up with our purposes to the idea that these purposes, when rationally weighed and organized, serve to define the nature of our good: The proposition that stands at the center of his theory of the good life is that "the rational plan for a person determines his good."[22] This statement is the epitome of the outlook I reject. It allows Rawls to conclude that happiness consists in the successful execution of a rational plan of life.[23] Yet the happy life, as I have been trying to bring home, cannot be in this way so much a matter of our own making. And not merely because of the fact that, as Rawls himself notes, the conditions under which we draw up a life plan are never under our complete control, and may in some cases

---

when rational, their individual good in a systematic fashion, even if really they would be unwise to live their lives in this constricted way. I am unsure whether my criticisms touch the more circumscribed role Rawls then assigned to the idea of a life plan. Here, in any case, I shall be examining his views in their original form, since as such they provide the most careful statement available of the attitude toward life I am challenging.

[21] Josiah Royce, *The Philosophy of Loyalty*, (New York: Macmillan, 1908), p. 168.

[22] Rawls, *A Theory of Justice*, p. 408; also pp. 421, 424.

[23] *Ibid.*, pp. 93, 409, 548–560.

prove too unpropitious for the design of any life worth calling happy. Instead, my objection is that we are never in a position to grasp in advance the full character of our good, even in its broad outline, since it has no such character prior to the actual business of living. Our happiness encompasses not only the anticipated good we manage to attain, but also the unexpected good that enters our lives in ways we could not anticipate – perhaps as the unforeseen result of our own actions or as the boon that circumstances or others' actions send our way. It includes, in fact, this very experience of surprise.

What then is the line of thought by which Rawls arrives at his thesis that a person's rational plan of life determines his good? It is important to retrace his steps carefully so that we may locate where precisely the error occurs. As will be apparent, his argument builds explicitly on the assumptions that we saw unspokenly at work in Socrates' thinking.

Rawls' idea of a life plan grows out of a general theory of the good, a theory that seeks to explicate goodness in terms of rationality. In general, he writes, "A is a good X, if and only if A has the properties (to a higher degree than the average or standard X) which it is rational to want in an X."[24] In the same spirit, he goes on to say that something will be good for a person – will not just be good, but will also form part of that person's good – if and only if the thing has the properties it is rational for that person to want in it, "given [his] circumstances, abilities, and plan of life (system of aims)." This last phrase introduces the term at issue, but it does so in a rather misleading way, suggesting as it does that a person's "plan of life" is one among several factors serving to establish the makeup of his good. In reality, a person's plan of life, if rational, will have required a careful appraisal of his circumstances and abilities, as well as of his interests, of course. If well thought out, so we have seen Rawls claim, it should suffice all by itself to determine the nature of the person's good. The question is thus twofold: Why does he believe that a rational plan of life is able to fix the nature of our good? And what does he think is involved in ensuring that a life plan is rational?

A plan of life, Rawls writes, is a "system of aims." It is important to realize that he has a rather ambitious notion of "system" in mind. Each of us inevitably pursues a number of goals that we arrange according to relations of means and ends, part and whole. Some of our aims we only espouse because they advance or belong to our pursuit of other aims, and sometimes we find ourselves obliged to specify further the relations among them. To this extent, none of us can fail to have a "system of aims," whatever their degree of coherence or detail. However, a life plan, as Rawls conceives it, purports to systematize our ends in so comprehensive a way as

[24] *Ibid.*, p. 399.

to shape the course of our life overall. Why does he think that we need to plan on so broad a scale?

In part, the answer is that each of us has his whole life before him and feels a stake in how it turns out. Rawls, like Socrates, is convinced that a person's life as a whole is a proper object of evaluation, as a life lived well or otherwise, since we cannot help but care about our own lives in precisely these terms. But he is equally of the view that a life is to be led, not allowed to simply happen to us – "the question of what to do with our life is always there," he writes.[25] Consequently, he also shares the Socratic assumption that how well our life goes is at bottom up to us, and that whether we attain our good depends on the steps we take in order to secure it. Does he hold this view because, again like Socrates, he supposes that the character of our good is something already settled, awaiting our discovery and our efforts to achieve it? That, as we have seen, is along with the preceding assumption the essential underpinning to the idea that we ought to live our lives in accord with a rational plan of life. Rawls, I believe, endorses it too. But to see at just what point in his argument he makes this fatal assumption, we must look closely at his account of what it is for a life plan to be rational.

In general, such a plan is rational, in Rawls's view, when it accords with the principles of rational choice (by which he means, essentially, the maximization of expected utility) and is such as would be chosen by the person with "full deliberative rationality – that is, with full awareness of the relevant facts and after a careful consideration of the consequences."[26] Let us examine in some detail what all this means.

In one sense, he admits, the life plan that determines a person's good turns on the purposes he can formulate at the time of the plan's conception. Thus there is an essential reference to the present in the reasoning by which life plans are to be constructed: "A person's future good on the whole [is] what he would now desire and seek if the consequences of all the various courses of conduct open to him were, at the present point of time, accurately foreseen by him and adequately realized in imagination."[27] Yet the role this proposition gives to the present is held to entail no more than the trivial fact that it is always in the present that we deliberate. What we are reflecting about clearly extends beyond the present. Moreover, the way we are to carry out our deliberation aims at neutralizing any substantial kind of dependence on the given moment. According to Rawls, we are to give full consideration to all our possibilities and to look to our future good as

---

[25] *Ibid.*, p. 413.

[26] *Ibid.*, p. 408. More exactly, a person's plan is "subjectively rational" if based on an accurate conception of his existing wants and the available knowledge concerning the consequences of his actions; it is also "objectively rational" if the future actually goes as he supposes (pp. 417, 422).

[27] *Ibid.*, pp. 416–417.

a whole. That means that we are not to determine the nature of our good by appealing simply to our commitments at the time, for they too must be pondered and weighed. Reflecting upon our life as a whole, we are to stand free from the perspective of any particular moment within it. We are no less our later selves than the person we are now, and so our choice of a life plan should find its footing in our identity across time.

Deliberative rationality, so Rawls gives us to understand,[28] is impartial, not just in its basis, but in its object too. That is, it also requires that we show an equal regard for all moments of our life. No life plan is rational if it resorts to "pure time-preference." It may not accord greater weight to interests we have at one time rather than another simply because of their difference in time – and that means in particular because they are interests we have now or will have in the near future. On the contrary, the preference given to some interests over others must reflect the belief that they contribute more to our overall good, considered as a whole.

Rawls' idea of what it is to deliberate rationally about our good corresponds to the second key assumption I showed to underlie the Socratic outlook – namely, that the properly examined life is one we reflect upon in a kind of timeless way. But even more illuminatingly, it could be said that this "deliberative rationality" is really the age-old notion of prudence under another and rather inelegant name. It means the careful management of life's affairs. Our good, so Rawls is essentially claiming, consists in that way of life we would choose were we always to think prudently about what we ought to do. Prudence, to be sure, is no guarantee of success. Our plan of life, though rational, may be defeated by events we could not possibly have anticipated. But in Rawls' view, prudence does ensure that, should disappointment occur, we still will have nothing to blame ourselves for. We will have done the best we could. We will have rightly discerned the character of our good and done all we could to try to achieve it. A rational person, he observes,

does what seems best at the time, and if his beliefs later prove to be mistaken with untoward results, it is through no fault of his own. There is no cause for self-reproach.[29]

For Rawls as for others, this sort of satisfaction appears to provide one of the chief motivations for the idea that we should live our lives in accord with a rational life plan.

4. SOME OTHER OBJECTIONS

Such, at first approximation (more details will be necessary), is the line of argument by which Rawls develops his account of a rational life plan and

[28] See *ibid.*, p. 420.
[29] *Ibid.*, p. 422.

gives it the pivotal role in his theory of the good life. A number of steps might seem contestable – not simply the neglect of unexpected goods that I have been concerned to emphasize. Before showing at what stage this error makes its appearance, I want to consider two other objections that Rawls' argument has provoked. These criticisms are important, even if they do not latch on to what is crucially amiss. They provide, in fact, a helpful contrast to the objection I regard as far more fundamental.

The first of these objections is that Rawls has lost touch with the natural rhythm of human finitude. By defining an individual's good in terms of a life plan, he contradicts the shape our lives inevitably take by virtue of the fact that we are born and die.[30] We begin life as children, and though children should certainly imagine and act out various ways of life, those who trade this play for planning, weighing their interests and capacities, making up their mind about their goal in life and devoting themselves to achieving it, are a dreary lot who have missed the blessings of childhood. Prudence about life is a "relative virtue," as Michael Slote has observed: it does not fit every period of life. It is desirable when we are grown up, but not when we are young. To say that our rational plan of life determines our good cannot therefore be right as a general claim. It forgets that we were not always adults.

It also forgets – so the objection continues – the other end of our finite condition, the fact that we die, and die at a roughly foreseeable age, at least in the natural course of events. On Rawls' telling, a rational plan of life gives equal weight to all the moments of one's life; it refuses pure time-preference, as he says. But, in reality, a proper sense of our mortality makes us anything but impartial with respect to time. Not only should we accord greater importance to that part of our life when we are at the height of our powers than to childhood or senescence, but we should also give priority within this period to later moments over earlier ones. That is because we rightly prefer the life in which failure gives way to success to one marked by success and failure of a similar magnitude, but occurring in the opposite order. Recognizing that our lives must end, we naturally want them to end well. We want them to achieve a form of completion, to see a lifetime's efforts be finally rewarded, instead of watching early triumphs give way to years of labor that ultimately lead nowhere.[31] If our life extended indefinitely before us, we would not regard the order of success and failure, if of finite duration, as inherently significant, for after every failure there would always be more than enough time to make up for it by starting anew.

This objection has a mixed validity. Though "earlier" and "later" may well possess a different weight within the prime of life, the sort of pure

---

[30] This objection is nicely developed by Michael Slote, in *Goods and Virtues* (Oxford: Oxford University Press, 1983), Chapters 1 and 2.

[31] Cf. Robert Nozick's reflections on the "narrative direction" of the happy life, in *The Examined Life* (New York: Simon and Schuster, 1989), pp. 100–102.

time-preference that Rawls excludes is not thereby legitimated. If success can count for more in virtue of when it occurs, then not because of temporal position alone, but because the biological givens of birth and death, plus our very consciousness of time, impart to the human good a certain directionality. Since we live from the past into the future, and into a future that is inescapably limited, our life takes on the pattern of a story – each moment building on what has come before, its significance modified by what comes afterward, so that the shape of a life only comes fully into view when it is over and done with. Everything else being equal, therefore, a life goes well to the extent that it turns out well, its trajectory going upward rather than downward. Yet this asymmetry does not conflict with the impartial exercise of practical rationality that Rawls deems essential to the construction of a life plan. It figures instead among those fundamental features of the human condition that such deliberation must regard as the premises from which it starts. Indeed, this first objection does not really question the primacy of prudence in the makeup of the good life. Though it rightly observes that a life plan has no proper place among the concerns of childhood, it says nothing to challenge the assumption that mature persons should bring their lives under the rule of a rational plan.[32]

The second objection to Rawls' argument also takes issue with the idea that deliberative rationality ought to be impartial. This time, however, the target is not the axiom forbidding "time-preference" in the content of a life plan, but rather the ambition of transcending the local perspective defined by our present concerns as we think about how our life as a whole ought to go. If the first objection urges us to retain a sense of the finitude of the life we deliberate about, the second seeks to remind us that in this matter, as in others, deliberation is always situated, dependent upon the beliefs and interests that are ours at the time.

This objection we have met before. It is Bernard Williams' complaint about the timeless form into which Socrates cast the question, "How should one live?" And Williams has brought the very same charge against Rawls' conception of what it is to devise a life plan. "The perspective of deliberative choice on one's life," he complains, "is constitutively *from here*."[33] In other words, the fact that our deliberation takes place in the present is not so trivial as it may seem. The results of practical deliberation – so I understand the gist of Williams' argument – cannot be more substantive than the premises from which it sets out. Present commitments can be weighed and

---

[32] Michael Slote develops some interesting criticisms of this assumption as well (op. cit., pp. 43–45), though they seem to turn on the point that some goods such as spontaneity or love cannot be the object of planning. On the limitations of this objection, see §1. There is also a very suggestive critique of this assumption in Martin Seel, *Versuch über die Form des Glücks* (Frankfurt: Suhrkamp, 1996), pp. 102–113, which comes closer to the criticism I have been propounding.

[33] Bernard Williams, *Moral Luck* (Cambridge: Cambridge University Press, 1981), p. 35.

sometimes revised, but never in a wholesale fashion, for the examination of some must rely on others that provide the standards of appraisal. Even when surveying critically our life as a whole, we must always draw our bearings from our present perspective. We cannot jump over our own shadow.

With remarks of this tenor, I am certainly in accord. There is no way for reason to transcend the particularities of our time and place so as to resolve, once and for all, the way in which we ought to live. Many philosophers deny or choose to forget this fact, talking as though we must throw off the weight of history if we are to grasp the true character of the right and the good. So apparently the point cannot be underscored enough.[34] No doubt the resistance betokens another deep-seated philosophical prejudice. Nonetheless, my earlier discussion of Socrates should have shown that this line of argument, despite the important truths it embodies, does not really yield a decisive objection to the idea of a life plan. Even though we must rely on inherited forms of thought and our own limited experience, we can still believe that we should do the best we can to work out on their basis a comprehensive view of how we should set about living our lives.

A useful way to confirm this result, deepening it at the same time, is to look at another, related conclusion that Williams draws from the rootedness of all deliberation in the here and now. In his view, it implies that practical reason must be understood as pursuing a different sort of aim from theoretical reason. Our scientific beliefs seek to describe the world as it is in itself, as independently as possible from our historical or local context: they seek to take up, as it were, the point of view of the universe. Reflection on how we should act, by contrast, focuses essentially on what we should do as the particular beings we are, having the beliefs and interests that are ours at the moment. It would be a misconception, he claims, to suppose that in practical deliberation we should proceed by first determining how anyone ought to act in the given situation, abstracting from our own perspective and judging things (as Henry Sidgwick indeed said) from "the point of view of the universe." Williams writes:

My life, my action is quite irreducibly mine, and to require that it is at best a *derivative* conclusion that it should be lived from the perspective that happens to be mine is an extraordinary misunderstanding. Yet it is the idea that is implicitly contained in the model of the point of view of the universe.[35]

A dichotomy of this sort between theory and practice is completely unfounded, however. As I emphasized before (§2), all our thinking, be it

---

[34] I have argued the point myself in *The Morals of Modernity* (Cambridge: Cambridge University Press, 1996), particularly Chapter 2.

[35] Williams, *Making Sense of Humanity* (Cambridge: Cambridge University Press, 1995), p. 170; see also his *Ethics and the Limits of Philosophy*, pp. 67–69.

theoretical or practical, draws its premises from the resources that tradition and previous experience happen to have given us, and yet reasoning from within our present perspective is precisely our way, our only way, of determining the way things really are. The conclusions we find reason to endorse are conclusions we are entitled to regard as true, and since all truth is essentially timeless and absolute (if a proposition is true, then it has always been and always will be true), we could just as well say that our conclusions are true "from the point of view of the universe." Scientific inquiry does not lose its claim to objectivity, to be uncovering the way the natural world really is, once it is recognized that our conception of nature always depends on the existing state of doctrine and on standards and methods we have so far found reason to consider reliable. So, too, the fact that practical deliberation must proceed on the basis of given beliefs and interests does not stand in the way of our rightly taking our conclusions, when justified, to be valid absolutely speaking – or again, "from the point of view of the universe." After all, we cannot believe we have reason to act or live in a certain way unless we suppose that anyone, under similar circumstances, would equally have reason to do so.[36] All our conclusions about how we should behave are necessarily "derivative" in this sense, without it being any the less the case that the particular action or way of life we then choose is "irreducibly ours," one that we alone, no one else in our place, are undertaking. The only real difference between theoretical and practical reason, so it seems to me, is the difference in their subject matter: the one focuses on what we are to believe, the other on what we are to do.

Naturally, deliberating about what we are to do depends on beliefs about the nature of the good and the right. But in precisely this respect it becomes plain that the essential situatedness of practical deliberation does nothing by itself to undermine the view that we ought to live our lives in accord with a rational plan of life. Everything depends on what we actually believe. If we are persuaded that our good is something already settled, existing independently of the way our life happens to go, and that it must in principle lie within the reach of our own efforts, then devising a rational plan of life will appear to be a very sensible endeavor – even though we have no choice but to rely on our past experience and present powers of imagination to figure out what is the character of our good. Why then should the fact that "the perspective of deliberative choice on one's life is constitutively *from here*" seriously compromise the idea of a life plan?

Williams' principal argument is that it undermines the precept propelling Rawls, like many others, to embrace that idea – namely, the precept that the rational person lives prudently so as to avoid self-reproach. That this is a primary motive for thinking that we should live in accord with

---

[36] For some more detail, see Chapter 5, §6.

a well thought-out plan of life is certainly true. Rawls himself says so explicitly (see the passage quoted at the end of §3), and it is in general easy to suppose that avoiding the possibility of self-reproach means taking charge of our lives, to the extent of our power, so that they always go in the best way we can manage. The trouble is, Williams protests, our decisions can never enjoy an immunity from our criticism in the future, since our later self will judge our earlier choices on the basis of the preferences that then will be ours and that will have arisen in perhaps unforeseeable ways from what we have been and done in the meantime. *From there*, in the light of all that we have become and of how we then think about the world and ourselves, we may find cause to blame ourselves for not having chosen otherwise, even if we cannot now (*from here*) envisage or identify with the reasons for those self-recriminations.[37]

This objection might be taken in two different ways, and if understood in the first, it does not seem very persuasive. Surely there can be no use in reproaching ourselves for not having deliberated better than we could have done in a given situation. Consider the parallel case of our attitude toward others: should we not judge the rationality (though not perhaps the worth) of another's decision in the light of his view of the world and not our own? Examining in hindsight some decision we made, we might certainly regret that we did not make a different one, given our present self-understanding. But this regret cannot properly take the form of reproaching ourselves for the way we deliberated, if it was the best we could do under the circumstances.

On another construal, however, the objection has a great deal more force. We might rightly reproach ourselves for having been prudent at all, for having so carefully deliberated about what to do. In retrospect, we may think that, instead of weighing our options judiciously, we ought to have acted impulsively, letting ourselves be carried away by the passions of the moment, since then a good would have become ours whose worth we only now can truly appreciate. So construed, the objection embodies the very truth about the importance of unexpected goods on which I have been insisting. However worthy a trait it may be, prudence is not a supreme value, since in fact – so one may say more broadly – no single value enjoys that status: nothing is so important that, in certain circumstances, something else may not matter more. A value pluralism having this sort of compass, recognizing that not just the things we consider pursuing but our very deliberation about which to pursue are goods that can conflict with others, is very much a part of the view I am advocating. It provides the best framework for understanding how the prudent person cannot be certain to escape self-reproach.

---

[37] Williams, *Moral Luck*, pp. 33–36.

Williams, however, appears to have understood his objection along the lines of the first version I outlined. For he was chiefly concerned to present what seemed to him a more sensible analysis of deliberative rationality, one that keeps in mind the situatedness of reflection even when directed toward the course of one's life as a whole. This truth, he believed, is incompatible with Rawls' idea of a life plan, but that is really not so. Rawls' mistake is not his account of prudence or deliberative rationality. It lies instead in whatever impelled him to believe that prudence should be the rule of life.[38]

5. PRUDENCE AND WISDOM

Neither of the objections discussed in the previous section goes deep enough. Quarreling with one or another aspect of Rawls' understanding of deliberative rationality, they do not directly challenge the principle that a person's good consists in what he would choose were he to deliberate correctly. Rawls' fundamental mistake occurs long before he explains what it would be to devise a rational plan of life.

Recall (from §3) the somewhat misleading statement with which he first delineates what it is for something to belong to a person's good: "A is a good X for K (where K is some person) if and only if A has the properties which it is rational for K to want in an X, given K's circumstances, abilities, and plan of life."[39] The statement was poorly worded, since a rational plan of life would supposedly take into account one's circumstances and abilities (and interests too) in setting out what one has reason to pursue. More accurately formulated, Rawls' basic position is this: something belongs to a person's good if and only if the person has reason to pursue it, given his circumstances, abilities, and interests, duly weighed together in an overall plan of life.[40] And it is precisely this definition, and not his subsequent explanation of how those factors are to be weighed together in deliberation, that contains the fatal error. What is amiss, moreover, is not the equation between the elements of a person's good and what he has reason to pursue. I myself defended earlier (in §1) a kindred view, arguing that a good is something that a person has reason to desire. No, the mistake

---

[38] There is an important distinction between regret and reproach: to regret something we did is to wish that we had or could have done otherwise, whereas to reproach ourselves for it is to believe that we were wrong to do as we did. As Williams made plain in a number of his writings, we may sometimes, as in the case of choosing a lesser evil, regret having done what we do not reproach ourselves for doing. However, it is also important to keep in mind the distinction between how we may have deliberated in acting as we did and how we acted, deliberatively or not. It is this distinction that Williams missed in trying to explain how the prudent person may fail to avoid self-reproach.

[39] Rawls, *A Theory of Justice*, p. 399.

[40] Cf. the more careful formulation at ibid., p. 407.

is the idea that a person's good is what he has reason to pursue, *given* his circumstances, abilities, and interests. For this idea is taken to mean that a person's good is determined by conditions that are in principle knowable in advance – the circumstances, abilities, and interests that are truly his, and that the makeup of his good is therefore something already settled, prior to the person's actually living his life. This assumption, as we saw in the case of Socrates (§2), constitutes (along with the belief that this good lies within the reach of one's own efforts) the real source of the conviction that one ought to live in accord with a rational plan of life. And the truth it misses is that a person's good may itself change over time in ways he cannot foresee. Only because his life happens to take a particular turn does he come to have reason to regard certain things as part of his good.

I need to be as explicit as possible about the nature of the mistake. It is not that Rawls forecloses the possibility that we may find reason to modify our conception of our good. On the contrary, he can admit that we may fail to recognize our circumstances, abilities, and interests for what they are, or fail to reflect properly upon those facts, and thus arrive at an idea of our good that we would find reason to correct, were we to learn more about who we are or to think more deeply about what this entails. But such is not the point at issue. The crucial phenomenon is that our good itself can change, and unforeseeably so. Our plans, however well-laid they may be, can always be upset by the course of experience, since it may alter in ways we cannot anticipate those very circumstances, abilities, or interests of ours on which depends the character of our good. When this happens, our good assumes a new and unexpected form. Once we acknowledge, as surely we must, that the very act of living exposes us to influences beyond our foresight and control, changing in unpredictable ways our person and situation and thus the basis of what can count as our good, how can we suppose that the nature of our good is something determined in advance of how our life happens to go? It takes shape as a result of living itself. Consider, for example, the happiness that comes with having children. No doubt we can frame some idea of it beforehand. But we cannot appreciate that distinctive mix of love and pride that consists in helping another who is ours become able to stand on his own, nor realize how these feelings go on to color the value of other things we hold dear, except in and through the experience of being a parent.

Life is too unruly to be the object of a plan, and not simply because our schemes may founder when they come to be applied. Often we do fail to achieve the good we pursue. But equally important, and certainly more neglected by philosophy, is the fact, the happy fact, that the good we pursue, the good we have reason to pursue, is likely to fall short of the good that life has yet to disclose. From this insight we should not infer that the nature of the good life is a question not worth trying to answer since every answer will prove inadequate. It is natural to think about what elements go to make up our good, and my remarks have not been meant to deny that each of us lives, or ought to live, with an idea in mind of what it is to live well. The target of my criticism has been the view that any such idea must be of a life we have taken charge of and shaped so as to embody the purposes we can see reason to pursue, given who we are and where we find ourselves. The good life is not the life lived in accord with a rational plan. It embodies instead a sense of our dual nature as active and passive beings, bent on achieving the goals we espouse, but also bound to run into forms of self-fulfillment we could never have anticipated. A life lived in the light of this more complex ideal can accommodate, it will even welcome the way an unexpected good may challenge our existing projects. We will not thereby avoid being surprised (nor should we want to), but we will know enough not to be surprised at being surprised.

Nothing I have said should suggest that planning is wrong or futile. Prudence is an undeniable virtue, and not solely in the handling of the little things of life. We cannot hope to live well if we do not direct ourselves to achieving goals that have a ramifying significance, that organize our various activities and give our lives meaning. But we err if we suppose that prudence is a supreme virtue and that the good life is one that unfolds in accord with a rational plan.

Some may be tempted to reply that in constructing a life plan we could always set aside some room for the unexpected goods that may come our way. But this rejoinder misses the point. The sort of unexpected good whose importance I have been underscoring does not simply fill in a space left blank. It overthrows our existing expectations. No doubt we could plan for a bit of surprise, if that is what we wanted to do. But this plan, like any, would have to involve some scheme of ends and means. And such schemes may always be tripped up by the good that life has yet in store for us.

The belief in the supremacy of prudence is mistaken for two reasons. The key reason is that, if we give life a chance, it always turns out to be richer in possibilities than any conception we could have at the time of what it would be to flourish. To make our life the object of a plan, however well-informed and carefully arranged the plan might be, means closing our minds to the lessons that future experience will impart. But, in addition, there is the fact that our lives would mean less if they did not contain moments of wonder and redirection, when we find that earlier actions or new conditions have led to a happiness we could never have imagined, or see our existing purposes thrown into disarray by the realization that our fulfillment lies elsewhere. We would live less well if our projects, however rational, were never tripped up by unforeseen goods that impel us to rethink the way we live. For not only do we then encounter a good we could not foresee, but such experiences are themselves of inestimable value. They drive home an important truth about what it is to be human.

That truth is the essential contingency that lies at the heart of whatever, for each of us, happiness may signify. Precisely because the unexpected good can upset the most rational plans, it is to be understood, not as a part of what our overall good has always been (if unrecognized), but instead as a new turn in what our good has come to be. Had our experience gone otherwise, as it could well have done, our good itself (and not just our efforts to discern it) would have been different. Such is the invaluable insight that only such moments of surprise can truly provide us. We are creatures for whom the character of our good takes shape only through the act of living and with the impress of chance. At no point does our good exist as a finished end, waiting to be discovered and made the object of pursuit. The goodness itself of some human possibility may exist independently of its particular importance for our own lives; but when a good comes to form part of our good contrary to all we had hitherto reason to expect, our good has changed. It is in large part the fruit of experiences we stumble into, and thus as much the unintended result of our actions as the goal they may set out to achieve. The good life outruns the reach of planning because its very nature is to be the child of time. To recognize this truth is the beginning of wisdom, for it is to understand why wisdom is something more than prudence.

Index